Intellectual Disabilities
and 'Personality Disorder'
How Caring Relationships Can Support Individuals with Enduring Distress

Second edition

Zillah Webb, Vicky Lauté and Kirsten Collins

AF764677

Pavilion
PUBLISHING

Intellectual Disabilities and 'Personality Disorder'

How Caring Relationships Can Support Individuals with Enduring Distress

Second edition

© Pavilion Publishing and Media

The authors have asserted their rights in accordance with the Copyright, Designs and Patents Act (1988) to be identified as the authors of this work.

Published by:

Pavilion Publishing and Media Ltd
Blue Sky Offices, 25 Cecil Pashley Way
Shoreham by Sea, West Sussex
BN43 5FF

Tel: 01273 434 943
Email: info@pavpub.com
Web: www.pavpub.com

Published 2023

All rights reserved. No part of this publication may be reproduced, stored in a retrieval system, or transmitted in any form or by any means, electronic, mechanical, photocopying, recording or otherwise, without prior permission in writing of the publisher and the copyright owners.

A catalogue record for this book is available from the British Library.

ISBN: 978-1-803882-58-1

Pavilion Publishing and Media is a leading publisher of books, training materials and digital content in mental health, social care and allied fields. Pavilion and its imprints offer must-have knowledge and innovative learning solutions underpinned by sound research and professional values.

Authors: Zillah Webb, Vicky Lauté and Kirsten Collins

Editor: Mike Benge

Cover design: Tony Pitt, Pavilion Publishing and Media Ltd

Page layout and typesetting: Tony Pitt and Emma Dawe, Pavilion Publishing and Media Ltd

Printing: Independent Publishers Group (IPG)

About the authors

Zillah Webb worked as a clinical psychologist in a range of roles in the NHS and voluntary sector in services for adults with intellectual disabilities and paediatric services. Prior to training, she worked in support roles for people with intellectual disabilities or mental health problems. Her final NHS role, before retiring, was in a specialist inpatient service for individuals with intellectual disabilities and mental health problems.

Vicky Lauté is a Principal Lead Psychologist with experience of working in Adult Mental Health Outpatient Services and Community Teams for People with Learning Disabilities. She is experienced in supporting people with intellectual disabilities whose mental health needs and behaviours present a challenge to services.

Kirsten Collins is a clinical psychologist working for Surrey and Borders Partnership NHS Trust.

Acknowledgements

I would like to thank Pavilion for inviting me to create a second edition of *Intellectual Disabilities and 'Personality Disorder'* and for supporting me when I realised that it required a complete rewrite. Special thanks to Louisa Robertson for her patience, encouragement and problem solving. I would like to thank Karen Dodd for putting me in contact with Vicky Lauté and Kirsten Collins, whose generosity with their time and knowledge has greatly enriched this edition.

I would like to thank staff from Surrey and Borders Partnership Foundation NHS Trust: both those who helped me develop the ideas for the first edition and those working in the Intensive Support Service, whose work has inspired parts of this new edition.

Thanks are due to Rowena Rossiter for generously sharing her thoughts on the importance of names and putting me in touch with current issues within child and adolescent services. I would also like to thank Neus Bartual-Sola for her generosity in creating a number of illustrations for this edition.

Finally, thanks are due to Philip Hunt who has, again, patiently read and commented on each chapter many times in an effort to promote the consistency, coherence and logic of both the content and structure of this edition.

 Intellectual Disabilities and 'Personality Disorder' © Pavilion Publishing and Media Ltd and its licensors 2023

Contents

Intellectual Disabilities and 'Personality Disorder' © Pavilion Publishing and Media Ltd and its licensors 2023

Foreword

Dr Karen Dodd

I am delighted to have been invited to write the foreword for the second edition of this valuable book, that should be mandatory reading for everyone who supports a person with intellectual disabilities.

I have known the lead author, Zillah Webb, for over 40 years, having met as trainees on clinical psychology training at Surrey University where we bonded over being the only two trainees who were interested in understanding and supporting people with intellectual disabilities. Working closely together as qualified clinical psychologists, I was impressed with how Zillah worked with people with intellectual disabilities and their staff teams to understand the emotional turmoil that presents as behaviour that challenges and was commonly attributed to the person as having 'personality disorder', and to work collaboratively with staff and people with intellectual disabilities to help them resolve what seemed like insurmountable problems.

The first edition of the book was principally based on giving readers an understanding and recognition of basic human processes that apply to everyone, which can be a useful starting point for challenging thinking and opening possibilities for change. In addition, it provided practical information on how these problems arise and how they can be addressed. Zillah acknowledged her discomfort with the term 'personality disorder' and used this term only because there was, as yet, no widely understood and accepted alternative. She looked forward to a time when there will be a more accurate and less derogatory name for this constellation of difficulties.

This second edition is updated by Zillah in collaboration with two clinical psychologists working in my service. They are also powerful advocates for understanding the complexity of the lives of people with intellectual disabilities, particularly in their experience of poor attachment and enduring trauma that leads to an continuing pattern of emotional and cognitive difficulties, affecting the way they both relate to others and understand themselves.

The first two chapters are the building blocks to understanding this topic, and should be compulsory reading for anyone supporting a person with intellectual disabilities who has been labelled – or is at risk of being labelled – as having a 'personality disorder'. It explores why 'personality disorder' has become a controversial diagnosis, 'surrounded by unhelpful myths and associated with poor treatment and negative outcomes'. Being given an additional diagnosis of 'personality disorder' compounds the stigma and poor outcomes associated with having intellectual disabilities. Chapter 2 powerfully illustrates the additional vulnerabilities of having intellectual disabilities on the development, attachments and impact of adverse events as well as early and ongoing trauma, and how these can be misdiagnosed as 'personality disorder'. Within services for people with intellectual disabilities, we have worked tirelessly to promote the importance of seeing and keeping the person at the centre: seeing their strengths and their needs and not their diagnosis or labels. A diagnosis of 'personality disorder' contradicts this approach, with the person being seen in a negative or dysfunctional stereotype and to blame for their thoughts, feelings and behaviour. As the authors carefully point out, we need to focus on asking 'What has happened to you?' rather than 'What is wrong with you?'.

The remainder of the book focuses on how to work with people who may be at risk of being labelled as having a 'personality disorder'. Each chapter enables the reader to understand how to support the person and the timing and range of interventions to try. Section 2 applies these themes and gives clear examples of what should be available to the person, what is best practice and how these principles can be embedded in services that support people with intellectual disabilities. The learning points at the end of each chapter will help staff to consider their practice and that of their service and the wider systems around each person with intellectual disabilities who is at risk of having a diagnosis of 'personality disorder'.

I fully endorse this second edition. It is written in a way that will make sense to anyone working with people with intellectual disabilities in all settings. My hope is that it helps readers to understand each person as an individual who comes with a whole range of complex issues and experiences that are often out of their control, and to work with them in a way that gives the person support to develop a stable and positive sense of self and promotes positive interventions in capable environments.

Intellectual Disabilities and 'Personality Disorder' © Pavilion Publishing and Media Ltd and its licensors 2023

Section 1:
Understanding what is meant by *'personality disorder'* and how to provide positive support

Introduction

Some individuals with intellectual disabilities experience enduring and pervasive patterns of feeling and thinking that affect the way in which they relate to others and understand themselves. A small proportion of them may be overwhelmed by unbearable feelings and find it very difficult to navigate the daily challenges of life. Where the individual has mild intellectual disabilities, this may lead to them being given (formally or informally) a medical diagnosis of 'personality disorder'.

The diagnosis 'personality disorder' may be defined as:

> *'An enduring pattern of emotional and cognitive difficulties which affect the way in which the person relates to others or understands themselves.'* (Personality Disorder Commission, 2018)

'Personality disorder' has become a controversial diagnosis. It is surrounded by unhelpful myths and associated with poor treatment and negative outcomes, and being given a diagnosis of 'personality disorder' can compound the stigma and poor outcomes associated with having intellectual disabilities.

Enduring patterns of relating and behaving have their origins in the interaction between the individual's unique biological make-up and their life experiences, particularly developmental trauma and insecure attachments. Psychologically informed approaches help to explain how these experiences shape an individual's physiological responses, thoughts, feelings and ways of relating. Understanding the origins and functions of these enduring patterns challenges myths and helps develop and maintain empathy. This psychologically informed understanding also forms the basis for offering support and interventions that are designed to meet individual needs, that are positive, and that will enable individuals to live their best life.

The chapters in this section explore:

- What is meant by personality and 'personality disorder', why the label 'personality disorder' is controversial and the importance of using language thoughtfully.
- How individuals with mild intellectual disabilities may show enduring patterns of relationships and behaviour that can lead to them being given a diagnosis of 'personality disorder'.
- How a psychological approach can promote constructive, alternative ways of understanding 'personality disorder', help to build positive working relationships and promote engagement.
- How to create a positive and hopeful environment in which staff can work collaboratively to help individuals lead their best lives.
- How unconscious mechanisms can distort communications and create tensions, and how this can be understood and addressed through reflective practice.

Intellectual Disabilities and 'Personality Disorder' © Pavilion Publishing and Media Ltd and its licensors 2023

Chapter 1: What is meant by the term 'personality disorder' and how it can be understood in relation to individuals with intellectual disabilities

This chapter starts by establishing what is meant by 'intellectual disabilities'. It then explores what is meant by the terms 'personality' and 'personality disorder'. The term 'personality disorder' has become controversial. This is explored both as a label and a diagnosis. This chapter looks at the patterns of responding and behaving that might lead to a diagnosis. It looks at recent changes to diagnostic criteria and differences between diagnostic systems. It examines the impact of both the patterns of relationships and behaviour, and the diagnostic label for the individual. It looks at the particular challenges around the diagnosis of 'personality disorder' for individuals with mild intellectual disabilities. It stresses that, if a diagnostic approach is taken, it only provides a signpost: individual formulation is essential to identify the way forward.

Key topics

- Intellectual disabilities
- Personality
- 'Personality disorder' – a controversial diagnosis
- Diagnosis criteria
- Diagnosing 'personality disorder' when an individual has intellectual disabilities
- Occurrence
- Outcomes

Intellectual disabilities

'Intellectual disability' is a term used when there are limits to an individual's ability to think and learn at an expected level and to function in daily life. Intellectual disabilities have their origins in the developmental process. Factors in the individual's biology, before, during and after birth, and subsequent relationships and experiences, shape their ability to learn, their relationships and what they can achieve. Having intellectual disabilities will uniquely affect the trajectory of the individual's intellectual and emotional development. The biological limitations on their development may be ameliorated – for example, by effective early intervention – or exacerbated – for example, by deprivation.

The term 'intellectual disabilities' is used here synonymously with the term 'learning disabilities' and the diagnostic categories 'Disorders of Intellectual Development' (WHO, 2022; ICD-11) and 'Intellectual Development Disorders' (APA, 2022; DSM-5TR) to represent the presence of:

- a significantly reduced ability to understand new or complex information, to learn new skills (impaired intelligence), with;
- a reduced ability to cope independently (impaired social functioning); which started before adulthood, with a lasting effect on development.

The phrase 'mild intellectual disabilities' is used to represent individuals meeting these criteria whose intellectual functioning falls in the approximate IQ range of 50-69.

Estimates of the prevalence of intellectual disabilities vary. It is suggested that 1–2% of the population may have intellectual disabilities. The great majority of these individuals (more than 75%) will have mild intellectual disabilities (Emerson and Hatton, 2008).

Intellectual disabilities are not a mental health problem. However, a significant proportion of individuals with intellectual disabilities (15–52%) also experience mental health problems (Mencap, 2022). They are thought to be more at risk as a result of a number of factors including: biology and genetics, experiencing more trauma and adversity, having fewer resources and coping mechanisms, and the impact of others' attitudes and stereotypes.

 Intellectual Disabilities and 'Personality Disorder' © Pavilion Publishing and Media Ltd and its licensors 2023

Personality

A starting point for understanding 'personality disorder' in relation to individuals with intellectual disabilities is to explore what is meant by personality.

> *'Our personality is the collection of characteristics that make us distinctive as people.'* (Personality Disorder Commission (PDC), 2018).

Personality may be understood as the lasting characteristics that influence a person's thoughts, feelings and behaviour. It shapes a person's view of themselves (their identity), other people and the world in general. It influences how they engage in relationships. Personality also underpins how people respond, both emotionally and behaviourally, to situations and people, and how they cope with life's challenges. Personality comprises an integrated system of traits and attributes that characterise the individual.

Everyone's personality is unique. However, personality characteristics, or 'traits', can be seen as falling somewhere on a range. For example, people differ in how sociable they are, from the most extraverted and outgoing to the most introverted and reclusive. Box 1.1 shows the 'big five' – the overarching personality traits consistently identified in research and some of their sub-traits.

Box 1.1: The 'big five' personality traits

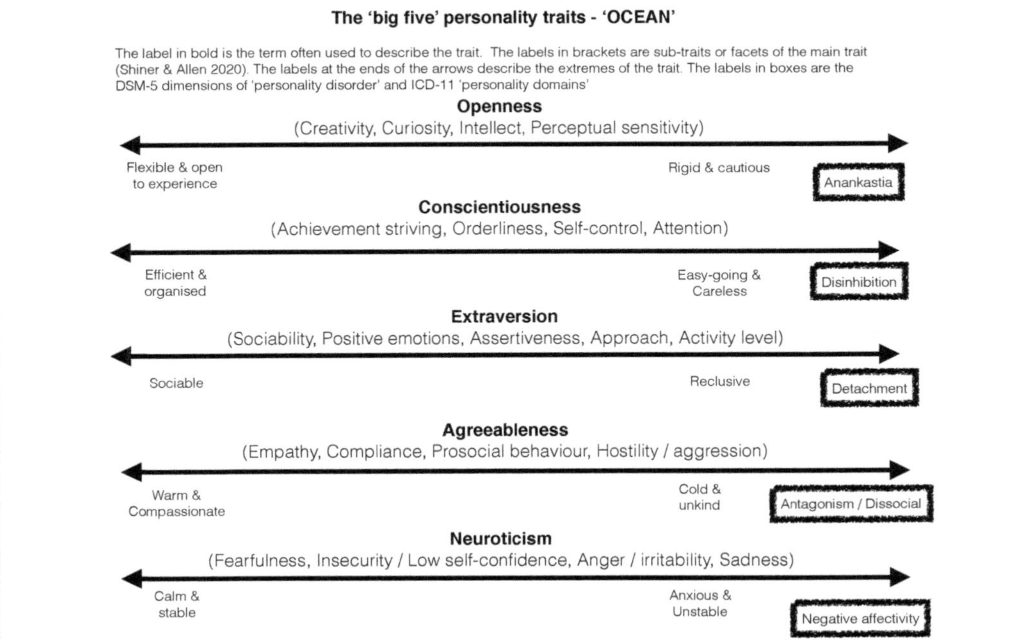

There is a social aspect to our understanding of personality: what we understand by personality will be shaped (and potentially misshaped) by our attitudes and values, and those of wider society. Some traits or personality styles may be more valued than others. There is also a risk that people may be categorised in ways that reduce their power or status (Johnson, 2019). Although personality may be viewed as a 'social construct', research shows that predictions based on personality measurement actually work to some degree. For example, observer judgments of personality predict a number of relevant, objectively measurable behaviours, such as delay of gratification, attitude change, creativity, aggression and dominance (Johnson, 2019).

Personality is a major influence on how people behave, but it is not the only factor. For example, people may be influenced by changes in their mood or the characteristics of the situation they find themselves in.

Personality develops from childhood as a result of the interactions between an individual's biology, relationships and experiences (Shiner and Allen, 2020). There appears to be a genetic component to personality, as differences in temperament are evident from birth. Babies have been shown to differ in characteristics such as activity, sociability and emotional reactivity. Other personality traits become apparent during childhood, but these are flexible and change as the individual develops and responds to experiences. These emerging traits, in turn, influence the types of experiences the child is likely to have (Shiner and Allen, 2020). A more consistent pattern of traits emerges in late teens or early adulthood. In adulthood, personality is much less flexible, but it can and often does change as people mature and undergo different life experiences. The development of personality can be influenced by a wide range of adverse physical, environmental, psychological, social or economic factors (Benefield and Haigh, 2020). These are explored in Chapter 2. An individual's personality may also change in adulthood, for example after the experience of a traumatic event (Tanaka, 2019) or as a result neurological changes arising from diseases such as dementia.

Personality traits and intellectual disabilities

Research suggests the experience of growing up with intellectual disabilities has a profound effect on the development of personality (Roy *et al*, 2015). Individuals with intellectual disabilities experience more failure, rejection and social deprivation than the general population. This can shape personality traits in ways that may impede learning and make the individual more vulnerable to depression and anxiety. The impact is such that Zigler *et al* (2002) concluded that individuals

Intellectual Disabilities and 'Personality Disorder' © Pavilion Publishing and Media Ltd and its licensors 2023

with intellectual disabilities show a different personality structure from the general population (see Box 1.2).

Box 1.2: Seven personality dimensions identified in children with intellectual disabilities

	Dimension	'Big five' (and other) personality traits that might be reflected in Zigler's dimensions
1	**Positive reaction tendency –** a heightened motivation to interact with and be dependent on a supportive adult	Extraversion Openness
2	**Negative reaction tendency –** initial wariness shown when interacting with strange adults	Extraversion Neuroticism
3	**Expectancy of success –** degree to which the individual expects to succeed or fail when presented with a new task	(Optimism)
4	**Outer directedness –** tendency to look to others for solutions to difficult or ambiguous tasks	(Dependence)
5	**Efficacy motivation –** the pleasure derived from tackling and solving difficult tasks	(Self-efficacy/achievement striving)
6	**Obedience**	Conscientiousness
7	**Curiosity/creativity**	Openness

Reference: Zigler *et al* (2002)

At first glance, these traits bear little resemblance to the 'big five'. These may reflect genuine differences in the personality structure of individuals with intellectual disabilities. However, they may also be influenced by characteristics of the research approach that developed them. These traits were identified in children, from observations of their approach to certain tasks and ratings by teachers. There was no attempt to talk to the participants to explore their inner worlds. The researchers were looking for traits that distinguished individuals with intellectual disabilities from their more able peers, and hence did not explore areas of similarity.

The language used to describe the traits may also reflect the unconscious bias of the researchers about the position of children with intellectual disabilities in society (see

Chapter 7). This may make the traits appear more different from the 'big five' than is perhaps the case. Box 1.2 shows how the dimensions might relate to personality traits identified in the general population. Widely held, unhelpful beliefs and stereotypes of intellectual disabilities (explored in Chapter 7) are also likely to have a direct impact on shaping the personality development of all individuals with the label 'intellectual disabilities'.

The traits described by Zigler *et al* (2002) as positive and negative 'reaction tendency' may also reflect ambivalent and avoidant insecure attachments (see Box 2.6).

Overall, it is most helpful to think of individuals with intellectual disabilities as having personalities that fall on the 'big five' spectrum, but to be mindful of how this will have been shaped by their experiences.

Personality functioning

For most people, their developmental experiences facilitate personality traits that help them successfully navigate their lives. This has been termed 'personality functioning' (Rishede *et al*, 2021). This enables people to:

- have a stable and coherent sense of themselves (identity) and sense of self-worth
- have coherent internal experiences (perceptions, emotions and thoughts)
- manage impulses and emotions and direct their behaviour
- have a stable sense of other people
- form successful relationships
- function interdependently (manage some things independently, seek and accept help when needed)
- function in groups
- function in wider society.

For some individuals, their experiences and biology interact to shape their development in ways that have a pervasive impact on their ability to navigate their lives. Some of these issues are given in Box 1.3, together with some composite examples.

Intellectual Disabilities and 'Personality Disorder' © Pavilion Publishing and Media Ltd and its licensors 2023

Box 1.3: Issues that may contribute to individuals being given a diagnosis of 'personality disorder':
Frequent crises e.g. placement breakdown or admission to hospital
Self-harm including self-injury and self-poisoning
Emotional dysregulation e.g. intense, changeable emotions
Interpersonal difficulties e.g. unstable relationships, conflict, lack of empathy
Difficulties with self-direction and impulsivity including substance misuse and offending behaviour
Distorted thinking
Low self-esteem or fragmented sense of self
Composite examples* of how individuals might present to services:
'Susan' was referred urgently as being at risk of placement breakdown as a result of self-harm and verbal and physical aggression to carers and threats to harm others. Allegations about staff (that proved unfounded on investigation) were making it very difficult to provide the support Susan needed. Susan also had multiple physical health issues, including poorly controlled diabetes.
'Elizabeth' was referred following increasing concern about her chaotic lifestyle and the risks she was exposed to, including financial and sexual exploitation. She was living on her own with community-based support but other services had been responding to repeated crises.
'Margaret' was referred after being treated in A&E for an over-dose of over-the-counter medication and self-harm.
'David' was referred following an incident where the police were called to the local pub, where he was being verbally aggressive and refusing to leave. He was reported to have also been making abusive comments to carers and the other people he lived with.
*Examples have been created from clinical experience and the literature. They are not based on specific individuals.

These issues can be understood in different ways, and this is explored fully in Chapter 2. However, within the medical model, they may be interpreted as 'impairment of personality functioning'. This can lead to an individual being given a diagnosis of personality disorder. This diagnosis may be given to individuals who also have mild intellectual disabilities. However, similar issues experienced by individuals with more severe intellectual disabilities are more likely to be viewed as 'behaviours that challenge' (see Chapter 8).

Personality disorder: a controversial diagnosis

Before further exploring what is meant by a diagnosis of 'personality disorder', it is important to understand that this has become a controversial term that evokes strong reactions. The debate around 'personality disorder' is polarised, with passionate advocates both for its continued use and its total eradication.

Concerns about a diagnosis of 'personality disorder' encompass general issues about the impact of labels and the appropriateness of applying the medical model to mental health. There are also issues specific to a diagnosis of 'personality disorder'.

The label 'personality disorder'

Some positive and negative characteristics of labels are given in Box 1.4.

Box 1.4: Positive and negative characteristics of labels

A label: a classifying phrase or name, especially one that is inaccurate or restrictive	
Label – General Issues	
Positive	Negative
Shared language – enables conversations. 'Shorthand' – one or two words replace a long description.	Over simplification. May trigger stereotypes, biases. Poor choice of words may misrepresent issues.
Pride, positive identification.	Sense of shame, embarrassment, fear.
Reduced sense of isolation *'I am not alone'*. Sense of belonging, shared experiences Access to a community, peer support.	Isolation, increased sense of difference from general population.
Recognition, acceptance from society.	May be devalued, stigmatised, judged. Experience prejudice and discrimination.

 Intellectual Disabilities and 'Personality Disorder' © Pavilion Publishing and Media Ltd and its licensors 2023

'Personality disorder' Label – Specific Issues	
Validation (see Chapter 11)	Adds to earlier experiences of invalidation.
	Implies that your whole being is wrong or ill, is experienced as pejorative. Inaccurate, does not reflect the origins or real nature of the difficulties experienced.
	Triggers a set of unhelpful assumptions about the person and how to support them: That it is an untreatable, life-long condition. That individuals are 'manipulative', 'attention seeking', will not benefit from/do not deserve help, that they bring their problems upon themselves.
References: Rossiter and Arena (2021), Sibbald (2020), BPS (2018).	

The words 'personality disorder' convey a powerful message that an individual's whole being is seen by others as bad or dysfunctional. There is widespread agreement that the label 'personality disorder' does not reflect the true nature or origins of the difficulties experienced by individuals given this diagnosis and has become stigmatising (PDC, 2018). Box 1.5 summarises types of stigma and how these impact on the individual and those around them.

Box 1.5: Definition of stigma	
Stigma: ■ A mark of disgrace or infamy ■ A set of negative and often unfair beliefs that a society or group of people hold about something	
Public stigma	Stereotypes: e.g. seen as 'attention seeking' or 'manipulative' Prejudice →

	Discrimination: e.g. insulted, denied of support/access to services, lowered expectations May lead to 'label avoidance' – refusing services/support to avoid being labelled
Self-stigma	Internalising public stigma and believing it is true of oneself. May lead to: ■ lowered self-esteem, depression ■ social isolation ■ secrecy and avoidance of help ■ feeling unworthy of love/support
Associative or vicarious stigma	Families may feel blamed, judged or tainted by association Pain from seeing impact of public stigma on loved one
Structural stigma	Need for services overlooked, lack of funding Reduced efforts to provide high quality service
Reference: Sheehan *et al* (2022)	

For individuals who also have intellectual disabilities, there is a particular concern about the additional stigma attached to the 'personality disorder' label. The Royal College of Psychiatry RCP (2006) cautioned:

> *'The term personality disorder however should be used with care; it can be used pejoratively in people* [with intellectual disabilities] *whose behaviours are intractable, are considered socially unacceptable, or invoke strong emotional responses in others.'*

For individuals with intellectual disabilities, the 'personality disorder' label can lead staff to rely on unhelpful assumptions rather than seeking to understand the individual and their own reactions to them. For example, behaviour may be seen as conscious and planned, despite the individual's mental capacity, social skills and planning abilities being significantly impaired. Staff may assume that their skills in supporting individuals with intellectual disabilities are not relevant and that the individual needs to move to a new setting, or to a team where staff have a different skill set.

Intellectual Disabilities and 'Personality Disorder' © Pavilion Publishing and Media Ltd and its licensors 2023

Finding and agreeing on an alternative name for 'personality disorder' has proved difficult. It is difficult to capture such a range of issues and perspectives in a brief phrase. For example, the phrase 'persistent cognitive, emotional, behavioural, or relational problems that cause significant distress' (Paterson, 2022) captures many of the issues but is too unwieldy for general use.

As there is not yet an agreed, non-pejorative alternative, the PDC (2018) suggest using the phrase: 'given a diagnosis of personality disorder' to separate the diagnosis from the individual. However, it is essential to keep in mind that changing a label does not on its own remove stigma. Box 1.6 highlights how stigma needs to be directly confronted.

Box 1.6: Challenging stigma and myths

Changing a label, in isolation, will not remove stigma:

'...stigma often ignores science and runs its own pathological course. If we hide behind our fear and do not mention the 'disorder-that-should-have-no-name' [personality disorder], we only serve to promote stigma. Once it is recognised by health professionals, the general public and those with lived experience of personality disorder that all of us are on a single personality spectrum ... we can first reduce and then eliminate stigma.' (Tyrer, 2022)

Stigma should be tackled directly:

'History shows that all forms of discrimination (e.g. racism, sexism and homophobia) can be improved with the right campaigning.' (Cannon and Gould, 2022b)

Pervasive myths about 'personality disorder' need to be challenged:

- It is **NOT** life-long.
- It **DOES** respond to interventions.
- Individuals should **NOT** be seen as 'attention seeking' or 'manipulative'. They are showing survival skills and are trying to meet overwhelming needs in the only ways that are available to them.

Individual professionals and professional bodies should:

- Recognise the culture of bigotry and discrimination that exist in many services.
- Take a robust stance on promoting positive approaches.
- Ensure fair access to support and intervention.
- Challenge myths though staff training.

Adapted from: Chanen (2022), Cannon and Gould (2022b) and Schmeck (2022)

The diagnosis 'personality disorder'

The recognised limitations of medical diagnoses (see Box 1.7) are particularly apparent when applied to 'personality disorder'.

Box 1.7: Positives and negatives of diagnosis	
Diagnosis: the process of identifying a disease, condition, or injury from its signs (objective phenomena that can be identified by another person) and symptoms (subjective experiences that cannot be identified by anyone else).	
(Mental Health/Psychiatric) Diagnosis – General issues	
Positive	Negative
May change individual's perceptions of being 'mad' or 'bad' and bring relief from not knowing.	Can change what people feel, think and do into something they have (e.g. 'schizophrenia') or are (e.g. 'a schizophrenic') leading to feeling diseased or disordered.
	Imposed by professionals, creates sense of being 'done to'. Asks 'what is wrong with you?' not 'what has happened to you?'
Knowledge promotes understanding of self, thoughts, feelings and behaviour.	Professional knowledge may not reflect 'lived experience'.
'Signposting' – identifies which services are most likely to help.	Mis-diagnosis may lead to unhelpful care pathway. Meeting some but not all diagnostic criteria can deny access to potentially helpful interventions.
First step to evidence-based 'treatment'.	First step in a 'psychiatric career' with feelings of hopelessness, exclusion, and disempowerment. Can lead to an emphasis on medication. Medical model can create passivity – 'someone will cure me'.
Facilitates recovery	Can lead to feelings of hopelessness and being unable to change.
Facilitates research – identifying people with the same pattern of signs.	Privileges narrow focus on biological issues over experiences.

 Intellectual Disabilities and 'Personality Disorder' © Pavilion Publishing and Media Ltd and its licensors 2023

Shared understanding of issues.	Narrow interpretation as a 'medical' problem can miss important personal issues such as life experiences.
Diagnosis of a 'personality disorder' – Specific Issues	
Captures the breadth of issues.	Lacks validity e.g. diagnostic criteria may not relate to research on personality, arbitrary thresholds.
Includes trauma without this necessarily being the primary focus.	Is unreliable; different assessors/different assessment tools can lead to the same individual being given different diagnoses.
	May be refused access to services.
	Pathologising, being blamed for own distress.
	'Dustbin diagnosis' (given if don't recover/don't respond to medication/complain).
	Based on implicit assumptions about how personality should be. Given to those who challenge social norms.
References: Rossiter and Arena (2021), Sibbald (2020), BPS (2018), Bach and First (2018)	

The medical model is based on the assumption that a 'disorder' has a specific cause and progression; these assumptions are questionable for all mental health issues. The fit is particularly poor for 'disorders' such as 'personality disorder', which arise from the complex interactions of multiple factors (Livesley and Larstone, 2020a). The diagnostic criteria for all mental health problems are agreed by committees. This makes them vulnerable to unconscious bias and assumptions by the committee members about what constitutes appropriate behaviour. The criteria for 'personality disorder' may be seen as comprising the opposite of an idealised 'normal' personality (Leising *et al*, 2009). The diagnostic process may be seen as labelling people as 'disordered' if their behaviour does not comply to these idealised norms.

However, for some individuals, being given a diagnosis of 'personality disorder' helps make sense of their experiences and is perceived as the starting point of their recovery (Ng *et al*, 2019). The diagnosis helps ensure that the wide range of presenting issues are addressed in a coherent manner rather than separately. It acts as a signpost, pointing towards relevant research and evidence-based interventions and can facilitate access to appropriate services and peer support.

These advantages and disadvantages are equally applicable to individuals with intellectual disabilities. Currently, the diagnosis 'personality disorder' is still used in adult mental health services. Despite its many disadvantages, to unilaterally cease using this diagnosis with individuals with intellectual disabilities carries risks. It risks individuals with intellectual disabilities being seen as 'other' (different rules apply to them), being unable to access mainstream services (where appropriate) and breaking the link to research and development for the general population that might be helpful. The balance of pros and cons of giving a diagnosis will be different for each individual in their unique setting. Hence, decisions about the language to use should be made thoughtfully and collaboratively.

Diagnostic criteria

As the diagnosis 'personality disorder' remains in use, it is helpful to understand how 'personality disorder' is currently defined within the medical model. (Seeking to understand the diagnosis does not imply acceptance or agreement with the term.) Unfortunately, this is not straightforward as there are different approaches, and diagnostic systems are evolving in response to criticism and research developments.

Historically, 'personality disorder' was diagnosed by allocating a category based on the patterns of thoughts, feelings and behaviour shown by the individual. These are shown in Box 1.8, together with ways the categories may be grouped. Categories are retained in the current version of the American Psychiatric Association's Diagnostic and Statistical Manual of Mental Disorders (APA, DSM-5 TR, 2022). There are many weaknesses to this approach (Ofrat *et al*, 2020) including individuals meeting the criteria for several categories or not fitting in any category, despite having a number of issues. Specific issues with applying these categories to individuals with intellectual disabilities are also shown in Box 1.8.

Box 1.8: Category approach to personality disorder and issues when applied to individuals with intellectual disabilities (ID)

Label, cluster and behavioural category	Main characteristics	ID comments
A. Odd/eccentric	**Internalised**	
Paranoid	Distrust and suspicion of others.	Experiences of abuse/ exploitation and being lied to are common for people with ID.

→

 Intellectual Disabilities and 'Personality Disorder' © Pavilion Publishing and Media Ltd and its licensors 2023

Schizoid	Lack of social connection and limited emotional expression.	Limited opportunities/ overlap with Autism Spectrum Disorders (ASD).
Schizotypal	Social discomfort, cognitive distortions and behavioural eccentricities.	Overlap with ASD.
B. Dramatic/erratic	**Externalised/'acting out'**	
Antisocial/Dissocial	Ignore and break the rights of others. Lack concern for others feelings. Low tolerance of frustration. Low threshold for aggression.	Level of moral development, learning history – lack of consequences for behaviour.
Borderline/ Emotionally Unstable	Impulsive behaviour, unstable relationships and emotions.	Impulsivity can be due to ID.
Histrionic	'Excessive' emotion and need for attention.	ID can impact on emotional regulation and need for social interaction.
Narcissistic	Patterns of grandiosity, need for admiration and lack of empathy.	Impact of ID on self-image may lead to need for admiration. Lack of empathy may overlap with ASD.
C. Avoidant/fearful	**Internalised**	
Avoidant/Anxious	Social inhibition, feel inadequate, oversensitive to criticism.	Overlap with ASD. Frequent experience of failure.
Obsessive-compulsive	Need for order, perfection and control.	Overlap with ASD.
Dependent	Excessive need to be cared for, unassertive, 'clinging', fear of separation, difficulties with decision-making, taking responsibility and initiating projects.	Signs can arise directly from growing up with ID. Distinguish between appropriate (to ability level) interdependence and maladaptive, over-dependence.

To address the weaknesses of the categorical approach, there is a move towards a dimensional approach. The World Health Organization's International Classification of Diseases (WHO, ICD-11, 2022) recognises a spectrum of personality function (see Box 1.9). DSM-5 TR (APA, 2021) includes an Alternative Model of Personality Disorders, described as a hybrid model with aspects of dimensions and categories. Both of these approaches include looking at whether an individual shows traits that are in the extreme range of the 'big five' personality traits (ICD-11 'domains', DSM-5 'dimension', see Box 1.1).

Box 1.9: ICD-11 Diagnosis of 'personality disorder'*

Step 1: General requirements (for a diagnosis of 'personality disorder')	An enduring 'disturbance' characterised by problems in functioning of aspects of the self (e.g. identity), and/or interpersonal dysfunction (e.g. ability to develop and maintain relationships) that: ■ Has persisted over time (e.g. 2+ years). ■ Comprises patterns of cognition, emotional experience, emotional expression, and behaviour that are 'maladaptive' (e.g. poorly regulated). ■ Is shown across a range of personal and social situations (i.e., is not limited to specific relationships or social roles), though it may be consistently evoked by particular types of circumstances but not others. ■ Are not developmentally appropriate and cannot be explained primarily by social or cultural factors, including socio-political conflict. ■ Are not due to medication or another mental or physical health problem. ■ Is associated with substantial distress or significant impairment in personal, family, social, educational, occupational or other important areas of functioning.
Step 2: Severity	Mild Moderate Severe

 Intellectual Disabilities and 'Personality Disorder' © Pavilion Publishing and Media Ltd and its licensors 2023

Step 3: Trait qualifiers (optional descriptors from 5 domains)	**Negative Affectivity –** A tendency to experience a broad range of negative emotions with a frequency and intensity out of proportion to the situation. **Detachment –** A tendency to maintain interpersonal distance (social detachment) and emotional distance (emotional detachment). **Dissociality –** Disregard for the rights and feelings of others, encompassing both self-centredness and lack of empathy. **Disinhibition –** A tendency to act rashly based on immediate external or internal stimuli (i.e. sensations, emotions, thoughts), without consideration of potential negative consequences. **Anankastia –** A narrow focus on one's rigid standard of perfection and of right and wrong, and on controlling one's own and others' behaviour and controlling situations to ensure conformity to these standards.
* The wording in this table reflects that used in ICD-11. This is not the language the authors would choose to describe these experiences.	

Age

Previous versions of ICD and DSM specified a lower age limit for diagnosing 'personality disorder', of 18 years, as, before this age, personality is still very flexible and developing. However, it has been argued that early identification of personality difficulties can facilitate self-advocacy and promote the offering and acceptance of evidence-based treatment (Chanen, 2022; Cannon and Gould, 2022a and b). Schmeck (2022) draws parallels with early intervention in psychosis – suggesting that early identification and access to treatment might mitigate negative outcomes. Hence, DSM-5 alternative model and ICD-11 have removed age-related caveats, allowing a diagnosis of 'personality disorder' to be given to teenagers. However, this is controversial, and strong arguments being made both for and against this practice (Hartley *et al*, 2022).

Diagnosing 'personality disorder' when an individual has intellectual disabilities

Applying the diagnostic criteria for 'personality disorder' to individuals with intellectual disabilities is problematic (Cowan, 2018a; Fletcher *et al*, 2016). Some characteristics shown by individuals with intellectual disabilities can be confused with symptoms of 'personality disorder' (see Box 1.10).

Box 1.10: Issues that complicate diagnosing 'personality disorder' in individuals with intellectual disabilities

Area of concern	Comments
Delayed maturity.	Difficult to distinguish lasting traits from 'immature' behaviour that will resolve with development.
Some signs of 'personality disorder' are also characteristic of having/growing up with intellectual disabilities.	■ Immaturity ■ Dependence ■ Impulsivity ■ Suggestibility ■ Sensitivity to criticism
Overlap with Autism Spectrum.	Difficulties with social relationships, social communication, social imagination (empathy) or obsessionality can be misdiagnosed as 'personality disorder'.
Restricted lives – limit access to formative experiences.	Restricted opportunities for: ■ Intimate/sexual relationships ■ Decision-making ■ Independence ■ Employment/vocational experience
Abnormal living environments e.g. living in institutions, multiple placements.	May foster/reinforce behaviours that appear maladaptive outside that environment.
Sense of self.	Shaped by negative self-evaluation in relation to non-disabled peers and experience of stigma.
Accessing historical information.	Communication difficulties and inadequate records may mean important historical contextual information is not accessible. Individual may have a limited understanding of time.
Accessing thoughts, feelings and perceptions.	The more severe their intellectual disability, the more difficulty an individual will experience with: expressive and receptive communication, understanding abstract/complex ideas.

Intellectual Disabilities and 'Personality Disorder' © Pavilion Publishing and Media Ltd and its licensors 2023

Some behaviours that indicate personality disorder are similar to behaviours that challenge.	■ Aggression ■ Self-harm/self injury
Both intellectual disabilities and 'personality disorder' are developmental disorders.	Artificially trying to allocate certain behaviours to a 'disorder' when they arise as a result of influences during development.
High levels of Adverse Childhood Experiences in both intellectual disabilities and 'personality disorder'.	Artificially trying to allocate behaviours to a disorder when they are the consequences of trauma or disadvantage.

To address this, guidance specifically for intellectual disabilities has been developed for both ICD and DSM criteria (Barnhill *et al*, 2017; Deba *et al*, 2021; RCP, 2001). The RCP (2001) highlighted the importance of being confident that any specific sign of 'personality disorder' cannot be explained by the individual's intellectual disabilities or them also having an Autism Spectrum Disorder (ASD). They also recommend diagnosis of a general 'personality disorder' rather than using categories. This is compatible with the ICD-11 approach. Although guidance improves reliability, it does not address other valid concerns about diagnosing 'personality disorder' in individuals with intellectual disabilities.

Assessment

Where individuals with intellectual disabilities show enduring patterns of relationships and behaviour that might be given a diagnosis of 'personality disorder', it is important that these be thoroughly assessed.

The patterns of relationships and behaviours that might lead to a diagnosis of 'personality disorder' are not in themselves unusual; it is their frequency, severity, intensity and duration that make them problematic. Many issues may come and go depending on the situation the individual is in. Consequently, an assessment needs to look for patterns over time and in different situations.

Most authors suggest combining interviews, questionnaires, informant information and direct observation. It is best practice that the assessment team has a thorough knowledge of both 'personality disorder' and intellectual disabilities (RCP, 2020). Once assessment is completed, it may be more appropriate to develop a formulation (see Chapter 4) to understand the origins and functions of the pattern, rather than giving a diagnosis. However, if a diagnosis of 'personality disorder' is given, it should only be when these sources give a consistent picture of pervasive difficulties that cannot be explained by other factors. Box 1.11 gives a possible wording for giving a diagnosis.

Box 1.11: Possible wording if giving a diagnosis of 'personality disorder':

... currently shows a pattern of thoughts, feelings and behaviour that could be given a diagnosis of 'personality disorder'. This means that their experiences (such as early and persistent trauma, poverty and deprivation), their attachment and relationship history have interacted with biological vulnerabilities. This means that they will experience distress, may be overwhelmed with unbearable feelings and find it very difficult to navigate the daily challenges of life. This pattern may be temporary but there are intervention strategies that can help reduce/manage immediate distress and improve long term outcomes. We have agreed to call these difficulties ________ and together have agreed the following course of action______'

Adapted from Tyler (2022)

If a diagnostic approach is taken, it is important to keep in mind that reaching a diagnosis is not the end point. Rather, a diagnosis is a signpost to help identify areas that need in-depth assessment and, potentially, intervention. This mirrors the approach with other developmental disorders such as the TEACCH approach to ASD (Mesibov *et al*, 2004).

If an individual's troubling thoughts, feelings and behaviours do not cross the threshold for a diagnosis of 'personality disorder', these issues may still need to be addressed. Part of the problem with diagnosis is that it imposes an artificial cut-off on a spectrum of functioning; one side is considered 'normal' and the other 'abnormal'. Where an individual is not given a diagnosis, it is still helpful to think about the traits or patterns of responding that the individual shows and to progress to formulation.

Reviewing a historic diagnosis

Sometimes, an individual already has a diagnosis and it is important to consider how to take this forward. Given the multiplicity of diagnostic systems, it is important to be aware not only of the diagnosis an individual has been given, but also which system of diagnosis was used and the patterns of relating and behaving that led to the diagnosis.

 Intellectual Disabilities and 'Personality Disorder' © Pavilion Publishing and Media Ltd and its licensors 2023

If a pre-existing diagnosis of 'personality disorder' is accepted without question, it can have a serious negative impact on the support received by the individual. Improved living conditions, appropriate intervention and increased maturity may mean that the individual no longer shows the behaviours that resulted in the original diagnosis but still carries the label and associated stigma. The outdated diagnosis may trigger false assumptions about their behaviour ('they are manipulative'), their motivation ('they choose to behave this way') and their response to treatment ('nothing will change'). Consequently, interventions may not be offered, be inappropriate or be pitched at an inappropriate intellectual level. Any diagnosis should always be reviewed regularly to ensure that it is still applicable to and helpful for the individual.

Occurrence

Research suggests that 5–15% of the general adult population could be given a diagnosis of 'personality disorder' (Morgan and Zimmerman, 2020). Personality disorders occur in similar numbers in men and women. However, under the category system, 'borderline personality disorder' is more commonly diagnosed in women while 'antisocial personality disorder' is more commonly diagnosed in men (Morgan and Zimmerman, 2020). There are some differences in rates of diagnosis between different ethnic groups (Mulder, 2020). However, it is not clear if these reflect cultural differences or just reflect differences in diagnostic practices (for example, the influence of gender or other stereotypes).

The number of individuals with intellectual disabilities who might be given a diagnosis of 'personality disorder' is unclear, mainly as the result of difficulties with research in this area. Andersen's (2015) review of studies of the general population of people with intellectual disabilities, concluded that the prevalence of 'personality disorder' ranged from 0.7–35%. However, rates of up to 50% have been found within forensic services for people with intellectual disabilities (Lindsay, 2007). The most frequently identified categories of 'personality disorders' in this population are 'antisocial' and 'borderline personality disorder', possibly because the behaviours that can lead to these diagnoses are more likely to be referred to services.

Outcomes

Many individuals given a diagnosis of 'personality disorder' experience a wide range of negative outcomes. Box 1.12 gives favourable and unfavourable outcomes for individuals with 'personality disorder' and factors influencing these outcomes.

Box 1.12. Outcomes and factors associated with them

OUTCOMES	
Favourable outcomes	**Unfavourable outcomes**
Patterns of behaviour become more 'mature' until the diagnosis is no longer applicable. Respond well to longer-term intervention (min 15 months) such that they no longer meet diagnostic criteria.	Increased vulnerability to: Living precarious and isolated lives e.g. homelessness, unemployment. Physical health problems e.g. cardiovascular disease, obesity, diabetes. Mental health problems e.g. anxiety and depression Misuse of alcohol and drugs. Reduced life expectancy: 18 (men) and 19 (women) years shorter. Raised risk of 'unnatural deaths' (suicide, homicide, accidents). Raised risk of 'natural deaths' (e.g. infections, cardiovascular disease). Reduced access to health care compared to other mental health 'diagnoses' e.g. 'psychosis'. Risk of imprisonment: In the prison population, it is estimated that 60–70% might be given a diagnosis of 'personality disorder'.
FACTORS ASSOCIATED WITH OUTCOMES	
Short term	
Favourable	**Unfavourable**
Mild symptoms. Early and rapid progress in interventions. Supportive relationships. Friendliness and 'likability'.	Chronic/severe symptoms. Having additional mental health problems e.g. depression. Greater impulsivity. Impaired relationship with parents. Disability. Poor physical health.

 Intellectual Disabilities and 'Personality Disorder' © Pavilion Publishing and Media Ltd and its licensors 2023

Long term	
Higher intelligence. Physical attractiveness. Artistic talent. Self-discipline. Involvement in 12-step program (e.g. AA) if have addiction.	Chronic hostility and irritability. History of antisocial behaviour. History of severe parental abuse. Severe jealousy. Poverty. Addiction but not in 12-step programme.
References: Kreisman and Straus (2004), PDC (2018)	

The factors associated with favourable and unfavourable outcomes in 'personality disorder' in the general population suggest that individuals with intellectual disabilities who might be given a diagnosis of 'personality disorder' are at risk of having poor outcomes. Individuals with intellectual disabilities are more likely to have additional physical health problems (see Chapter 17) and disabilities, to be poor and socially isolated. They are often more dependent on their families and have greater difficulties 'stepping out' of family relationship patterns, for example where there has been exploitation or abuse. They are also at risk of 'over medication' if their difficulties are not correctly recognised and the required support is not given (Bradford *et al*, 2018).

The negative outcomes experienced may lead to increased contact with health services. One study found that 59% of individuals with intellectual disabilities identified as meeting the diagnostic criteria for 'personality disorder' had had at least one hospital admission in the previous five years and had needed intensive behavioural support (Khan *et al*, 1997). One case study reported an individual who had over 100 admissions as a result of self-harm (Wink *et al*, 2010).

Individuals may make frequent use of services such as accident and emergency departments, and often have contact with many different services. Sadly, they often receive poor care as the result of staff misunderstanding or holding prejudices about 'personality disorder'. They may also be excluded from accessing some services. These experiences may compound existing difficulties with trusting others and seeking help.

As a result of their patterns of relationships and behaviour, individuals can provoke strong emotional reactions in those trying to help and support them. Staff members may feel de-skilled, 'manipulated' ('tricked' into doing something they would not have otherwise done), powerless or angry. Members within a team may have very different images of the individual and there may be conflict or 'splitting' within and between teams. These patterns need to be understood and addressed if individuals are to get the help and support they need. These issues are explored in Chapter 7.

However, outcomes are not always negative. In the general population, 'personality disorder' is not always life-long. Research shows that 'personality disorder' is most common in younger age groups (Morgan and Zimmerman, 2020), indicating that many individuals 'mature out' of the 'diagnosis' by their mid-30s. This has been recognised in ICD-11, where guidelines explicitly state that 'personality disorders' are only 'relatively' stable (Bach and First, 2018).

It is a myth that 'personality disorder' does not respond to intervention. Many individuals respond well to longer-term, structured-intervention approaches (see Chapter 3). Case studies (Iversen, 2019) suggest that, once appropriate support and interventions are given, outcomes can improve significantly. For example, individuals may be on fewer medications and at lower doses, they may have fewer admissions to hospital, and may have better relationships with family members and the staff who support them. However, progress was dependent on them being given consistent support; those lacking such support did not improve. Approaches to intervention and support that can enable individuals to live their best lives are explored in the subsequent chapters.

Key learning points

- Personality is the collection of enduring personal characteristics that make us distinctive as people.
- Individuals with intellectual disabilities share the same personality traits as the general population. However, these are shaped by their experiences of failure, rejection and social deprivation. This impacts on how they interact with others in their adult life, including how they interact with caregivers.
- 'Personality disorder' is a medical diagnosis that refers to an enduring pattern of emotional and cognitive difficulties which affect the way in which the individual relates to others or understands themselves.
- 'Personality disorder' has become a pejorative label. It is associated with stigma, triggers negative assumptions and can lead to exclusion from services. However, there is not yet agreement on alternative language.

 Intellectual Disabilities and 'Personality Disorder' © Pavilion Publishing and Media Ltd and its licensors 2023

- Using the diagnosis 'personality disorder' is controversial; it lacks validity, is unreliable and pathologising. However, it can provide a coherent explanation of difficulties, capture the breadth of issues involved, and can be a signpost to appropriate intervention and research.
- There are several different sets of diagnostic criteria and it is important to look beyond a label to see what patterns of thoughts, feelings, behaviours and relating contributed to a diagnosis.
- The application of 'personality disorder' with individuals with intellectual disabilities is complex and controversial. If diagnosis is considered appropriate, it should be supported by guidelines specific to people with intellectual disabilities and draw on multiple sources of information.
- A diagnosis of 'personality disorder' is not an endpoint. It must be accompanied by a formulation of the factors contributing to the pattern of thoughts, feelings and behaviour that led to the diagnosis to provide a hopeful way forward.
- While many individuals given a diagnosis of 'personality disorder' experience negative outcomes, there is evidence that many 'mature out' of the diagnosis and that others can respond to longer-term supportive interventions.

Chapter 2: Understanding the development of patterns of relating and behaving that can lead to a diagnosis of 'personality disorder'

This chapter explores how patterns of relating and behaving develop. It looks at the developmental process and how it can be shaped or delayed by an individual's biology, attachments and life events. It highlights that individuals given a diagnosis of 'personality disorder' and those with intellectual disabilities experience higher rates of trauma than the general population. It explores the effects of trauma including changes to neurological and physiological pathways, attachments and learning opportunities. It shows how this can lead to patterns of thoughts, feelings and behaviour that can affect an individual's mental and physical health. It shows how 'personality disorder' is one of many possible outcomes of the developmental process.

Key topics

- Human development
- Delayed or disrupted development
- Adversity, trauma and attachment
- Trauma in adulthood
- Disrupted development, trauma and mental health

Human development

'All features of the individual are constructed during development…' (Livesley and Larstone, 2020). This includes the patterns of relating and behaving that can lead to an individual being given a diagnosis of 'personality disorder'. Patterns of relating and behaving arise as the result of complex interactions between multiple factors, from genes to culture (Hang and Vernon, 2020; Shiner and Allen,

2020). There is no single developmental pathway: factors that appear to have been influential for one individual may have had a smaller or no apparent impact on another (Shiner and Allen, 2020). There are no factors that are unique to the 'personality disorder' pattern. Individuals having similar experiences might have many different outcomes including: being given a diagnosis of 'personality disorder', experiencing depression or being superficially unaffected by those experiences. The exact outcome for any individual will be influenced by multiple factors, including personality traits and biological vulnerabilities, resilience and the timing and nature of any adverse experiences.

Hence, to understand the origins of 'personality disorder', it is necessary to adopt a 'whole-person, whole-life' perspective (Benefield and Haigh, 2020). The developmental process may be likened to the chaotic dynamics of the weather. There is no single causal chain of events and consequences, rather, events interact and change the way people may respond in the future (see Box 2.1).

Box 2.1: The interplay of biological and psychological development

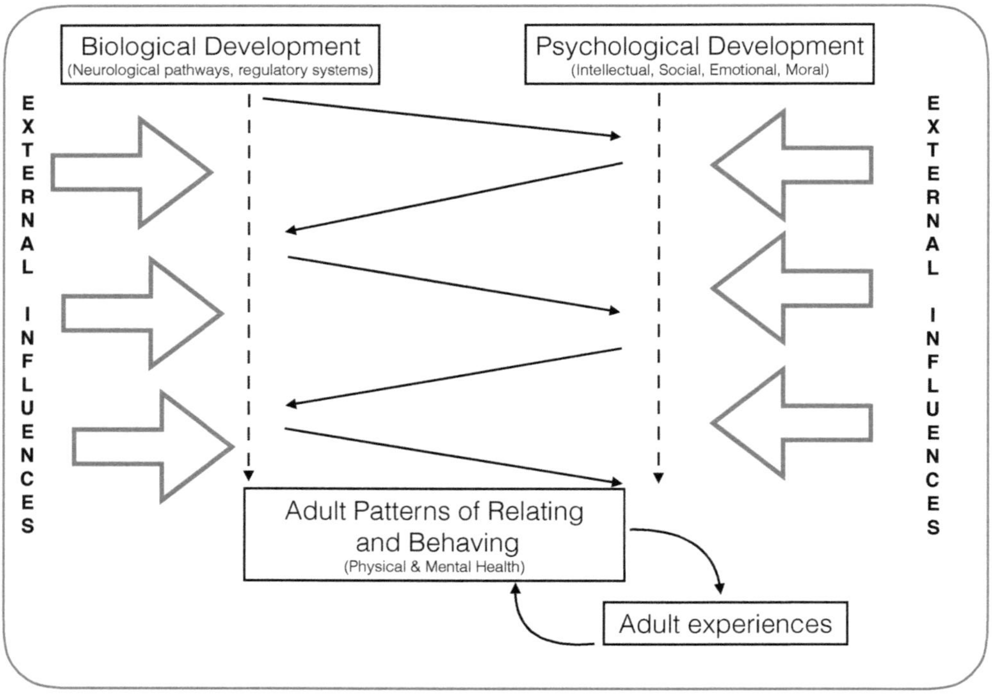

 Intellectual Disabilities and 'Personality Disorder' © Pavilion Publishing and Media Ltd and its licensors 2023

In this process, *the nature of relationships between people is as important as the characteristics of the individual themselves*. For example, a particular temperament trait evident at birth may or may not interfere with parental bonding, depending on the characteristics of the parent and their support system. The process of parental bonding or attachment is explored more fully later in this chapter (see Box 2.6). If attachment is affected, the trait may be amplified and go on to have a negative effect on peer relationships, which may further amplify the trait (Paris, 2020). Within this approach, every event will be understood as having a unique effect depending on the context, the timing and how it is perceived by the individual. Even superficially minor negative events may have a huge impact on vulnerable or hypersensitive individuals. This may result in them experiencing mental health issues despite appearing to have experienced relatively 'normal' childhoods (Paris, 2020).

> *'For example, an early adverse event which appears objectively trivial may have disproportionate and severe consequences throughout somebody's life. This could be something unpleasant said at school, a moment of perceived rejection by a parent, a pervasive atmosphere of disquiet - or any number of potential experiences. Such an event will not have a single definitive effect, but will also modulate further development by changing the way in which experience is perceived and responded to. And so on ad infinitum.'* (Benefield and Haigh, 2020)

This multiplicity of outcomes is possible because of characteristics of the developmental process (see Box 2.2 for definitions of the terms used).

Box 2.2: Some terms relevant to the developmental process	
Epigenetics	Chemical changes at the cellular level that alter gene expression but do not alter the genetic code. Factors present in an individual's external environment (e.g. neglect) influence the expression of their genes and thus shape their physiology and influence all aspects of their functioning. More active during early life. (Jones *et al*, 2021)
Brain development	Begins before birth and continues into young adulthood. An ongoing process with periods of more rapid development (critical periods): ■ Early childhood 0-5 years. ■ Adolescence and early adulthood 12–25 years. ■ Positive experiences and interactions and positive stress (appropriate challenges and learning opportunities) help form connections between neurones and build pathways. Pathways that are used will strengthen while unused connections may be pruned.

→

Stages of development	Distinct transitions in physical and psychological functioning occurring in age-specific life periods. Individuals progress through stages in the same order but different rates, and some may not achieve the later stages. Different areas of development e.g. physiological, intellectual (see Box 15.7) and emotional (see Box 11.1), progress in parallel and are shaped by and influence each other.
Neuroplasticity	Flexibility in the developmental process that allows brain development to respond to the individual's unique physical and social environment. The brain is most plastic in childhood. However, it retains some capacity to recover, adapt and change across adulthood.
'Hard wiring'	Used to describe the way biological and behavioural changes can become built into the nervous system. When an individual has been exposed to prolonged stress, the systems that control the stress responses, enable learning, memory and regulate attention and emotion do not automatically reset when a situation improves.
Neurodiversity	Different ways of thinking and learning that emerge as a result of an individual's biology and their interaction with their physical and social environment. There is no single 'right' way of thinking, just different profiles. Profiles traditionally thought of as deficits are re-evaluated to see their potential benefits and associated strengths. Originating the field of Autism, it has been applied to other ability patterns such as dyslexia. (Baumer and Frueh, 2021; Wiginton, 2021; Madebydyslexia)
Resilience	Most individuals exposed to a particular experience do not have serious negative outcomes. Factors that can provide some protection: ■ Positive personality traits. ■ Intelligent. ■ Having positive relationships outside the family. ■ Having the support of safe and available adults. ■ Having positive experiences. Multiple, sequential adverse events may overcome resilience (Paris, 2020).

 Intellectual Disabilities and 'Personality Disorder' © Pavilion Publishing and Media Ltd and its licensors 2023

Development unfolds from before birth and continues into early adulthood, progressing through a series of stages. However, this process is flexible. Adaptations to an individual's unique physical and social environment are facilitated by neuroplasticity. This allows neural pathways and the reactivity of systems, such as stress pathways, to be shaped to fit the environment. Adaptations are also aided by the process of epigenetics, which changes the expression of genes in response to external influences. As development progresses, these adaptations become increasingly 'hard wired' and are built into the individual's nervous system. This is manifest in characteristics such as the individual's personality profile. Each individual will develop patterns of thinking and learning with associated strengths. These differences may be referred to as 'neurodiversity' and influence both their functioning and their understanding of the world.

Delayed or disrupted development

Development may be facilitated by positive factors or delayed or disrupted by adverse factors.

Although adverse events can disrupt or delay development, this is not inevitable. Most individuals have a degree of resilience, while others may be much more vulnerable. The metaphor 'dandelions and orchids' fits well here: orchids flourish only with special care, while dandelions will thrive in almost any conditions (Kennedy, 2013). However, resilience may be overcome by multiple, sequential adverse events or where resources are depleted by adverse social conditions.

Where development is delayed, an individual may not progress through subsequent developmental stages, and the biological process underpinning thoughts, feelings and behaviour may be altered. Delayed or arrested development in one area will impact on other areas. For individuals with intellectual disabilities, such delays may be perceived as arising from their intellectual disability and therefore inevitable, whereas sometimes they may in fact respond to supportive interventions designed to help their development progress (Frankish, 2021).

When development has been disrupted or delayed, there will still be the potential to change, adapt and develop. For example, there is evidence that adolescence gives a window to repair damage from earlier childhood. However, sometimes it is not possible for an individual to achieve their full potential. When this occurs, it is important to understand the impact this disrupted neurodevelopment has on the individual's thoughts, feelings and behaviour to ensure they receive appropriate support.

Factors contributing to delayed or disrupted development

The timing in the life cycle, type, duration and intensity of the disrupting factor(s) will all shape the resulting changes to development. It is beyond the scope of this book to explore all of the multiple factors that can disrupt or delay development (Benefield and Haigh, 2020). However, the effects of attachments, childhood adversity and trauma are particularly important in understanding the development of patterns of relating and behaving that can lead to a diagnosis of 'personality disorder' and are discussed in the following sections.

A very high proportion (50–80%) of individuals given a diagnosis of '(borderline) personality disorder' show the attachment pattern (see Box 2.6) described as 'disorganised' or 'unresolved' (Agrawal *et al*, 2007). Childhood trauma is a common experience for this group. In a meta-analysis of 97 studies, Porter *et al* (2020) concluded that individuals given a diagnosis of '(borderline) personality disorder' are more than 13 times more likely to report trauma in childhood (particularly neglect and emotional abuse) than non-clinical controls and three times more likely than individuals with other mental health diagnoses.

Individuals with intellectual disabilities are also at increased risk of childhood trauma. Children with intellectual disabilities are 2.5 to 11 times more likely to experience abuse than children without disabilities. They are at high risk of emotional abuse and neglect, are more likely to experience severe maltreatment and to be victims of more perpetrators (Dion *et al*, 2018; McDonnell, 2019; Morris *et al*, 2020). They are more likely to experience social deprivation such as low income and poor housing and have a higher risk of having their resilience compromised (Wigham and Emerson, 2015). Individuals with intellectual disabilities are also more likely to experience trauma during birth and infancy, for example being hospitalised. Although children with intellectual disabilities are able to form secure attachments, they are more likely to show disorganised attachments than children without intellectual disabilities (Hamadi and Fletcher, 2019; Vanwalleghem, 2021).

Individuals with intellectual disabilities are particularly vulnerable to the effects of trauma in childhood. Their intellectual impairment reduces their ability to think about and process their experiences and to learn new ways of responding. They have narrower social networks which reduce the likelihood of forming protective relationships. The effects of failure, rejection, discrimination and stigmatisation are cumulative.

The experience of childhood abuse can lead to children being taken into the care system. Sadly, paid carers may not provide good enough parenting. 'Looked

Intellectual Disabilities and 'Personality Disorder' © Pavilion Publishing and Media Ltd and its licensors 2023

after' children may experience multiple relocations and placement failures, with associated trauma.

Adversity, trauma and attachment

Adversity and trauma are overlapping terms that refer to negative events and experiences. The use of the term 'trauma' rather than 'adversity' has been criticised for having medical overtones and creating the '*...potentially misleading impression of discrete, possibly very unusual, extreme or life-threatening events impinging from outside, rather than, as is often the case, of* ***continuous or repeated very negative experiences, embedded in people's lives and relationships...***' (BPS, 2018 emphasis added). Despite these concerns, the word 'trauma' will most often be used here, for compatibility with the 'trauma-informed care' approach (see Chapter 3).

A broad definition of trauma is:

> ***'Individual trauma results from an event, series of events, or set of circumstances that is experienced by an individual as physically or emotionally harmful or life threatening*** *and that has lasting adverse effects on the individual's functioning and mental, physical, social, emotional, or spiritual well-being.'* (SAMHSA, 2014, p.7, emphasis added)

Trauma covers a wide range of events and experiences, and different terms have been developed to capture particular aspects, such as complexity or age at occurrence. These are described in Box 2.3 and their interrelationships are shown in Box 2.4.

Box 2.3: Aspects that influence the effects of trauma

Dimension	Terms	Description
Who the event happened to		■ Experienced by the individual.
	Vicarious/ secondary	■ Indirect exposure through first-hand account e.g. listening to individual talking about the abuse they have experienced.
	Historical	■ Previous generations.
Type of event	Neglect/ deprivation	■ Omission – something didn't happen e.g. neglect, poverty.
	Abuse	■ Commission – something active was done e.g. assault, shouting insults.

➔

	Type 1/single incident Adversity	■ Accident, terrorist attack, natural disaster. ■ Wider social stressors – family adversity/ breakdown.
Who or what caused the trauma	Relational/ interpersonal	Parent or partner/important relationship. Other person(s) in social network. Stranger. Multiple placements.
Objective severity		Risk to life, physical injuries.
Subjective severity		How individual perceived what happened to them – may dismiss objectively traumatic events or experience apparently neutral events as traumatic (subtle relational).
Timing	Historical Developmental Developmental Adult	■ Previous generations – ongoing impact of events e.g. slavery, the Holocaust. This can add another layer of complexity to the experiences of individuals from minority groups. ■ Pregnancy – impact of trauma experienced by mother e.g. malnutrition, drug misuse. ■ Infancy – adolescence – delayed or distorted development, influences whether memories can be accessed. ■ 25+ main development is complete (described by characteristics of trauma e.g. type 1/ relational/complex).
Duration	Type 1/single incident Type 2/ complex	One-off event. Ongoing or multiple incidents.
Pervasiveness		How much of life is affected. Whether some part of life is safe e.g. time at school. Whether escape is possible.
Context	Resilience	The impact of any event will be influenced by the individual's level of support and personal resources.

 Intellectual Disabilities and 'Personality Disorder' © Pavilion Publishing and Media Ltd and its licensors 2023

Box 2.4 Interrelationship of types of trauma.

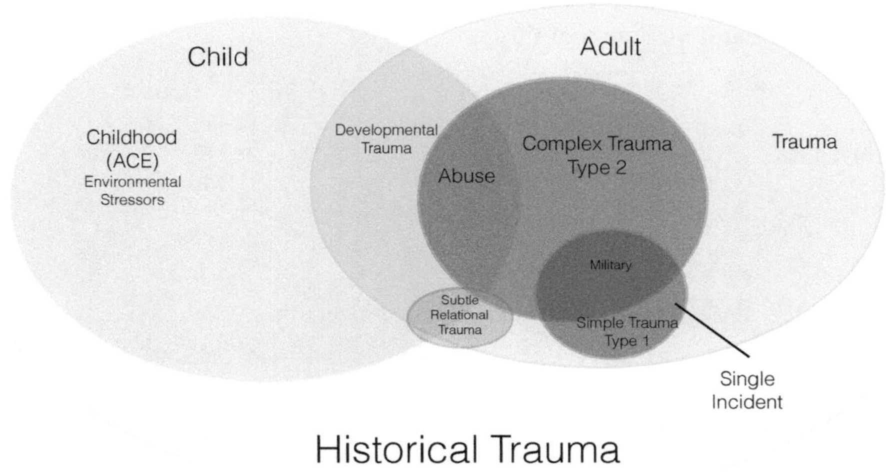

Adapted from NHS Education for Scotland

Trauma has both short-term and long-term effects. These are shaped by factors such as the characteristics of the individual, the situation and the trauma itself. Trauma triggers adaptive biological and behavioural responses to high-threat/high-challenge environments that interact and affect each other. If trauma is experienced in childhood, when brain development is very active and incomplete, it shapes the development of multiple systems, pathways and behaviour patterns. These changes can become 'hard wired' and continue to shape responses long after the traumatic experience itself is over. Trauma in childhood also impacts on relationships, on the individual's ability to learn and the learning opportunities they have access to.

Trauma and biological systems

Regardless of the source, when trauma is experienced, biological responses to short- and long-term stress are activated (see Box 2.5).

Box 2.5: Neurological pathways and physiological systems that are shaped by attachments and trauma

The perception of and response to threat:	
Short term response (The Fight/Flight or survival cascade)	Rapid: Increase in heart rate and breathing. Decrease in digestive activity. Liver released glucose for energy.
Long term/ chronic stress response The Hypothalamic Pituitary-Adrenal (HPA)	Slow: Releases energy and suppresses inflammation. The interaction between the hypothalamus, pituitary gland, and adrenal glands. 'An intricate, yet robust, neuroendocrine mechanism' (Sheng *et al*, 2021) that mediates the effects of stressors by regulating numerous physiological processes, such as metabolism, immune responses, and the autonomic nervous system. It releases hormones that tell the adrenal glands to release cortisol. The immune system is suppressed while this happens.
Experiencing and regulating emotions and how these shape decision-making and planning	
Remembering, including memories described as affective or emotional	
Experiencing and regulating different levels of arousal/attention	
Reward pathways	
States of consciousness: extreme events may trigger different states of consciousness such as dissociation – where the system reacts to overload by cutting off from an otherwise inescapable situation (see Chapter 8)	
Reference: DCP (2018) Smith and Pollak (2020)	

These systems switch off higher-level cognitive functioning and focus attention on perceived threats (Smith and Pollak, 2020). An individual who does not feel safe primarily 'lives' in their fight/flight (survival cascade) responses in order to survive the real or perceived danger they face (these are explored more fully in Chapters 8 and 9). They will struggle to engage, reason and learn. Extreme, unescapable situations may lead to changes in states of consciousness e.g. dissociation (see 9.4). Prolonged activation of stress responses can suppress the immune system leading to physical ill-health. It can also disrupt the development of neurological and physiological systems that regulate arousal, emotions and behaviour (see Box 2.5).

Intellectual Disabilities and 'Personality Disorder' © Pavilion Publishing and Media Ltd and its licensors 2023

The resulting social, emotional and cognitive changes can contribute to the adoption of high-risk behaviours. These, in turn, contribute to illness, disability and social problems (NHS Education for Scotland).

Trauma and attachments

Forming relationships and developing emotional bonds is an essential part of human development and a child's relationship to their parent(s)[1] is both central to this process and vital for the child's survival. This relationship bond is referred to as 'attachment'. It develops from the interaction of a child's instinctive strategies for engaging adults to elicit comfort and care (care-seeking behaviour) and their parents' care-giving behaviour. When parents respond to these strategies by meeting care needs, the child develops a secure attachment. A secure attachment allows the child to develop a number of abilities and skills (see Box 2.6), provides a basis for future relationships (see Chapter 12) and is also protective against the effects of trauma.

Box 2.6: Attachments in childhood and implications for adulthood

Child category (% general population)	Expression in adult relationships and patterns of behaviour
Secure (60%): Confident attachment needs will be met and return quickly to explore and play once they have been comforted. Child develops: ■ A safe and secure base. ■ The ability to engage and learn. ■ The ability to share enjoyment. ■ The ability to be comforted at times of stress and anxiety. ■ The ability to notice, label and organise feelings. ■ A sense of self as loveable.	Values attachment relationships. Comfortable with intimacy, interdependence and independence. Is likely to have a coherent sense of self and the ability to: ■ Feel safe – be sensitive to safety cues. ■ Engage with others and enjoy life. ■ Form secure, mutual relationships. ■ Self-soothe and regulate emotions. ■ Take comfort from others. ■ Empathise and understand others. ■ Regulate behaviour and control impulses. ■ Integrate thoughts, feelings and memories. **These become 'hard wired' and automatic.**

→

1 The terms parent and parenting is used to include all those who care for children under the age of 18, including biological, step, foster and adopted parents and paid carers. The terms carer / care staff / staff are used for those supporting individuals over 18 years.

Avoidant (10–15%): Maintain proximity to their caregiver by apparently 'self-managing' and not signalling a need for comfort, thereby avoiding rejection.	Minimises the importance of attachment relationships and experiences and stress their own independence and ability to cope. May repeatedly rebuff approaches from others.
Ambivalent (8–10%) Maintain proximity to the caregiver by extensive use of attachment behaviours, which may be of high amplitude, and it may become difficult to reduce arousal levels at times of distress.	Overly concerned with past family relationships and may present as passive and childlike, overwhelmed or conflicted and angry.
Disorganised (15-19%) Afraid of their parent or their behaviour. Children are conflicted if they need comforting. May show fear/apprehension when approaching their parent which leads to them 'freezing'. May appear confused and disorientated.	May switch between rebuffing approaches and frantic efforts to maintain contact. Is likely to: ■ Have a negative and/or fragmented sense of self. ■ Feel unsafe, be insensitive to safety cues. ■ Have difficulty engaging and enjoying life. ■ Form insecure or disorganised attachments (anxious, avoidant, chaotic). ■ Be unable to self-soothe or regulate emotions. ■ Be unable to take comfort from others. ■ Lack empathy and understanding of others. ■ Have difficulty regulating behaviour and controlling impulses. ■ Struggle to integrate thoughts, feelings and memories (use unconscious mechanisms to protect self). **These become 'hard wired' and automatic.**
Adapted from: BPS (2017)	

However, the formation of attachments can be disrupted by adversity and trauma. For a variety of reasons, a parent may be absent, less available or may

 Intellectual Disabilities and 'Personality Disorder' © Pavilion Publishing and Media Ltd and its licensors 2023

respond inconsistently or with hostility. When this happens, the *child learns that adults cannot be trusted* and will use different attachment strategies to try to get their needs met. They may work hard to invite a response from the parent and maintain the connection. They may try to meet their own needs as best they can without the adult, or flip between strategies (Hughes, 2017). Where the parent is a source of threat, for example when abuse is occurring, the child will both need the parent and be afraid of them. This will lead to them being conflicted and confused; they may freeze or respond in a disorganised way. They may try different strategies, but whatever strategies they adopt, their needs are rarely met. Over time, the strategies adopted come to characterise the child's wider attachments (BPS, 2017). These are called insecure attachments (ambivalent, avoidant and disorganised, see Box 2.6). *While adaptive in a threat situation, when these strategies persist in safe situations they are unhelpful.* Chronic disruption to attachments also means the child does not develop the abilities fostered by secure attachments, with consequences for their intellectual, emotional and social development. This influences their ways of relating and thinking, regulating emotions and managing arousal (BPS, 2018).

Learning opportunities

Trauma and disruption to attachments alter the child's learning environment in a number of ways:

- Reduced opportunities to learn about positive emotional experiences.
- Over exposure to intense emotional experiences, for example anger or fear.
- Reduced opportunities (through neglect or over-protection) to learn positive coping skills.
- Shaping of behaviours that are not adaptive outside of the survival situation.
- Switching attention to survival, making it hard to absorb new information, concentrate or problem-solve.

Consistent and caring parents help children to understand their own and others' actions. Parents explain the child's emotions to them and signal that it is OK to feel that way. They also explain why others might have behaved in certain ways. For example, 'John hit you because he was tired of waiting for a go on the swing, you are upset because it was your turn'. This develops into the ability to understand actions by working out on their own what is going on, and 'best guessing' what is going on in other people's minds (Fonagy and Luyten, 2020). This process is called 'mentalising' or 'social cognition'.

Without these experiences, a child will not learn to understand their own and others' thoughts, feelings and behaviours. Without the ability to mentalise, their own behaviour and emotions and those of others will often be experienced as confusing, unpredictable and frightening. Lacking this ability may make it very hard for an individual to consider others' needs; they may even be totally oblivious of the pain they cause others.

Children who are neglected or abused often learn to think only of themselves. They need to be selfish and ruthless to protect themselves and get as much as they can in situations where there is not enough to go round. Children who are exposed to harsh or neglectful parenting will absorb negative views of themselves and the world. They will also learn a narrow range of unhelpful ways of interacting with others. For example, individuals may adopt the role of either victim or bully depending on who they are interacting with, and be unaware that there are other ways of behaving in these situations.

The combined result of the impact of developmental trauma and attachments is summarised in Box 2.7. This looks very similar to a list of 'symptoms' of 'personality disorder'.

Box 2.7: Combined effects of trauma and disruption to attachment

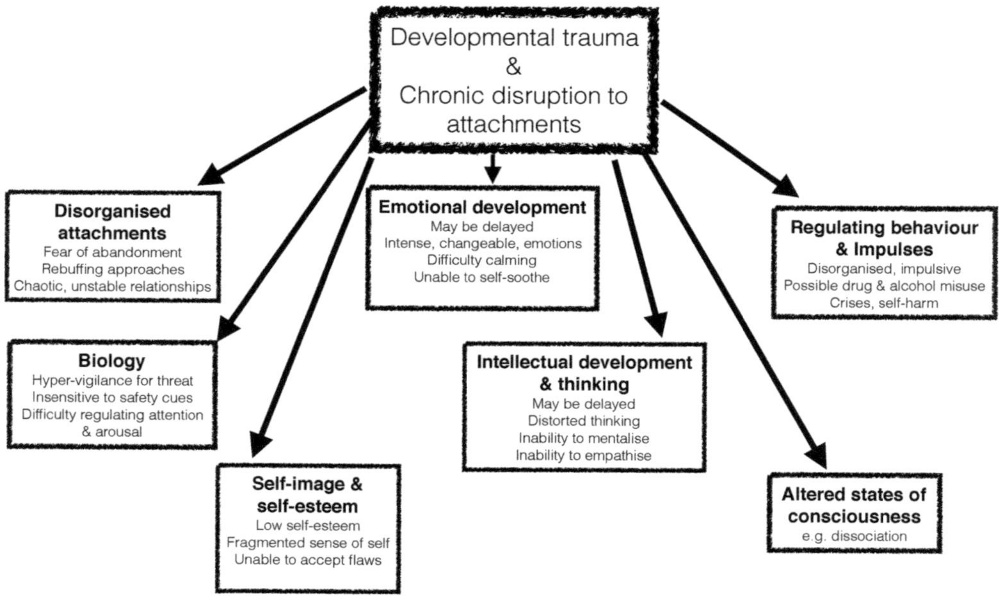

 Intellectual Disabilities and 'Personality Disorder' © Pavilion Publishing and Media Ltd and its licensors 2023

'Subtle' relational trauma

The term 'subtle relational trauma' can be used to describe apparently trivial interpersonal events that impact development in a similar way to more obvious trauma. For example, a well-meaning carer may be distracted by other demands and might fail to recognise a child's emotional needs, see things from their perspective or respond to them consistently. A child might be ridiculed, left out of a friend group, bullied by a classmate or shamed by a teacher (Kushnick, 2018). There may be subtle messages that the child is a disappointment or unloveable. These experiences will impact on all children. However, for vulnerable children (orchids), they may result in similar outcomes as more obvious relational trauma such as abuse.

Individuals with a diagnosis of 'personality disorder' may have experienced subtle relational trauma in their interactions with parents. Linehan (1993) explored the concept of an 'invalidating environment' where children with greater needs are hypersensitive to parents who dismiss their feelings and their need for support (see Chapter 11).

Children with intellectual disabilities may experience subtle relational trauma within their attachment relationship to 'good enough' parents. Their parents may experience emotional distress in response to their child's disability, have difficulty understanding the child's communications and developmental level, and experience increased levels of stress. These may influence the sensitivity of their responses (BPS, 2017) and result in the child's needs not being met.

Although the term 'subtle relational trauma' can be criticised for being almost impossible to define, it is helpful in understanding the cumulative effects of slights and criticism. It also enhances the development of empathy with individuals who show enduring distress without a history of more obvious trauma.

Trauma in adulthood

The experience of trauma is not confined to childhood: findings suggest one in six adults will have experienced significant trauma. How an individual presents as an adult will be a combination of their childhood and adult experiences. Both simple and complex trauma can happen for the first time in adulthood, for example experiencing rape or domestic violence after a secure childhood. For other individuals, the adverse experiences of childhood may persist into adulthood. Earlier relational trauma can make the individual more vulnerable to further abuse, exploitation and deprivation. Experiences as adults may trigger memories of earlier trauma.

Sometimes, adults are traumatised by the services that are intended to help them, and individuals with a diagnosis of 'personality disorder' may experience relational trauma as a result of the way services are designed and delivered. They may have repeated experiences of being excluded, unheard, disbelieved, demonized or dismissed (Ball, 2020).

> *'I have been treated abominably by some staff in A&E: having my feet slapped; told my bed is for an ill person, not for those who overdose. Being told that I have 'personality disorder' so it must be all my fault…'* (Sibbald, 2020)

Individuals with a diagnosis of 'personality disorder' comprise around 70% of those detained in secure facilities where they are exposed to a variety of restrictive interventions (Ramsden, 2020), which are traumatic to experience.

Being in receipt of life-long support may pose particular risks to the psychological well-being, emotional safety and quality of care of people with intellectual disabilities (BPS, 2017). They may experience staff shortages, frequent changes of staff and often multiple placements. Secret filming by BBC's *Panorama* series has exposed the appalling abuse of some adults with intellectual disabilities and complex needs. They found evidence of toxic staff cultures, falsification of medical paperwork, individuals being taunted, provoked, bullied, sworn at and slapped, inappropriate use of restraint and seclusion. Lessons from previous scandals do not appear to become embedded in service culture, allowing the same patterns of abuse to emerge again and again.

Disrupted development, trauma and mental health

Adults who do not make secure attachments are at increased risk of psychological distress including paranoia, distressing intrusive thoughts, depressive thoughts and feelings, and are more likely to receive formal psychiatric diagnoses including depression, obsessive-compulsive disorder, schizophrenia, and a range of 'personality disorders' (BPS, 2017).

Trauma can lead to patterns of thoughts, feelings and behaviour that can be given a number of psychiatric diagnoses including post-traumatic stress disorder (PTSD) and complex PTSD (see Box 2.8). There is substantial overlap between the diagnoses complex PTSD and 'personality disorder', particularly the category 'borderline personality disorder'. This has led to suggestions that 'personality disorder' should be subsumed under the complex PTSD label.

Intellectual Disabilities and 'Personality Disorder' © Pavilion Publishing and Media Ltd and its licensors 2023

Box 2.8: Types of trauma in relation to diagnoses

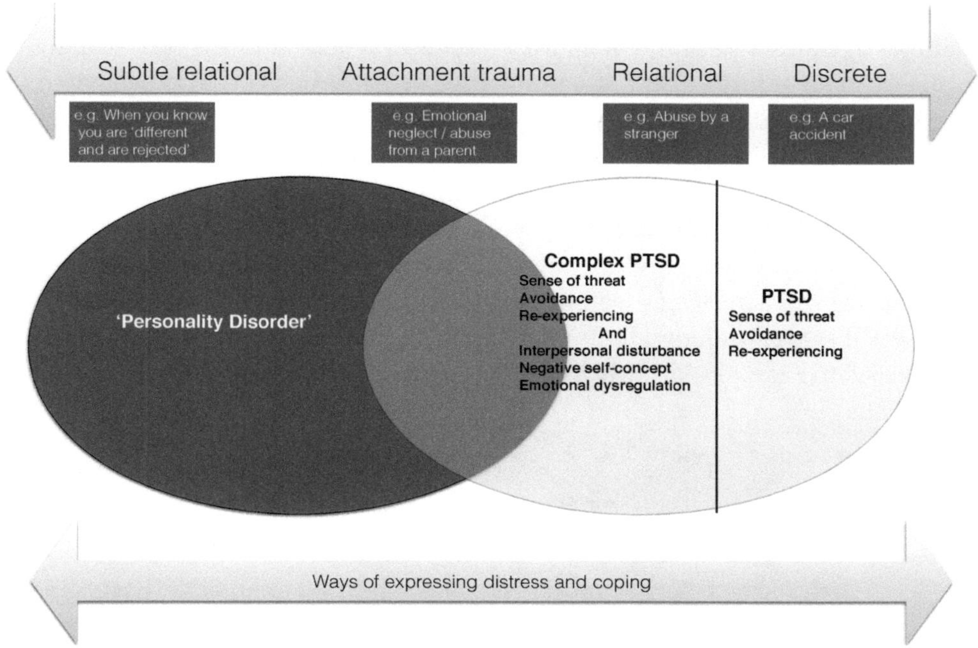

However, some individuals given a diagnosis of 'personality disorder' do not see trauma as being central to their difficulties and find this alienating (Cannon and Gould, 2022b). Others may have experienced more subtle negative experiences for which the label 'trauma' may not feel an appropriate description or have vulnerabilities that made them more sensitive to life events. The Personality Disorder Commission (2018) comment that:

> *'It is important to recognise, however, that people may not have experienced major trauma and yet still have needs best met through therapeutic approaches. In the absence of trauma histories, their needs may be particularly hard to recognise as they don't even attract the sympathy and concern which is often afforded to those with trauma histories. Many of them will have some measure of physically based developmental difficulties including foetal alcohol syndrome, general or specific intellectual disabilities, autistic spectrum disorders and/or attention deficit hyperactivity disorders.'*

The pattens of thoughts, feelings and behaviour that can lead to a diagnosis of 'personality disorders' can be conceptualised as sometimes being the outcome of the interaction of relational trauma with temperamental and trait variants that predispose to behavioural and affective issues (Paris, 2020).

The effects of trauma on individuals with intellectual disabilities is increasingly recognised (Beail *et al*, 2021). It often underlies presentations such as behaviours that challenge, obesity and depression (McNally *et al*, 2021; Wigham and Emerson, 2015). Individuals with intellectual disabilities may experience PTSD which may present overtly (McCarthy *et al*, 2016) or may be overshadowed by behaviours that challenge, including misdiagnosis as 'personality disorder' (Bakken *et al*, 2014). It is likely that the interaction of relational trauma with personality traits and biological vulnerabilities will sometimes lead to presentations that are given a diagnosis of 'personality disorder' in individuals with intellectual disabilities (see Chapter 1). Some composite examples of early experiences are given in Box 2.9.

Box 2.9: Composite examples* of experiences of individuals	
'Susan'	■ She was the youngest of several children born close together. ■ Her father was away with work during much of childhood. ■ She had multiple health problems, which led to repeated hospitalisation during childhood with periods at home recovering from surgery. ■ She was sexually assaulted as a teenager. ■ As an adult she has moved repeatedly as apparently suitable, placements broke down.
'Elizabeth'	■ She was taken in to care as a baby; the reasons for this are not clear. ■ She experienced multiple foster placements, may have been considered for adoption but it did not proceed. ■ As a teenager she had a number of 'boyfriends' much older than herself and she was sometimes treated for injuries she reported as accidental.
'Margaret'	■ She grew up in her birth family with her younger brother. ■ She attended mainstream school, with support, where she was bullied for being 'slow'. ■ Her brother describes her as being 'sensitive' and says his parents found her 'difficult'. ■ Their father died from suicide when she was in her early teens which their mother hinted might have been due to 'the strain' of raising Margaret.

 Intellectual Disabilities and 'Personality Disorder' © Pavilion Publishing and Media Ltd and its licensors 2023

'David'	■ He grew up with his mother; sometimes the two of them, sometimes a boyfriend also lived with them. ■ There were concerns about neglect - neighbours reported David being left alone or taking food from bins, but other times things seemed OK.

* Examples have been created from clinical experience and the literature. They are not based on specific individuals.

The patterns of thoughts, feelings and behaviour that can lead to a diagnosis of 'personality disorder' are one of many possible outcomes of the complex process of human development. They are shaped by the interaction of the individual's biological make-up and their experiences of trauma and attachment, and may be viewed as adaptations for living in a harsh world (Hughes, 2017). This highlights the importance of asking 'What has happened to you?' rather than 'What is wrong with you?' (BPS, 2018). For some, the trauma may be easily recognised and may need to be directly addressed (see Chapter 3). For others, because of heightened sensitivity, subtle, apparently innocuous events may have had a profound, cumulative effect on their development. Rather than making assumptions based on a diagnosis, an understanding of the origins of an individual's pattern of thoughts, feelings and behaviour should be sought through collaborative formulation (see Chapter 4).

Key learning points

- 'Personality disorder' is one of many possible outcomes of a complex developmental process. It arises from the complex interaction of multiple factors from genes to culture.
- Relationships with other people, particularly parents, are as important as the characteristics of individuals themselves, in the outcomes of the developmental process.
- Each individual will have their own unique developmental pathway and unique cognitive profile that will shape relationships, their functioning and their understanding of the world.
- Development may be disrupted or delayed. For some individuals, these respond to supportive interventions. For others, it is not possible overcome them. When this occurs, it is important to understand the impact this has on the individual's thoughts, feelings and behaviour to ensure they receive appropriate support.
- Individuals with intellectual disabilities are at greatly increased risk of experiencing trauma, both as children and adults. They are also more vulnerable

to the effects of trauma as a result of reduced ability to think about and process their experiences, narrower social networks and experiences of failure and stigma.

- The term 'trauma' encompasses a wide variety of events and circumstances. An individual's perception of an event is important: apparently innocuous events may have a profound impact on sensitive individuals.
- Trauma impacts on all aspects of development as the individual adapts to a high-threat environment. These changes can become 'hard wired' as a result of neuroplasticity, and persist when the individual is in a safe environment.
- Trauma can disrupt the formation of secure attachment between children and their parents. This can lead to distrust and feeling unsafe. Individuals may experience a wide range of difficulties including: forming secure relationships, self-soothing and regulating emotions, taking comfort from and understanding others, regulating behaviour and impulses and integrating thoughts feelings and memories.
- Trauma can result in patterns of thoughts, feelings and behaviour that are given many different diagnoses including 'personality disorder'.
- A diagnosis of 'personality disorder' should alert those supporting the individual to look closely at whether the individual has experienced trauma and whether this has been appropriately addressed.

 Intellectual Disabilities and 'Personality Disorder' © Pavilion Publishing and Media Ltd and its licensors 2023

Chapter 3: An integrated approach to intervention: the right support and intervention at the right time

This chapter draws on models of the stages of intervention to understand how to give the right support at the right time. It shows how different interventions are appropriate to the stages of **R**egulate, **R**elate and **R**eason. It highlights the need for long-term planning and longer-term interventions. It considers the role of trauma-informed care and Positive Behavioural Support in creating an overarching framework for delivering these interventions. It examines therapeutic approaches for individuals with complex needs including trauma, and those for individuals given a diagnosis of 'personality disorder'. It looks at the use of a 'toolbox' approach as an alternative to specific therapies. It highlights the importance of non-specific therapy factors in facilitating change.

Key topics

- Stages of intervention: the right time
- Overarching framework
- The right support and interventions
- The toolbox approach
- How it is done: the right way

In their statement of what individuals given a diagnosis of 'personality disorder' should expect from services, the Personality Disorder Commission (2018) state:

The '*Right treatment / right place / right time*

> *I have the right to receive evidence-based treatments delivered from a suitable venue in a timely fashion from services that offer an integrated approach to my care throughout my life.'*

This statement about 'treatment' is equally applicable to the support and interventions offered to individuals with intellectual disabilities who might be given a diagnosis of 'personality disorder'. The 'right place' is discussed in Chapter 6.

Stages of intervention: the right time

Individuals with intellectual disabilities who might be given a diagnosis of 'personality disorder' often present with multiple difficulties, sometimes in crisis. It can be hard to work out what is 'the right help at the right time'. The importance of offering the right help at the right time has been recognised in a number of approaches to supporting individuals who have experienced trauma or have been given a diagnosis of 'personality disorder' (Beail, 2021; Golding and Hughes, 2012; Herman, 1992; Livesley, 2005). A number of different stages have been identified; these are sometimes represented as a pyramid to emphasise that the early stages form the foundations for later work. An integrated summary of these stages, tailored to individuals with intellectual disabilities, is given in Box 3.1.

Box 3.1: Integrated stages of intervention

	Focus	Goal
Stage 1: Crisis: keeping safe. **'Regulate'**	The present. Risk management. Behaviours of concern. Containing emotions.	Safely contain risky behaviour. Provide physical/bodily regulation. Provide emotional containment. Minimise re-traumatisation. Build trust.
Stage 2: Building stability. **'Relate'**	The present. Developing relationships. Co-regulating emotions. Establishing person-centred routines.	Build working relationships. Relief from emotional pain. Emotional containment. Prevent re-escalation.
Stage 3: Maintaining stability. **'Relate/Reason'**	The present. Understanding and learning. Skill building.	Develop collaborative working. Achieving stability in emotions and relationships. Building a shared understanding of issues.

Intellectual Disabilities and 'Personality Disorder' © Pavilion Publishing and Media Ltd and its licensors 2023

Stage 4: Developing new ways of thinking, behaving and relating, and or addressing difficult memories. **'Reason'**	The present and the past.	Work collaboratively to explore thoughts, behaviour, relationships and memories.
Stage 5: Building understanding of self and developing healthy interdependence. **'Reason'**	The present and future. Healthy boundaries.	Work collaboratively to develop a healthy sense of self and others. Build healthy interdependence.
Adapted from: Beail (2021), Golding and Hughes (2012), Herman (1992), Livesley (2005), Perry (2020)		

There are some differences between the models, for example the number of stages and whether to address building a healthy sense of self before or after addressing difficult memories. However, there is much more overlap. They all recognise the importance of tailoring interventions to the individual's state of mind (Chapters 8, 9 and 11 explore this more fully). The phrase '**R**egulate, **R**elate, **R**eason' (3 Rs) nicely captures the order of interventions (Perry, 2020). First **R**egulate and calm the fight/flight (survival cascade) response and avoid overwhelming the individual's capacity to process information. Then connect through attuned and sensitive relationships (**R**elate). Only then can work on reflection, remembering, resolving and learning be considered (**R**eason). This is a slight oversimplification as regulation is actually achieved through relationships via the process of co-regulation (see Chapter 11). However, the 3 Rs makes the primary focus of each interventions stage very clear.

The application of this staged model is key to achieving success: often, the primary focus of those supporting an individual is to address skills deficits or try to resolve the emotional effects of traumatic experiences. However, the individual will be unable to engage with such work if the stages of **R**egulate and **R**elate have not been achieved (Perry, 2020). Indeed, if these stages are achieved, specific therapeutic interventions may not be needed.

Identifying the stage an individual is currently experiencing is explored in Section 2, particularly Chapters 8 and 9. It will be indicated by a combination of factors including emotional arousal, verbal and non-verbal communication, behaviour and attachment strategies. Staff teams can develop a shared understanding of the appropriate intervention stage through the process of formulation (see Chapter 4).

Feeling safe

The staged approach stresses the need to help individuals *feel* physically and emotionally safe before any other work can be undertaken. If therapy is offered before an individual's need for safety and emotional containment have been met, they will not be able to engage. This risks an individual being labelled as 'untreatable' or 'uncooperative'. In fact, they might have been able to engage and benefit from interventions if their needs for containment and stability were addressed and the foundations for a working relationship were developed. Individuals may also move up and down through the stages, for example if a longstanding and trusted member of staff leaves or the individual experiences a significant life event. Hence, it is important to be vigilant for times when they no longer feel safe and may be destabilised. The approach used needs to be sensitively and flexibly adjusted to accommodate these fluctuations.

It is not enough that the setting is safe (although this is important to address, particularly in service settings where a number of individuals showing behaviours that challenge share living space): it needs to be experienced as safe. Chapter 6 explores ways of promoting a sense of safety through the physical structure and philosophy of a service. (Note that helping an individual to feel safe is not the same as avoiding risk. Collaborative, thoughtful, positive risk-taking allows opportunities to build connections and experience joy. This can contribute to building a sense of emotional safety.)

Building relationships is an important part of feeling safe. If staff are able to build relationships with the individual, they can begin to 'co-regulate' emotions (caregivers respond sensitively to cues of the individual's changing emotional state while remaining warm and calm themselves). This is explored further in Chapter 5 and is a theme running through Section 2.

Process through the stages

For some individuals, progress through all stages may not be possible. Their intellectual disabilities may prevent them from learning and implementing the necessary skills or from thinking about some of the abstract concepts involved in the work at later stages. For others, their experiences may have resulted in very significant emotional delays, such that the work to build relationships is, in itself, a life-long process. However, by managing crises, building positive working relationships and giving long-term stability, it is possible to greatly increase an

Intellectual Disabilities and 'Personality Disorder' © Pavilion Publishing and Media Ltd and its licensors 2023

individual's quality of life and promote optimal functioning. This also creates an environment where further emotional development may be possible (Frankish, 2021).

Some individuals may never achieve the early stage of safety; they remain dependent on those around them to manage their emotions and behaviour. For these individuals, it is important to create a long-term plan to keep them and those around them safe while minimising restrictions and maximising their quality of life. Thoughtful work may be required with the system around the individual to maintain a positive approach in the absence of hope for improvement (see Chapter 7 on reflective practices).

Where an individual is stable, is it possible to explore whether they are able to and wish to undertake the work required to progress to further stages. Herman (1992) suggests that, for some people, achieving stability will be sufficient to meet their goals and that they may choose not to take the risks and potential pain of exploring difficult memories. It is important to recognise that individuals may perceive their situation differently from the staff or relatives who support them, and may not wish to address issues or change their behaviour at that time. If not recognised, such a mismatch makes it more likely that the individual will feel misunderstood or that they are being controlled by staff. They are then less likely to engage with staff.

Time scale

The pervasive and enduring nature of the issues experienced by individuals who might be given a diagnosis of 'personality disorder' mean that short interventions are likely to be ineffective. Interventions specific to 'personality disorder' will usually take place over months. and some expect to take one to three years (Livesley and Larston, 2020b). Individuals are also likely to need more general support for extended periods and to have multiple episodes of care. This requires a thoughtful approach within services that are designed to offer time-limited interventions. The PDC (2018) recommend 'sustainable long-term planning' within a life-long service pathway and this need is recognised in the Community Mental Health Framework for Adults and Older Adults (NHS England 2019).

Overarching framework

The longer-term nature and complexity of work within the staged model means that it is important to have an appropriate overarching framework to ensure the necessary coherence and consistency of the approach across stages.

An intervention framework guides staff as to what they need to know and what they need to do; it gives a structure and outline of the work that needs to be carried out. It also provides principles and a shared language that promote understanding and consistency.

Two approaches are particularly relevant when considering a framework to direct work with individuals with intellectual disabilities who might be given a diagnosis of 'personality disorder'.

A trauma-informed approach has been recommended to guide interventions for individuals given a diagnosis of 'personality disorder' (PDC, 2018). While the Positive Behavioural Support (PBS) framework is recommended for supporting individuals with intellectual disabilities (NICE, 2015, NG11). Fortunately, these approaches share many core values and have complementary strengths.

Trauma-informed care

Trauma-informed care is a well-developed approach (SAMSHA, 2014; Office for Health Improvement and Disparities, 2022) that spells out its principles (see Box 3.2) and offers guidance for implementation (see Box 6.3). It seeks to address the barriers that people affected by trauma can experience when accessing health and care services. This approach is embedded in the Community Mental Health Framework (NHS England, 2019).

Box 3.2: Trauma-informed care: principles

Principle	Description
Recognise	Realising that trauma exposure affects people's neurological, biological, psychological and social development, that trauma is experienced by both using and those providing services, and that, if this is not addressed, individuals will not be able to engage with services and staff will not be able to perform to their potential.
Safety	The physical, psychological and emotional safety of both individuals and staff is prioritised. Services are collaboratively designed to avoid re-traumatisation.

Intellectual Disabilities and 'Personality Disorder' © Pavilion Publishing and Media Ltd and its licensors 2023

Trustworthiness	Transparent policies and procedures build trust among staff, individuals and the wider community by: ■ the organisation and staff explaining what they are doing and why. ■ the organisation and staff doing what they say they will do. ■ the organisation and staff not overpromising.
Choice, collaboration and empowerment	Recognise that the experience of trauma can make people feel controlled, excluded and powerless, and to directly address this by listening to and involving individuals and staff in all aspects of the organisation e.g. service planning and design as well as the delivery of support.
Cultural consideration	The impact of cultural stereotypes and biases (e.g. gender, sexual orientation, age, religion, disability, geography, race or ethnicity) contributes to traumatic experiences and need to be actively addressed.
Adapted from: SAMSHA (2014) and OHID (2022)	

Trauma-informed care recognises the pervasive impact of trauma on *both those using and providing services* and *the capacity of services to traumatise and re-traumatise* the individuals they seek to help. It is based on an understanding of how trauma exposure affects people's neurological, biological, psychological and social development (see Chapter 2). It recognises that trauma can make it difficult for individuals to feel safe and to develop trusting relationships both in their personal lives and in their interactions with services.

While recognising the benefits of understanding trauma and trauma-specific interventions, the approach stresses that this is not enough. Trauma-informed care recognises that the damage arising from traumatic relationships needs to be addressed through every aspect of contact with a service. It stresses that *everyone has a role to play in healing and someone doesn't have to be a therapist to be therapeutic*. The professional relationships individuals develop with all staff (not just those considered therapists) become the primary agents for fostering safety and hope. More recently, the approach has highlighted *the need for compassion at all levels of the system* (NHS Education for Scotland, 2021). Trauma-informed care gives the strong message that how things are done is at least as important as what is done.

Considering thoughts, feelings and behaviour through a trauma-informed lens can contribute to a greater understanding of why some individuals experience difficulties with relationships, learning and behaviour. It shifts the emphasis from 'What is wrong with you?' to 'What has happened to you?' (BPS, 2018) and 'What do you need?' (OHID, 2022).

However, looking at the whole system (staff, building, policies, clinical practices) can give a richer picture. For example, reflecting about the trauma experienced by members of a staff team both directly and vicariously, can help understand why they might be struggling to support an individual (see Chapter 7). The approach also shifts the emphasis from changing the individual to changing the emotional and physical environment that surrounds them and the systems that support them.

To be effective at the clinical level, trauma-informed care principles must permeate all levels of the organisation (SAMSHA, 2014). This is explored in Chapter 6.

Positive Behavioural Support

Positive behavioural support (PBS) is an evidenced-based, values-led approach to addressing behaviours that challenge. It provides a framework that includes values, a theory and evidence base, and a process. These elements combine to inform all aspects of intervention.

Some important elements of the approach are presented in Box 3.3. The approach is explored more fully in Chapter 8.

Box 3.3: Positive Behavioural Support: Aims to understand what behaviours that challenge tell us so that the individual's needs can be met in better ways	
Values led	Person-centred, whole-person, whole-life approach. Collaborative: working with individual and their family. Treats people with respect and dignity. Positive and proactive.
Evidence based	Behavioural science-based techniques e.g. functional analysis.
Comprehensive	Incorporates other evidence-based approaches and draws on a multi-disciplinary knowledge base.
Understand behaviour	Behaviours that challenge have a meaning and arise from unmet needs.
Individualised assessment	Assesses the individual and their environment to identify unmet needs and find better ways of meeting them.

 Intellectual Disabilities and 'Personality Disorder' © Pavilion Publishing and Media Ltd and its licensors 2023

Promotes quality of life	Safety, choice, least restrictive options, help achieve potential and thrive, meaningful activities through Active Support (see box 5.7). Happy, healthy, involved.
Making systems work for the individual	Changing the system rather than trying to change the individual. Creating capable environments (see Chapter 6).
Positive behaviour support plans	Co-produced to meet needs, improve quality of life and teach new skills. Using positive language, includes strengths, likes and wishes. Provides a vehicle to promote consistent implementation of multi-competent interventions.
Adapted from: Gore *et al* (2013)	

PBS has its origins in behavioural science but has developed to become a comprehensive approach that can incorporate other evidence-based therapies and interventions. The core principle of PBS is that behaviours that challenge (see Box 8.1) have a meaning and arise from unmet needs.

It looks beyond the individual and stresses the need to look at the wider system around them. PBS aims to work aims to work collaboratively to enhance the individual's quality of life, keeping them and those around them safe, using the least restrictive option. Fitting with the PDC (2018) recommendation, it aims *to give the right support at the right time so individuals can thrive to their potential* (BILD, 2022). This information is then used to create a PBS plan to deliver interventions (see box 8.12).

A collaborative approach to developing PBS plans has been used successfully with individuals given a diagnosis of 'personality disorder' both with (Toogood, 2017) and without intellectual disabilities (Brown *et al*, 2017). However, several authors have highlighted the need for PBS to be extended if it is to successfully support individuals who have experienced trauma (Harding, 2021; Paterson, 2017) or have insecure attachments (Skelly, 2017). This can be achieved by integrating the principles of trauma-informed care and attachment theory within PBS to create a trauma informed framework. For example, an awareness the effects of trauma can help identify behaviours rising from the need to create a sense of safety (see Chapter 8).

Harding (2021) highlights how a trauma-informed PBS plan can extend healing experiences beyond the therapy setting, by integrating positive interactions across the individual's whole day. A PBS plan can also promote engagement in meaningful activities. Meaningful activities include creative and leisure activities, exercise, self-care and community access activities. They have been found to have multiple benefits for mental health (Harflett *et al*, 2017), including creating a sense of identity, building self-esteem and increasing social interaction. Engagement with meaningful activities was identified as a key component of their recovery by individuals given a diagnosis of 'borderline personality disorder' (Ng *et al*, 2019).

What works: the right support and intervention

Working within the framework of trauma-informed PBS, it is then necessary to identify the right support and interventions to offer for each intervention stage. Box 3.4 gives some suggestions for interventions appropriate to each stage. Interventions for **R**egulate and **R**elate are discussed in detail in the chapters indicated and will not be explored further in this chapter.

Box 3.4: Stage-appropriate interventions

		Interventions*
Stage 1: Crisis: keeping safe '**R**egulate'	Feel	Crisis plan, boundaries and emotional containment, minimise re-traumatisation, Build trust. Chapter 9 – Getting through: helping everyone survive crises. Chapter 10 – Suicidal behaviour, self-harm and self-injury. Chapter 11 – Containing and regulating emotions.
Stage 2: Building stability '**R**elate'	Sa	Develop TI PBS plan, Build relationships. Chapter 5 – Building positive, respectful working relationships. Chapter 8 – Applying PBS. Chapter 13 – Compassionate supportive relationships.
Stage 3: Maintaining stability '**R**elate/**R**eason'	fe	Avoid overwhelming capacity to process information, begin to explore individual's ability and wish to move towards more active work, for example building understanding though active listening and psycho-education.
Outcome of stages 1-3: A foundation of understanding, safety, stability and emotional regulation.		
Individual may choose not to or may be unable to proceed to stages 4 and 5. Where this is the case, look at how the support needed for stability can be provided for the long term.		

 Intellectual Disabilities and 'Personality Disorder' © Pavilion Publishing and Media Ltd and its licensors 2023

Stage 4: Developing new ways of thinking, behaving and relating and or addressing difficult memories '**R**eason'	F e e l	Active listening, psycho-education, tool-box approach. Chapter 15 – Unhelpful core beliefs and patterns of thinking. Chapter 14 – Regulating impulses. Specialist techniques.
Stage 5: Building understanding of self and developing healthy interdependence '**R**eason'	S a f e	Active listening, psycho-education, tool-box approach. Chapter 16 – Building a positive and stable sense of self. Chapter 12 – Interpersonal relationships.
* Chapters will also contain interventions appropriate for other stages.		

There is a growing evidence base looking at the efficacy of interventions for individuals who reach the **R**eason stage, and in some areas, national guidance, to help make decisions about what interventions to offer. There is considerable overlap between effective approaches, particularly in their positive core values and attitudes towards the individuals they are intended to help. Specific interventions designed for individuals given a diagnosis of 'personality disorder' and those designed to address the effects of trauma may be helpful. A flexible 'toolbox' approach may also be used.

The interventions described below may be helpful once the individual has reached the **R**eason stage, but they are specialist and require specialist training (Jones, 2021). However, it is important to be aware of evidenced-based options. It is also important to be aware that the effectiveness of these interventions will be enhanced if they take place in the context of a trauma-informed PBS plan that ensures the individual receives the right support in addition to the specific intervention. Where individuals also experience more specific difficulties, for example with anxiety or depressed mood, evidenced-based approaches for these issues need to be incorporated into the overall framework, rather than addressed in a fragmented way.

Trauma-specific interventions

There are a number of interventions developed to overcome the effects of trauma, for example trauma-focused cognitive-behavioural therapy (TF-CBT) and eye movement desensitization and reprocessing (EMDR). For the general population, these approaches are more effective than pharmacological interventions in improving sleep quality and reducing PTSD symptoms (Coventry *et al*, 2020). Both EMDR and TF-CBT have been successfully adapted for individuals with intellectual disabilities, although more research is needed to establish their effectiveness (Byrne, 2022). Exploring these approaches is beyond the scope of this book. However, it is important to be aware that these approaches should be considered where an individual has reached the **R**eason stage and shows specific trauma-related symptoms e.g. flashbacks or nightmares.

Dyadic Developmental Psychotherapy (DDP)

DDP was developed by Hughes (2007; 2017) to help children who had experienced trauma in their birth family and were unable to thrive within their safe foster families. It draws on theories and research of attachment, intersubjectivity (the give and take in relationships), interpersonal neurobiology, and trauma. This gives a coherent explanation of how the child's adaptations to surviving parental abuse block their ability to trust, take comfort from and experience joy within their new, safe relationships. Hughes then shows how the child's blocked or misplaced mistrust disrupts the feedback process that helps the new parent to build a caring relationship with the child. Care becomes 'blocked' and parents go into survival mode. They become defensive, reactive, get stuck in unhelpful patterns of responding, focus on correcting behaviour rather than understanding it, and feel rejected. Working with both the parents and the child, DDP aims to build an understanding of and overcome the child's misplaced mistrust though playfulness, acceptance, curiosity and empathy (PACE).

There are clear parallels between the processes Hughes identifies between child and foster parent and those between individuals with intellectual disabilities and their paid carers. Jones (2021) shows how DDP was helpful in addressing the needs of two young women with intellectual disabilities experiencing highly chaotic and risky lives. The approach brought improvements over time, where other approaches had been unsuccessful.

The concepts of misplaced mistrust and blocked care can be very helpful in understanding what is happening in the **R**elate intervention stage, and in understanding what can go wrong in relationships between individuals and the

 Intellectual Disabilities and 'Personality Disorder' © Pavilion Publishing and Media Ltd and its licensors 2023

staff who support them. These concepts are discussed in Chapter 5. PACE may also be helpful in creating engagement.

'Personality disorder' specific approaches

A number of specialist therapies have been developed to help individuals given a diagnosis of 'personality disorder', with most designed for the pattern of difficulties classified as 'borderline'. Livesley and Larstone (2020b) identified seven approaches that had at least one random control trial to support their efficacy. Of these, Dialectical Behaviour Therapy (DBT) (Linehan, 1993) and DBT skills groups, Cognitive Analytic Therapy (CAT) (Ryle, 1997) and Mentalization-based Therapy (MBT) (Bateman and Fonagy, 2004) have been adapted for use with individuals with intellectual disabilities. There is limited evidence of their efficacy with this client group (McNair *et al*, 2017; Lloyd and Clayton, 2013; Horsham and Grantham, undated).

The evidence base in this area is evolving. However, currently, no one of these specialist approaches has been found to be better than any other (PDC, 2018). More significantly, specialist therapies do not work significantly better than the 'systematised and manualised' clinical care or supportive therapy provided to control groups in studies (Livesley and Larstone, 2020b). Rather, what has emerged from the research is the importance of using a structured approach (Livesley and Larstone, 2020b). This finding is likely to be equally applicable to individuals with intellectual disabilities. This is supported by the finding that individuals with intellectual disabilities who have been given a diagnosis of 'personality disorder' can be successfully supported within specialist services for individuals with intellectual disabilities (Alexander *et al*, 2010).

Where such specialist approaches are available, they should be offered to individuals with mild intellectual disabilities (NICE, 2009). However, where they do not already exist, the development of specialist services need not be a priority. Rather, the focus should be on developing skilled staff working within a well-structured approach.

A toolbox approach

The PDC (2018) suggest that a wide range of interventions specific to 'personality disorder' should be available, but that:

> '*A toolbox approach designed around the core problems of the individual delivered skilfully by competent and compassionate clinicians may be as helpful for some people* [as specific interventions], *with a clinician needing to be responsive to the current issues, using a flexible and holistic approach.*'

A toolbox approach offers the flexibility to support individuals with intellectual disabilities. It allows the inclusion of other therapy approaches that have proved helpful for individuals with intellectual disabilities but that are not 'personality disorder' or trauma specific. For example, there are a range of Acceptance and Commitment Therapy-based exercises that help individuals with intellectual disabilities understand, accept and regulate thoughts and feelings, and build self-compassion (Williams and Jones, 2022).

There is evidence to support a toolbox approach from case studies (Wink *et al*, 2010; Cowan, 2018b). They show that the needs of individuals with intellectual disabilities who had been given a diagnosis of 'personality disorder' could be met through an individualised, multidisciplinary, multi-modal approach that considers medication and psychological and behavioural interventions. These studies have also highlighted the importance of a consistent, containing environment with a stable and skilled staff group.

Section 2 contains a range of approaches that can be tailored to make a toolbox within the framework of a trauma-informed PBS plan.

How it is done: the right way

The finding that no one specialist intervention is more effective than any other, or 'gold standard' structured clinical care (PDC, 2018; Livesley and Larstone, 2020b) draws attention to the importance of the non-specific factors of therapy.

Any intervention can be seen as having two types of components: specific (what is done) and non-specific (how it is done).

Specific factors are the active techniques that are special to a particular approach, derived from a theoretical model or to address specific issues. These are added on to the non-specific elements of therapy to create different models of therapy or intervention.

Non-specific factors relate to the characteristics of the therapist, their relationship with the individual seeking help, and the situation in which the intervention takes place. They are common across different approaches (see Box 3.5). They are often not mentioned but may be embedded in the values espoused by an approach.

Intellectual Disabilities and 'Personality Disorder' © Pavilion Publishing and Media Ltd and its licensors 2023

Box 3.5: Non-specific factors in interventions

Therapist (staff member) characteristics	Competence/skills e.g. active listening/training. Professionalism. Personal style – warmth, empathy, genuineness, non-judgemental, respect, non-contingent positive regard.
The therapeutic alliance (working relationship)	The building of trust and collaboration
Hope/expectancy	Both the individual's natural frame of mind and that created by the therapy process
The structure	Appointment times, session lengths, being consistent, boundaries
Support and containment	That someone is there for you, regular contact
The environment	Noise levels, distractions, physical comfort

Warmth, empathy and genuineness have long been identified as important qualities for therapists to be effective (Rogers, 1957). The therapeutic alliance (working relationship) and positive expectancy (hope) function as active ingredients of intervention, leading to better outcomes (Zilcha-Mano *et al*, 2019). For individuals who have experienced trauma, who find relationships very difficult and who struggle to contain emotions, the non-specific elements of interventions are highly important. Attention to consistency, relationships and environments seem to be necessary for the success of interventions (PDC, 2018): if these are not met, individuals may not even attend. This is explored more fully in Chapter 5. The combination of these non-specific factors acts to create what has been termed a 'reparative relationship' (Clarkson, 2003).

Interventions for individuals with intellectual disabilities who might be given a diagnosis of 'personality disorder' should be designed and delivered in ways that maximise the contribution of these non-specific factors to create reparative relationships. Put simply: *How things are done may be at least as important as what is done*.

Key learning points

- There are different stages to interventions. Using **R**egulate, **R**elate, **R**eason will help to choose the right support at the right time.
- No one can engage with staff or interventions if they feel physically or emotionally unsafe.
- It is important to recognise that not everyone wants to or is able to work through all the stages. It is still possible to create PBS plans that keep people safe, maximise their quality of life and give opportunities for emotional development.
- Interventions for individuals who might be given a diagnosis of 'personality disorder' need to take place within sustainable, structured, longer-term planning.
- An overarching framework such as trauma-informed PBS provides guidance and promotes understanding and consistency when working with a multi-stage, multi-component approach to intervention.
- A trauma-informed PBS plan is an effective vehicle for delivering interventions, including preventing and resolving crises, promoting positive interactions and engagement in meaningful activities.
- There is evidence for the effectiveness of trauma-specific interventions for individuals experiencing trauma-related experiences such as flashbacks. Concepts from these approaches are also helpful in understanding interactions between individuals and staff.
- There is evidence to support the efficacy of a number of specialist treatment approaches for individuals who have been given a diagnosis of 'personality disorder', for example DBT. Where these are available, they should be considered for individuals with mild intellectual disabilities.
- A toolbox approach designed around an individual's core issues, delivered skilfully by competent and compassionate clinicians within the framework of a trauma-informed PBS plan, is highly useful, and especially beneficial in settings where access to specialist interventions is limited.
- The way an individual is supported is at least as important as the interventions chosen. Emotional containment and positive working relationships are essential for interventions to succeed.

 Intellectual Disabilities and 'Personality Disorder' © Pavilion Publishing and Media Ltd and its licensors 2023

Chapter 4: Formulation: collaboratively creating a shared understanding and a way forward

This chapter looks at what formulation is and how it can be helpful when working with individuals with intellectual disabilities who might be given a diagnosis of 'personality disorder'. It looks at ways of ensuring that formulation is a collaborative process. It looks at some approaches to formulation and considers their different strengths.

Key topics

- What is formulation?
- Using formulation
- Making formulation trauma informed
- Using the tree of life as a formulation
- Formulating within a Positive Behavioural Support framework

What is formulation?

> '*...however unusual, confusing, risky, destructive, chaotic, overwhelming, frightening or apparently irrational someone's thoughts, feelings and behaviours are, there is a way of making sense of them.*' (BPS, 2018, p304)

Individuals who have been given a diagnosis of 'personality disorder', are experiencing enduring distress, or have insecure attachments may behave in ways that make no sense, to themselves or others, unless the behaviours are put in context. Formulation is central to achieving this. The Personality Disorder Commission PDC (2018, p16) highlight that everyone given a diagnosis of 'personality disorder' should expect:

> *'A person-centred, individualised trauma-informed formulation of the reasons for my psychological distress that I have co- produced.'*

Formulation is the evidenced-based process of creating a person-centred, shared understanding of an individual's distress which offers a way forward (Division of Clinical Psychology (DCP), 2011; BPS, 2018). It can also form a narrative or story of an individual's life (Cameron, 2015). Although an on-going process, the formulation at any one time is often captured in the form of a diagram to help draw out themes and patterns. Some characteristics and benefits of psychological formulation are given in Box 4.1.

Box 4.1: Characteristics of formulation and their benefits

	Characteristics of formulation	Advantages/benefits
Evidence based	Grounded in psychological theory and research. Draws from a range of models and causal factors.	Enhances theory-practice links.
Listening	Seeks to hear what people have to say rather than imposing expert opinion.	Feel validated. Enhances engagement.
Respectful	Non-judgmental, values all contributors and contributions.	Helps redress imbalances of power. Builds self-esteem.
Collaborative	Listens to everyone involved in the process, it seeks to be inclusive.	Promotes engagement. Share knowledge and skills.
Accessible	Jargon free, uses vocabulary of those involved.	Promotes communication. Reduces misunderstandings.
Shared/ transparent	Is shared with those involved, not filed away or kept exclusive to professionals.	Promotes trust. Helps manage risk.
Meaning	Looks beyond the 'facts', explores how they are perceived and understood. Captures events in a way that is satisfactory to those involved.	Builds shared understanding. Has conviction.
Reflective	Open and curious.	Facilitates learning, insights and change.

 Intellectual Disabilities and 'Personality Disorder' © Pavilion Publishing and Media Ltd and its licensors 2023

Coherent narrative	Tells a story rather than listing facts. Answers 'Why is this happening now?'	Draws out themes and makes connections.
Way forward	Indicates a plan of intervention, drawing on evidence and shared narrative OR that no further intervention is needed.	Gives direction to intervention.
Best guess	A working hypothesis about the nature and origins of an individual's distress.	Acts to contain anxiety about uncertainty.
Usefulness	Offers a plausible account that looks for a useful way forward.	Promotes hope.
Person-centred/whole person	Considers an individual's experiences in context rather than focusing on 'the problem'.	Holistic approach. Recognises strengths.
Experience based	Focuses on the thoughts, feelings, behaviour experienced by the individual not on a psychiatric diagnosis.	Flexible. Does not pathologise the individual. Normalises experiences.
Context aware	Considers cultural perspectives and the wider societal context.	Reduces risk of unconscious biases. Tailored to individual's cultural context.
Open process	An ongoing process, not a single event. Is revised as new information arises.	Identifies issues to be explored. Evolves and changes.

Formulation may be used with individuals, families and groups. It is used by professionals to inform a particular intervention with an individual (individual formulation). It can also be used with a staff group supporting an individual and in multidisciplinary teamwork (team formulation). The focus of formulation is on the needs of a specific individual, and it is intended to inform their care. Teams may also want to reflect on the challenges team members face working with a specific individual i.e. the team is the focus (reflective case discussion). Although superficially similar, team formulation and reflective case discussion are different processes and require different approaches to collaboration and confidentiality (see Box 4.2 and also Chapter 7).

Box 4.2: Types of formulation and case discussion

Format	Who is involved	Purpose
Individual formulation	Individual and 1-2 staff members.	■ Collaboratively develop an understanding of/ make sense of an individual's difficulties and needs. ■ Listen to and understand the individual's own way of making sense of their experience. ■ Enhance individual's self-compassion. ■ A process in which the individual can feel heard and understood, enhancing the working relationship. ■ May offer psycho-education. ■ Shared with others, with consent.
Team formulation	Individual (present or views represented in an agreed way) and staff team/ Multi-disciplinary team (MDT) working with the individual (facilitator).	■ Develop a compassionate understanding from multiple perspectives, central to which is the individual's history and their way of making sense of experience. ■ Support a compassionate understanding of unhelpful repeated patterns and inform potential intervention plans. ■ Develop ideas to explore further in individual work. ■ Create a summary of ideas to support continuity of care created with and shared with individual.
Reflective case discussion	Staff team/MDT (facilitator).	■ Share experiences working with the individual and barriers faced in that work. A safe space to discuss emotional impact of working with the individual. Confidential to the team but feeds back into formulation process for the individual.

Adapted from: Ebrahim and Sams (2022)

Although intended to identify a way forward, a formulation can, in itself, bring about change. Individuals may feel listened to and properly heard for the first time (Yeandle *et al*, 2015), facilitating new insights into their behaviour:

Intellectual Disabilities and 'Personality Disorder' © Pavilion Publishing and Media Ltd and its licensors 2023

> *'It was like a recipe, explaining how I came to be who I am, and a personal instruction guide. The ... formulation made what has always seemed illogical, logical, and what seemed disordered and messy, ordered and clean. It gave my feelings validity and helped me to see myself as a whole rather than fragmented pieces.'*

Formulation can help increase the empathy felt by often hard-pressed staff (Yeandle *et al*, 2015). It can dissipate staff beliefs such as that they are not skilled enough or that the individual needs to use a different service. It can promote sharing of skills from different backgrounds and improve risk management (DCP, 2011; Hollingworth and Johnstone, 2014). Within teams, formulations may contribute to changes in culture and promote different ways of working (DCP, 2011).

Using formulations

There is no set time to capture a formulation. However, the stage of intervention (see Chapter 3, Box 3.1) the individual is at, may influence how much they can collaborate in the process.

Collaboration

An individual in crisis will be in their 'emotional mind' (see Chapter 9) and will struggle to see beyond their present pain and distress to engage in formulation. For an individual first encountered in crisis, an initial 'working hypothesis' may be created by the staff team to guide the assessment process and think about how best to support the individual. A structure with boxes to fill can often be helpful at this stage: empty boxes indicate areas the team need to explore. This can prompt further assessment. When only partial information is available, it is important to avoid being caught up in a generalised story of 'what usually happens', as this can lead to key information being missed (Brown *et al*, 2017). Speculating about the missing parts of the 'jigsaw' is an important part of the formulation process. However, the ideas generated must held as 'possibilities' to be explored that may or may not be true, and need to be updated as new information emerges.

As the individual moves through the stages of intervention, the formulation process will become increasingly collaborative. Difficulties with communication and understanding can make it more challenging to involve the individual, however these may be addressed by thoughtful use of total communication strategies (Page, undated, see further reading) and choice of formulation format. There may also be concerns that the individual may be distressed or re-traumatised by participating in the formulation and (where they lack capacity to choose) that it may not be in their best interests to take part. If no way can be found to actively engage them, thought needs to be given to how the individual's perspective can be included. For example, Gregson and Delaney (2021) describe how they sought to remain person-centred despite 'Jane' not being able to collaborate in the formulation process:

> *'... we sought to use questions that elicited Jane's voice and perspectives, such as "what would Jane's perspective be?", "what would Jane want to be different?" We hoped that this could keep us grounded to Jane's voice...'*

Box 4.3 summarises some of the issues that can arise when seeking collaboration and how these might be addressed. Issues with collaboration are likely to arise where an individual's history has made it difficult for them to trust others. Building trust and positive working relationships are explored in Chapter 5.

Box 4.3: Promoting meaningful involvement: *'Nothing about me without me'*	
Informed choice about involvement	Individual makes an informed choice about whether they engage in developing a formulation with the team: understanding, feeling safe and choice. Best-interest process used when individual lacks capacity at that time to make an informed choice.
Understanding the process	*'Why use a word nobody understands* [formulation]? *It's a bad word, find a better word. Maybe person-centred plan'** Provide understandable, accessible information about team formulation, and give support to understand how it might be helpful for them. Give information about different ways of participating in the process. Use words that make sense to the individual. Ensure there is time for the individual to hear and process information.
Feeling safe to participate in the formulation process	Acknowledging formulation may be stressful, individuals may feel exposed or intimidated or be re-traumatised – 'someone's life story being laid bare' ■ Explore individual's concerns and what might help them feel safe. ■ Ensure the individual understands the process – prepare in advance. ■ Presence of person (family, trained peer supporter, chosen staff member) who helps the individual feel safe. →

Intellectual Disabilities and 'Personality Disorder' © Pavilion Publishing and Media Ltd and its licensors 2023

	■ Make the environment as informal as possible e.g. with comfortable chairs, rather than around a table. ■ Use the space where team formulation takes place for leisure activities to help individuals feel comfortable and familiar in the environment.
Choice	Individual chooses how to participate (be creative): ■ Lead on telling their story. ■ Co-deliver with chosen staff member of trained peer. ■ Share an individual formulation they have developed in other work. ■ Attend and listen. ■ Prepare e.g. a letter, in advance, for trusted person to share at the meeting. ■ Be represented by chosen family member or carer. ■ Be given feedback after the meeting.
When an individual is not involved in the meeting due to lacking capacity and best interest decision:	
Representative or advocate	Be thoughtful – some relatives or carers may not know the individual's story or represent their needs or wishes. Acknowledge different perspectives.
Where individual has capacity but does not want the team to talk about them:	
Policy and rationale	If policy is to go ahead with the team-formulation meeting, then the reasons for this need to be explained to the individual, and continued support provided to listen to their concerns, and to resolve them as far as possible e.g. confidentiality. If meetings don't go ahead, there must be a clear process for ensuring the team have a shared understanding and way forward for their work with the individual. Ensure all steps are taken to help the individual understand the process and gently revisit to see if they now wish to take part.
Adapted from Ebrahim and Sams (2022). * p.17	

Choice of format

There is no single 'right' format for a formulation: rather a format is chosen on the basis of 'best fit' for each individual and team. It is important to be flexible and creative (PDC, 2018). Some formulation formats are linked to specific treatment models, others aim to be applicable across different treatment models, and some are unique creations that resonate for specific individuals or teams. Some example formulations for individuals experiencing different issues are given in Section 2.

The format chosen will depend on factors such as the training and professional backgrounds of those involved and the approach taken by particular services or organisations. For teams where there is a focus on the medical model, biopsychosocial formulation (see Box 4.4) can fit very well. This also fits well with the approach to assessment within the Community Mental Health Framework (NHS England, 2019). The biopsychosocial model also combines well with the 5 Ps model (see Box 4.8) and has been successfully used to help junior doctors understand the impact of trauma (Cappleman *et al*, 2021).

Box 4.4: Biopsychosocial model

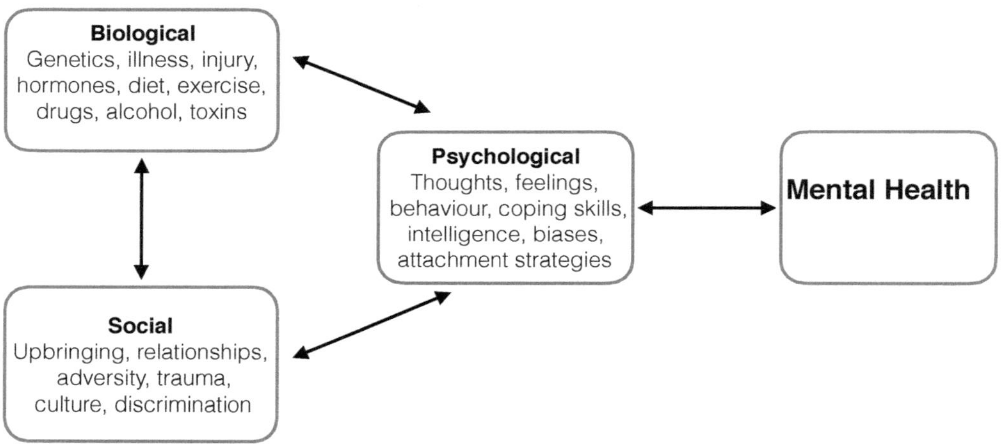

The format should also be tailored to the strengths and needs of the individual. Approaches that use drawing, pictures or symbols can work well for individuals who struggle to put things in words or talk about themselves, for example 'talking mats' (Murphy, 1998) and the 'tree of life' (Ncube, 2006). The tree of life also elicits and recognises strengths, positive memories and resources within the individual's network. Its use can reduce the risks of re-traumatisation when exploring distressing events and telling difficult stories. The 'extended hot-cross bun' framework (adapted from McGill *et al*, 1996) can be useful for addressing complex challenging behaviour. These approaches are discussed in more detail below.

Intellectual Disabilities and 'Personality Disorder' © Pavilion Publishing and Media Ltd and its licensors 2023

When creating an individual formulation with someone who has been given a diagnosis of 'personality disorder', Yeandle *et al* (2015) advocate including a member of staff not working directly with that individual. Having a triad consisting of the individual, a staff member working directly with them and an independent person, helps manage the relational and psychological issues that can arise in the formulation process.

Overcoming obstacles

Formulation is now widely accepted as best practice. However, there can be barriers to it working effectively. These include practical issues such as time pressure and staff availability in busy services. Different professions may have different interpretations and expectations of the process. The amount of collaboration involved means team formulation can expose professional rivalries and tensions. However, Baird *et al* (2017) comment that:

> *'It is perhaps the lingering perception that formulation is difficult, labour intensive and "specialist" that is the bigger obstacle to its wider use.'*

Addressing barriers may require both attention to service design (see Chapter 6) and to team dynamics (see Chapter 7). However, participating in well-led formulation meetings is a positive, empowering process. Often, just the experience of taking part can dispel negative perceptions.

Co-creating formulations of behaviours that challenge can be intellectually and emotionally demanding. This is explored in Chapter 8, and Box 8.7 gives a few thoughts on how to keep on track.

Making formulation trauma informed

The high frequency and severity of trauma experienced by individuals given a diagnosis of 'personality disorder' and those with intellectual disabilities means that thinking about the impact of trauma is an important component of formulation, whatever format is used. The PDC (2018) specifically recommend that formulation should be 'trauma informed'.

There is no single 'right' way of doing this. Rather, thinking about the impact of trauma should be a part of whatever approach is adopted.

McFetridge *et al* (2017) recommend that:

> *'Any therapeutic intervention (for complex PTSD) should be informed by careful formulation of the effect of the specific traumatic experiences endured by the particular individual at their age and stage of life, in these circumstances and contexts, and with a specific level of support and personal resources.'*

This appears equally as applicable to work with all individuals with intellectual disabilities. This ensures that the hard wired and soft-wired neurological effects of trauma and impact on attachments are central to the formulation. Box 4.5 gives a structure that might be helpful in exploring the impact of trauma.

Box 4.5 Impact of Trauma and vulnerability factors: formulation diagram

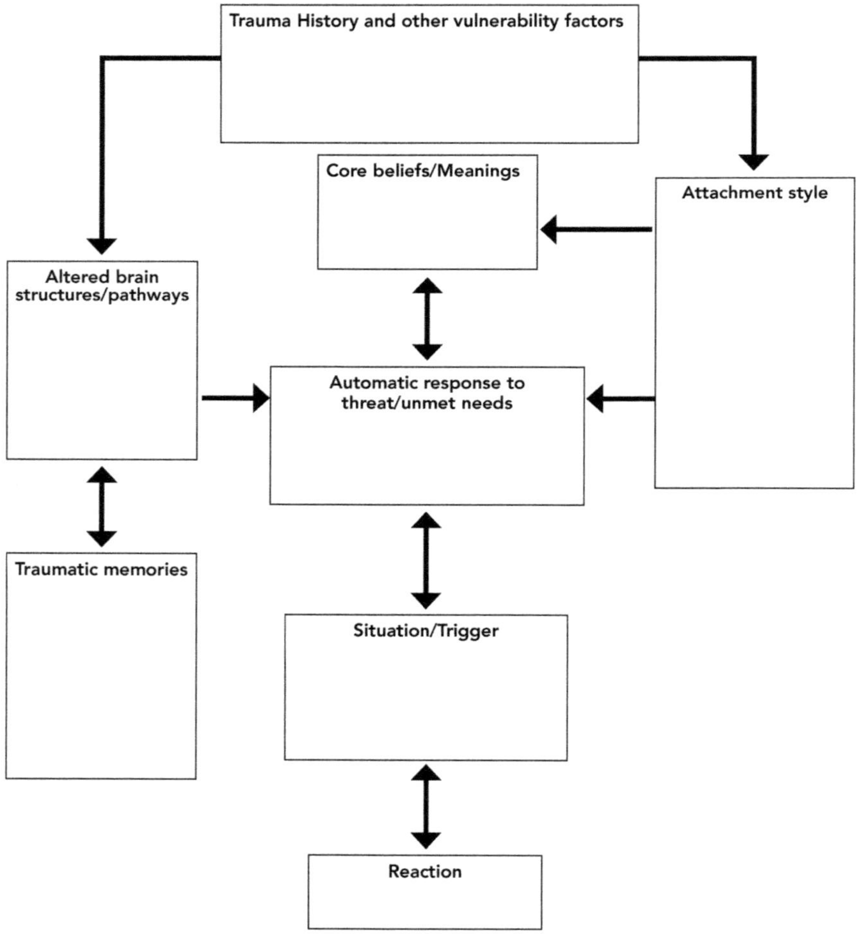

Intellectual Disabilities and 'Personality Disorder' © Pavilion Publishing and Media Ltd and its licensors 2023

Questions developed within the BPS Power Threat Meaning (PTM) Framework (2018) can be used to develop an understanding of events from the individual's perspective on trauma in their life (see Box 4.6.) These can be used collaboratively with the individual to find out about and make sense of their experiences, finding links between past events and present experiences. They can also be used with staff teams to help normalise the experiences of the individual, to increase empathy and compassion.

Box 4.6: Formulation questions from PTM framework

Questions to ask the individual	The themes the questions aim to explore
What has happened to you?	Exploring the relational and social adversities the individual may have experienced.
How did it affect you?	E.g. being physically hurt, afraid, shamed, withdrawing, avoiding.
What sense did you make of it?	Beliefs about why things happened or why people behaved as they did.
What did you have to do to survive?	What the individual thought and did.
AND:	
What are your strengths?	Access to healing resources.
What is your story?	A coherent narrative that conveys meaning and hope.

Adapted from PTM Framework (BPS, 2018)

Using the tree of life as a formulation

The tree of life is a narrative (story telling) approach developed by Ncube (2006). It is a constructive approach to the impact of trauma and loss. It is flexible and can be used either as an assessment or an intervention (Lock, 2016), and lends itself to use as a formulation. It uses the metaphors of a tree and a forest to create a full picture of someone's life (tree) and create a sense of community (forest). Each part of the tree is linked to a part of their life (see Box 4.7).

Box 4.7: The tree of life

Roots – where I come from	Influential people, places, experiences, culture.
Ground – present life	Where I live now, activities, what happens in my everyday life.
Trunk – skills and interests	My skills, caring and kindness. Where I learnt them and who taught me.
Branches – hopes, dreams, wishes	History of hopes and dreams – how they link to people and experiences. How I have held on to them during times of challenge.
Leaves – important people in my life	Why this person is important to me, lovely times I had with them (includes people who are alive and those who have died).
Fruit – gifts given to me	Material gifts and acts of kindness, or care, or love from others. Why I was given this. What the giver values about me.
Storms – challenges	There are storms in all lives. How do I respond?

Image credit: Neus Bartual

 Intellectual Disabilities and 'Personality Disorder' © Pavilion Publishing and Media Ltd and its licensors 2023

The tree is created collaboratively. Thoughtful questioning is used to help the process. If done in a group, trees are shared with and commented on by other group members and brought together to make a forest. The process of creating the tree can be engaging and the structure it provides can make communication easier. The inclusion of elements such as skills, gifts and important people puts trauma and loss into context, helping individuals to feel more able to cope and move forward. It gives a way of honouring people important to the individual who have died and taking good memories of them into the future. The approach has been found to be helpful in engaging with 'hard to reach' populations (Lock, 2016; Kasmani, 2021) and has been successfully used with individuals with intellectual disabilities (Randle-Phillips, 2016).

The tree of life approach provides an accessible and engaging way of organising and integrating information about someone's life. It provides a visual reminder of strengths and positive relationships that may be a resource at times of distress. As it does not use the language of trauma or bereavement, it can also be used with individuals who do not see trauma as a major theme in their lives. It also gives an integrated representation of the whole self, which can be helpful for individuals without a clear self-concept. Finally, by capturing elements of an individual's past, present and possible future, the tree of life helps to place periods of distress within the context of their whole lifespan.

Formulating within a Positive Behavioural Support framework

PBS has its origins in behavioural science. Working from its core principle that all behaviour has meaning, it uses the process of 'functional analysis' to determine that meaning. As the approach has broadened, it has added the concept of formulation. The PBS framework allows for integration with any evidence-based approach to formulation. One that fits well and is often used is the Five Ps approach (Greentree and Beth Kruger, 2019). The Five Ps are described in Box 4.8.

Box 4.8: The Five Ps model for formulations	
Presenting problem:	The behaviour/issues of concern.
Predisposing:	Characteristics that make the individual vulnerable to developing that problem.
Precipitating:	How the problem started, its triggers or antecedents.
Perpetuating:	Things that maintain the problem, what keeps it going, the consequences of the behaviour.

→

Protective:	Factors that stop the problem occurring, reduce its severity or could be used to help address the problem. These might include characteristics of the individual, the situation or the people and services around them.
Reference: Weerasekera (1993)	

The 'extended hot-cross bun' diagram (Box 4.9) (Webb, 2014) builds on the CBT formulation often referred to as the 'hot-cross bun' by integrating the 5 Ps' concepts and the behavioural science ABC approach (Antecedents, Behaviour, Consequences – explored in more detail in Chapter 8).

Box 4.9: The extended hot-cross bun

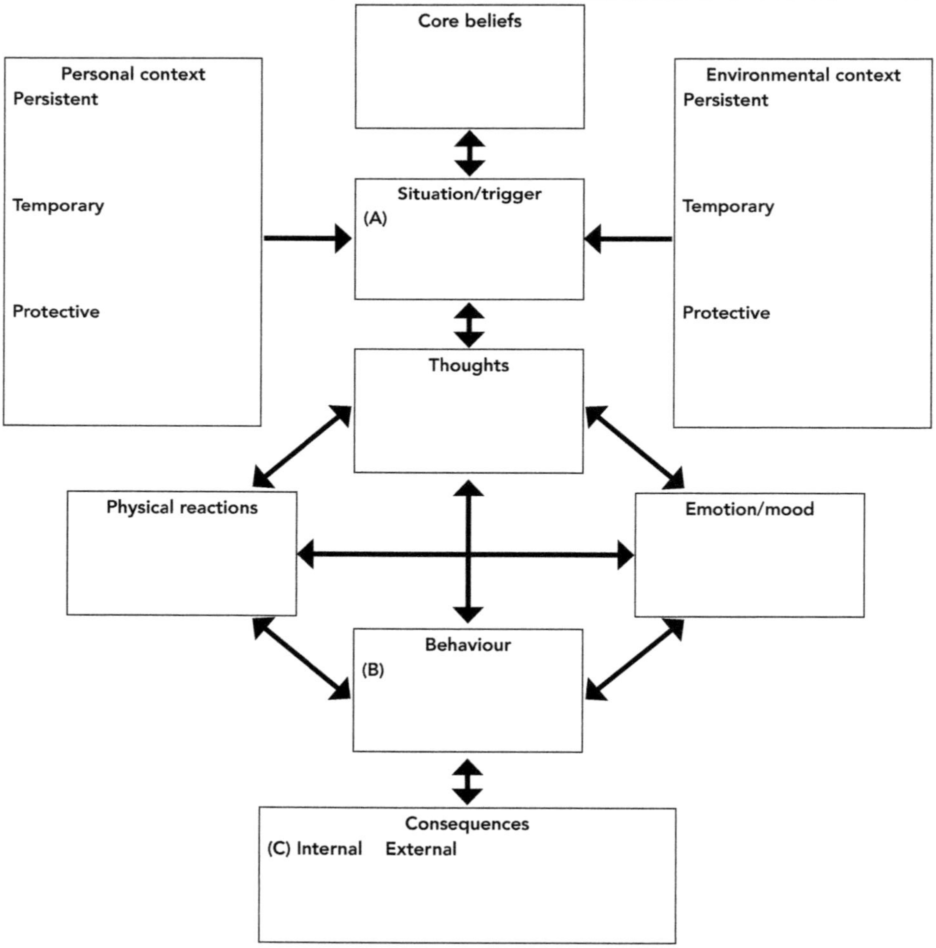

Intellectual Disabilities and 'Personality Disorder' © Pavilion Publishing and Media Ltd and its licensors 2023

This formulation format is helpful for understanding complex behaviours as it translates easily into a PBS plan. As it does not focus directly on the effects of trauma, this approach needs to be informed by an understanding of how trauma may have affected the individual. For example, considering how behaviours might act to create a sense of safety or protect the individual from attachment loss, hurt and abandonment. This may be achieved by using one of the trauma-informed approaches presented earlier in this chapter. Making the PBS framework trauma informed is explored further in Chapters 3 and 8.

Key learning points

- A psychologically informed formulation is an essential part of all individual and team interventions.
- Formulation is a collaborative way of creating a shared understanding of and integrating information about how an individual's patterns of thoughts, feelings and behaviour arose in the context of their unique life story.
- Making a formulation is a flexible and creative process that is judged by its usefulness: it should promote understanding and suggest ways forward.
- Although superficially similar, team formulation and reflective case discussion are different processes and require different approaches to collaboration and confidentiality.
- Formulation is an on-going process. Thought should be given to ensure the approach used evolves with the individual's progress though the stages of intervention, creating maximum opportunities for collaboration with the individual.
- There is no one right format for a formulation. The format chosen and the way it is communicated should fit the individual and the team supporting them.
- Formulations should always be trauma informed but this can be achieved in different ways. Trauma may be integral to the format, for example the tree of life, or explored by using the PTM questions in addition to the chosen format.
- When formulating within a PBS framework, it is important to widen the focus to consider the impacts of trauma, the need for a sense of safety and psychological needs such as protection against attachment loss, hurt and abandonment.

Chapter 5: Building positive, respectful working relationships and facilitating engagement

This chapter explores what is meant by 'engagement'. It examines the importance of engagement and positive working relationships as the foundation for therapeutic endeavour. It looks at the barriers to engagement faced by individuals with intellectual disabilities who might be given a diagnosis of 'personality disorder'. It considers how to build and sustain positive working relationships and engagement. It explores how past experience of trauma can block the building of trust, which in turn can block the development of a caring relationship. It highlights the importance of formulation, reflective practice and supervision to support staff in overcoming these challenges.

Key topics

- Engagement
- Engagement and 'personality disorder'
- Engagement and intellectual disabilities
- Building engagement and positive working relationships
- Sustaining engagement
- What might be happening when individuals do not engage despite being offered good support
- What can happen to staff when an individual does not respond to the 'good care' provided

Engagement

> *'In my early professional years I was asking the question: How can I treat, or cure, or change this person? Now I would phrase the question in this way:*
>
> ***How can I provide a relationship which this person may use for*** [their] ***own personal growth?'*** (Rogers, 2012, p32 emphasis added)

Engagement is the healthy, mutual connection between an individual and those who support them. It can be used to describe an individual's connection to a service as well as their commitment to a specific therapeutic activity. Engagement allows people to work together to achieve mutually agreed objectives and solve problems. It has a number of elements (see Box 5.1). An important element of engagement is the working relationship (therapeutic alliance) between the individual and the staff working with them. Engagement is visible through an individual's behaviour, for example joining in an activity, but is mediated by their thoughts and feelings. Although engagement is most often discussed in the context of therapy, it is essential in all areas of support, including help with activities of daily living.

Box 5.1: Engagement and positive working relationships

Engagement: the healthy, mutual, dynamic and collaborative connection between an individual and those who support them, that allows them to work to achieve mutually agreed objectives and solve problems.	
Elements of engagement	
Bond (therapeutic alliance)	Forming a positive working relationship between the individual and the people supporting them. It comprises: ■ the collaborative nature of the relationship (ability to work together and reach agreements). ■ the affective bond between individual and professional (how they feel about each other).
Objectives	Agreeing what is to be achieved.
Task	Agreeing what is to be done to achieve the objectives.
How engagement is experienced by the individual:	
Behaviour	Adherence: attending appointments, taking part in therapeutic activities, using suggested strategies, carrying out agreed tasks in the agreed way. Effort: actively communicating relevant information, real-life behaviour change.
Thoughts	Agreement: with the intervention rationale, seeing the interventions as suitable to meet their goals.
Feelings	Interest: in the intervention content. Attention: paid to the intervention. Response: how the intervention makes them feel.
Adapted from Bijkerk *et al* (2022), Dixon *et al* (2016), Stubbe (2018)	

 Intellectual Disabilities and 'Personality Disorder' © Pavilion Publishing and Media Ltd and its licensors 2023

The word 'engagement' implies that it is a one-off event. However, engagement is an on-going, dynamic process; it must first be created and then actively maintained. Levels of engagement fluctuate throughout the course of an intervention (Chowdhury, 2019) and disengagement may occur at any point. Sometimes things go wrong: a previously successful working relationship may falter, for example as the result of a misunderstanding (Schenk *et al*, 2021). This is referred to as a 'rupture'. This is a common experience and is to be expected. However, a rupture needs to be thoughtfully 'resolved' to prevent it leading to disengagement.

When objectives have been achieved, thought needs to be given to how to end the working relationship. The aim is that the individual does not feel abandoned or rejected but instead feels satisfied with the process. The ending should make it more likely that the individual would engage in future if they were to experience difficulties again. Box 5.2 shows some points of engagement for community and residential services.

Box 5.2: Points of engagement	
Engagement doesn't just happen at the beginning:	
Community	Seeking help. First contact with service. First contact with each individual member of staff. Every, subsequent contact with each member of staff. Starting a piece of therapeutic work. Finishing that work. Ending episode of care. Seeking help at a later date.
Residential	'Choosing' where to live. Moving in. First contact with each member of staff. Every, subsequent contact with each member of staff. Carrying out activities of everyday living. Carrying out activities that are a source of enjoyment. Every time a member of staff leaves. Moving out. 'Choosing' where to live.

If an individual does not engage, or stops attending, this needs to be managed in a way that makes future engagement more likely. For example:

> '[member of staff] *would make an appointment with me and I wouldn't turn up. She didn't get angry… she just kept trying and waited until I was ready'* (Ng *et al*, 2019).

There is no 'one-size-fits-all approach' (Dixon *et al*, 2016): engagement occurs in the context of an individual's unique personality, social and life circumstances, within the context of a specific service and particular members of staff at a particular time in the individual's life. A broad focus, 'person-centred' approach is the key to achieving engagement (Dixon *et al*, 2016; Henderson *et al* 2020). In particular, the impact of developmental trauma on the development of trust and attachment needs to be considered. Some of the multiplicity of factors that influence engagement are given in Box 5.3.

Box 5.3: Some of the factors that influence engagement

Social context

- Attitudes – towards the problem and those who seek help.
- Stigma – the negative perception of individuals with particular characteristics.
- Taboos – things that cannot be talked about.
- Consequences of engaging with services e.g. impact on work opportunities.

Service characteristics

- Physical and emotional safety – does the individual feel safe when they use the service?
- Visibility – do people know the service is there?
- Outreach – the degree to which it takes services to people, links with the community.
- Accessibility e.g. location, transport links, opening times.
- Flexibility e.g. different options for keeping in contact.
- Confidentiality.
- Gate-keeping (who is referred/which referrals are accepted).
- Allocation of resources (money, facilities, priority given to service).

 Intellectual Disabilities and 'Personality Disorder' © Pavilion Publishing and Media Ltd and its licensors 2023

Staff characteristics and behaviour (their ability to form a positive working relationship)
■ Personal qualities e.g. personality, warmth, empathy, positive regard. ■ Collaborative approach – working with people, not imposing on them. ■ Skills e.g. building rapport, listening skills, creative solutions, building motivation, maintaining hope. ■ Attitudes e.g. being hopeful, accepting and non-judgmental. ■ Continuity – being able to see the same person over a long period of time. ■ Persistence – not easily giving up. ■ Adaptability – being able to work in different ways to reflect individuals' needs. ■ Managing interactions (ability to contain emotions and make individual feel safe). ■ Managing endings (so the individual feels able to return if necessary).
Characteristics of the intervention
■ Collaborative and person-centred, good fit with individual's objectives. ■ Match with where the individual is on the intervention process (see Box 3.1). ■ Appropriate for individual's cognitive and emotional development – makes sense to the individual. ■ Ease of implementation. ■ Speed of results – how quickly does the individual start to feel better?
Characteristics of the individual
■ Personal circumstances – homelessness, poverty, illness, being in crisis. ■ Experience of developmental trauma, particularly the impact on trust and attachment. ■ Ability to organise self e.g. to get to appointments, to put plans into action. ■ Quality of previous contact with services – impact of past negative experiences, including abuse. ■ Attitude towards professional helpers/services. ■ Attachment – ability to form stable relationships. ■ Degree of trust, shyness or embarrassment. ■ Recognising that others might be able to help and comfort, accepting help. ■ Belief that they are deserving of help. ■ Belief that the problem can be changed (hope).

Intellectual Disabilities and 'Personality Disorder' © Pavilion Publishing and Media Ltd and its licensors 2023

The order of the categories in the table has been consciously chosen to emphasise the importance of looking beyond the individual to the impact of contextual factors. Focusing only on the characteristics of the individual can lead to them being seen as the cause of any difficulties with engagement, absolving staff and services from considering the impact of their own practices. In particular, some client groups are sometimes described as 'hard to engage'.

Reflecting on the experiences of people using services, Hibbins (2017) comments:

> '*The phrase* [hard to engage] *makes it sound as though it is a failing or a difficulty within us – an inability that we have to make good use of the service being provided to us. In reality, the likelihood is that the service was not providing what we needed so we didn't engage. That's not a criticism of the service, but rather a recognition that we are all individuals with our own unique needs.*'

When an individual has not engaged with a piece of work or the wider service, it is important to explore what the service could have done differently. Box 5.4 has some questions to start this exploration. It is to be hoped that the more joined up and flexible approach embedded in the Community Mental Health Framework (NHS England 2019) will help overcome some of these service-related issues.

Box 5.4: Important questions for services to ask themselves if someone does not engage with the service:
Why have we been unable to engage them?
What do we need to do to make it possible for them to engage with our service?
How can we ensure that we do provide what they need?
Or: If we feel we can't provide what they need, then how do we help them to access a service which can?'
Adapted from Hibbins (2017)

There is a robust finding that the therapeutic alliance accounts for only a small part (about 7%) of the outcome of therapy (Stubbe, 2018). However, engagement is essential if an individual is to access the wider benefits of an intervention and also if services are to successfully help individuals thrive and fulfil their potential (Bigby and Beadle-Brown 2018). Without it, individuals may struggle with problems on their own. Or, if they are at risk of harming themselves or others, they may have interventions imposed on them, with the associated risk of re-traumatisation and further damage to trust in staff and services.

Engagement and 'personality disorder'

The Personality Disorder Commission (2018, page 9) comment that:

> *'People given the diagnosis of personality disorder have often experienced complex social and system failures early in life, leading to chronic difficulties in developing and maintaining sustainable adult identity and functioning which can affect how they engage with all services – not just those focused on mental health'.*

Individuals with a diagnosis of 'personality disorder' face a number of barriers to engagement with services and staff as a result of their developmental and life experiences. Some important barriers are given in Box 5.5.

Box 5.5: Barriers to engagement for individuals given a diagnosis of 'personality disorder'	
Stigma	The diagnosis of 'personality disorder' carries many negative associations in society (see Chapter 1). Individuals may avoid services for fear of being labelled. They may also be embarrassed or ashamed to use mental health services. These feelings can make individuals more reluctant to seek help and more likely to drop out of treatment.
Attachment needs/ relationship skills	Developmental trauma may have shaped their ability to form relationships, they may rebuff others to avoid being rejected, repeatedly seek contact but not appear to be benefiting from it or may be unresponsive to approaches (see Chapter 12).
Misplace mistrust	Developmental trauma may have taught them that others cannot be trusted. Negative experiences with services may have acted to reinforce this position. Misplaced mistrust describes how the originally valid mistrust of an abusive or neglectful parent is applied to everyone the individual interacts with, including those worthy of trust.
Need for control	Being in control can create an illusion of safety, even when exercising it closes the door to help.

→

Cycle of rejection	Where staff hold negative views about 'personality disorder', individuals are likely to feel that they are blamed for their problems. Individuals may feel that staff are prejudiced against them, are belittling or patronising them. Consequently, individuals may feel rejected, that they are a nuisance or that there is no point attending appointments as there is nothing that can be done to help them.
Low self-esteem	Individuals may feel that they do not deserve or would not benefit from help.
Intense and overwhelming needs	Individuals may feel so desperate that, at some point, even the best care cannot make them feel supported and valued. This may be mis-understood as 'unrealistic' expectations of what services or staff can offer, and can lead to disengagement through despair.
Lack of hope	An individual's experiences may have led to the belief that their difficulties are permanent and unchangeable. There is no point trying to change them or engaging in interventions.

Although overcoming these barriers is challenging for both the individual and those working with them, the potential benefits are great. Individuals with a diagnosis of 'borderline personality disorder' identified engagement (with meaningful activities, relationships and services) as a key element of their recovery. Engaging in meaningful activities and relationships can provide a sense of belonging and connectedness, the opportunity to practice new skills, reflect upon emotional reactions and build a sense of self (Ng *et al*, 2019). Good outcomes from therapy are characterised by the working alliance growing over time (Folmo *et al*, 2021). Although more ruptures to engagement may be experienced when working with individuals given a diagnosis of 'personality disorder', the process of resolving ruptures appears to actively bring about change (Schenk *et al*, 2021). In effect, a rupture in a positive working relationship is a powerful opportunity to experience firsthand new ways of relating and resolving conflicts and difficult emotional reactions. Rather than being seen as a cause of concern, ruptures are better seen as natural, expected events that can be resolved and will, over time, lead to a stronger working relationship.

Maintaining engagement should be an objective in its own right and given as much attention as the 'therapeutic' activities being delivered (Desrosiers *et al*, 2020). Supporting engagement with meaningful activities should receive as much attention as engagement in specific therapeutic interventions (Ng *et al*, 2019). Promoting engagement with meaningful activities needs to be a focus for everyone who supports the individual; it is not just the business of 'therapists'.

Intellectual Disabilities and 'Personality Disorder' © Pavilion Publishing and Media Ltd and its licensors 2023

Engagement and intellectual disabilities

Individuals with intellectual disabilities who might be given a diagnosis of 'personality disorder' face the same barriers to engagement as more able individuals. In addition, barriers can arise directly from their intellectual disabilities. These can include difficulties with attention, understanding, expressive and receptive language, memory and executive functioning (Unwina *et al*, 2016). These barriers are well understood and there are well-established approaches to overcoming them (Porcelan, 2019; see Box 5.6). Although identified in the context of psychological therapies, these adaptations are likely to be effective in facilitating engagement in a wide range of therapeutic and meaningful activities.

Box 5.6: Overcoming barriers to engagement arising from intellectual disabilities (ID)	
Beliefs about ID:	Staff beliefs about and reaction to ID will affect the process of engagement. These should be explored through supervision and in reflective practice (see Chapter 7).
Power imbalance:	Impact of life experiences on individuals with ID can lead to them being more dependent on others for direction (see Chapter 1). Staff will need to be more directive but also attentive that this does not make the individual feel powerless and 'done to'. Role models are a powerful influence because of increased dependence.
Collaboration:	Look at involving concerned others e.g. family, direct support staff e.g. in sessions, supporting homework or helping to get to activities. **BUT:** be aware of power imbalance between individual and carers – ensure individual is properly heard and given an opportunity to answer for themselves. Actively help carers to adopt a supporting role e.g. teaching them about active listening (see Chapter 13).
Expectation of failure:	Individuals with ID may be fearful that they will fail in a new activity. Provide encouragement and positive feedback and praise for effort.
Reduce complexity:	Divide into smaller units, use short, direct phrases e.g. 4-5 words – matched to individual's own communications, use concrete language, avoid 'psychobabble' and jargon.

→

Fit explanations to developmental level:	Most individuals with mild ID will struggle with abstract ideas. Give clear and specific explanations. Check the literal meaning of what you say.
Tailor to sensory needs:	Adjust environment for the sensory needs of the individual.
Facilitate communication:	Consider using pictures, symbols, drawing, role-play, games (always tailored to the individual). Actively teach helpful vocabulary e.g. names of feelings.
Length of activities:	Match length of sessions/activities to attention span, consider using breaks.
Enhance memory:	Use repetition to aid retention and generalisation, and clarify, recap and summarise. Collaboratively build an accessible, permanent record of work.
Length of intervention:	Allow a longer period of time for the intervention.
Augmentation:	Support therapeutic work with other activities that reinforce the message/give learning opportunities.

The way individuals with intellectual disabilities are supported can also form a barrier to engagement. If individuals are 'done to' or 'cared for' their opportunities to engage in activities, interactions and relationships are reduced. Active Support (see Box 5.7) is a person-centred approach that 'works with' individuals to maximise their successful engagement in activities of daily living, everyday interactions and social networks (Ockenden *et al* 2014, BILD 2023). This enables them to fully participate in all aspects of their lives. Although not explicitly mentioned in the Active Support literature, effective use of this approach is still mediated by the creation of an effective working relationship.

Box 5.7: Active Support: 'working with,' not 'caring for'	
Active Support	Support that focuses on enabling each individual to engage and participate in all areas of their life. It prioritises individuals doing things for themselves as much as they can over having things done to or for them. It focuses on doing things with people, providing whatever support is necessary to ensure the experience of engagement is successful. →

Intellectual Disabilities and 'Personality Disorder' © Pavilion Publishing and Media Ltd and its licensors 2023

	Working within the framework of person-centred routines to provide predictability and consistency, it proposes four essential components to promote engagement in activities, interactions and relationships: ■ Every moment has potential ■ Little and often ■ Graded assistance ■ Maximising choice and control
Every moment has potential	All environments and every situation hold potential to promote engagement. Real and naturally occurring opportunities for engagement can be identified within: ■ The things everyone needs to do as part of their home life and work responsibilities ■ Activities individuals enjoy or aspire to at home and in the community ■ Conversations and interactions with all the people around an individual.
Little and often	Every activity and interaction that happens throughout the day is made up of smaller parts or steps. In order to successfully complete the activity or interaction it is necessary to identify: ■ Parts an individual can do for themselves ■ Parts they will need help with ■ Parts that will need to be done for them To promote engagement, active support: ■ Starts small ■ Supports individuals to engage in parts of an activity or interaction ■ Enables individuals to dip in and out of activities and interactions ■ Provides many shorter opportunities for engagement throughout the day rather than solely focus on single, lengthy events ■ Adapts the way things are done to provide more opportunities for an individual to be involved

→

Graded assistance	The level, type and timing of support is tailored to individual need. Too much and they will be over-supported, too little and they will be unsuccessful. The approach highlights the importance of using a range of types of support e.g. environmental cues, visual prompts, gestures and facial expressions rather than over-relying on spoken instructions. When supporting individuals, the aim is to shift (or grade) the amount of assistance provided so that the individual receives just enough help. If one level of assistance is not working then staff move on to the next level or add a different type of help so that the individual is successful in the activity or relationship.
Maximising choice and control	In any situation there are opportunities for an individual to express their preferences and be listened to. Choice has to be balanced with the responsibilities of domestic life, working and/or being part of a family and community. Hence there are some things that have to be done. However individuals can still be supported to exercise a choice about when, where and how they are done.
References: BILD (2023), Ockenden *et al* (2014), United Response (2015)	

There is a risk that individuals with intellectual disabilities may misunderstand staff roles and view them as friends or potential partners (see Chapter 13). Such confusions over roles can complicate the process of engagement.

For the most able individuals, living relatively independent lives, their intellectual disabilities are likely to make it more difficult for them to understand their own needs, to seek help and to organise themselves to see interventions through. Some of these individuals may feel stigmatised by being viewed as having intellectual disabilities and may avoid services with this in their title. They may prefer to use mainstream services. Some individuals may feel doubly stigmatised if given both 'personality disorder' and 'intellectual disabilities' labels, and may want to avoid both mental health and intellectual disabilities services. It requires a thoughtful and creative approach to overcome these issues.

Building engagement and positive working relationships

The key to enhancing engagement with individuals with intellectual disabilities who might be given a diagnosis of 'personality disorder' is that staff must actively

 Intellectual Disabilities and 'Personality Disorder' © Pavilion Publishing and Media Ltd and its licensors 2023

facilitate the process. *Individuals are not in a position to change how they respond to staff or services.* Box 5.8 gives some important areas to consider when seeking to engage individuals, including some basic practicalities that are easily overlooked.

Box 5.8: Facilitating engagement with individuals with intellectual disabilities	
The right help at the right time: '**R**egulate, **R**elate, **R**eason'	Ensure that the interventions offered are appropriate for the stage the individual is at (see Chapter 3, Box 3.1). Individuals at the '**R**egulate' stage will not be ready to form a working relationship; they need comfort and emotional containment (see Chapters 9 and 11). Be sensitive to fluctuations in mood and emotional availability – adjust approach for good and bad days.
Physical and emotional safety	Individuals cannot engage if they feel threatened. Promote physical and emotional safety (see Chapter 6 for service design promoting safety).
Practicalities	Set up the situation to make it as easy as possible for the individual to engage e.g. choice of venue, means of transport, appropriate surroundings, support of key people in the individual's life, time of day.
Abilities profile	Identify barriers arsing from the individual's abilities profile and tailor input to accommodate them (Box 5.6).
Person-centred	Ensure best fit with individual's preferences and wishes (be creative). Prioritise empowerment and respect (Dixon *et al*, 2016).
Hope, expectations and endings	It is important to let the individual know you believe there can be a positive outcome, however small the steps or long the process. It is also important to be explicit about what the intervention comprises e.g. number and location of sessions, when staff are available and what they can do, when it will end. Avoid misunderstandings and disappointments.
Core skills – staff	Build skills that promote engagement – e.g. Active support (see box 5.7), SET, emotional validation, motivational interviewing, compassionate and containing support style (see Chapter 13).
Resolving ruptures	Shift focus from the intervention to the working relationship with the aim to re-establish the collaboration (Eubanks *et al*, 2018; Schenk *et al*, 2021). Validate individual's perspective, acknowledge own role and agree solution e.g. using SET.

→

Understanding individual	What might be happening when individuals do not engage despite all of the above.
Understanding self	Understanding the natural, automatic reactions that are triggered in all care-givers when the individual they are caring for does not respond to the 'good care' provided.

If an individual's first contact with services is during a crisis, it is unlikely that they will be ready to engage with staff. Staff will first need to support them to regulate their emotional state. If this is done sensitively, with an eye to the future (see Chapters 9 and 11), individuals will be more likely to engage when they reach the **R**elate stage (Perry, 2020, and see Chapter 3).

Emotional safety

The first interactions with an individual will set the tone for their work with that service or member of staff. From the start, it is important to make the individual feel that they are safe, both physically and emotionally. This is important because, when anxious or afraid, an individual will be focusing on keeping safe and will not be open to engaging with staff. Creating a sense of safety involves a combination of the physical environment (see Chapter 6) and the emotional climate created by staff behaviour and responsiveness. Some key elements of emotional security are given in Box 5.9. As an individual gradually builds trust in staff, they may be able to use staff as a secure base – a source of comfort if they are distressed and a launching pad when they feel able to explore and test things out.

Box 5.9: Creating a sense of safety/emotional security (a secure base)	
Physical safety	An environment that keeps the risk of physical harm or neglect to a minimum.
Availability and predictability of support	Familiar staff available through good staffing practices. Needs for food, drink, activity or interaction are consistently met. Staff are able to comfort and provide emotional containment when individuals are stressed or distressed. Individual feels seen, heard and accepted without judgment.
Warmth	There is a two-way, positive emotional connection, conveyed though body language, posture, facial expression, eye-contact, tone of voice, choice of words and actions e.g. offering a cup of tea.

 Intellectual Disabilities and 'Personality Disorder' © Pavilion Publishing and Media Ltd and its licensors 2023

Shared positive feelings	Opportunities to enjoy interactions and activities.
Shared reflection and exploration	Ensure that exploring and learning about difficult issues has some fun in as well as being challenging.
Adapted from Skelly (2017)	

Warmth is an essential component in creating a positive working relationship; it makes individuals feel welcome and encourages relaxation. It is also important that the individual feels that they are being listened to and that staff can be trusted. This can be difficult to achieve at a time when the individual may be distressed and staff have a lot of information they wish to convey. Often, the message staff are trying to convey gets lost in distressed feelings and misunderstandings, which jeopardises engagement. However, using effective communication strategies can help. It is important that the individual is made aware that the staff member is trying to help them. This may seem too obvious to put into words. However, when individuals are hypersensitive to threat and unable to pick up safety signals, it helps to gently remind them why staff are there. Then it is important to recognise and validate their emotions and views. This helps show that staff are listening. At this point, the individual is more likely to hear the information staff wish to communicate. The acronym SET (support, empathise, truth) summarises this approach. SET and validating emotions are explored more fully in Chapter 13.

Emotional safety can also be promoted by thinking creatively about what will make each individual feel safe. For example, using a playlist of their favourite songs and having familiar objects around them. 'Breathing room', an approach that recognises that standard therapy settings can feel unwelcoming and unsafe for many individuals, is described in Box 13.11.

Expectations and endings

In early interactions staff should also make clear how they see the future of this intervention. This is an opportunity to make clear that staff are hopeful that things will improve, and that the individual is deserving of help and support to achieve this. They can explain that the individual will, when ready, be expected to work with the staff team to agree goals and to eventually do more for themselves. For individuals at the **R**eason stage (see Chapter 3), it may be helpful to work together to draw up a contract or a more general plan with stages in it. If the individual will be expected to leave the service or the intervention is intended to come to an end, this should be gently mentioned in the earliest stages. For example, 'When you are feeling better, we will work together to find you a new placement. We will support you until you get to know the new staff'. This is important as it avoids the individual making up their own plan and then feeling let down when it does not reflect reality. This also helps foster a healthy sense of interdependence and autonomy, which can improve self-esteem.

If an individual has successfully engaged with a service and this has been sustained, it is easy to forget about the importance of ending work thoughtfully. While some individuals will do so well that they never need services again, many will have multiple episodes of care. Endings need to be managed sensitively so that the individual feels that they can return if they need to, without feeling they have failed or let people down. Equally, attention needs to be given to the feelings triggered by the ending. However well the individual may appear, ending can leave them feeling rejected and abandoned. Such feelings may result in the re-emergence of difficulties or make it hard for them to return if they become unwell in the future. Within an individual's full and varied life, the people, emotions and activities encountered during an episode of care may or may not go on to be significant in their future. However, thoughtful planning can maximise the chances of any connotations being positive.

Leaving an inpatient setting after a period of intervention, can be particularly difficult and needs to be managed sensitively. Ideally, there should be a carefully planned transition period with the opportunity to build relationships with new staff or build links with the community. Individuals may have spent a lot of time telling staff how much they hate being in hospital and how much they want to leave. It can then be very difficult for them to admit how scared they are about forming new relationships and leaving behind the security of staff who have (hopefully) supported them with compassion during a very difficult time. It can be very helpful for individuals if staff raise these issues in a matter-of-fact and considerate way. Gentle humour is often helpful at these times. Staff might make comments such as, 'I know you are well-fed up with all of us but it is always difficult to make a new start. Everyone feels a bit frightened when they have to make new relationships.' This would help create an environment in which the individual feels comfortable to acknowledge their fears. (Difficulty leaving is only one of a number of reasons why inpatient care needs to be avoided whenever possible. Chapter 6 shares a service model that minimises the risk of individuals needing inpatient stays, and where this is unavoidable, promotes prompt and successful discharge.)

Intellectual Disabilities and 'Personality Disorder' © Pavilion Publishing and Media Ltd and its licensors 2023

Sustaining engagement

Once things have got off to a good start, it is important to pay attention to sustaining engagement. Individuals with experience of relational trauma and little hope need thoughtful support if engagement is to be sustained. An individual may stop attending appointments consistently, may not make the progress expected, may stop co-operating with efforts to help them or may experience repeated crises. As individuals move though the stages of intervention (**R**egulate, **R**elate, **R**eason), engagement may change. For example, an individual may have developed confidence in staff to go about their activities of daily living with support (**R**elate) but may not wish to work with staff to develop skills to improve their self-management (**R**eason).

Lack of engagement can be less visible in residential settings. An individual may be willing to continue to live in a setting, but closer examination shows that they spend little time engaged in constructive activities, let others do things for them that they are able to do themselves and do not participate actively in efforts to promote 'independence'. The system may have unintentionally placed them in a safe, passive and dependent role. 'Helping' can sometimes inadvertently lead to helplessness and disempowerment (Gregson and Delaney, 2021). This can be difficult to challenge as direct efforts to encourage independence and activity can be experienced as rejection and abandonment. Gregson and Delaney (2021) describe helping a compassionate staff team shift towards drawing an individual 'in' to feel safe and connected, as opposed to encouraging them 'away' through pressure for greater independence. By building the individual's sense of safety and self-esteem, they may be better able to work towards exploring more independence and reaching their potential.

Other individuals may show their lack of engagement with residential settings by seeking to move home after the initial 'honeymoon' period is over. This is often related to underlying core beliefs the individual holds about 'perfect care' and 'black-and-white thinking' such that small, inevitable disappointments are seen as proof that the placement is no good. Rather than simply finding a series of new placements for the individual, it may be helpful to explore their thinking with them using the approaches in Chapter 15.

All ruptures need to be thoughtfully explored, with the individual wherever possible, and addressed. Reflective practice and supervision (see Chapter 7) may help formulate what has led to the rupture. It is important to hold in mind that, when individuals do not engage, or subsequently disengage, their responses are instinctive, automatic reactions to interactions (however well intentioned) that they experience as threatening. It is up to staff to find a way of making the individual feel safe enough to engage again.

It is important to understand that, even when staff and services get things right, individuals may not engage fully with the service. It may take several contacts for the individual to build up trust and be in the right place, mentally, to work with a service. Some may be so fearful that they only engage when compelled to, for example, being detained under the Mental Health Act. The secret is to do the right things and keep doing them, in the knowledge that they are most likely to engage the individual in the longer term. Always include the questions in Box 5.4 in this process. It is easier to keep trying if staff understand some of the barriers that can make it very difficult for individuals to engage despite staff's best efforts and being offered good support.

What might be happening when individuals do not engage despite being offered good support

Individuals who have experienced severe developmental trauma (whatever medical diagnosis they may have been given) can become trapped by the survival strategies that helped them during very difficult experiences. For such individuals, the world is not a safe place and no one can be trusted. To open up and acknowledge their needs is to let others know how to hurt them most easily.

Their brains may have become hard wired to look for threats (see Chapter 2); they are hypersensitive to threat, picking up the slightest hints and expecting it where it does not exist. However, they are slow to register, or completely miss, signs that the situation is safe (sometimes called 'safety blindness'). When individuals are so threat-focused, they are unable to respond to, and may not even notice, friendly invitations to engage. Such individuals may repeatedly appear oblivious to efforts to engage them. This has been described as 'blocked trust' (Hughes, 2017).

Developmental trauma can also lead to individuals developing insecure attachments (see Chapters 2 and 12). Using insecure attachment strategies can inhibit the development of engagement (see Box 5.10).

 Intellectual Disabilities and 'Personality Disorder' © Pavilion Publishing and Media Ltd and its licensors 2023

Box 5.10: Attachment and engagement	
Attachment	Response to efforts to engage.
Secure/autonomous	Open to engagement, learning and enjoyment.
Insecure:	
Avoidant/Dismissive	Rejecting. I may repeatedly rebuff you as I expect you to rebuff me. I may be completely 'cut off' or unresponsive to social communication.
Ambivalent/Preoccupied	Anxious. I will want to engage with you but worry that you will go away. However much you reassure me, it only lasts briefly then I will need to be reassured again. I will be hyper-sensitive to signs you are angry, don't like me. I will find it hard to let go when it is time to end an intervention.
Disorganised/Unresolved	I will chaotically and unpredictably switch between seeking reassurance and contact and rejecting you. You never know what to expect, or just when we seem to be forming a bond, I will reject you.

Although individuals may hear staff's words, they are not in a place to receive the social and emotional message that staff can be trusted and are safe to engage with.

What can happen to staff when an individual does not respond to the 'good care' provided

When staff repeatedly try their best to engage individuals without success, it can undermine their job-satisfaction and lead to a number of different reactions. Staff may, naturally, experience feeling rejected, frustrated, inadequate, angry, helpless or hopeless. Without good enough support, staff may struggle to relate to the individual. They may withdraw or focus only on trying to control or manage behaviours that challenge.

Harding (2021) draws parallels between this situation and the concept of 'blocked care'. Hughes (2017) uses this phrase to explain the response of foster carers when the child they are looking after is experiencing 'blocked trust' and does not respond to the good care the parent is offering. Without positive feedback from the child, foster-parents can gradually become emotionally disengaged. They 'do their job' but without the emotional connection needed to benefit the child (see Box 5.11). This process is mediated by automatic neurological processes, hence it happens despite the carer's best intentions. It can be combated by actively seeking to understand what is happening and consciously choosing to behave differently. This requires motivation and support.

Box 5.11: Characteristics of blocked care

Characteristics of blocked care	Unblocking care and promoting good care
■ In survival mode. ■ Defensive, not open and engaged. ■ Social-emotional apathy. ■ Focus only on behaviour not its meaning. ■ Reactive, not proactive or responsive. ■ Repeat doing what is not working. ■ Only see the need to correct, not connect. ■ Sensitive to rejection.	■ Cultivate compassion. ■ Muster warmth. ■ Stay in the game: it's not a sprint, it's a marathon. ■ Recognise rejection for what it is: **MISPLACED MISTRUST** ■ Enhance your 'approachability', work at making yourself safe to be near and fun to engage with. ■ Strengthen your capacity for deep relaxation. ■ Identify and desensitise your 'hot buttons' (see Chapter 13). ■ Maintain a good support system. ■ Importance of team formulation, supervision and reflection. ■ Use PACE: **P**layfulness: light, hopeful, open **A**cceptance: Unconditional **C**uriosity: Non-judgemental, not knowing, active interest in their experience **E**mpathy: build understanding of where the behaviours of concern comes from

Adapted from Hughes (2016)

Staff teams need to develop a good understanding of themselves, for example their own most-used attachment strategy, what motivates and de-motivates them. They need to build the skills to manage their own emotional reactions to repeated rebuffs and rejection. They need the emotional resilience to bounce back again and again.

 Intellectual Disabilities and 'Personality Disorder' © Pavilion Publishing and Media Ltd and its licensors 2023

They also need to understand that the way that individuals cope with intense needs and fears can trigger difficult emotions and unhelpful behaviours in those supporting them (see Chapter 7).

Key learning points

- Engagement is the healthy, mutual connection between an individual and those who support them. It allows people to work together to achieve mutually agreed objectives and solve problems.
- Engagement is influenced by a wide range of factors including the social context, the characteristics of the service, the staff and the intervention as well as the characteristics of the individual.
- Engagement is important as, without it, individuals struggle with problems on their own or, if they seek help, interventions may not be completed. This increases the risk of crises and of negative outcomes.
- The experience of stigma can lead to an individual avoiding contact with mental health or intellectual disabilities services.
- A 'person-centred' approach is the key to achieving engagement. However, when a service struggles to engage an individual, it should first ask itself questions about what it needs to do differently.
- An understanding of the effects of developmental trauma on trust and attachment is necessary to understand why staff may struggle to engage some individuals despite their best efforts.
- Persisting in the presence of misplaced mistrust is challenging. Staff teams need good training and support if they are to continue to provide good care while being repeatedly rebuffed and rejected.

Chapter 6: Services – the right place at the right time

This chapter explores why individuals with intellectual disabilities who might be given a diagnosis of 'personality disorder' are at risk of placement breakdown and admission to hospital. It explores the characteristics of services that promote well-being and avoid crises. It looks at the need to embed these principles throughout the service. It explores how the physical environment can help reduce the need for restrictive interventions. It presents an example of a flexible, integrated intensive support service that works to prevent placement breakdown and avoid admissions to hospital.

Key topics

- What goes wrong?
- What works?
- Enhanced capable environments
- The physical environment
- Services to prevent and resolve crises

What goes wrong?

Individuals with intellectual disabilities who might be given a diagnosis of 'personality disorder' are at increased risk of placement breakdown and of being admitted to hospital (Toogood, 2017). The characteristics of the services that support them, both every day and at times of crisis, play a significant role in this risk. Many services operate a short-term approach, within a simplistic medical model. This can result in support being reduced or stopped when the individual appears settled and stable. This makes them vulnerable to tipping into crisis if even small things go wrong for them. Individuals frequently struggle in services that offer a great degree of personal freedom and choice and expect high levels of personal independence (Gregson and Delaney, 2021). A mismatch between the support style an individual's needs and the philosophy of the service they are placed in may lead, sooner or later, to placement breakdown.

It has long been recognised that some services are more likely than others to lead individuals to meet their needs through behaviours that challenge, and are less able to respond constructively when this occurs. Some of these service characteristics are given in Box 6.1. Some arise from the philosophy of care, others from the way the service operates, or a combination of the two.

Box 6.1: Service characteristics that may create and maintain behaviours that challenge
Inability to respond to individual need (e.g. are not person-centred, lack of resources, inflexibility, lack of creativity).
Believe the causes of behaviours that challenge lie solely in the individual showing the behaviour (i.e. rigid medical model).
Lack relevant training (e.g. positive behavioural support, person-centred approaches).
Over-emphasis on learning and using reactive strategies (e.g. restrictive physical interventions).
High staff turn-over.
Poorly organised staff teams with lack of clarity about priorities of work.
Lack of team work leading to inconsistent support.
Poor or inaccurate record-keeping (making it difficult to find out what is happening).
Over-controlling OR chaotic and lacking organisational structure.
Difficulties working with competent external professionals. Have preconceived belief that professionals do not understand the demands of their job. Believe that they cannot implement the advice given as it does not reflect the limitations of their situation.
References: Bigby and Beadle-Brown (2018) Royal College of Psychiatrists (2006)

Many families speak of how quickly their family member reaches crisis point when things go wrong. However, rapid early intervention (Families and Mencap, 2021) is often not available. For the most able individuals, there can also be confusion or disagreement at such times as to whether they should be supported by services for people with intellectual disabilities or adult mental health services (RCP, 2021). This can lead to their not receiving support in a timely manner. In the absence of responsive 24/7 community support and local alternatives to hospitals, individuals may be admitted to (usually non-NHS) assessment and treatment units, often far from home. Once there, issues such as distance, lack of suitable placements and

Intellectual Disabilities and 'Personality Disorder' © Pavilion Publishing and Media Ltd and its licensors 2023

perverse financial incentives, can make it difficult to achieve a successful return home: stays can be protracted. Sadly, the support they receive there may not be of high quality and they are vulnerable to abuse.

The abuse of individuals with intellectual disabilities at Winterbourne View (assessment and treatment unit), uncovered in 2011 by Panorama, triggered a number of responses from government, including the Transforming Care Agenda (DoH, 2012). These were intended to facilitate the speedy discharge of those already in hospital and prevent re-admission. They also hoped to prevent new admissions by developing enhanced, intensive community support.

However, progress towards these aims has been slow. Ten years after Winterbourne View, the families of the individuals involved, together with Mencap (2021), reviewed the progress made. For example, the average length of stay for people with intellectual disabilities and/or ASD in inpatient units was 5.6 years in 2021. They concluded:

> *'Over the course of the past 10 years, not one of the targets the government have set for themselves has been achieved.'*

It is beyond the scope of this book to explore the reasons for the slow progress. However, the understanding of how to successfully support individuals with complex behaviours that challenge continues to grow, offering hope for how change can be achieved.

What works?

For individuals to thrive, a number of factors need to be in place in the services that support them both on a day-to day basis and when they are in crisis (see Box 6.2).

Box 6.2: Key factors to enable individuals to thrive	
The right approach	See Chapters 3 (What works) and 8 (PBS).
Right time 3 **R**s	Services delivered promptly, at the time they are needed, at the right stage of the intervention cycle (see Box 3.1). Ability to respond rapidly when needed.
Flexible	Able to respond agilely and creatively to fluctuating needs, ability to respond 24/7.

→

Longer-term	Understand that issues may be life-long and that withdrawing support will destabilise the individual.
Support style	Provides compassionate emotional containment. Neither too permissive or too controlling. Person-centred, consistent and predictable, providing emotional security. Uses Active Support (see box 5.7).
Collaborative	Inclusive – work with individuals and their families, value individuals, promote choice, empower, respect.
Focus	Promoting quality of life and positive relationships, preventing the need for behaviours that challenge and facilitating healthy interdependence.
Knowledgeable	Understand behaviours that challenge, the impact of trauma and different attachments. Interventions informed by an appropriate model e.g. trauma-informed-PBS.
Skilled	Have appropriate skill set e.g. active listening, emotional validation, de-escalation.
Well organised, well managed and well led	Appropriate staffing levels and shift patterns, cover for holidays, supervision and team reflection built into work patterns. Consistent and reliable.
Integrated and inter-connected	Good links with other services and other teams also commissioners. Where appropriate, seamless transitions between different parts of services.

These apply equally to the services that provide day-to-day support and those that respond to specific needs, for example the community team for people with learning disabilities (CTPLD) and crisis services. Services need to work smoothly together so that crises are prevented whenever possible and that individuals have access to additional support and respite if needed. If respite is needed they are supported to return home or to a new placement in a timely and constructive manner.

Enhanced 'Capable Environments'

The first step is ensuring that individuals have the right support in their everyday lives. The phrase 'capable environments' is used in Positive Behaviour Support PBS (see Chapter 8) to highlight the importance of service settings in preventing, minimising and managing behaviours that challenge. Capable environments provide the key elements described in Box 6.2. They are knowledgeable, structured but flexible, person-centred and active. They will have staff with a good understanding

Intellectual Disabilities and 'Personality Disorder' © Pavilion Publishing and Media Ltd and its licensors 2023

of the factors that make individuals vulnerable to developing behaviours that challenge, the functions that challenges may serve and an understanding of how to promote positive behaviours.

These core PBS qualities need to be enhanced with understanding of relational issues such as attachment (Skelly 2017) and an understanding of trauma (Harding 2021). Progressing from traditional PBS to trauma-informed PBS involves a widening of the main focus, away from behaviours that challenge to explore 'what happened to you?' (see Chapter 8).

> *'This can be a radical shift in some services: sometimes requiring not just multi-agency endorsement but also service commissioners and senior managers to support this innovative way of working'.* (Jones 2021 p146)

Goad (2021) explores the process by which a culture-shift to the values of trauma-informed care can be achieved within services for individuals with intellectual disabilities. She highlights the importance of support from the top of the organisation to reduce barriers to change and ensuring that change is carried out in such a way that staff feel included rather than imposed upon.

For effective attachment and trauma-informed PBS to be delivered consistently and sustainably, it needs to be supported across all elements of the service, including non-clinical functions such as finance and human resources (SAMSHA, 2014). Services need to be structured, organised and delivered in ways that promote safety, build trust and prevent re-traumatisation. Understanding relationships, trauma and positive support needs to become embedded in the culture. Some of the actions required to achieve this are given in Box 6.3

Box 6.3: Trauma-informed PBS: 10 Implementation domains

Domain	Key elements
1. Organisation governance and leadership	Investment in implementing and sustaining the approach. There is an identified organisational lead/champion. There is a peer voice at organisational level.
2. Policy	Trauma-informed-PBS is 'hard wired' into the practices, policies and procedures of the organisation, not relying only on training workshops or a leader.

→

3. Physical environment	Must be designed and maintained so that it is experienced as safe and inviting by staff and individuals.
4. Engagement and involvement of past and current service users and their families	Significant involvement, voice, and meaningful choice at all levels and in all areas of the organisation.
5. Cross-sector collaboration	Individuals with complex needs often access multiple services or have contact with different service sectors. A referral to a trauma-insensitive programme could undermine the progress of the individual.
6. Screening, assessment, treatment services	Practitioners use assessments and interventions based on the best available empirical evidence and science, are culturally appropriate, and reflect principles of a trauma-informed approach.
7. Training and workforce development	Ongoing training on trauma and peer support. Trauma-informed principles run through hiring, supervision, staff evaluation; procedures are in place to support staff with trauma histories, vicarious trauma.
8. Progress monitoring and quality assurance	There is ongoing assessment, tracking and monitoring of trauma-informed PBS principles and effective use of evidence-based trauma specific screening, assessments and treatment.
9. Financing	Includes resources for all elements of trauma informed PBS e.g.: staff training on trauma and positive support, development of appropriate and safe facilities; establishment of peer support.
10. Evaluation	Specifically evaluates progress and effectiveness of trauma informed PBS.

The physical environment

There are strong links between the physical environment and both physiological and emotional arousal. Creating a safe and inviting space for both individuals and staff is the foundation for delivering trauma-informed care (SAMSHA, 2014). Although this seems obvious, it is easy for this to be overlooked in situations where time and money are both in short supply. Well-designed and maintained environments promote mental well-being and create a sense of safety (Gill 2019). Thoughtful layouts can also

Intellectual Disabilities and 'Personality Disorder' © Pavilion Publishing and Media Ltd and its licensors 2023

promote collaboration and openness. When supporting individuals with behaviours that challenge, attention to layouts and sufficient space make it much easier to keep everyone safe. Trauma-informed design (TID) explores how to create spaces that achieve these objectives. Some of the key areas addressed by TID are given in Box 6.4. Although some features need to be incorporated at the design stage, many others can be achieved at low cost by thoughtful use of existing resources. The involvement of individuals who live in or use a service in reviewing the physical environment can maximise the potential for change and innovation, so that it is genuinely guided by the insights of lived experience (Oostermeijer *et al*, 2019).

Box 6.4: Creating a trauma-informed environment	
Spatial layout	Spaces with clear sight-lines and few barriers create a sense of safety and calmness. Capacity to support distressed individuals away from others for their privacy and to minimise the impact on those observing their distress.
Space and choice	Avoid overcrowding, create personal space e.g. arms on chairs and choice e.g. more chairs than people.
Minimise barriers	For example: sitting face-to-face across a desk or table may be perceived as confrontational. Sitting corner to corner invites conversation and interaction.
Visual interest	Some detail but not overcrowded. An appropriate quantity of objects, symmetry and regularity in their arrangement alleviates stress and promotes well-being. Choose art carefully to avoid risk of triggering distressing memories or distress.
Colour	Cool colours have a calming effect e.g. soft blues, greens and natural shades. Avoid deeply hued warm colours that may arouse negative emotions. Avoid stark brilliant white.
Furniture	Comfortable, durable and easy to clean. Its arrangement should enhance safety and promote positive interactions. Seating that faces out from a sheltering wall creates a sense of safety.
Lighting	Natural light makes rooms appear less crowded. Soft lighting is more comfortable and less stressing than bright harsh lighting.
Smells and sounds	Loud noises and unpleasant smells make people uncomfortable.
Bring in nature	Views of nature are calming – make the most of the outlook e.g. strategically planted trees, bring nature in e.g. pictures of landscapes or house plants.

→

Temperature	Both too hot and cold are stressful.
Tidy and organised	Messy workplaces are perceived as unprofessional and out of control.
Maintenance	Well-kept places feel safer than tired and neglected ones. Fix flickering lights and change blown bulbs.
Ease of movement, finding way around	People feel safer if they understand where they are and how they can leave, and can easily locate important things such as reception area, exits and toilets.
Summarised from: Trauma-Informed Design How the Physical Environment Supports Recovery from Homelessness https://cotsonline.org/wp-content/uploads/2018/04/Trauma-Informed-Design.BOD_.pdf	

Individuals with a diagnosis of 'personality disorder' are at greater risk of being restrained or placed in seclusion (Hansen *et al*, 2020). Seclusion is a restrictive practice intended to protect the individual or others from harm. However, it can result in trauma-related harm as it is both unpleasant in itself, can trigger memories of abandonment and neglect, and can leave individuals with nothing to distract themselves from intrusive thoughts or intense feelings. There is evidence that a number of environmental features act to reduce the need for seclusion and restraint. Oostermeijer *et al* (2019) found that a beneficial physical environment (e.g. access to gardens or recreational facilities), sensory or comfort rooms and private, uncrowded and calm spaces were all helpful in reducing the use of restraint or seclusion.

De-escalation rooms

A de-escalation room is an environmental feature that can reduce the risk of crises and create a sense of safety. They may also be called sensory rooms, Snoezelen rooms or comfort rooms, depending on the client group and setting they have been designed for. They provide a safe, quiet environment that offers low levels of pleasant stimulation, designed to reduce over-arousal and create a sense of well-being. They can be equipped with features to promote relaxation, for example music, lighting and sensory stimulation. The controls can be designed so that the individual can tailor the stimuli to their needs, for example through the use of specially designed interactive whiteboards. Individuals may be supported to use the room by staff. However, individuals can also actively choose to use the room when they feel stressed or anxious.

 Intellectual Disabilities and 'Personality Disorder' © Pavilion Publishing and Media Ltd and its licensors 2023

The Safety Pod™ beanbag

The Safety Pod™ (see Box 6.5) is an example of how a well-designed piece of furniture can transform care and reduce trauma. It is a specially designed bean bag developed to make physical restriction safer and less traumatic. It replaces 'supine' or 'prone' restraint (restraint of an individual in a face-up position on their back on the floor or another surface, and with physical pressure applied to the body to keep that position). Rather than being held on the floor, the individual is seated in the Safety Pod™. The pod maintains a body angle at 135 degrees, which optimises chest expansion and lung function, and minimises head trauma during restraint. Use can be supported with a knee cushion, to safely contain the individual's legs, if needed. Safety Pods™ have been medically risk assessed and clinically approved by a member of the Royal College of Emergency Medicine and the Royal College of Surgeons. Staff need to be trained in the use of the pods and their use must be part of a PBS plan (see Chapter 8). The pods also need to be carefully maintained to ensure they continue to be safe to use.

Box 6.5: Safety pod™ beanbag

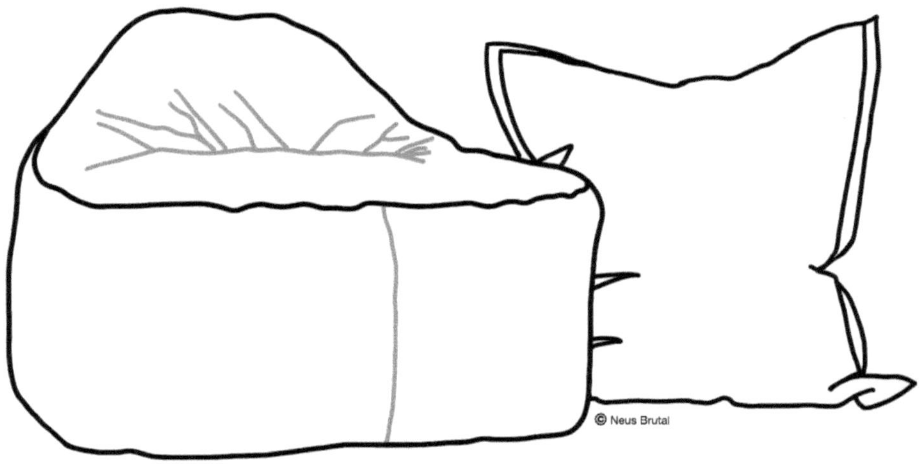

Image credit: Neus Bartual

Service audit data show that, when used as part of a PBS plan, the pods significantly reduce or eliminate the need for prone restraint (CQC, 2019; UK Pods, 2022). They also reduced the number of staff needed to safely contain an incident. The pods are easy to move, so staff can manoeuvre the pod to where it is needed, avoiding the risks of moving the individual. The pods are viewed positively by both staff and individuals and staff feedback showed 100% agreed the Safety Pod™ was easy and safe to use, compared to only 9% saying supine restraint was easy and safe to execute.

An individual who was supported with a Safety Pod™ said: *'Safety Pod is good, it feels comfortable and is very relaxing.'*

It appears that the pod may be meeting a need for proprioceptive feedback (which helps regulate arousal) or a need to be held and contained both physically and emotionally. Hence, using the pod replaces a traumatic experience with one that is intrinsically calming.

Services to prevent and resolve crises

To successfully support individuals during crises, a service needs to be able to respond quickly and flexibly to the situation, provide the right additional support and, where necessary, have access to local crisis support/respite beds. The importance of this approach is recognised in on-going developments in mental health care including the Community Mental Health Framework (NHS England, 2019), Health and Care Act (2022) and the NHS long-term plan (2023-24). The service needs to be fully integrated with services for both intellectual disabilities and mental health (RCP, 2021), with the flexibility to respond to the individual's needs and preferences.

An example of such a service is the intensive support service (ISS) described by Dodd *et al* (2021). The ISS is an integrated, seven-day-a-week crisis intervention and support service for individuals with intellectual disabilities and severe and complex mental health needs and/or behaviours that challenge, requiring urgent specialist assessment and intervention. The ISS comprises an Intensive Support Team (IST) and Intensive Support Beds/crisis beds (ISB) provided within an assessment and treatment unit on a local intellectual disabilities services hub (see Box 6.6).

 Intellectual Disabilities and 'Personality Disorder' © Pavilion Publishing and Media Ltd and its licensors 2023

Box 6.6: Intensive Support Service Model

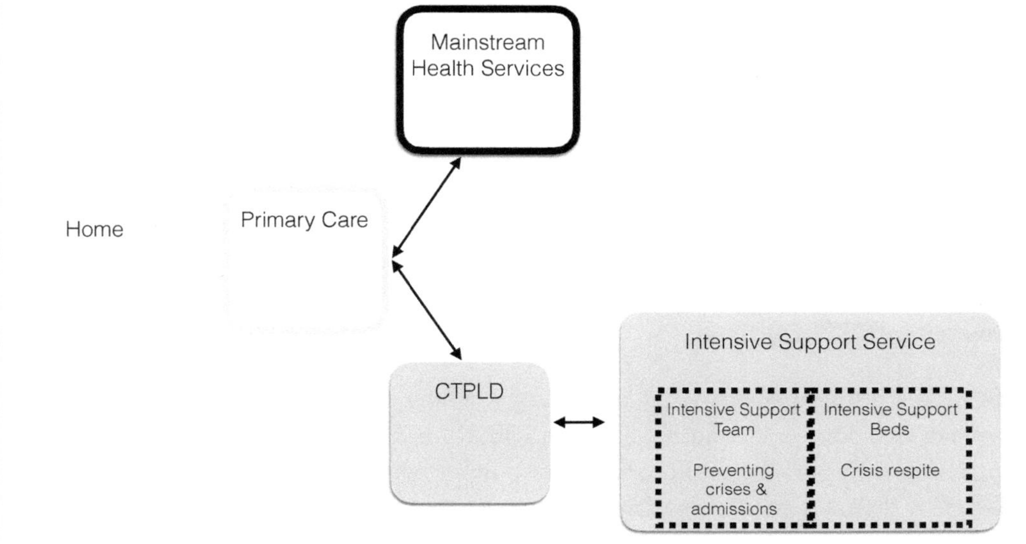

The ISS works to prevent inappropriate admissions and keep people in their homes. It supports them with familiar staff if they need admission, and facilitates timely discharge to their home wherever possible. Where individuals cannot be supported at home, one of three options is chosen depending on need (see Box 6.7). This approach is particularly helpful for individuals with intellectual disabilities who might be given a diagnosis of 'personality disorder' as it is able to support them in the setting that best meets their needs and preferences.

Box 6.7: Options when an individual cannot be safely supported in their home or placement

Option 1:	Support the individual at home or in their current placement with an additional support package from commissioners and social care with intensive support from the IST and CTPLD.
Option 2:	Support the individual in a local non-inpatient unit using residential or short break services with input from the IST.
Option 3:	Arrange admission into a local inpatient service in the CCG area. Either: Individual with a mild ID to access a mainstream working-age adult ward where possible, with additional support from ISS if needed. →

	Or: Individual with moderate or severe ID, admission would be arranged within the Intensive support respite beds*.
*Intensive support respite beds	In an ATU. Located within the county served. Accessible to transport links, local shops and town centre, safe outside space, multi-sensory de-escalation room, soft colour scheme, shared and private areas, domestic kitchen.

The IST works closely with the CTPLDs to identify people most at risk of inpatient admission, then joins with them to provide a more intensive approach than can be delivered by CTPLDs alone.

A flexible staffing model is used, with staff working across both elements of the service. If someone is admitted to an ISB, then the IST staff who had been supporting that person would continue to support them in the ISB until they settle. There is a robust discharge pathway. Discharge planning starts at admission and involves all stakeholders, including commissioners. Placement staff are supported to understand the individual's needs and how to support them. An individual is not discharged from the ISS until they have settled within that placement and placement staff have demonstrated they are able to respond appropriately to meet the individual's needs. This reduces the risk of re-admission.

The IST also provide out-of-hours advice to the 136 suite (a place of safety for people who are detained by the Police under Section 136 of the Mental Health Act), crisis line, emergency duty team and psychiatric liaison in acute hospitals. This ensures that individuals with intellectual disabilities receive appropriate support during a crisis, whatever service is their first point of contact.

The ISS works primarily within the PBS model. All nurses and care support workers receive training in PBS and some have attended PBS coaches training through BILD. This range of skilled staff allows the ISS to offer rapid advice on de-escalation and risk management, devise an initial multidisciplinary formulation, and recommend practical support strategies. The service has a multidisciplinary team including psychiatry, psychology, occupational therapy, speech and language therapy and specialist nurses.

Data indicates that the majority of people referred to the service avoid both admission to an inpatient unit and placement breakdown. This contrasts strongly with the previous service (a stand-alone, Assessment and Treatment Unit), where all

 Intellectual Disabilities and 'Personality Disorder' © Pavilion Publishing and Media Ltd and its licensors 2023

seven beds were usually occupied, and stays could be as long as two years. Dodd *et al* (2021) comment:

> '[Few services] *have an integrated model of intensive support combining both the community and inpatient aspects within one service. It is this integration that gives our model its strength, with all staff working as one team; and having investment in making the system work for people with* [intellectual disabilities] *to prevent admission where possible…'*

Key learning points

- Individuals with intellectual disabilities with patterns of relationships and behaviour that might be given a diagnosis of 'personality disorder' are at increased risk of placement breakdown and of being admitted to hospital.
- Services with a short-term focus that see the cause of difficulties being within the individual, that are inflexible or slow to respond, can lead to crises and placement breakdowns.
- Lack of suitable local crisis respite beds can mean out-of-area placements with the risk of long stays and, potentially, of experiencing abusive treatment.
- Enhanced 'capable environments' can help promote well-being and help reduce the risk of crises.
- The principles of trauma-informed PBS need to be embedded throughout the organisation to ensure consistent support.
- Well-designed physical environments can enhance well-being and reduce the need for restrictive interventions.
- The Safety Pod™ is an example of a well-designed piece of furniture that can make managing an incident safer and less traumatic for both the individual and the staff supporting them.
- An integrated intensive support service can reduce placement breakdown, reduce the need for admission and facilitate prompt and successful discharge.

Chapter 7: Building positive, collaborative working relationships within and between teams

This chapter explores the ways in which interactions between individuals can be distorted. It looks at unconscious mechanisms, such as projection and splitting. It shows how past relationships can shape interactions in the present through mechanisms such as transference and reciprocal roles. It considers how stereotypes allow speedy decision-making at the cost of failing to perceive people as individuals. Although everyone uses these mechanisms, this chapter highlights that they are more likely to be used at times of high stress and by individuals who have difficulty managing and accepting intense emotions and those who experienced difficult relationships early in life. These mechanisms impact on interactions between staff and individuals and within and between staff teams. It shows that, although these mechanisms are unconscious, their influence can be identified and addressed through practices such as team reflection. It explores how reflective practices can improve working relationships within and between teams.

Key topics

- Processes influencing interactions between people
- The impact of unconscious mechanisms on interactions at work
- Promoting positive interactions within and between teams
- Reflective practice

Processes influencing interactions between people

Interactions and conversations between people appear deceptively simple: one person has something they wish to communicate, they share it with the other person. The second person hears and understands what is communicated and makes a response. The process continues in this way with each person understanding the other. However, the process is by no means so simple in real life. A number of factors can contribute to misunderstandings and some mechanisms actively distort the process of communication and shape how people behave. Some of these factors are given in Box 7.1.

Box 7.1: Factors influencing interactions between people
Diversity factors e.g. differences in age, gender, sexuality, race, ethnicity, social class and cultures, which influence how we understand others and the assumptions we make.
Motivation to communicate (or not) and opportunities to communicate e.g. not being invited, being talked over, lacking confidence to speak up in meetings.
Ability to understand own thoughts, feelings and motivations (mentalising) (Chapters 11 and 15).
Ability to express thoughts, feelings and concepts e.g. in words, signs, writings.
Ability to interpret the content of communications, both verbal and non-verbal.
Ability to interpret others' thoughts, feelings and motivations (mentalising) and style of mentalising (Chapters 11 and 15).
Impact of core beliefs, stereotypes, prejudices and cognitive distortions on how situations/communications are understood (Chapter 15).
Impact of the emotional state of the person on their thinking (emotional mind/ reasonable mind/wise mind) (Chapters 11 and 15).
Impact of past experience, especially developmental trauma (Chapter 2).
Unconscious mechanisms, for example projection and transference.

Unconscious mechanisms used by individuals

Much of our understanding of how communications can, unconsciously, be distorted, developed within psychotherapy, starting with the work of Freud and Breuer (1895). The concepts evolved to understand what was happening within therapy sessions both within the individual (for example, projection and transference) and the therapist (counter-transference), or to make sense of patterns of interaction (e.g. reciprocal roles). Other concepts about how perceptions can be biased have their origins in social psychology (e.g. the effects of stereotypes). Box 7.2 gives definitions and examples of a number of unconscious mechanisms that can distort communications. These mechanisms act to protect individuals from unacceptable feelings, give automatic ways of responding to

Intellectual Disabilities and 'Personality Disorder' © Pavilion Publishing and Media Ltd and its licensors 2023

interactions and provide mental shortcuts that reduce how much time is expended thinking about how to respond to new people and different situations.

Box 7.2: Unconscious mechanisms that can distort interactions	
Splitting: AND Projection:	A psychological defense (a way of keeping safe) when it is too unbearable for an individual to consider that a person (including themselves) or experience includes both positive and negative aspects. Thinking of the person or experience as an imperfect whole is too painful; instead, the individual thinks of them as EITHER good OR bad. The disowned part has to be pushed away (projected), and attributed to others. Ideas, groups, other people or the self are then viewed in absolute terms. There are no shades of grey; once an imperfection is recognised, it will 'flip' from being 'good' to being 'bad'. It is a way to make sense of and simplify experiences that are complex, confusing or threatening. **Examples:** Either good or bad; Either right or wrong; Best friend or arch enemy. When someone is unable to accept, cope with or process difficult and unwanted feelings, they may unconsciously attribute them to or 'project' them on to others. They may also misinterpret well-meant comments as showing that others feel about them in the way they find unacceptable. **Examples:** ■ Instead of facing the fact that they dislike a person, an individual thinks that they are disliked. ■ An individual cannot accept their own anger and accuses another person of having anger-management issues. ■ An individual who is cheating on their partner becomes very suspicious of their own partner.
Transference	When a past relationship shapes an individual's perceptions of a different person in the present. They feel about, relate to and behave towards that person in the way they responded to someone significant in their past e.g. a parent, sibling, life partner or person in authority This may reflect fear, hate or anger (negative transference) or love (positive transference). The pattern of feeling and behaving is unconsciously 'transferred' from the person in the past to a different person in the present. →

	Example: An individual becomes furious when their therapist suggests practicing mindfulness at home and shouts *'Homework? NO, I am not at school anymore'*. They respond to the therapist as if they were responding to their verbally abusive Year 7 teacher.
Reciprocal roles: (relationship roles)	Ways of interacting, learnt in childhood, that become automatic ways of responding to others. Everyone has reciprocal roles, many people use these flexibly to navigate their relationships. Others have a limited range or rigid reciprocal roles. Roles come in pairs. Each reciprocal role can be enacted in three different ways: others do it to me, I do it to myself, I do it to others. Roles may be healthy or unhealthy. For example, an individual neglected as a child, may perceive and act towards to other people as if they were neglecting the individual. They might also neglect those they care for or neglect their own needs. **Examples:**

Healthy	**Unhealthy***
Carer – Cared for	Abuser/Bully – Abused /Victim
Comforter – Comforted	Rejecting/Rejected
Teacher – Learner	Rescuing/Cared for
Supporter – Supported	Damaging/Damaged
Empowering – Empowered	Abandoning/Abandoned
Valuing – Valued	Special/Perfect to Learning Disabled
	Controlling/Controlled

Adapted from: Jenaway (2019) Madeson (2021) ReGain (2022) and Yashinsky (2022) * Psaila and Crowley (2005) most frequent roles found in sample of individuals with intellectual disabilities

These concepts highlight how, in any interaction, people's responses are not just shaped by the present situation. They are also influenced, unconsciously, by each person's past experiences and their ability to accept and manage thoughts and emotions they find threatening. As these mechanisms work unconsciously, individuals are unlikely to be aware of what is happening. The effect of these mechanisms can be benign, for example treating a stranger kindly without realising that they reminded you of your grandmother. However, *they always mean that we are not seeing or responding to the individual in front of us*. This often has a negative impact on interactions and may cause confusion, misunderstandings, frustration and anger. At the extreme, they can result in blame-shifting and believing that innocent people are guilty of wrongdoing.

Intellectual Disabilities and 'Personality Disorder' © Pavilion Publishing and Media Ltd and its licensors 2023

These mechanisms can perpetuate negative experiences from the past and can often become self-fulfilling. They are also resistant to change (Gelso *et al*, 2013) causing individuals to become stuck in unhelpful patterns of thinking and interacting. For example, an individual may continue to behave towards a member of staff as if they are uncaring despite evidence to the contrary. This may be because the individual's perceptions are preconceived, and hence the contradictory evidence is not noticed. It may also be because the pattern is an automatic way of dealing with stress, learnt during childhood, that provides a sense of safety despite being unhelpful in the present situation.

These processes may be encountered in interactions in any setting. For example: between family members, within personal relationships, between staff and the individuals they work with and between staff members. However, the extent to which individuals use these mechanisms varies greatly. People with positive past relationships, secure attachments, a positive sense of self and an acceptance of their own imperfections, may not use them to any noticeable degree. Such individuals are likely to have been exposed to positive role models while growing up and will have internalised a range of healthy, flexible reciprocal roles, giving them options to constructively interact in different settings. They may only use unconscious mechanisms at times of great stress.

However, people with difficult past experiences and insecure attachments may unconsciously use several mechanisms to help them deal with overwhelming and unwanted feelings, thoughts and behaviours. They may have a poorly developed sense of identity, low self-esteem and may not understand or feel comfortable with strong emotions. Hence, they are vulnerable to experiencing strong feelings but have limited ways of dealing with them. These feelings may be unconsciously avoided by using projection or splitting. Individuals may have unresolved issues with past relationships, making them likely to experience transference. Their exposure to positive reciprocal roles may be restricted by negative life experiences such as loss, deprivation or abuse. As well as limiting opportunities to develop helpful roles, such experiences make individuals vulnerable to absorbing and rigidly enacting roles that are unhelpful or harmful outside of the survival situation in which the role was learnt (Jenaway, 2019; Lloyd and Clayton, 2013). Together these experiences make it very difficult for individuals to hold balanced, integrated, stable views of themselves or other people. They will struggle to respond to others as unique human beings; rather they are responding as if to parents or carers from their past. Through no fault of their own, the triggers can be generalised similarities such as hair colour, spoken accent or wearing a certain scent. These combine to distort their relationships with others, causing conflict and preventing open communication.

Unconscious mechanisms and professionals

All professionals are human and hence may sometimes use the unconscious mechanisms discussed above. However, two unconscious mechanisms are particularly important in understanding the relationships staff have with the individuals they support. These are counter-transference and stereotypes.

Counter-transference

Counter-transference is an unconscious mechanism that is often at work when a professional finds themselves responding to and wanting to behave towards an individual in ways that are not characteristic of their usual professional behaviour. Box 7.3 describes some types of counter-transference and gives examples.

Box 7.3: Counter-transference	
Counter-transference	The professional's emotional response to the individual that draws them towards behaving and reacting to the individual in a way that is not characteristic of their usual professional behaviour. This may come from the professional's unresolved issues. Alternatively, it may be a reaction to the individual, which the individual characteristically triggers in those they interact with.
Comes from the professional	The professional's own unresolved issues are the cause: the professional is responding to the individual as if they were someone significant from the professional's past. Reflecting on this can help the professional understand themselves better.
	Positive: The professional is over-supportive, trying too hard to befriend the individual, and disclosing too much. There is a risk of forming inappropriate relationships. This can damage the working relationship. Example: A member of staff becomes concerned when they develop protective feelings for an individual and worry about them when they are not at work. On reflection, they realise that the individual reminds them of their younger sister who was vulnerable and looked to them for protection.
	Negative: The professional acts out against uncomfortable feelings in a negative way, including being overly critical and punishing or rejecting the individual. Example: A member of staff becomes concerned when they repeatedly find themselves exasperated with an individual. On reflection, they realise the individual's behaviour reminds them of an ex-partner, who repeatedly left messes for the member of staff to sort out.

 Intellectual Disabilities and 'Personality Disorder' © Pavilion Publishing and Media Ltd and its licensors 2023

Comes from the individual:	The professional's behaviour changes in response to the individual's transference. Reflecting on this can help understand the individual better. Example: Despite creating lots of opportunities to sit and chat with an individual, a member of staff finds that they are still tempted to chat with them when attempting to engage in work they have agreed to do together. On reflection, they remember being told about the individual's parent's difficulty accepting how hard it was for the individual to learn new skills. Expecting anger at failure, the individual was repeating a pattern of distracting their parent by pleasant chatting.
Adapted from: Fritscher (2021)	

Although counter-transference is mostly discussed in the context of therapy or counselling, it is now recognised that counter-transference can occur in other types of interactions including between carers and the individuals they support and within staff teams. It can be damaging if not identified and addressed. However, counter-transference is to be expected and, if reflected on and understood, it can help make sense of what is happening within a working relationship. It can give insight into areas a member of staff needs to address in themselves and can also give insights into unhelpful patterns in an individual's relationships. This, in turn, can inform thinking about how best to support them.

Stereotypes of intellectual disabilities

Stereotypes are an unconscious mechanism that allow us to respond rapidly to situations without having to evaluate each person we meet, at the expense of failing to see them as individuals. Stereotypes also influence how we interpret ambiguous situations. For example, the behaviour of someone who belongs to a group we assume is aggressive will be more likely to be seen as threatening than that of someone from a group we assume is friendly.

Historically, individuals with intellectual disabilities have been stereotyped in many different ways. Some examples of these stereotypes are given in Box 7.4.

Box 7.4: Stereotypes of individuals with intellectual disabilities (ID)	
Stereotypes:	■ A fixed, over-generalised belief about a particular group or class of people. ■ An unconscious assumption that an individual has all the characteristics and abilities that we attribute to members of that group. ■ Allow rapid responses without having to evaluate each situation. ■ Simplify the social world and reduce the amount of thinking needed. ■ Make us ignore differences between individuals; making unfounded generalisations. ■ *Are self-perpetuating* – things that fit the stereotype are attributed to the individual. Things that don't fit are attributed to the situation or temporary causes. ■ Behaving towards the individual as if they will behave in the way we expect often triggers that behaviour, hence reinforcing the stereotype.
Historic stereotypes	■ Eternal child/innocent. ■ Object of pity/victim. ■ Object of charity – a burden on society. ■ Source of profound wisdom. ■ Object of ridicule/clown/court jester – butt of jokes. ■ Outcast – not part of society, should be hidden. ■ Less than fully human – not part of the human race, different. ■ Object of fear, horror, or menace to society. ■ Unfeeling, without the same emotions or experience of physical and emotional pain. ■ Non-sexual being.
More modern stereotypes	■ Friendly. ■ Vulnerable/in need of help. ■ Unintelligent (and hence de-valued because of the value placed on intelligence).
Reference: Block (2022), McLeod (2015) Momene (2015) and Pelleboer-Gunnink *et al* (2021)	

 Intellectual Disabilities and 'Personality Disorder' © Pavilion Publishing and Media Ltd and its licensors 2023

Attitudes to individuals with disabilities have become more positive with greater contact and education (Wang *et al*, 2021). However, many individuals with intellectual disabilities are aware that others view the label negatively and express feelings of shame, anger and powerlessness about their disabilities (Logeswaran *et al*, 2019). Negative stereotypes of people with disabilities and mental health issues are still prevalent in the media (Aruma, 2022). Hence, it is likely that most staff have been exposed to many of the historic stereotypes and even the more benign stereotypes may prevent them responding to an individual's unique needs. *The activation of stereotypes occurs rapidly, involuntarily, and often without any awareness that it is taking place*. It is therefore easy for a professional to be unaware of how preconceived views of intellectual disabilities may have influenced their practice. Rather, there is a continual need to ensure practice is genuinely person-centred and tailored to individual need.

Impact of unconscious mechanisms on interactions at work

Individuals with intellectual disabilities who show the patterns of relating and behaving that can lead to a diagnosis of 'personality disorder' are highly likely to (unconsciously) use projection, transference and splitting. As a result of experiences during development, they are likely to have insecure attachments, have a fragile sense of self and to have difficulty managing intense emotions and stressful situations. They are likely to have limited experiences of healthy reciprocal roles but may have experienced unhealthy patterns of interaction. This means that they may switch between extreme behaviours such as being totally controlling or totally passive. *As a result, their patterns of relating to others may be inconsistent, unpredictable and may make little sense if interpreted only within the present context. Rather, they are unconsciously responding to a misperception of the situation that is distorted by their own emotions, thoughts and past relationships.* Depending on the template activated, they may interact with different staff in such different ways that each member of staff may form entirely different perceptions of them, with associated emotional reactions. Where splitting occurs, staff may be confused to find themselves suddenly treated in a completely different way as the result of an apparently minor issue. These switches can happen in response to the behaviour of others but also in response to thoughts, memories or mood changes. The impact of all these processes is to make the individual's behaviour appear unpredictable and unreasonable to the member of staff interacting with them. Everything a staff member says or does seems to be misunderstood and does not have the effect they intended or hoped for. Box 7.5 gives some indicators that unconscious mechanisms may be influencing interactions.

Box 7.5: Questions to help identify when unconscious mechanisms may be in action

Is there a mismatch between your comments and the individual's reactions?

Is it hard to make sense of their reaction to you?

Does it feel as if they are seeing or hearing something beyond/different from the message intended?

Does the person's reaction seem out of proportion?

- Saying '*you are the best ever…*' having only just met you?
- Bursting into tears at the thought of you having a day off?
- Exploding with anger and saying you don't care when you are a few minutes late because of traffic.

Do you find yourself wondering:

- *What on earth have I done to make them feel like this about me?*
- *Whatever did I say to make them think that?*
- *Why does the person think everything I say and do is wrong?*

Does the individual have strong preferences about who they work with?

Are they very warm and friendly to some people and very distant with others?

Do they switch rapidly between seeming to love and hate people?

Do team members have very different views of the individual?

If the answers to any of these questions are YES, it may be helpful to explore unconscious mechanisms in a reflective setting.

Maintain curiosity – is there something they are finding hard to accept or is a past experience re-emerging?

Together, the effect of these unconscious processes, within both the individual and those supporting them, create pressure to repeat unhelpful patterns from the past. There is a risk of staff being drawn into a reciprocal role and acting out parts that are unhelpful for the individual or even unprofessional (see Chapter 13). Individuals may be seen in negative ways and their survival behaviours given inaccurate and pejorative labels such as 'demanding', 'manipulative', 'attention-seeking' or 'over-dependent'. Staff may feel rejected, powerless and incompetent. They may become demoralised, lose empathy with and compassion for the individual (compassion

 Intellectual Disabilities and 'Personality Disorder' © Pavilion Publishing and Media Ltd and its licensors 2023

fatigue see Box 11.12). This can lead them to become emotionally and physically exhausted, creating the state called 'burnout' (see Box 13.7), or may cause them to leave their job, creating issues with staff turnover.

Sometimes, the reaction of one staff member will be reflected throughout the whole team. The team may work heroically to rescue the individual or will unite in rejecting them as not being suitable to work with. More commonly, the action of unconscious mechanisms will trigger different reactions in each staff member the individual comes into contact with. Staff members will then see the individual in very different ways, leading to tensions and conflict about how best to support them. These conflicts can be severe: staff members who usually work well together can find themselves arguing or questioning each other's competence. Team members may begin to pull in different directions, criticise each other and cease to work in a co-ordinated way. Such conflicts can lead to fragmented, uncoordinated and inconsistent support for the individual. This can lead to individuals or their families being justifiably dissatisfied with the care they have received. This, in turn, can lead to criticism, anger and complaints. Where care is fragmented and uncoordinated, risks may go unnoticed or not be effectively managed. This can place individuals or staff members at risk and, in extreme situations, may lead to harm.

A common reaction is for team members to 'split' around an issue, such as whether or not to use the term 'personality disorder' or whether the individual's needs would be better met in another service. Rather than collaboratively building a shared understanding of the individual, staff may become stuck trying to resolve their differences. These differences can also create tensions between teams. For example, an intellectual disabilities team may advocate an individual use adult mental health services at times of crisis. However, the crisis team may say that individuals with intellectual disabilities should be excluded from their service as the team lack the skills to support individuals with intellectual disabilities. Where an individual comes into contact with multiple services, they can end up being given conflicting and inconsistent advice in an atmosphere of chaos, fear or anger, or not receive a service from any of the teams.

Promoting positive interactions within and between teams

A good starting point in resolving conflicts and building positive relationships within and between teams is to acknowledge that individuals with complex needs can be successfully supported by a confident and united team that works professionally, within clear boundaries, and develops the necessary skills base. This can be promoted by learning about the causes of the patterns of relationships and behaviour that can lead to a diagnosis of 'personality disorder' (Chapter 2), understanding how to give the right support at the right time (Chapter 3), using psychologically informed formulation (Chapter 4), and understanding the most effective service models and philosophies (Chapter 6). The Royal College of Psychiatrists (RCP, 2021) highlights how local expertise can be developed flexibly to fit local service structures. Where gaps in services are recognised, these should be addressed through the appropriate channels, for example discussions with commissioners.

Positive working relationships within and between teams will be greatly enhanced by basic good practice. Some areas that are important are given in Box 7.6. It is beyond the scope of this book to explore all of these. However, areas such as teamwork and supervision are addressed by professional bodies such as Royal College of Nursing, Health and Care Professions Council (HCPC), the British Psychological Society and the Royal College of Psychiatrists. Current initiatives to increase collaboration and integration of services at all levels, for example the Community Mental Health Framework (NHS England 2019) and Health and Care Act (2022), may also facilitate positive relationships and closer working.

Box 7.6: General factors for promoting positive interactions within and between teams

Working with commissioners	To ensure that a local service is developed with the skills to support individuals with intellectual disabilities and mental health needs and is fully integrated with other local services (see Chapter 6).
Effective working relationships with other teams	Agreed protocols for responsibilities in complex cases, develop shared, collaborative ways of working.
Building effective teams	Shared vision, good communication, conflict tolerated and resolved.
Developing effective team leadership skills	Conflict resolution, effective decision-making, validating and containing emotions, motivating, engaging, maintaining professional boundaries.
Professional development	Understanding unconscious processes, self-awareness.

 Intellectual Disabilities and 'Personality Disorder' © Pavilion Publishing and Media Ltd and its licensors 2023

Supervision	Protect supervision time and ensure that it happens. Create an environment where it is safe to discuss (negative) emotional reactions, explore counter-transference and professional boundaries. Provide a range of clinical supervision opportunities e.g. peer supervision.
Access to confidential counselling service	Promote a culture where staff are actively encouraged to seek help for personal issues that might impact on work relationships.
Team formulation	Gives a shared, collaborative understanding of individuals (Chapter 4).
Reflective practices	Built into service, used proactively to prevent conflicts and splitting. Provide space for staff to reflect on challenges within the care environment.
Secure bases	For all members of staff (at all levels of seniority) to feel they have supportive management and seniors, who 'have got their back' and are able to provide a safe space where strong emotional responses can be explored without fear of seeming unprofessional or incapable.

Formulation

Developing a collaborative team formulation with an individual will often make clear the nature and origins of their patterns of interacting and identify any unconscious mechanisms that are occurring. This will greatly reduce the risk of miscommunication and conflict. In particular, it can allow understanding of why an individual behaves in ways that staff struggle to understand and can identify ways in which interactions are distorted by the past. Chapter 4 highlighted how the formulation process itself can bring about change through developing a shared understanding and reframing patterns of interacting. Working through the questions in Box 7.5 before a team formulation meeting may help identify whether unconscious mechanisms are being used by an individual.

However, the process of formulation itself may be undermined by team issues such as power-imbalances, poor communication and poor attendance (Hymers *et al*, 2021). Services in which team formulation is not part of regular practice may seek consultation about an individual, when staff feel stuck or are struggling to support them. In such situations, the primary focus is often the team rather than the individual (BPS, 2011). The team may need space to explore and formulate their reactions to the individual they are working with. Hence, while the discussion may be centred around a specific individual, is not about the individual, it is about the team. In such situations, it may be harmful for the individual to be present during the discussion or for the outcome to be shared with them. While the format looks the same as team formulation, such meetings are in fact reflective case discussions (see Box 7.7) and need to follow the same principles of information sharing as professionals' meeting or supervision (BPS, 2011). The process of team reflection is discussed more fully in the following section.

Box 7.7: Distinguishing formulation and reflection

Format	Who is involved	Purpose
Individual formulation	Individual and 1-2 staff members	Develop a shared understanding of individual's experiences and agree a way forward for a specific piece of work together. Collaborative and shared with individual.
Team formulation	Individual (present or views represented in an agreed way) and staff team/ multi-disciplinary team (MDT) working with the individual (facilitator)	Develop a shared understanding of individual's experiences and agree a way forward for the team's work. Collaborative and shared with individual.
Reflective case discussion	Staff team/MDT (facilitator)	Share their experiences of working with the individual and barriers faced in that work. A safe space to discuss the emotional impact of working with the individual. Promote a shared, compassionate understanding of those experiences. Promote staff well-being and retention and enhance care quality. Confidential but feeds back into formulation process for the individual discussed.
Team reflection	Staff team/MDT (facilitator)	Develop a shared understanding of the organisational and systemic issues they face and how these might be overcome. →

 Intellectual Disabilities and 'Personality Disorder' © Pavilion Publishing and Media Ltd and its licensors 2023

Team reflection	Staff team/MDT (facilitator)	A safe space to discuss emotional impact of the work undertaken by the team. Help sustain compassion for self and others. Promote staff well-being and retention and enhance care quality.
Self-reflection	Individual staff member	Taking time to explore their own reactions to their work in general or with a specific individual. With the aim of enhancing practice and learning from experiences, identifying learning needs and issues to take to supervision.

Reflective practice

Reflection is the thought process whereby staff members consider specific experiences at work, to gain insights about their whole practice. Reflective practice is a common expectation for all health and care professionals (Joint statement, 2019). Self-reflection can be helpful for individual members to identify their own emotional reactions to and perceptions of individuals they support and their work colleagues. Using the questions given in Box 7.8 or templates such as that offered by the HCPC can help this process. These issues can then be explored in supervision.

Box 7.8: Questions about your reaction to the individual
Is this reaction characteristic for you? Do you feel like this much of the time? (*This is about you.*)
Is the response triggered by something unrelated to the individual you support? e.g. being hungry, tired, arguing with your partner, problems with the job. (*This is about you and your lifestyle.*)
Is the response related to the individual in a direct way? e.g. are you upset because they are screaming abuse and have broken the new TV? (*This is an obvious and natural response to the individual's behaviour.*)
■ Is there a specific characteristic of the individual that bothers you? ■ Do you dislike the individual for no apparent reason? ■ Do you dread seeing them, find yourself bored, irritated or contemptuous in their presence? →

- Do you really like the individual and prefer them to others?
- Do you find yourself thinking about them a lot?
- Do you find yourself feeling impulses to behave towards this individual in a way that is not usual for you? e.g. feeling critical, angry, impatient, controlling, frustrated, talking a lot about yourself.

Have you done any of the following?

- Inappropriately disclosed personal information, talked a lot about yourself.
- Offered too much advice (rather than helping the individual work out what is right for them).
- Broken professional boundaries.
- Been overly critical of the individual.
- Been overly supportive of the individual.

Have you survived a similar trauma or situation to the individual?

If the answer to any of these questions is YES, unconscious mechanisms may be in action

Explore these issues in supervision to promote well-being and professional conduct. Supervision may identify issues specific to an individual that can be shared in reflective practice.

Adapted from: Reidbord (2010), Madeson (2021) and GoodTherapy (2021)

However, team reflection is likely to be the most effective way of addressing the impact of distorted communications in teams. This may be done generally, for example by reflecting on who a team can and cannot support, or more specifically through reflective case discussion. Team reflection provides space to address challenging organisational, systemic or clinical issues (Ebrahim and Sams, 2022). The aim is to promote a shared, compassionate understanding of team members' experiences of working with individuals and organisational challenges. It supports staff to understand and to manage the emotional impact of the work on themselves and to create insights into the experiences of other team members.

There is no set format for team reflection, although standardised formats such as Schwartz Rounds can be used (Point of Care Foundation, 2016). The Cognitive Behaviour Therapy (CBT) 'hot-cross bun' (see Box 15.9) can be used to explore how an individual's behaviour influences staff thoughts, feelings, physical sensations and behaviour. It is important to consider the format in order to ensure that it meets the needs of a particular team, for example being tailored to the issues to be explored and also what is known to best suit a team's way of working. Thought

Intellectual Disabilities and 'Personality Disorder' © Pavilion Publishing and Media Ltd and its licensors 2023

should be given to factors that will promote an effective meeting. For example, choosing times, venues and strategies that promote attendance, choosing a comfortable and confidential setting and providing suitable refreshments (Wilcox, 2013). Where team reflection focuses on a specific individual, attention must be given to maintaining confidentiality, for example how and where the session is recorded. Thought should also be given as to how any action points or insights are fed back into the collaborative clinical work with the individual. Box 7.9 gives an example of a reflective case discussion for 'Susan' (see Boxes 1.3 and 2.9).

Box 7.9: Team reflective case discussion for 'Susan'*

The manager of the home where Susan lived expressed her concern to the clinical psychologist that the team were struggling to support Susan, were very worried by the unfounded allegations she had made and that a new placement might need to be found (see Box 1.3). On discussion they identified mixed feelings in the team with some wanting to find a way to make things work. The home manager expressed her willingness to give things 'another try'.

They agreed to hold a reflective case discussion, found a time slot which was convenient, using a comfortable room in a local NHS hub, with a good supply of tea, coffee and biscuits. The home manager and psychologist worked together to help the team explore what they knew about Susan, how it felt working with her and finally what Susan might be feeling. They created two 'word clouds' one for staff and one for Susan, made comparisons and then thought about where these feelings might be coming from. The psychologist shared some thoughts about the impact of Susan's experiences on her ability to form relationships with staff and her possible search for 'perfect care'. Staff were struck by the similarities between their own feelings and their guesses about Susan's feelings, including fear, confusion and rejection. Someone commented that they had been so busy fire-fighting and worrying about losing their job, that they had not had time to think about what Susan had 'been through' (see Box 2.9).

It was agreed that ideas about how Susan was feeling should be explored further and fed into her formulation and Positive Behavioural Support plan.

The session highlighted the need for the service to find ways of protecting staff from the effects of investigating unfounded allegations (whilst also keeping Susan safe), and for space to explore the feelings these caused. It also highlighted the need for regular team reflection to be built into their model of working.

A note that the session had taken place was added to Susan's file with the information to be fed into her formulation. A record of the session was anonymised to protect Susan's confidentiality before placing it in the staff supervision records.

* 'Susan' is a composite example created from clinical experience and the literature. She is not based on a specific individual.

It is helpful if team reflection happens regularly, has clear aims and purposes, and provides space for emotional expression and validation (Dallimore *et al*, 2016). Despite perceived benefits, there is a risk that reflective practice can be seen as 'escapism' from work as opposed to directly influencing clinical practice (Lye and Stedmon, 2020) and attendance may need to be actively promoted (Wilcox, 2013). Hence, it is important to build the team's understanding that reflection is an essential part of good clinical care. In many teams, there are formal and informal power dynamics that may limit the value and positive power of reflection unless facilitated carefully and respectfully – all views need to be respected and listened to (Joint statement, 2019). Some teams may require the sessions be facilitated by a professional highly skilled in managing group dynamics and conflict resolution.

Successful team reflection enables teams to address these difficult issues in ways that enrich their understanding of the individual and allows them to work together constructively to meet the individual's needs.

Key learning points

- Interactions between people are complex and can be distorted by a number of factors. In any interaction, people's responses can be shaped not just by the present situation but also by their own past experiences and the past experiences of the person they are interacting with.
- A number of psychological concepts are helpful in making sense of these distortions. These concepts include 'projection', 'transference', 'counter-transference', 'splitting' 'stereotyping' and 'reciprocal roles'.
- When interacting with individuals who have experienced developmental trauma, have insecure attachments and low self-esteem, it is highly likely that unconscious mechanisms will be activated. If this is not understood, their behaviour will seem unreasonable or incomprehensible, triggering strong reactions in those supporting them.
- These emotional reactions can create tensions and disagreements within and between staff teams. Splits may develop within and between teams. If these reactions are not understood and actively managed, staff teams may be unable to act together to constructively support the individual.
- If the difficulties persist, staff can become exhausted, frustrated and de-motivated, leading to compassion fatigue. There may be problems with staff turnover or burnout.

 Intellectual Disabilities and 'Personality Disorder' © Pavilion Publishing and Media Ltd and its licensors 2023

- Teams need to develop understanding of key psychological processes. This will help them to reflect on and resolve conflicts. Regular reflective practice, including self-reflection and team reflection, is essential and needs to be built into the everyday working environment.
- If this is done, teams will be able to manage these difficulties in ways that enrich their understanding of the individual and allow them to work together constructively to meet the individual's needs.

Section 2:
The 'support and intervention toolbox'

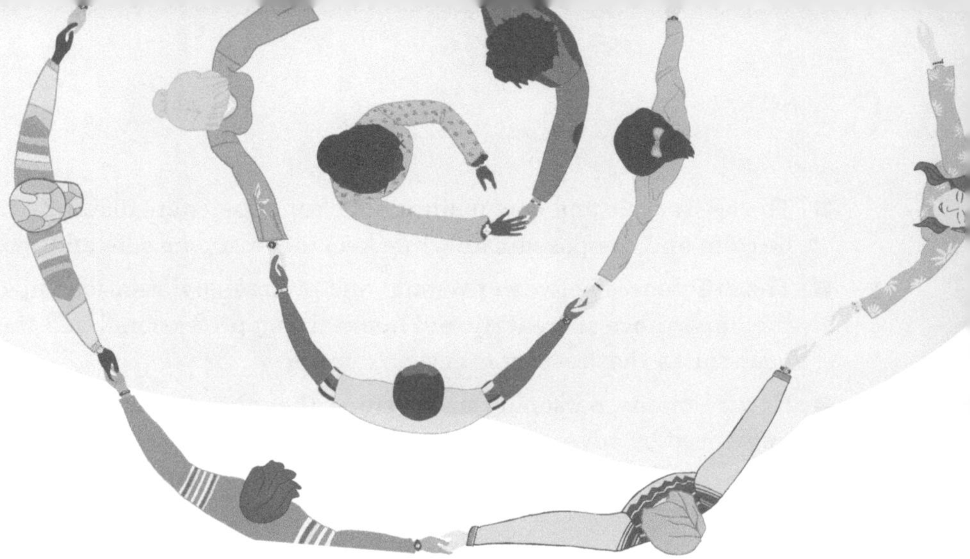

Introduction

The diagnosis 'personality disorder' may be defined as:

> *'An enduring pattern of emotional and cognitive difficulties which affect the way in which the person relates to others or understands themselves'.* (Personality Disorder Commission, 2018).

Section 1 has explored why this is a controversial diagnosis. It looked at the patterns of relating and behaving that can lead to some individuals with mild intellectual disabilities being given (formally or informally) a diagnosis of 'personality disorder'. It explored how these patterns can best be understood as having their origins in the developmental process and factors that influence development, particularly attachment and trauma. It looked at the importance of engaging individuals, and of giving the right support at the right time, in the right way and in the right place. It introduced the concept of the 3 Rs – **R**egulate, **R**elate, **R**eason – to help understand why different interventions are appropriate depending on an individual's current status.

Section 2 applies these themes to issues that are often encountered when supporting individuals with intellectual disabilities who might be given a diagnosis of 'personality disorder'. It shows how a proactive, compassionate and containing support style can provide a secure and hopeful base to help individuals navigate the challenges of daily life and live their best life.

The chapters in this section explore:

- How an attachment and trauma-informed Positive Behavioural Support (PBS) framework can promote the understanding of behaviours that challenge, including self-harm, and facilitate positive and proactive approaches.

- The crisis cycle and how maintaining 'compassionate distance' can enable staff to be calm and compassionate while keeping everyone safe and resolving the crisis.
- The differences between personal and professional relationships. It highlights the importance of creating and maintaining professional and therapeutic boundaries that respect everyone's needs.
- How emotions, personal relationships, thoughts, impulses, and sense of self are influenced by adverse early experiences. It highlights the importance of this understanding in helping to promote positive attitudes and identifying helpful strategies for intervention.
- How physical and mental well-being are interrelated. It explores health inequalities and the impact of trauma and adversity on well-being and shaping health-risk behaviours. It explores approaches to improving well-being, including Health Action Plans and Hospital or Care Passports.

 Intellectual Disabilities and 'Personality Disorder' © Pavilion Publishing and Media Ltd and its licensors 2023

Chapter 8: Applying Positive Behaviour Support

This chapter explores the concept of 'behaviours that challenge'. It looks at what behaviours that challenge can communicate about unmet needs and emotional distress. It shows how our understanding of behaviours that challenge can be enriched by taking a trauma and attachment informed perspective. It looks at how trauma-informed Positive Behavioural Support (PBS) can be used to work constructively with individuals with intellectual disabilities who might be given a diagnosis of 'personality disorder'. It looks at PBS assessment, formulation and writing PBS plans. It gives an example of a formulation and PBS plan for a behaviour that challenges. It highlights the importance of understanding and taking ownership to ensure that a PBS plan is interpreted intelligently and implemented consistently.

Key topics

- 'Behaviours that challenge'
- Safety first
- Applying Positive Behavioural Support
- PBS plans
- Which strategy when?
- A good plan is not enough

'Behaviours that challenge'

Positive Behavioural Support (PBS) is an evidenced-based, values-led approach to understanding, preventing and reducing the impact of behaviours (see Chapter 3) that may put individuals and those who support them at risk, damage relationships or reduce opportunities. Some examples might include intense anger, impulsivity, aggression and self-harm. Such behaviours are not valued by our society and can lead to people being restricted, punished or excluded. For individuals with intellectual disabilities, these behaviours can result in them being subject to abusive practices and having severely restricted living arrangements, including inappropriate hospitalisation. Such behaviours are sometimes thought to be under the individual's control, which may lead to them being seen as 'bad' and not worthy of good care or sympathy. This is more likely to happen to individuals given a diagnosis of 'personality disorder' than those given other diagnoses (Markham and Trower, 2010).

These behaviours are often seen as 'symptoms' of mental health problems, which can result in over-dependence on medication to 'treat' the 'symptom'. It can also leave staff feeling powerless to help. However, if behaviours that challenge are viewed from the perspective of attachment (Jones, 2021) and trauma-informed PBS (Paterson *et al*, 2017), it is apparent that they may have their origins in adverse life events, that they convey meaning about experiences, and that they are attempts to meet intense needs and manage emotions. This opens the way for constructive, positive and hopeful interventions.

Description and terminology

The term 'behaviours that challenge' will be used here when exploring these behaviours. The choice of terminology in this area can be difficult. The behaviours described are not socially valued: any name given to them quickly acquires negative connotations and has the potential to become a label leading to exclusion. However, the word 'challenge' captures the reality that these are difficult behaviours for both those experiencing them and those who seek to support them. A description of what is meant by this phrase is given in Box 8.1.

Box 8.1: What is meant by 'behaviours that challenge'?

Behaviours that are of such intensity, frequency or duration that they may:

- Trigger reactions of disapproval – are seen as culturally abnormal.
- Threaten the individual's quality of life.
- Threaten the physical and/or emotional safety of the individual.
- Threaten the physical and/or emotional safety of others.
- Lead to responses that are restrictive or aversive.
- Result in exclusion from ordinary society.

Behaviours that challenge:

- Have been shaped by adversity or trauma and the developmental process.
- Occur as a result of the interplay between the individual and their social and physical environment.
- Are not a characteristic of the individual.

Intellectual Disabilities and 'Personality Disorder' © Pavilion Publishing and Media Ltd and its licensors 2023

Behaviours that challenge have meaning or purpose, they:
■ Are a communication of threat, distress or unmet need. ■ Are ways of surviving in difficult circumstances (physical, emotional, relational and social survival).
Adapted from Emerson (1995), RCP (2006), BPS (2018, p.9)

This description combines elements from a number of sources. It is wider than Emerson's (1995) definition of 'challenging behaviour' and is intended to draw attention to the links between these behaviours and adversity and trauma. Many behaviours that challenge can be seen as '*intelligible responses to very adverse life experiences*' (British Psychological Society, 2018) and an individual's best way of coping (Harding, 2021). For this reason, they are sometimes referred to as 'survival strategies'.

The behaviours range from largely automatic biological responses (for example, survival cascade, fight–flight response) to more complex, learnt and culturally shaped behaviours, with the latter appearing later in the developmental process (British Psychological Society, 2018).

The meanings and purposes of behaviours that challenge

In PBS, behaviours that challenge are framed as having purpose or function; they are a way of communicating needs and seeking to have them met. They have their origins in the mismatch between an individual, the way they are supported, and the environment in which they live. Drawing on behavioural science, PBS has identified a number of functions that may be served by 'behaviours that challenge' (see Box 8.2).

Box 8.2: Meanings and purposes of behaviours that challenge

Function (source PBS or PTM framework)	Explanations and examples
Signalling or blocking physical pain (PBS)	Limited communication and resources may mean an individual shows pain through behaviour or acts in ways that block pain sensations.
Communicating about distress – eliciting care (PTM)	Self-harm*, unusual beliefs, voice-hearing, self-starvation.

→

Meeting emotional needs, self-soothing (PTM)	Rocking, self-harm, skin picking, use of alcohol/drugs, over-eating, compulsive sexuality.
Regulating overwhelming feelings (PTM)	Dissociation, self-harm, carrying out rituals, use of alcohol/drugs.
Initiating/accessing social interaction (PBS) Seeking attachments (PTM)	Need for interaction may be increased by limited communication skills, poor self-occupation skills, limited opportunities, short attention span. By idealisation, appeasement, seeking care and emotional responses, use of sexuality.
Accessing things needed or really enjoyed (PBS) ('I'm starving' 'I feel empty')	If basic needs are not met, individual may learn 'unacceptable' ways of meeting them e.g. stealing food. May be driven by psychological need e.g. emotional emptiness.
Escaping situations experienced as unbearable (PBS)	Where individual has little choice, lacks skills to excuse themselves, reduced tolerance, no sense that the situation will end.
Avoiding situations experienced as unbearable (PBS)	When denied choice, is unable to communicate choice, low tolerance of stress, narrow window of regulation (see Box 11.4).
Creating pleasurable sensations (PBS)	Self-reinforcing behaviours, intense need for stimulation, limited choice, limited opportunities.
Releasing tension (PBS)	A release of tension, stress or over-arousal. Low tolerance for intense emotions, lack skills to calm self.
Protecting against attachment loss, hurt and abandonment (PTM)	Rejection of others, distrust, seeking care and emotional responses, submission, self-blame, hoarding.
Protecting from a sense of danger (PTM)	Hyper-vigilance, isolation, aggression, suspicious thoughts, insomnia.
Maintaining a sense of control (PTM)	Self-starvation, rituals, violence, dominance in relationships.
Preserving identity, self-image and self-esteem (PTM)	Grandiosity, unusual beliefs, feeling entitled, perfectionism, dominance, hostility, aggression.
Finding meaning and purpose (PTM)	Unusual beliefs, over-work.
*See Chapter 10 for exploration of self-harm/self-injury terminology	

 Intellectual Disabilities and 'Personality Disorder' © Pavilion Publishing and Media Ltd and its licensors 2023

These are well-researched, robust concepts that are of proven usefulness with individuals with severe intellectual disabilities. Particularly important is the recognition that behaviour can be a communication about physical pain. However, if they are mapped onto Maslow's (1943) hierarchy of needs (see Box 8.3), it is apparent that they primarily focus on physiological needs.

Box 8.3: Maslow's hierarchy of needs

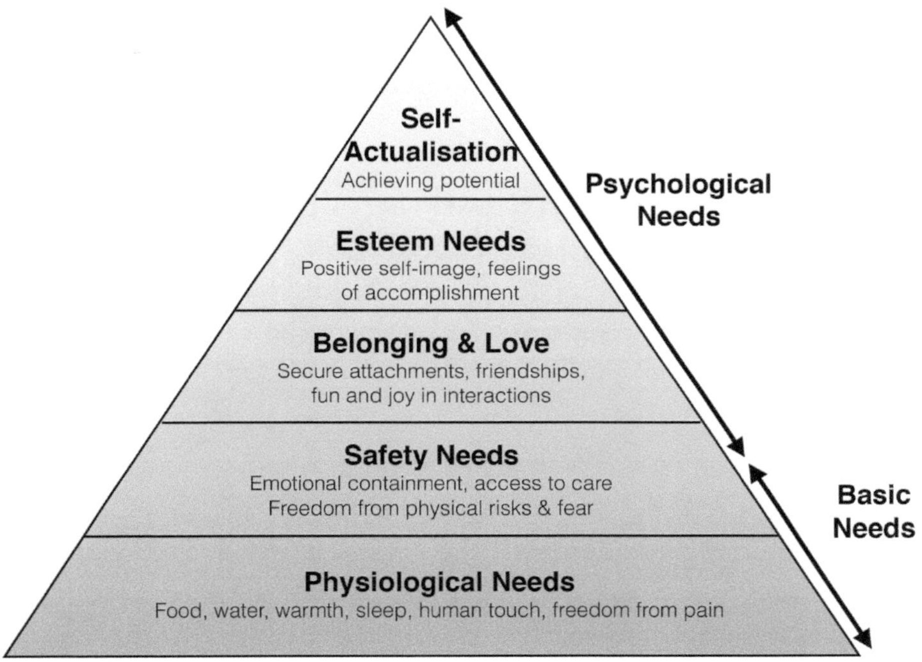

Drawing on research and theory about the general population, the Power Threat Meaning (PTM) framework (BPS, 2018) identifies a number of additional 'functional groupings' (see Box 8.2). These include functions that relate to a sense of safety and to psychological needs. The PTM-derived functions also highlight the importance of attachment as a driver of behaviours. This includes seeking attachments and also protecting against loss and abandonment by driving people away. This is important, as attachment issues have been positively linked to behaviours that challenge shown by individuals with intellectual disabilities (Rinaldi *et al*, 2022).

Combining functions from PBS and PTM covers all levels of Maslow's hierarchy. This makes it more likely that a formulation will show a helpful way forward for individuals with mild intellectual disabilities and enduring patterns of relationship and behavioural issues. Without this extension, the needs that are driving behaviours may be missed. For example, Dunn and Bolton (2004) describe how explaining an individual's threats of violence, purely in terms of his intellectual disability (unintentionally) invalidated his emotional distress. As the individual's underlying difficulties in emotion regulation (see Chapter 11) had been missed, the only way he could convey how he was feeling was by escalating his behaviour.

It is important to understand that there is no simple relationship between a behaviour and the function(s) it may serve: the function must always be determined through assessment and formulation. The different types of relationships possible are explored in Box 8.4.

Box 8.4: Possible relationships between behaviours and functions
The same behaviour shown by different people serves a different function for each person, e.g. getting drunk: Individual A – gets drunk to escape unpleasant memories. Individual B – drinks to release pent up tension.
Very different behaviours shown by different people serve the same function, e.g.: Individual A – gets drunk to escape unpleasant memories. Individual B – cuts their arms to escape unpleasant memories.
Very different behaviours shown by one person may serve the same function for them e.g.: Occasion 1 – Individual A gets drunk to escape unpleasant memories. Occasion 2 – Individual A uses very loud music to block out unpleasant memories.
A particular behaviour may serve different functions for the same person at different times e.g.: Occasion 1 – Individual B cuts their arms to escape unpleasant memories. Occasion 2 – Individual B cuts their arms to access the comfort of someone else treating the wounds.

Development and maintenance of behaviours that challenge

A number of factors have been identified that may make people more vulnerable to the development of behaviours that challenge. These factors arise from the individual's genetic makeup, personal characteristics, life experiences and social status. Trauma or adversity during the developmental period can both create intense

 Intellectual Disabilities and 'Personality Disorder' © Pavilion Publishing and Media Ltd and its licensors 2023

needs and shape the neurological pathways that underpin responses to threat situations, making individuals vulnerable to becoming dysregulated (see Chapter 11).

Groups who are marginalised, stigmatised, disempowered and excluded have reduced opportunities to meet their needs through socially valued behaviours (see Box 8.5), and their behaviour is more likely to attract disapproval (BPS, 2018). This increases the risk of them needing to meet needs through behaviours that challenge. This resonates with the experiences of individuals with intellectual disabilities (Bush and Griffiths, 2017; Sineson, 2021). For some individuals, behaviours that challenge may achieve some degree of control in an otherwise powerless situation (Bush and Griffiths, 2017).

Box 8.5: Influence of access to resources on responses to threat and unmet needs

	Individual's access to valued resources and ability to exercise socially approved forms of 'power'	
Is it likely that:	**More access**	**Less access**
They will be able to escape, avoid or constructively change their situation?	YES	NO
Responses will alleviate the problem?	YES	NO
Responses will bring support and concern?	YES	NO
Responses will compound problem?	NO	YES
Responses will bring disapproval?	NO	YES

There is a significant overlap between the factors that increase the risk of behaviours that challenge with those that lead to an individual being given a diagnosis of 'personality disorder' (see Chapter 2).

PBS recognises a distinction between the situation that may have given rise to a behaviour and the factors that cause the behaviour to continue. Behaviours that occur for one reason may become established in the individual's behavioural repertoire and may be triggered by other unmet needs. An understanding of trauma shows how behaviours that developed to survive difficult situations may persist, despite not being the most effective way of getting needs met in a safer situation. The automatic (hard wired) or over-learnt nature of responses may make it very difficult for the individual to discover that they are now safe; change may take months or years, or it may never occur.

Intellectual Disabilities and 'Personality Disorder' © Pavilion Publishing and Media Ltd and its licensors 2023

If the causes of an individual's behaviours are not understood, others may respond in ways that are unhelpful. For example, where behaviours such as aggression act to keep staff at arms-length, responses that isolate the individual mean they have little opportunity to experience positive interactions and hence to learn new ways of interacting (Harding, 2021). At their worst, responses to behaviours that challenge can re-traumatise individuals leading to intensification of the behaviours they were intended to contain (Bush and Griffith, 2017).

Safety first

By definition, behaviours that challenge carry risks for the individual and those who support them. Keeping everyone physically and emotionally safe and preventing further traumatisation needs to be a priority. However, a holistic assessment and formulation can be a lengthy process and needs to be carried out when the situation is stable (see Box 3.1). If the situation has reached crisis point, the approach given in Chapter 9 should be followed to stabilise the situation. In-depth, holistic assessment can then proceed safely.

Although self-harm and suicide attempts can be understood within a trauma-informed PBS framework, they are complex and anxiety provoking. For this reason, they are addressed separately in Chapter 10.

It is likely that an individual showing behaviours that challenge will need to be referred to a specialist intellectual disabilities service. Understanding behaviours that challenge often needs the involvement of a number of different professional disciplines, for example psychology, psychiatry, nursing, speech and language therapy and occupational therapy. These can be accessed by referral to local services such as a community team for people with learning disabilities (CTPLD). Support and supervision are also essential for staff to feel safe and confident at these difficult times (see Chapter 7).

Most individuals will understand that their behaviour is unhelpful for them and for other people, and hence they are likely to be willing for a referral to be made. This is important because the more the individual is involved in, understands and supports the plans to prevent and respond to the behaviour that challenges, the more effective the intervention will be. However, some individuals may refuse to seek help, for example through misplaced mistrust arising from past trauma or negative experiences with services in the past. This can paralyse staff teams if they think that intervening without consent infringes that individual's human rights.

 Intellectual Disabilities and 'Personality Disorder' © Pavilion Publishing and Media Ltd and its licensors 2023

Capacity, consent and duty of care

It is helpful to understand the legal framework around capacity, consent and duty of care. In the UK, this includes the principles of the Mental Capacity Act (2005), Mental Capacity (Amendment) Act (2019) and the Mental Health Act (1983, amended 1995 and 2007). These acts provide a framework for assessing capacity (see Box 14.5) and acting in the best interests of individuals who lack capacity (NICE, 2018). They also make clear when treatment and care can be given without consent. Where an individual has the capacity and refuses intervention, but the behaviour does not come under the Mental Health Act, it is also important to understand that there are still options that are open to staff teams. All services have a duty of care to the individuals they support and responsibilities for meeting professional standards (Royal College of Nursing, 2023). These allow them to set limits and uphold basic standards of behaviour expected of those who live in or use the service, even if the individual does not see their behaviour as problematic. It may also be an option to seek more general consultation, for example through team reflection (see Chapter 4).

Applying Positive Behavioural Support

Supporting individuals who show behaviours that challenge can feel overwhelming. However, taking a systematic, step-by-step approach can help to achieve a constructive understanding of the individual, their situation and the behaviours that challenge, leading to the development of a positive support package. This needs to be implemented using a proactive, compassionate and containing support style (see Chapters 9 and 13), within the PBS framework and a service structure that promotes the well-being of the staff team (see Chapters 6 and 7).

PBS Assessment

PBS takes an integrated, multi-disciplinary, holistic approach to assessment. It uses PBS-specific approaches drawn from behavioural science alongside other specialist assessments, for example assessments of language and cognitive skills. Box 8.6 gives some areas that may form part of a holistic assessment.

Box 8.6: Areas that might be included in an assessment of behaviours that challenge	
History *'What has happened to you?'* Trauma and loss Physical illness Mental health Intellectual and emotional development	Look at records – they often include key information that has been forgotten in the verbally conveyed 'story'. Listen to the individual – don't make assumptions about the 'truth' of what they say – they are telling you how they see things. Listen to those who know them – look for themes of similarity and difference. Look for subtle traumas and losses not just major ones, look for links to dates or times of year (anniversaries).
The individual	Strengths, weaknesses, vulnerabilities, coping strategies, likes, dislikes, aspirations, hopes and fears, self-image, self-esteem. Skills and abilities: expressive and receptive language, verbal and perpetual reasoning, executive functioning, activities of daily living, sensory processing, hyper and hypo sensitivities, attachments, emotional development, ability to regulate emotions. Core beliefs about self and others. Hard-wiring – what are their automatic stress responses? Do they struggle to stay within the 'window of regulation'? (see Chapter 11)
The behaviour: *What, when, where, with whom, for how long, how severe?* *'What is the behaviour telling us?'*	What does the individual do, think and feel (emotions and physical sensations)? What do staff think, feel and do about the behaviour? What fears and associations does this behaviour hold for the individual and the staff supporting them? Trauma and attachment informed exploration of purpose and meaning: basic and psychological needs e.g. emotional safety.
Current situation *'What kind of life are you leading?'* *'Why is this a problem now?'*	Look at physical and mental health. Current living arrangements and financial situation, relationships and activities. How are they supported? Staffing levels and skills, approach used, views on the current issues. What restrictions are being placed on the individual? Recent changes, life events, e.g. bereavement or other losses. Physical and emotional safety. →

 Intellectual Disabilities and 'Personality Disorder' © Pavilion Publishing and Media Ltd and its licensors 2023

Triggers, patterns and consequences	Triggers and patterns – escalating sequence, physical changes (e.g. going red or pale), build-up of tensions. Where there is trauma, triggers may be internal (thoughts, memories, flashbacks) and hence harder to identify. ABC analysis.
Relational risk (does the behaviour put the relationship between individual and support staff at risk?)	Does the behaviour threaten to break, damage or stress-load working relationships between individual and staff? Does working with the individual trigger feelings of hostility or ambivalence? Do staff feel emotionally unavailable or cut off from the individual? Is an earlier pattern of rejection and relationship breakdown happening again? Can staff find any warmth, shared joy and fun with the individual?
(From Skelly (2014), in Harding (2021)	

The assessment should be carried out sensitively, respectfully and collaboratively with the individual, those who are important to them and those who support them. Thought should be given to how to minimise the stress on the individual and to reduce the risk of re-traumatisation. Being repeatedly asked the same questions by different people understandably leads to feeling unheard and frustration at not moving forward. This applies equally to the individual, their family and support staff or carers. This can be avoided by carrying out joint assessments and sharing findings (NHS, 2019).

The core PBS approach of 'ABC' analysis can provide useful information. This considers what happened before (antecedents = A), the behaviour (B) and its consequences (C). When looking at ABC data, it can be helpful to try to look at the situation both objectively and through the individual's eyes. Consider the impact of trauma on thinking (see Chapter 15): could the individual perceive threats or insults where none were intended? Are there reminders of past traumatic experiences? Are they responding to the way something is done, for example the emotional state of the person interacting with them or overly controlling boundaries? It is also helpful to look at situations in which the behaviour does not occur as this may suggest ways of reducing the problem.

Exploring consequences helps to understand what the behaviour may be achieving for the individual. It is important to think about both external and internal consequences. For example, an apparently 'out of the blue' assault on another individual may appear to have achieved nothing externally but may have satisfied the individual's need to have revenge on that person for some previous (real or perceived) insult. Other incidents that occur apparently without triggers, can sometimes be explained by looking at how long the person has been left without active engagement, has been unsupported or felt alone for, prior to the behaviour occurring. Individuals who experience behaviours that challenge frequently experience loneliness and boredom (Nankervis *et al* 2020).

Where a behaviour appears totally unpredictable, it may be helpful to look at the time (hours, days and sometimes weeks) leading up to the event and consider the individual's level of arousal. Much behaviour that looks initially as if it is totally unpredictable turns out to be functioning to reduce over-arousal or manage emotional distress, particularly when an individual has a narrow 'window of regulation' (see Box 11.4). Rather like the straw that broke the camel's back, the 'trigger' event may have occurred many times without resulting in the behaviour of concern; the behaviour only occurs when the individual is so stressed or overwhelmed that they cannot cope with another stressor, however small. If this is suspected, it may be helpful to come up with a simple rating of stress for the individual, for example on a scale of 1 to 5. Staff can then rate the individual's stress before and after the incident. If the behaviours frequently occur when there is a high stress rating, and not when the rating is lower, arousal may be a key factor in triggering the behaviour.

PBS tools for identifying the functions of behaviours can sometimes be helpful. However, they only explore physiological needs and the need for interaction. When working with individuals with mild intellectual disabilities, it is important to also explore psychological needs and the need for emotional safety. Brown *et al* (2017) describe how the process of analysing the nature and role of a behaviour can be carried out through discussion between an individual and their support staff about the situations in which the behaviour has occurred.

It is also important to know when to pause assessment and progress to formulation. It is never possible to know everything about someone. A thoughtful and collaborative formulation will identify areas where further assessment would be helpful.

Formulation

Formulation is the process of organising and interpreting information that has been gathered in assessment. It creates a person-centred, shared, multi-disciplinary understanding of an individual's distress that shows a way forward (see Chapter 4). Working in a PBS framework does not require a specific approach to formulation:

 Intellectual Disabilities and 'Personality Disorder' © Pavilion Publishing and Media Ltd and its licensors 2023

the results of the assessment can be formulated in whatever way makes most sense to those involved. However, the 5 Ps approach and the extended hot cross bun are both easy to translate into a PBS plan.

Formulations of behaviours that challenge can be intellectually and emotionally demanding. It is possible that important factors could be missed or the formulation distorted by interpersonal processes (see Chapter 7). Box 8.7 gives a few thoughts on how to keep on track when using formulation to understand behaviours that challenge.

Box 8.7: Thoughts on formulating behaviours that challenge

Areas to think about	What these might be
Mis-matches?	Between different areas of functioning e.g. emotional vs intellectual. Between what people say and what they do. Between what is offered and what the individual needs/wants.
Unmet needs?	Physical health, pain management, emotional expression/containment, physical and emotional safety, attachment.
Functions?	Explore beyond the basic physiological functions, even if this has to be in the form of 'what if the behaviour is telling us…'
What are we missing?	Does this feel like the full picture? Are we missing something important?
Are we making assumptions?	Whose values and wishes does the formulation reflect?
Are we exploring hypotheses?	What else could it be? Is there another way to think about this?
Who or what are we focusing on? Does it look different from different perspectives?	Is the focus solely on the individual? Is it only considering certain people's perspectives? Are we being too objective or subjective?
Where is this leading?	Does this understanding give ideas for intervention? Does it convey hope?
What is the atmosphere?	How does it feel in the room? Collaborative? Hostile? Frightened? Is this getting in the way of creating a meaningful, hopeful formulation?

Intellectual Disabilities and 'Personality Disorder' © Pavilion Publishing and Media Ltd and its licensors 2023

Box 8.8 gives a possible formulation for Susan's physical aggression and threats to harm others.

Box 8.8: Formulation for Susan*

As suggested in Chapter 4, this formulation uses the PTM questions to explore the impact of trauma and combines this with the CBT hot cross bun to facilitate creation of a trauma informed PBS plan.

Part A: Exploring the possible impact of trauma on Susan* Using the PTM framework

What has happened to you?	I am the youngest of five children born close together. Dad was away with work during much of my childhood. I had lots of health problems (including diabetes) and operations so I spent a lot of time in hospital or at home recovering. Mum couldn't visit much because of my brothers and sisters but she made a fuss of me when I was at home, she let me do what I wanted and didn't help me stick to my diabetes plan. I didn't get to school much. I was a bit wild as a teenager and went to A&E lots (self-harm and diabetes related). Mum couldn't cope with me and neither could any of the places I went to live. I was raped at college but they didn't do anything, I don't think they believed me.
How did it affect you?	I hate other people telling me what to do. I'm really afraid of being on my own but I also find it difficult to be around people. I feel like I missed out. There's a lot I can't do and this makes me really angry.
What sense did you make of it?	I'm very confused. Sometimes I'm afraid and others I'm angry. None of it makes much sense to me. Am I a bad person? Did mum love the others more?
What did you have to do to survive?	I made a big fuss so the nurses would notice me. I hit out first to protect myself. I ignore my diabetes. I self-harm to get rid of the feelings and get people to look after me.
AND:	
What are your strengths?	Lots of interests, enjoy a joke, enjoy getting out and about.
What is your story?	See my life story book.

*Susan has been created from clinical experience & the literature. She is not based on a specific individual.

 Intellectual Disabilities and 'Personality Disorder' © Pavilion Publishing and Media Ltd and its licensors 2023

Part B: Formulation for Susan, patterns of relating and behaving

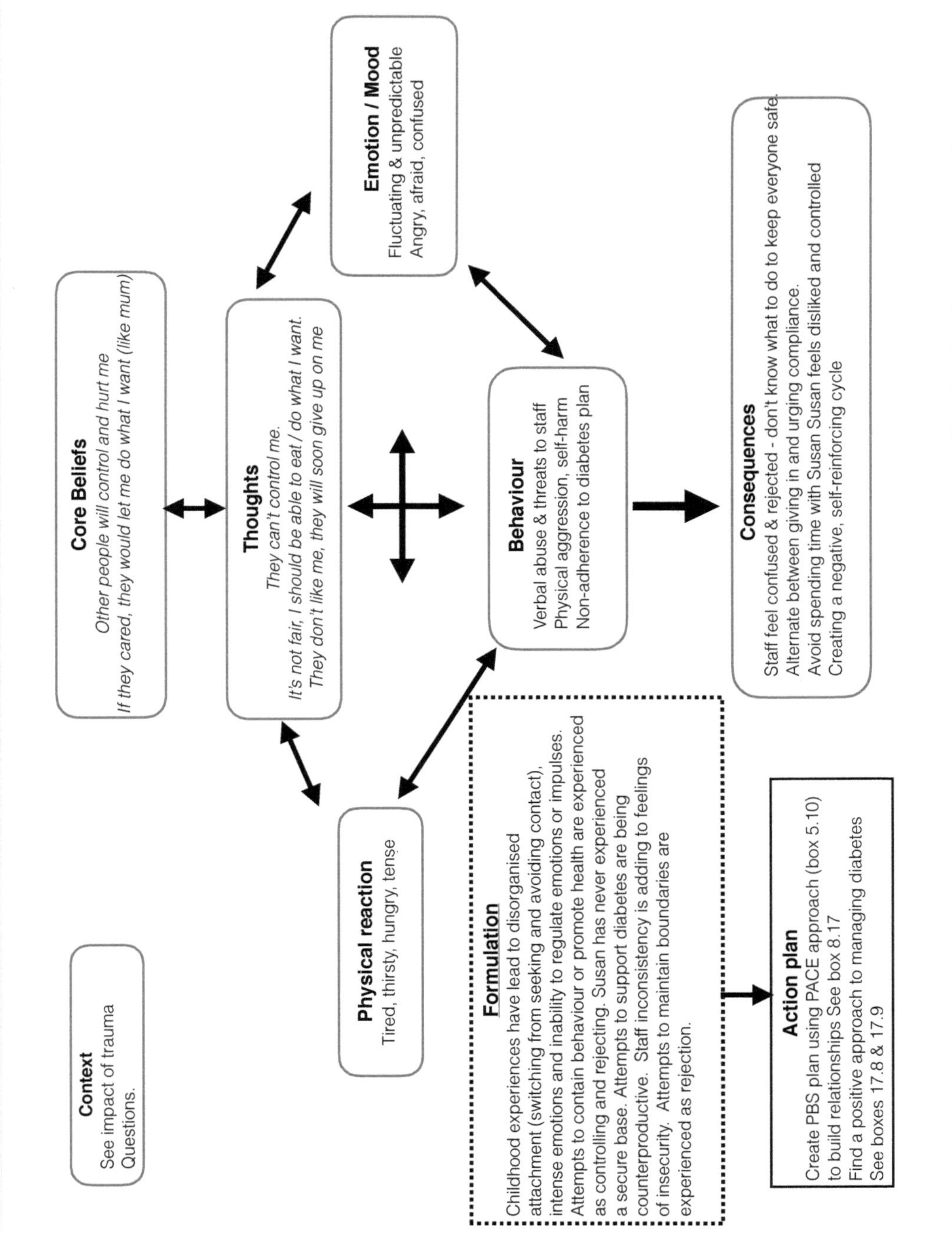

PBS plans

Assessment and formulation form the basis for collaboratively developing a Positive Behaviour Support (PBS) plan. A PBS plan is a document created to help understand behaviour and support behaviour change. It provides carers with a guide to making sure the individual has a good quality of life and has access to the things that are important to them. It includes tailored strategies to prevent or reduce the likelihood and impact of behaviours that challenge.

> *'What is important though is that ... people are assisted in coming to these decisions themselves wherever possible, rather than being 'prescribed' another treatment by their care team'.* (Brown *et al*, 2017)

A collaborative approach helps to ensure that the strategies selected will address the unique circumstances, needs, wishes and aspirations of the individual within their social setting. The priorities should be *maximising improvements in quality of life*, building relationships, addressing unmet needs and keeping everyone safe *in the least restrictive way possible*. Individuals who feel physically and emotionally safe and are enjoying themselves are much less likely to have to show behaviours that challenge.

A PBS plan brings together several elements (Harding, 2021):

- 'My best day' – preferred person-centred daily routine, enjoyable activities, preferred interaction styles.
- 'Understanding my behaviour' – an accessible summary of the formulation, telling everyone who reads the plan WHY these things need to be done.
- Proactive strategies – reducing the need for the behaviour to occur.
- Reactive strategies – resolving the behaviour as quickly and safely as possible.
- Positive risk-taking and risk-management plan: this identifies potential risks associated with the behaviour and its management, and minimises the risks to the individual, other people and the staff supporting the individual (Sellars, 2011).

A collaborative PBS plan will also meet the requirements of The Community Mental Health Framework (NHS England, 2019) for a *'co-produced and personalised care plan that takes account of all their needs...'*

 Intellectual Disabilities and 'Personality Disorder' © Pavilion Publishing and Media Ltd and its licensors 2023

The main PBS plan may be supported by shorter, more specific plans to help achieve specific goals (see Chapter 16) such as learning a new skill, or psycho-eduction such as learning about emotions. Where there are physical health issues, these will be addressed through the individual's Health Action Plan (see Chapter 17). Where an individual has experienced a crisis, the PBS plan should also be supported by a crisis and contingency plan (see Chapter 9) or risk formulation (see Chapter 10).

Which strategy when?

Chapter 3 highlighted the importance of using the right intervention approach at the right time. This principle applies equally to the use of proactive and reactive strategies. A helpful way of identifying which strategy to use is the time-intensity model (also called emotional arousal or assault cycle), first described by Kaplan and Wheeler (1983). Box 8.9 gives an adapted version of this model which also shows when an individual will be in their 'emotional mind' (see Chapter 15) or the **R**egulate phase. It also shows the points in the cycle when an individual may be in the **R**eason phase. (**R**elate does not map easily on to this diagram, as relating applies across the cycle but *the way staff relate needs to be adjusted* – this is explored in Chapter 9).

Box 8.9: Time – intensity model

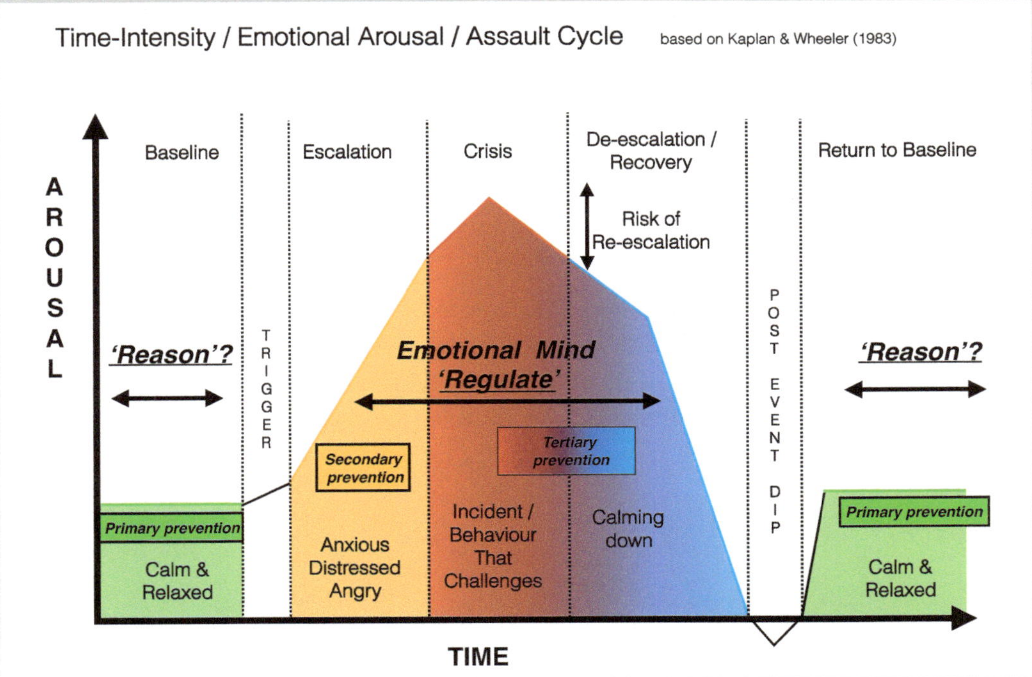

Behaviours that characterise each stage of the cycle can be identified with an individual, and when these are shown, the appropriate strategies can be adopted. This cycle has been likened to a traffic light and the stages colour-coded (see Box 8.10).

Box 8.10: Traffic lights

How stages of the emotional arousal/crisis cycle relate to the 'Traffic light' Positive Behaviour Support plan, prevention and types of strategies

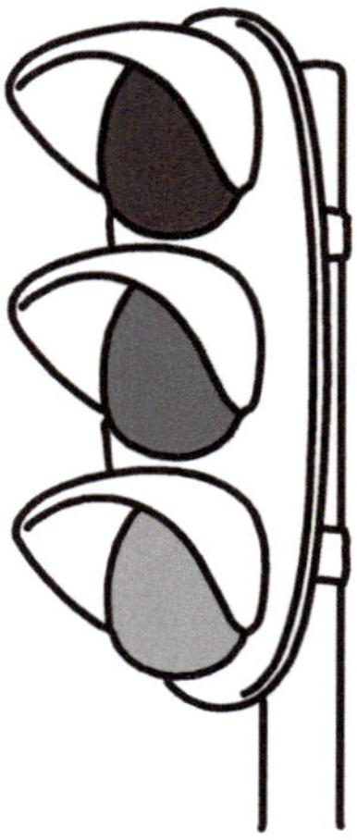

Green = Calm and relaxed/individual's typical arousal level	Primary prevention	Proactive strategies
Amber = Early signs of increasing arousal	Secondary prevention	Co-regulation and de-escalation
Red = Incident or crisis	Tertiary prevention (incident)	Reactive strategies: 'Hands off' Restrictive interventions
Blue = Calming down but vulnerable to re-escalating	Tertiary prevention – (post incident)	Post – incident support
Green = Return to calm and relaxed/ typical arousal level	Primary prevention	Proactive strategies

Challenging Behaviour Foundation (2022)

The PBS plans can also be colour-coded to link to the time-intensity stages. This helps clarify when to switch between the different types of strategies. An example 'traffic light' PBS plan format is given in Box 8.11. This basic framework can be adapted to make it accessible and relevant to each individual and the staff who support them.

 Intellectual Disabilities and 'Personality Disorder' © Pavilion Publishing and Media Ltd and its licensors 2023

Box 8.11 Format for a 'traffic light' PBS plan	
Personal details	
Places	Where the plan is to be used e.g. home, day centre.
Pen picture	Brief description of the individual. Their likes, dislikes, hopes and dreams. Their strengths and how they are when well and settled.
My best day	How to support the individual so that they feel safe and happy and their needs are met: ■ Preferred daily routine, activities of daily living. ■ Enjoyable and meaningful activities. ■ Preferred interaction styles. ■ Communication preferences. ■ Who they like to spend time with. ■ Working towards what they want to achieve in life (learning and building skills).
Understanding me	
Why?	Accessible summary of the formulation telling everyone who reads the plan WHY these things need to be done.
GREEN	**Helping me stay in a good mood/feel calm/feel safe and connected**
I'm in a good mood when I .... (How individual appears when they feel safe and their needs are being met)	Proactive strategies for when there are no signs of the behaviour – tailored to intervention stage. Promoting the 3 Rs: **R**egulate, **R**elate, **R**eason.
AMBER	**Helping me when I am getting loud/anxious/annoyed/fed up**
Early signs I'm getting...	How to spot the early warning signs and how to respond. What to say and do and how to do them.
RED	**Helping me when I am very upset/angry/might hurt myself or other people**
When I ... (behaviours of concern)	What to say and do to resolve the incident and keep everyone as safe as possible in the least restrictive way.
BLUE	**Helping me as I calm down**
When I ... signs of calming down)	What to say and do to avoid the situation re-escalating.

Proactive strategies

Proactive strategies, also known as 'primary prevention', identify what to do on a day-to-day basis, to help minimise the likelihood that the behaviour that challenges will occur. These are GREEN in a 'traffic light' plan. Proactive strategies consider all aspects of the person's life: they are about getting the individual's life right for them. They should aim to enhance the individual's quality of life and reflect their likes, wishes and dreams. Where an individual has reached the **R**eason stage, they may also include exploring issues and learning new skills across the domains of thoughts, emotions, attention, self, motivation, relationships and behaviour (Hayes and Hofmann, 2021). Proactive strategies should form the bulk of the PBS plan. Some examples of proactive strategies are given in Box 8.12. The Active Support approach (see Box 5.7) also contributes to primary prevention by promoting engagement with relationships and activities.

Box 8.12: Primary prevention strategies

GREEN = calm and relaxed: Primary prevention: proactive strategies for when there are no signs of the behaviour(s) of concern. Selection is informed by collaborative assessment and formulation

Individual factors	Examples
Physical well-being	Strategies to promote health (e.g. healthy eating, managing caffeine intake, fun physical activities, see Box 17.1) and reduce/manage physical pain.
Mental well-being	Strategies to promote mental health and reduce/regulate emotional pain (e.g. mindfulness, stress management, social contact, making friends, volunteering).
Creating a meaningful life	Building on strengths, wishes and aspirations to develop meaningful activities and a positive life.
Facilitating communication	E.g. developing a 'communication passport', accessible information, visual timetables, total communication.
Facilitating understanding	Develop compensatory strategies to overcome deficits e.g. use of memory aids, visual reminders, timely text messages.
Addressing skills deficits	Provide support for areas that can't be learnt and teach those that can.

 Intellectual Disabilities and 'Personality Disorder' © Pavilion Publishing and Media Ltd and its licensors 2023

Environmental Factors (ecological strategies)	
Arousal levels	Structuring day and designing environment to maintain optimum levels of arousal e.g. alternating physical activities with sedentary activities.
Living arrangements, environmental change	Support to find living arrangements that meet needs/ minimise triggers/temptations, create a sense of safety, manage sensory stimulation.
Support	Given the right amount of support by staff with the necessary skills and personal qualities, consider using small core teams of familiar staff. Use of Active Support (see box 5.7)
Interaction style	Supported in the style that is most helpful to them, tailoring style to mood.
Structure, routine and boundaries	Ensure individual feels safe, is physically and emotionally contained using positive person-centred structure and routines. Be consistent and predictable.
Modifying, minimising and avoiding triggers	E.g. be out or engaged at trigger times, have agreed strategies for dealing with difficult situations e.g. waiting for appointments.
Specific Functions	
Basic needs	Physiological needs: manage hunger, thirst, sleep, temperature and physical space, build access to pleasurable stimulation.
Emotional needs	Reduce emotional triggers, structure time to manage arousal levels, use of distraction techniques, constructive ways to let off steam – jogging, swimming, kick a ball about.
Attachment and relationship needs	Schedule interaction on basis on need e.g. regular contact where seeking attachment or regular respites where individual finds interaction difficult.
Esteem	Show interest and provide positive feedback, show respect, listen.

When selecting proactive strategies, it is important to look at the formulation as this will identify specific areas where the individual's life is not currently meeting their needs. It is also important to tailor strategies to the intervention stage the individual is being supported with (see Box 3.1). PBS rightly stresses the importance of teaching new skills. However, this should only be attempted once the individual feels safe, the situation is stable, and good working relationships have been established. People can only learn if they feel safe. Until this is achieved, the focus should be on co-regulating the individual's arousal level (see Chapter 11) and building secure relationships (see Chapter 5).

Sometimes, the actions necessary to prevent behaviours from occurring can feel uncomfortable for staff teams. For example, when behaviour is motivated by an overwhelming need for one-to-one staffing support, this should be given early on, before the behaviour occurs. However, this may feel like it is 'feeding' an 'unhealthy' need for staff input and is doing nothing to change the behaviour in the long term. In this case, 'giving in' should be seen as a 'holding response'. That is, it reduces the behaviour that challenges and gives a breathing space for the team to explore their understanding of this need (for example, attachment needs arising from trauma) and how this need could be met in more acceptable ways, and to identify other strategies to reduce the intensity of the need. As these actions are identified, they would also be included in the PBS plan.

Reactive strategies

Reactive strategies will form a smaller part of the PBS plan as they are specifically focused on the behaviour that challenges rather than improving the individual's quality of life. They may be divided into secondary and tertiary prevention.

Secondary prevention

Secondary prevention identifies early warning signs or the early stages in a behavioural sequence. It aims to prevent these from escalating into the behaviour that challenges by the timely use of interventions. These are AMBER in a 'traffic light' plan. Some examples of secondary prevention strategies are given in Box 8.13.

Box 8.13: Secondary prevention	
AMBER = Early signs of increasing arousal. Secondary prevention: reactive strategies responding to early warning signs or early stages of a sequence of behaviour. Selection is informed by collaborative assessment and formulation.	
Individual factors	
Physical well-being	Offering a caffeine-free drink or healthy, enjoyable snack. Timely use of painkillers* or pain management techniques.
Mental well-being	Active listening, familiar distraction (Box 15.15)/relaxation techniques (Box 11.16), timely use of 'as required' medication*.

 Intellectual Disabilities and 'Personality Disorder' © Pavilion Publishing and Media Ltd and its licensors 2023

Emotional arousal	Use of co-regulation and de-escalation techniques (Box 11.15). Familiar relaxation and self-soothing techniques (Box 11.17). Sensory regulating activities e.g. rhythmic actions.
Physiological arousal	Where there is a huge build-up of physical energy, this may need to be safely expressed before an individual can calm down. They may need to run, jump, tear up cardboard, hit a swing ball, pop bubble wrap. This needs careful assessment as for some individuals these activities might escalate their arousal.
Distressing thoughts	Use reassurance, acceptance, active listening (Box 10.13), restate key reassuring facts, familiar distraction, mindfulness. 'It has really upset you but it can't do any harm, it will go away in its own good time', how about we...'
Environmental factors	
Physical environment	Make changes e.g. switch music/TV on or off, open/close windows, remove objects.
Location	E.g. change rooms, go outside/come inside, go to a quiet area.
Specific functions	
Basic needs	Give needed item promptly then use distraction/de-escalation if needed.
Emotional needs	Active listening, familiar distraction/relaxation techniques, timely use of 'as required' medication*, leave stressful situations (if in care plan, expressive touch, see Box 13.13). Use familiar techniques to express emotions, e.g. pop bubble wrap, tear paper, write or draw concerns.
Seeking attachment and relationship needs	Increase support level, interact with individual, moving within eyesight, sitting near someone (if in care plan, expressive touch).
Protecting against attachment and loss	Reduce interaction, minimise number of people around, give space but don't isolate, show interest and care in body language e.g. turning towards, relaxed posture.
Esteem	Show interest, respect and listen.

*For some individuals, medication may have a limited but important role in managing acute distress. Where medication is used on an 'as required' basis, this should be supported by guidelines and reviewed after every use. Its use should be integrated into the PBS plan.

It is essential that secondary preventative strategies are identified from the formulation and not selected on an ad hoc basis. This is because what helps to calm one individual may push another individual into the behaviour it is intended to prevent. Also, randomly trying techniques to calm an individual is likely to make them feel insecure and hence increase the risk of them showing distressed and potentially challenging behaviours (see Chapter 9).

There is one important and deliberate omission from the list of secondary preventative strategies: 'ignoring' the behaviour. 'Ignoring' is sometimes suggested as an approach for responding to 'attention-seeking behaviour'. However, ignoring is disrespectful, potentially very distressing for the person ignored, and ineffective. It is more likely to lead to an increase in the behaviour that challenges. It is better to frame such behaviour as interaction or attachment-seeking and look for ways to help the individual to feel emotionally safe, listened to, cared for and supported.

Tertiary prevention

Tertiary prevention comprises actions taken once the behaviour is occurring. These actions aim to resolve an incident as quickly and safely as possible and to minimise the risk of it escalating or having serious negative outcomes. *It is important to recognise that, by this stage, there is nothing that can be done to stop the behaviour from occurring*. Effective tertiary strategies make the individual feel safe and cared for, provide physical and emotional containment, keep staff and other people safe, and build the foundations for positive working together once the incident has been resolved. These are RED in a traffic light plan. Having a clear plan of what to do when the behaviour is happening helps those supporting the person to act quickly, work together and, very importantly, to remain calm. Some examples are given in Box 8.14.

Box 8.14: Red tertiary prevention	
RED = Crisis or incident happening. Tertiary prevention: reactive strategies used once the behaviour is occurring with the aim of resolving an incident as quickly and safely as possible and to minimise the risk of it escalating or having serious negative outcomes. **MUST BE THE LEAST RESTRICTIVE OPTION**	
'Hands-off' strategies	Reduce social and sensory demands on individual e.g. fewer people, quieter, remove demands. Co-regulation and de-escalation techniques (see Box 11.15). Distraction (Box 15.15).

 Intellectual Disabilities and 'Personality Disorder' © Pavilion Publishing and Media Ltd and its licensors 2023

	Redirection e.g. *'Chairs are for sitting on, come down and we can go for a walk'*. Give the individual space (but stay within eye-sight). Access a calming space, e.g. de-escalation room, garden. Low-arousal disengagement techniques if individual makes contact with staff member.
As required medication*	If prescribed and not used previously.
Restrictive practices: limit individual's freedom of movement = 'use of force' [Risk assess: ■ Physical health problems and physiological contraindications. ■ Psychological risks e.g. a history of abuse. ■ Biomechanical risks, e.g. musculoskeletal risks. ■ Sensory sensitivities, such as a high or low threshold for touch.]	Low-arousal physical-intervention techniques to prompt or guide an individual to a safer area, then give space. Using clinical holding techniques to restrict movement e.g. supporting to use safety pod™. [Restrictive practices also include: ■ Rapid tranquillisation. ■ Seclusion – isolating a person and preventing them from leaving e.g. by locking the door. ■ The use of objects or equipment to restrict movement e.g. the use of arm splints.]

*For some individuals, medication may have a limited but important role in managing acute distress. Where medication is used on an 'as required' basis, this should be supported by guidelines and reviewed after every use. Its use should be integrated into the PBS plan.

Tertiary preventative strategies should comprise the smallest part of the PBS plan. If this section is longer than the other parts of the plan, it indicates that insufficient attention has been paid to meeting the individual's needs and improving their quality of life. Such a plan would be unprofessional, would not comply with national standards (NICE, 2015a; 2015b) or the Mental Health Units (Use of Force) Act 2018 (MHU Act). Appropriate training in positive and safer approaches to behaviour, such as that provided by the training organisation Maybo, enable staff to choose *the least restrictive option* from a range of low-arousal options, from 'hands off' strategies, through disengagement, guiding and prompting to clinical holding. The innovative Safety Pod™ bean bag (see Chapter 6) offers an alternative to traditional physical restraint that appears to reduce the potential for trauma for all involved (when properly maintained and used by trained staff). It appears that the pods promote calming by meeting a need for proprioceptive feedback (which helps regulate arousal) or a need to be held and contained both physically and emotionally. Hence, using the pods replaces a traumatic experience with one that for some individuals is intrinsically calming. Box 8.15 gives a generic care plan explaining the use of the Safety Pod.

Box 8.15: Safety Pod Care Plan

While you are using our services, staff will always try to keep you safe and work with you to get better.

There may be times when you become distressed or angry. Staff will always support you at these times and try to help you to become calm again.

Sometimes this might not be possible. If you were to become very distressed or angry then that behaviour may place yourself and others at risk.

At these times staff may have to hold you to ensure your safety as well as the safety of others.

Staff are trained to do this safely.

This is a Safety Pod™

It helps you to stay safe and to become calmer. It is safer for you as you are sitting down and not on the floor.

At least 2 staff will support you while you are in the Safety Pod.

They will stay with you until you are calm.

The safety pod is comfortable and enables you to relax.

Based on the Deacon Unit's generic Safety Pod™ care plan (SABP NHS Trust 2022). This plan can be personalised with illustrations for each individual to help accessibility. Staff can be photographed modelling how it would be used with the individual e.g. with or without use of knee cushion.

Image credit: Neus Bartual

Intellectual Disabilities and 'Personality Disorder' © Pavilion Publishing and Media Ltd and its licensors 2023

The MHU Act defines the use of physical, mechanical and chemical restraint, seclusion and long-term segregation as *the use of force*. This language reflects the intensity of, and risks associated with, these practices. Individuals with intellectual disabilities report all conventional restrictive interventions to be painful and stressful. Fear, anger, desperation, upset, anxiety and sadness were frequently reported as the consequence of being restrained. *This led to distrusting staff, disliking the placement and feelings of powerlessness*, which in turn made behaviours that challenge more likely to occur (Bush and Griffiths, 2017). Being restrained can re-traumatise individuals who have experienced abuse. It also carries risks to the physical and emotional well-being of both the individual and the staff members involved. Hence, it must only be used when absolutely necessary if a person is likely to cause harm to themselves or others.

If included, the use of restrictive physical interventions must comply with national guidance (NICE, 2015a and b) and they should only be used by appropriately trained staff. When used in a 'mental health unit', use must also comply with the requirements of the MHU Act. Their use should be recorded on a database that captures multiple aspects of the event (RCP, 2018) that allows meaningful analysis of incidents. When restrictive interventions have been used, staff must also follow their organisation's internal procedures, which may include reporting to a manager and completing an incident form. They should be reviewed after every use, with the aim of working towards less restrictive options. As Paterson *et al* (2017) phrased it: '*We seek to transition from physical to relational holding*'. The Challenging Behaviour Foundation (2023) gives advice on actions to take to reduce the use of restrictive interventions. This highlights the importance of using safeguarding procedures and reporting to the Care Quality Commission if anyone has concerns that restrictive physical interventions are causing harm to the individual. Where restrictive interventions are used, the17-Stepp Plan (RDasH, 2014) may help ensure risks are managed proactively. The MHU Act provides a framework of leadership, policy and data review that aims to ensure force is used as little as possible and as safely as possible, including staff training and the provision of information.

Tertiary prevention also includes strategies to help the individual return to their usual level of arousal, to avoid 're-igniting' the incident after it appears to have been resolved. These are BLUE in a traffic light plan (see Box 8.16). Once an individual has returned to their normal arousal level, the incident should be reviewed for any learning that can be taken from it. Everyone involved should be offered post-incident support.

8.16: Blue tertiary prevention	
Blue = cooling down. Tertiary prevention: Reactive strategies used once the incident is safely resolved to help the individual return to their usual level of arousal, to avoid 're-igniting' the incident.	
Physical well-being, basic needs	Offering a drink, ensure individual is not too hot or cold. Low-arousal physical activity e.g. stretching, walking.
Mental well-being	Active listening, *familiar* distraction, relaxation self-soothing or mindfulness techniques (Boxes 10.13, 15.15, 11.16, 11.17, 15.16).
Emotional arousal/ needs	Use of co-regulation and de-escalation techniques (Box 11.15). Active listening, *familiar* distraction/relaxation techniques. Use *familiar* techniques to express emotions e.g. pop bubble wrap, tear paper, write or draw concerns. Using sensory activities known to calm individual. Rhythmical physical activities e.g. walking, swinging. Listen to relaxing music.
Low-arousal interaction	Give quiet time alone. Chat about familiar topics. Speak quietly, use relaxed body language, move slowly.
Re-engage	Offer preferred low arousal activities.
Accept the incident	Don't try to talk about what has just happened. Wait until fully recovered and back to usual settled self. Accept any apology. Make a fresh start.

Box 8.17 gives an example of a brief traffic light PBS plan for Susan based on the formulation in Box 8.8.

 Intellectual Disabilities and 'Personality Disorder' © Pavilion Publishing and Media Ltd and its licensors 2023

8.17: Example PBS plan for 'Susan'	
Pen picture	I am 'Susan', only my friends and family call me 'Suzie'. I love going out and seeing my family. I love dogs, watching TV, doing crafts and puzzles. I enjoy a good joke. I have a good memory. I would like to have a job somewhere I would meet lots of people – like in a cafe. I prefer to forget my diabetes as I hate needles and finger-prick tests.
My best day	I like to know the plan for the day ('Now doing x… 'Next' doing y…) Let me do things my way, (even if it takes longer than your way). I like to go out every day but also having time to chill and time to chat. Patting a dog makes my day!
Understanding me	
Why?	I had a tough start to life, with lots of health problems including diabetes, stays away from my family and lots of moves (ask me to show you my life story book). I've missed out on a lot and struggle to form relationships, regulate my emotions and look after myself. I need you to follow these guidelines to keep us all safe, help me stay calm and give me a chance to build positive relationships and learn about having a stable home base.
GREEN	Helping me stay in a good mood/feel calm/feel safe and connected Think PACE: **P**layfulness, **A**cceptance, **C**uriosity, **E**mpathy
I'm in a good mood when I smile, joke and chat cheerfully and when I am doing my puzzles.	Use 'now' and 'next' to tell me about my day but make sure the next is something nice. Mix up quiet and lively activities, so I don't get over excited or bored. If I am reluctant to do things like shower or do my blood test, don't nag, just say *'I know this is tough for you but as soon as its done we can_______ (something fun).* Praise me – big smile and a high 5 when the job is done. Make sure I get to the craft shop once a week to choose things to do. Give me jobs to do so that I can help you about the house and work alongside me, tell me how helpful I am – more smiles and high 5s. Find time to chat with me and get me to tell you jokes. Tell me some (there is a big joke book in the office for ideas). When we meet a dog out walking ask the owner if I can pat it and then let me do this for as long as the dog owner is happy. Let me do puzzles for 30 minutes and then check if I would like to do something different – I may get lonely and think you have forgotten me…

→

AMBER	Helping me when I am getting loud/anxious/annoyed/fed up
Early signs I'm getting upset – I stop smiling, make comments like '*it's not fair*', my voice gets louder, I may glare at someone	Let the other staff know I am upset in case I don't calm down and you need help. Take a deep breath and shake out your tension – it really helps if you stay calm and show me how its done. Use active listening to find out what is upsetting me. Sort it out if you can or offer me a choice of two things we can do e.g. go for a walk or have a cup of tea. Sometimes it helps if we list all the dog breeds we can think of (I love it when you make mistakes like saying 'tiger' or 'hippopotamus'). Let me choose an activity off my calming menu and do it together (exaggerate your breathing a bit as this makes me laugh). If I don't calm down switch with another member of staff – (sorry, but I may just be fed-up with you at the moment).
RED	Helping me when I am very upset/angry/might hurt myself or other people
When I shout at people	Stay calm, keep your body language relaxed. Help me get to a quiet room, away from other people. Listen to me, remind me you are here to help. Don't get too close or talk too much. Don't ask questions, don't tell me to 'calm down'.
If I try to assault someone or hurt myself	Support me to use the safety pod™. Don't talk much but tell me I will soon be calm and it will be OK. I find the pod relaxing and you will soon feel when I am ready to get up.
BLUE	Helping me as I calm down
When I relax and my voice comes back to normal	Offer me a cool drink and put on something from my relaxing music list. Do a word search or two together. Then ask if I would like to go for a walk (gentle exercise helps get rid of my tension). Then offer me my now and next.

A good plan is not enough

To be effective, PBS plans need to be implemented consistently. This is essential to gain the trust of the individual; it can be very frightening and confusing for the individual if they are unable to predict how staff will respond to them. Frightened and confused individuals are likely to show more, rather than fewer, behaviours that challenge. This is particularly important for individuals who could be given a diagnosis of 'personality disorder': consistency is one of the core principles of effective services identified by the Personality Disorder Commission (2018, p10). Chapter 13

Intellectual Disabilities and 'Personality Disorder' © Pavilion Publishing and Media Ltd and its licensors 2023

explores how collaboratively creating and maintaining therapeutic boundaries helps create a hopeful and secure base.

Research shows that a behaviour that is successful some of the time, but not all of the time, (intermittent reinforcement) is much more difficult to change. Occasional success sends the message that the needed outcome will eventually occur. If staff are inconsistent in their response to the behaviour, there is a risk of unintentionally strengthening it.

The PBS plan also needs to be compatible and consistent with any other plans in place, for example a Health Action Plan. If plans conflict, everyone will be confused and neither plan is likely to be effective.

Strategies must also be implemented intelligently and flexibly. No plan can account for all situations. The staff implementing the plan need to understand the individual and the reasoning behind the strategies. In this way, they can act in the spirit of the plan in the absence of specific guidance for a new situation.

Finally, the more the individual and their support team 'own' and understand the plan, the more likely it is to work. This can be enhanced by using the language of an individual and their care network in the plan, ensuring that it is accessible to the people who need it most.

Key learning points

- Behaviour is described as challenging when it is culturally abnormal, threatens the quality of life and/or the emotional and physical safety of the individual or others, and is likely to lead to responses that are restrictive, aversive or result in exclusion.
- All people have physiological and psychological needs. Behaviours that challenge arise as ways of meeting needs, when more socially acceptable means of meeting the needs are not accessible.
- Behaviours that challenge have meaning or function (purpose) and are not a characteristic of the individual.
- Some behaviours that challenge can be understood as 'survival strategies' that developed to meet needs in situations where the usual, acceptable approaches did not work. Survival strategies may persist even when the traumatic situation has ended.

- PBS looks at the interaction between the individual, their underlying human needs, their environment and the people around them. It highlights the relationship between behaviours that challenge and the setting in which they occur.
- PBS is very different from the medical model. The medical model sees specific behaviours as 'symptoms' and looks for the clusters of symptoms that are characteristic of particular physical or mental health problems.
- Trauma-informed PBS examines the effects of trauma when carrying out assessment, formulation and intervention.
- The use of a structured formulation such as the adapted 'hot cross bun' can make sense of the large amount of complicated information that is often generated by a thorough assessment. It can also identify areas where further assessment might be needed and helps identify which interventions might be most helpful.
- A PBS plan includes both proactive and reactive strategies. It aims to prevent the behaviour that challenges wherever possible by improving the individual's quality of life and building skills. Where the behaviour cannot be prevented, it uses reactive strategies to resolve it as quickly and safely as possible.
- Restrictive interventions are traumatic, leading to individuals distrusting staff, disliking placements and increasing feelings of being powerless. This can make behaviours that challenge more likely to occur. Where restrictive interventions cannot be avoided, they must be the least restrictive option and every effort should be made to reduce their use.
- To be effective, PBS plans need to be implemented consistently and must be compatible with the individual's other plans. Ownership and understanding of the reasons behind the plan help it to be implemented intelligently and flexibly to address unforeseen situations.

 Intellectual Disabilities and 'Personality Disorder' © Pavilion Publishing and Media Ltd and its licensors 2023

Chapter 9: Getting through – helping everyone survive crises

This chapter looks at what a crisis is and the factors that can make individuals vulnerable to experiencing crises. It shows how crises may be experienced in different ways and how they affect thoughts, emotions and behaviour. It explores how to support individuals through crises and how to support staff to do this successfully. It shows how being curious and non-judgmental about a crisis allows learning, which can reduce the likelihood and severity of future crises. It looks at how to support individuals at the **R**eason stage to select, learn and use coping skills. It highlights the importance of evaluating the effects of interventions and the risks of forgetting lessons learnt when crises have been prevented for a period of time.

Key learning points

- Crises
- Impact of crises on individuals
- Supporting individuals in crisis
- Supporting the supporters during a crisis
- Learning from the crisis
- Is the approach working?

Crises

A crisis is an unstable period, especially one of troubling or dangerous events. When applied to people, crises may take the form of a sudden change, usually for the worse, in their social functioning, physical or mental health. Crises may be triggered by a wide variety of events that lead to the person being overwhelmed by internal or external stressors (see Box 9.1). Within the mental health field, a crisis has been described as a '*multidimensional subjective experience, which also contributes to distress for family carers and professionals*' (Warrender *et al*, 2021).

Box 9.1: Crises: Possible vulnerabilities, warning signs and triggers

Triggers:

- Life events e.g. loss, deaths, redundancy, relationship breakup, house move, homelessness, in trouble with the police, being attacked or abused, being reminded of past trauma.
- The anniversary of a loss or negative life event.
- Anticipated downturn in personal circumstances e.g. worrying about being made redundant.
- Practical changes e.g. level of support, changes to finances.
- Staffing changes e.g. familiar staff leaving, high staff turn-over.
- Changes to support style e.g. relaxing boundaries, inconsistent responses.
- Physical health e.g. onset of new illness or deterioration in existing condition.
- Mental health e.g. onset of new or deterioration in existing condition.
- Pain (physical and emotional).
- Medication: changes, not taking correctly, not taking at all, adding in unhelpful medications.

Vulnerabilities:

- Low or lack of self-esteem.
- Lack of practical skills and knowledge.
- Unhelpful thinking patterns.
- Lack of skills to manage intense emotions, narrow window of regulation (see Box 11.4).
- Small social network.
- Few sources of enjoyment and fulfilment in their life.
- Drug or alcohol misuse.
- Support services struggling to engage them.
- Insufficient support or a mismatch between type of support given and that needed.
- Support staff lacking skills/knowledge/attitudes to support individual when in difficulties.

Warning signs:

- Increase or decrease in phone calls and or contacts with services.
- More missed appointments.

→

 Intellectual Disabilities and 'Personality Disorder' © Pavilion Publishing and Media Ltd and its licensors 2023

- Erratic attendance at job or other day time activities.
- Talking more about problems and concerns.
- Talking less.
- Decline in personal hygiene.
- Increase in use of alcohol or drugs.
- Self-harm.
- Change in general demeanour e.g. more angry, sadder, more irritable.
- Change in personal appearance (hair, dress, weight loss/gain).
- Change in pattern of behaviour (sleeping more/less, eating more/less, going out more/less).

Sometimes, individuals experience cycles in which a seemingly minor event triggers a series of other events until the situation spirals out of control. This applies across their physical health, mental health and everyday lives. Appointments are missed, treatments are not followed accurately or important actions are not taken. In this way, an individual can ricochet from one crisis to the next. When difficulties continue for a long time or behaviour escalates beyond a containable level, living and support arrangements may break down.

Crises will happen at times in everyone's lives. How people are able to respond to these crises depends on a number of factors, including characteristics of the services that support them day to day (see Box 6.1) and those that are accessed in times of crisis (see Chapter 6), the individual and their circumstances.

Individual vulnerabilities

Some people are more psychologically resilient than others. They can manage their emotional reactions, bounce back from negative events, solve problems and adjust well to things they cannot change. This enables them to stay within the 'window of regulation' in which they can reason, empathise, reflect, learn and remember in difficult situations (see Box 11.4). People also cope better with crises when they have a strong social support network, a financial buffer, and access to good physical and mental health services.

Other individuals are more vulnerable to experiencing crises (see Box 9.1). They struggle to stay within the 'window of regulation' and are quickly overwhelmed. This may be because they have fewer social or financial resources, have limited skills, or struggle to regulate emotions and impulses. This can be as a result of social deprivation, childhood adversity and past or current trauma. Childhood adversity also contributes to poor physical health, making individuals vulnerable to health-related crises (see Chapter 17).

Trauma during the developmental period can lead to changes in how the brain reacts to threats. These changes lead to individuals being hyper-vigilant to danger, more responsive to danger cues, quicker to respond to perceived dangers and less aware of safety cues (Harding, 2021). Consequently, they may perceive danger in situations others experience as safe. They are more likely to respond to cues by going into crisis, to escalate more quickly, and find it harder to recover from the crisis. A crisis may also bring back difficult memories or cause the individual to re-experience traumatic events from their past, intensifying their reaction to present events. Trauma can also impact an individual's ability to trust others, making it difficult for them to seek or accept help. Some mechanisms individuals use to cope with crises may exacerbate the situation. For example, using drugs or alcohol, or seeking support from inappropriate people. The intensity of emotional distress experienced may be overwhelming and can lead individuals to self-harm or attempt suicide (see Chapter 10).

Given the high rates of trauma experienced by individuals with intellectual disabilities and those given a diagnosis of 'personality disorder', it is not surprising that they experience high rates of crises. Individuals given a diagnosis of '(borderline) personality disorder' may experience recurrent crises, often having a quick onset and associated with self-harm or concerns about suicide (Warrender *et al*, 2021). Individuals with intellectual disabilities also experience higher rates of crises than their peers, with a significant proportion of these crises occurring outside of the nine-to-five, five-day working week (Kalb *et al*, 2021). In the study by Kalb *et al* (2021) crises most frequently centred around aggressive behaviour, but a small proportion arose from thoughts of suicide. Crises were more frequent in those with mild intellectual disabilities, young adults, those who identified their gender as 'other', were not employed or who had previously been admitted to hospital. The health inequalities experienced by both groups also make them more vulnerable to becoming acutely physically ill and at risk of receiving poorer care at such times (see Chapter 17).

Crises often seem to 'come out of the blue'. However, even for crises that have a rapid onset, there are often warning signs that all is not well (see Box 9.1).

 Intellectual Disabilities and 'Personality Disorder' © Pavilion Publishing and Media Ltd and its licensors 2023

The impact of crises on the individual

Being in crisis is accompanied by a range of changes in how people think, feel and behave, and the physical sensations they experience (see Box 9.2).

Box 9.2: Effects of being in crisis	
Thoughts (see Chapter 15)	**Emotional mind:** Instinctive, impulsive, beyond control. Actions and responses are automatic, based on habit/instinct/ immediate situation. **Unable to reason, process information, problem solve or think longer term.** Unable to concentrate. Or: shut down and disconnected. May hear voices or see things not actually present.
Feelings/ emotions (see Chapter 11)	Anger (may be driven by fear), fear, terror or numbness. Intense, over-whelming emotional pain. Helplessness, hopelessness. May switch suddenly between emotions.
Physical sensations	Depends on the combination of hormones released. May include: ■ Feeling sick, pounding, racing heart, sweating, breathing rapidly. ■ May feel as if having a heart attack or physical illness. ■ Loss of appetite. ■ Heightened senses due to hyper-vigilance for signs of danger. ■ Increased physical tension, pent up energy. ■ May experience intense physical pain or not notice physical injury.
Behaviour (see Chapters 8 and 10)	Restless, agitated, erratic, unable to sleep. Running away, verbal and physical aggression to others, damaging property, self-harm or suicide attempts, suicide. Inactive, neglecting self, not washing, eating or drinking.

These changes are associated with biological survival reactions to perceived threats called the 'survival cascade' or 'defence cascade'. There are a number of possible responses depending on the characteristics of the situation and the possibility of escape (see Box 9.3) and an individual's past experience of trauma. These reactions are the result of the interaction of the sympathetic and parasympathetic nervous systems (the two parts of the autonomic nervous system) preparing the body to defend itself, for example through changes to heart rate and the release of stress hormones such as adrenaline and cortisol. *They are not conscious choices.*

Box 9.3: The survival cascade:

The survival cascade: involuntary bodily responses to perceived threat with associated physiological and psychological changes. *The brain automatically activates these responses* based on an unconscious assessment of the situation and what it has done in the past:

Fight	Attack behaviours – increased heart rate, blood flow to muscles. Unconscious assessment = *I am bigger, stronger and can win against this person. I will stand my ground and win.*
Flight	Flee, runaway. Unconscious assessment = *I am smaller and will not win, I can get away, so I'm going to run.*
Freeze	Attentive immobility. Conscious but unable to move – decreased heart rate and increased muscle tension. Unconscious assessment = *I can't get away and I can't win, I'll freeze because if I don't respond they may lose interest and go away.*
Flop/faint	Become physically and mentally unresponsive.. Unconscious assessment = *They aren't going away, if I stay frozen it's going to hurt more so I'll flop and look dead then it will be over and they'll go away.*
(Be)Friend	Seeking help from others or trying to befriend the assailant. Unconscious assessment = *I can't stop it, maybe if I keep them on my side and keep them happy they won't hurt me as much.*
Dissociate	Altered states of consciousness that allow the mind to distance itself from inescapable situations (see Box 9.4). Unconscious assessment = *This is unbearable, I can't get away physically, so I must get away mentally.*

The most commonly experienced states are the fight-flight states, which are the result of the action of the sympathetic nervous system. These are associated with a steep increase in arousal and physical tension, and usually follow the time-intensity model (see Box 8.9). Individuals may experience switches between fear and anger, resulting in changes of behaviour from running away to attacking. If they

 Intellectual Disabilities and 'Personality Disorder' © Pavilion Publishing and Media Ltd and its licensors 2023

mistakenly perceive them as a threat, some individuals may show verbal or physical aggression towards people trying to help or care for them. If pent-up energy is not released, it can make it very difficult for individuals to calm down and can make them vulnerable to 'flaring up' again at the smallest provocation.

In contrast, freeze, flop and dissociation are characterised by different types of shutting down and becoming unresponsive or 'absent' from the situation. In these states, the parasympathetic system (rest and digest) is also active or dominant. These states may persist for longer than fight-flight responses. This may lead to individuals neglecting themselves, putting their physical health at risk.

Dissociation is an altered state of consciousness which is characterised by feelings of disconnection. It may occur when an individual is completely overwhelmed by an inescapable traumatic situation, as a means of bearing the unbearable, and is associated with having experienced trauma. Think of it as acting like a shield between the individual and the situation they cannot escape. Individuals who have experienced trauma may come to automatically dissociate in response to any stressful situation or anything that triggers painful memories. Box 9.4 gives a summary of how to recognise dissociation and how to support someone during this experience.

Box 9.4: Dissociation	
Dissociation: Automatic altered states of consciousness that allow the mind to distance itself from inescapable situations.	
A more extreme version of the everyday experience of 'zoning out' or being on 'auto-pilot' e.g.: ■ Being so absorbed in a book you forget where you are. ■ Arriving at your destination in a car with no recollection of the drive.	
Everyone's experience of dissociation is different but it may include:	
Disconnection	Between areas of functioning that usually work together: consciousness, memory, identity, awareness of self and environment, sensory experiences.
Depersonalisation	Feel as if you are looking at yourself from outside. Feel: ■ As though you are watching yourself in a film. ■ As if you are just observing your emotions. ■ Disconnected from parts of your body or your emotions. ■ As if you are floating away.

→

	■ Unsure of the boundaries between yourself and other people. ■ That you are carrying out actions but are not in control of what you do.
Derealisation	Experience the world around you as unreal: ■ Feel detached or separate from the world around you. ■ See the world as 'lifeless' or 'foggy'. ■ See objects changing in shape, size or colour. ■ Feel like you're seeing the world through a pane of glass. ■ Feel like you're living in a dream. ■ Feel as if other people are robots (even though you know they aren't).
Memory	Lose periods of time, not remembering what happened.
Coping	Some individuals may use self-harm as a way to stop themselves dissociating or to reconnect with feelings after dissociating.
Signs	May appear dazed or spaced out, may seem not to hear what is said to them, may act or speak differently, may suddenly switch emotions and or behaviour, may lose memory of events. '*We saw her glance changing, we could not make any contact any more, she did not response to her name…* (van den Bogaard *et al*, 2018 individual 'M')
Support	**Respond with kindness and patience.** Use co-regulation strategies (see Box 11.15). Their 'auto-pilot' will shut down once it assesses the situation is safe. Aim to make them feel safe and comfortable. Using a warm, gentle tone of voice, tell them they are safe and that you will look after them, that you are there and it will be OK, use their name. It may help to make neutral comments e.g. talk about the colour of the room, how comfy the chairs are, the items on the shelves. Self-monitor to ensure your tone does not convey anxiety, frustration or authority. These feelings may make the situation feel unsafe to come back to. For individuals who reach the **R**eason stage, Grounding techniques* (mental and physical exercises that help refocus on the present) may be helpful (see Box 10.16).
Adapted from MIND (2023a)* see Raypole (2022)	

 Intellectual Disabilities and 'Personality Disorder' © Pavilion Publishing and Media Ltd and its licensors 2023

Once the threat has resolved, the person's thoughts, emotions and physical sensations gradually return to their usual state. The person may become aware of pain from injuries they were not aware of sustaining. They may struggle to remember or make sense of what happened during the crisis. This may be because their behaviour during the crisis became instinctive rather than reason-based and hence is difficult to recall and, even if it can be recalled, makes little sense when looked at from a calmer perspective.

Once the crisis is over, individuals may feel ashamed or embarrassed about their behaviour. Shame and embarrassment are uncomfortable emotions and unconscious psychological mechanisms may be triggered to protect individuals from them (see Chapter 7), making it difficult to think or talk about the crisis. While bringing short-term relief, such responses leave individuals vulnerable to future stresses.

Supporting individuals in crisis

In an ideal world, no one would experience a full crisis as they would be able to quickly access appropriate support at the earliest stages, or the signs would be spotted by others and support put in place. If crises did happen, the individual would be well known, and staff would be aware of how best to support them. Developments in services mean that this ideal may be coming closer (see Chapter 6). However, in the real world, individuals may encounter services for the first time when in crisis or may move to a new area or service, leaving behind all that is known about how best to support them at difficult times. Supporting an unknown individual and being supported by unfamiliar staff are both anxiety-provoking and can escalate a situation.

Proactively and compassionately supporting individuals in crisis comprises the first stage of the integrated model of intervention (see Box 3.1), characterised as '**R**egulate'. The focus of this stage is on getting the individual and those who support them through a very difficult time in a way that minimises the trauma they experience and lays the foundations for positive working relationships once the crisis is resolved. The support needed by the individual will depend on the nature of the crisis and the survival cascade response they are experiencing. Crises related to physical and mental well-being and 'shutting down' responses can be supported using the approach described in Chapter 17.

Crises characterised by intense distress and 'acting out' responses, where the fight-flight responses are predominant, can be very worrying for everyone involved. The primary focus in these crises is to keep everyone safe and avoid escalating the

Intellectual Disabilities and 'Personality Disorder' © Pavilion Publishing and Media Ltd and its licensors 2023

situation. Intense emotions such as anger, terror and grief, and behaviours such as physical aggression and self-harm, need to be contained in ways that build trust as well as keeping people emotionally and physically safe.

The aim is to manage the environment and use interaction styles to create an atmosphere of emotional and physical safety in which co-regulation can help the crisis to resolve itself. If this is achieved, the individual's unconscious assessment of the situation will come to recognise that there is no longer a threat and that the survival cascade can be 'switched off'.

The key to achieving this atmosphere is to act promptly and calmly to contain worrying behaviour and intense emotions while remaining warm and caring towards the individual as a person. Losing sight of the individual risks leading to restrictive practices and, potentially, abuse or leaving them feeling uncared for, vulnerable and alone. An inability to contain behaviour despite caring about the individual, risks spiralling into chaos. These different patterns of responding to crises are shown in Box 9.5 (also, see Chapter 13 on support styles).

Support in a crisis needs to be delivered within the attitudes, values and priorities of Positive Behavioural Support PBS (see Chapters 3 and 8). The strategies used during a crisis are tertiary prevention (the red and blue sections of a traffic light PBS plan). As highlighted in Chapter 8, *these strategies must not form a standalone approach*. Rather, they aim to stabilise a situation to allow a holistic assessment and formulation to take place. They should go on to form the smallest part of a wider PBS plan that focuses on primary and secondary prevention. Box 9.6 shows how the process of supporting an individual through a crisis feeds into the process of developing a PBS plan to improve their quality of life and achieve their potential (see Chapter 8).

The following sections give details of an approach that can be described as proactive and compassionate containment. As highlighted in Chapter 3, this approach recognises the importance of both what is done (the right intervention) and how it is done (the right way). However, at the peak of a crisis, the 'right way' becomes of critical importance because of the need for all actions to be experienced by the individual as both containing and non-threatening.

 Intellectual Disabilities and 'Personality Disorder' © Pavilion Publishing and Media Ltd and its licensors 2023

Box 9.5: Service responses to crises

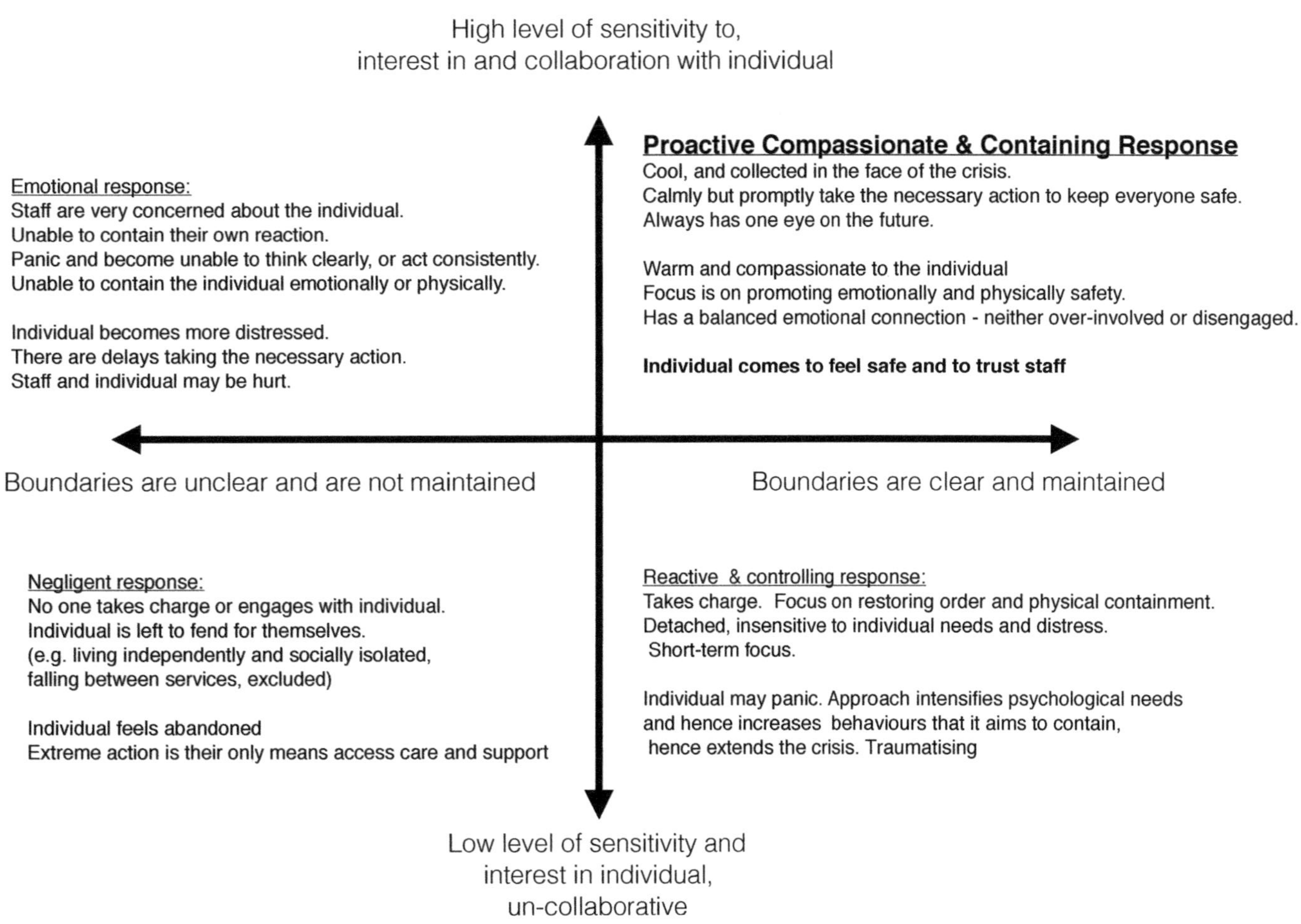

Adapted from Cameron & Maginn (2009)

Box 9.6: Linking intervention strategies to the crisis cycle and parts of the traffic-light PBS plan

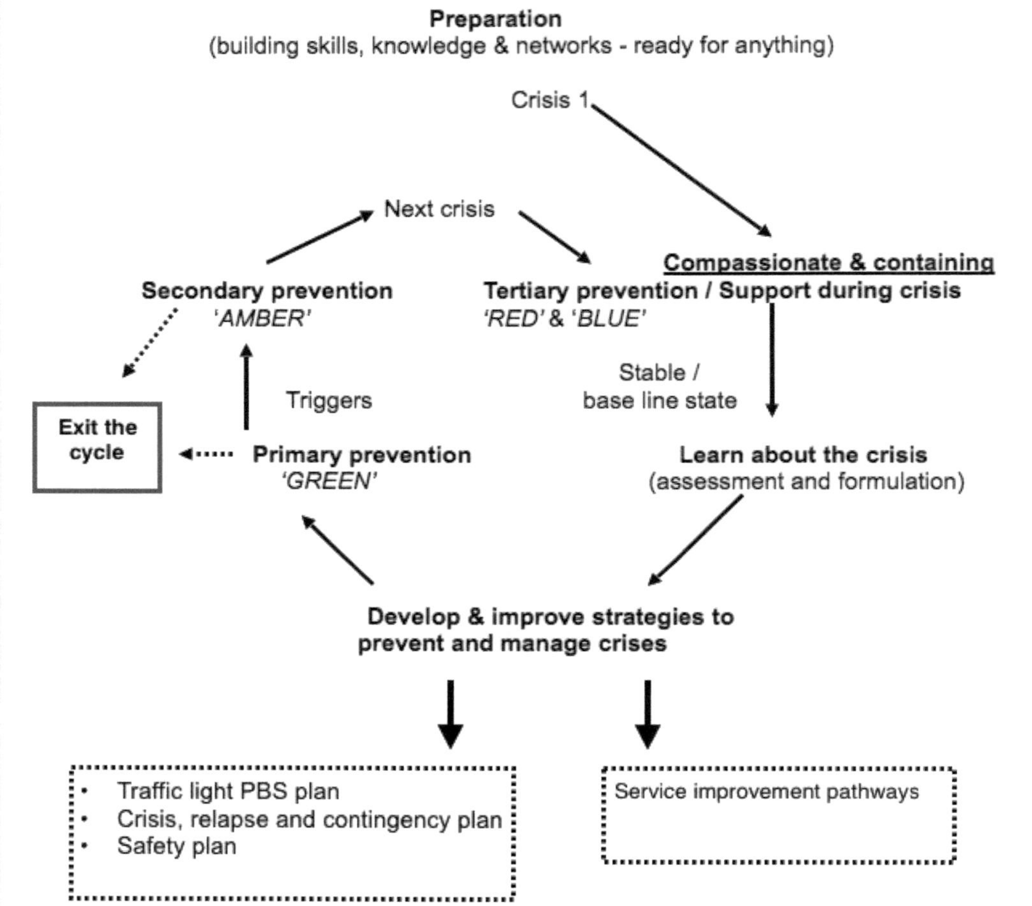

Safety first

When responding to a crisis, it is important to ensure that everyone is safe. This means considering the immediate and longer-term safety of the individual, those who live with or support them, and the general public. Decisions need to balance the risks to all involved, considering both physical and emotional safety to decide on the best course of action for each individual.

Safety may be achieved in a number of ways depending on the severity of the crisis, the individual's preferences and their insight into the risks. It might be sufficient

Intellectual Disabilities and 'Personality Disorder' © Pavilion Publishing and Media Ltd and its licensors 2023

to reduce demands and give increased physical and emotional space. An intensive support team might be able to provide the short-term skilled support needed in the individual's home.

However, sometimes crises cannot be managed safely at home. The setting may be too small, the impact on others living there too great or the setting intrinsically too risky. In such situations, support needs to be given in another more suitable setting (see Box 6.7). The individual might wish to stay in a crisis house for a brief period of respite or be supported to stay in a local mental health facility. There are significant long-term risks of admission to hospital for individuals with intellectual disabilities, particularly out-of-area placements (see Chapter 6). Hospital admission should be avoided wherever possible and, if unavoidable, this should be as short and as local as possible (Transforming Care agenda, DoH, 2012).

If the individual needs to move to another setting, this should be managed in a way that makes it as positive as possible for the individual (see Box 9.7) and helps them feel comfortable in the new setting.

Box 9.7: If it is necessary to move someone to keep them safe during a crisis

Finding space within the chaos to do the following will make the experience as positive as possible for the individual:

Explain what is happening:

- Use short sentences and a calm positive tone.
- Give honest information.
- Do not call it a 'holiday' this will destroy trust and intensify distress when they realise it is untrue.

Take time to collect essentials:

- Hospital or Care passport – a well-made passport will help everyone involved get off to the best start (see Chapter 17) maintaining familiar, person-centred routines will help individual to settle.
- Crisis, relapse and contingency plan – will contain helpful information on what works.
- Current medication.
- Several changes of day clothes and underwear.
- Slippers or light shoes for indoors.
- Toiletries (shower gel/soap, shampoo, deodorant, favourite scent, toothbrush, toothpaste).

→

■ Night clothes. ■ Hairbrush/comb. ■ Bath and hand towel. ■ Small amount of money in a purse or wallet. ■ Coat/jumper if weather is cold. ■ Comforter – any item e.g. soft toy, snuggly sweater, photo that would make individual feel at home.
Be cautious about valuable items that might be lost, damaged or stolen as this could add to distress.
Check if it is OK to take a mobile phone. If so, remember the charger and check credit.
Ensure any dependents/pets are cared for and key people informed. Let individual know this has been done.
Keep in touch and visit – let them know they are not forgotten.

Whatever setting the individual is supported in, any reactive strategies used to keep the individual or others safe must be the *least restrictive* methods and should be carried out by trained staff. (However, it important to be aware that, in an extreme situation, everyone is allowed by law to use reasonable and proportional force to escape a situation if they believe they are endangered.)

Psychotropic medication may also be prescribed in a crisis '*in the very short term to alleviate a serious risk to the safety of the [individual] or others while other, non-pharmacological programmes are implemented to manage the behaviour*' or '*if an independent mental illness or disorder is diagnosed*' (Faculty of Psychiatry of Intellectual Disability, 2016). However, individuals with intellectual disabilities are at serious risk of remaining on high doses of multiple medications (NHS England, 2016). There is a risk that medication prescribed in the 'short term' may continue beyond the crisis and be increased or added to in subsequent crises.

However distressed the individual is, it is important to help them understand what is happening and why, to seek their consent for actions deemed necessary, and to respect their wishes as much as possible, as this will increase their sense of being in control (Warrender *et al*, 2021) and hence reduce anxiety. Sometimes, individuals in crisis may not understand or accept the need for help, intervention or moving to a safer place. The law deals effectively with many of these situations through the Mental Health Act, The Mental Capacity Act, the Mental Capacity (Amendment) Act

 Intellectual Disabilities and 'Personality Disorder' © Pavilion Publishing and Media Ltd and its licensors 2023

and the common law Duty of Care. However, decisions can be complicated and need to be made promptly, hence it is important to have ready access to legal advice (NICE, 2022). In extreme situations, the police may need to take someone to a place of safety. When such actions are taken, it is still important to help the individual understand what is happening, listen to them and respect their wishes wherever possible to minimise the trauma of having actions imposed on them. The Challenging Behaviour Foundation (CBF, 2020) report 'Broken' vividly describes the lasting trauma experienced by individuals and their families who have experienced such situations.

Emotional safety and regulation

It is important to pay attention to making the individual feel safe. This is because the more frightened and out of control the individual feels, the longer and more intense the crisis will be. If crises are managed with too little attention to emotional safety, there is a risk that the approach will become reactive and controlling, perpetuating the behaviours of concern, traumatising everyone involved and making crises more likely in the future (see Box 9.8).

Box 9.8: Different approaches to worrying behaviours such as physical aggression and self-harm

Reactive and controlling	Proactive, compassionate
Overall approach	
Focus on containing the behaviour.	Focus on collaboratively understanding the individual and addressing the needs that drive their behaviour.
Aim to stop behaviours when they occur.	Aim to reduce the need for that behaviour and minimise the impact when it cannot be prevented.
Prioritises physical safety.	Recognise the interrelationship of emotional and physical safety.
Actions and interventions	
Increase levels of observation e.g. within eyesight.	Adjusting style of interaction to calm/distract/engage. Use PACE: **P**layfulness, **A**cceptance, **C**uriosity, **E**mpathy.
Increase staffing ratio e.g. 1:1.	Adjusting amount of interaction (up or down) to calm/distract/engage.

→

Spaces adapted to prevent behaviours e.g. anti-ligature, padded walls, furniture fixed to the floor. Seclusion room.	Spaces adapted to promote sense of emotional safety and relaxation. Access to relaxing spaces e.g. de-escalation room, garden.
Controlling movements e.g. locked doors.	Promoting engagement in meaningful activities.
Limiting access to items e.g. locked drawers removing items from room.	Facilitating access to items and area that can help e.g. easy access to safe garden with trampoline.
Use of medication.	Co-regulation strategies. Support to use strategies for regulating emotions e.g. breathing exercises. Channelling physical energy e.g. running, kicking a ball. Releasing/expressing emotions e.g. popping bubble wrap. Managing thoughts, focusing attention e.g. support to engage in distracting/grounding/mindfulness activities.
Over-emphasis on restrictive physical interventions, may include seclusion and rapid tranquillisation, mechanical restraints.	Low-arousal approach, 'hands off' techniques and innovative approaches to clinical holding e.g. use of safety pod™ (see Chapter 6).
Focus on the present.	Awareness that how things are done now will shape relationships in the future.
May become 'blocked' (see Box 5.10) and repeat things that are not working.	Reflection and openness means the approach is thoughtfully adjusted to reflect new understandings about the individual.
How individual might feel	
Controlled, blamed, punished, trapped, disempowered, 'done to', spied on, hopeless, helpless, inadequate, angry, frightened.	Involved, engaged, empowered, understood, hopeful, supported, safer, cared for, valued, worthwhile.

Intellectual Disabilities and 'Personality Disorder' © Pavilion Publishing and Media Ltd and its licensors 2023

Being in a setting that feels safe to them, in a warm atmosphere, and with regular and predictable staff, all help to create a sense of security despite the crisis (also see Box 5.9). Supporting an individual in crisis may require additional staff support. This needs to be done thoughtfully. Ideally, an individual would be supported by a small core team of familiar staff, who have been freed from other responsibilities by additional staff who are familiar with the setting. Being supported by constantly changing strangers who do not know the individual or the setting they are working in (as can happen if agency staff are used) is highly likely to escalate rather than improve the situation.

Individuals in crisis need staff to be both warm, caring and compassionate towards them, and cool, calm and collected in the face of the crisis and behaviours that challenge. This balance between emotional connection and emotional distance has been described as maintaining a '*compassionate distance*', '*let people affect you, but don't join them in the drowning*' (Pitonyak, 2008) or '*staying warm and keeping your cool*' (Bell, 2005). This can be promoted through training but does not come naturally to everyone; Box 9.9 summarises Pitonyak's (2009) description of the characteristics of staff who cope well with crises. This is helpful to consider when choosing which staff should comprise the core support team.

Box 9.9: Characteristics of staff who cope well with crises

- Not easily overwhelmed.
- Prepared for the worst.
- Know what to do when things get tough.
- Able to remain calm (emotionally regulated) even when the situation appears impossible.
- Able to convey verbally and non-verbally that they are OK and will do what is needed to make sure no one gets hurt (co-regulation).
- Have been through tough times before.
- Almost always have a sense of humour, but would consider jokes at the individual's expense a serious character flaw.
- Project a sense of hope to the individual about the future.

Summarised from Pitonyak (2009)

The way this core team of staff relate to an individual in crisis is central to making an individual feel secure. Box 9.10 summarises the attitudes, skills and techniques that staff can develop and use to help individuals feel safe, valued and hopeful during a crisis. These will be most effective when used within the framework of key factors that enable individuals to thrive (see Box 6.2).

Box 9.10: Supporting an individual in crisis. **The 'right way'**: *Every interaction aims to build a human connection, acknowledge distress, and leave the individual feeling more supported and hopeful about the future.*	
Do:	Reason:
Maintain compassionate distance: 'Staying warm and keeping your cool'.	Conveys the message that everything will be alright soon, however impossible that seems now.
Convey a sense of calm, normality and hope: Using body language, tone of voice, posture etc.	Emotions are 'catching'. Staff fear, anxiety or anger will increase those emotions in the individual.
Be respectful at all times: Show this in words, tone of voice, facial expression body language and 'social graces' (please, thank you).	This gives the message that the individual is valued despite the crisis and lays foundations for trust and working relationships once the crisis is over.
Attribute behaviour to distress: Be curious about/remember the individual when well: this is not who they are. '*This will pass and we will both be OK*'.	Focusing on acute distress enhances empathy and hope for change, in contrast to personal attributions which encourage blame and hopelessness.
Supporting an individual in crisis. **The 'right things'**:	
Do:	Reason:
Validate emotions: Says that their emotions are real and that it is alright to feel that way.	Helps the individual feel understood and builds a connection – they are not alone (see Chapter 11).
Co-regulation and de-escalation techniques: verbal and non-verbal strategies which reduce arousal.	Convey a sense of calm interest (see Chapter 11). Individual will unconsciously mirror staff calm.
Simplify communications: Keep interactions short and matter-of-fact. Use short, grammatically simple sentences. Share essential information. Use communication strategies known to help the individual e.g. signing, use of written symbols.	At the peak of the crisis the individual will not be able to absorb or process much information. Information overload and complex questions increase emotional distress. →

Intellectual Disabilities and 'Personality Disorder' © Pavilion Publishing and Media Ltd and its licensors 2023

'*Now and next*' will help explain what is happening.	Understanding: ■ Key messages will help them feel safe. ■ Where they are and what will happen next will help reduce anxiety.
Keep choices simple: Give choice over everyday things e.g. would you like a drink now? Tea or coke zero? (A choice of two known likes).	Individual will not be able to process information to make more complex choices. These can wait. Too many options may feed a sense of chaos. **But** giving no choices will make individual feel powerless and controlled.
Space or company?: '*Would you like me to stay with you?*' Observe: do they relax or tense up if staff move slowly towards or away from them?	Some individuals are calmed by having someone close, but others calm better if they are given more space.
Agree on and follow a plan of support: (use crisis plan if they have one)	Consistency helps create a sense of safety, build confidence and trust. Change and inconsistency increases anxiety.
Only use established, over-learnt calming techniques.	Learning new skills is stressful, difficult and can make people feel like a failure. These feelings will only add to the crisis. '*You don't teach swimming lessons to a drowning [person].*' (Pitonyak, 2009)
Respond promptly but calmly to extreme behaviours	Promptly using the least restrictive option. Using low-arousal approaches minimises trauma.

How well staff are able to respond to a crisis is also dependent on the support they receive; if an individual is to be successfully helped through a crisis it is necessary to '*support the supporters*' (Pitonyak, 2009).

Intellectual Disabilities and 'Personality Disorder' © Pavilion Publishing and Media Ltd and its licensors 2023

Supporting the supporters during a crisis

Crises have a significant impact on both family and professional carers around the individual (CBF, 2020; Warrender *et al*, 2021). Where an individual is supported by family carers, a 'whole family' approach should be taken (The Care Act, 2014) and the impact of the individual's needs on the family must be considered. This comprises four steps: think family, get the whole picture, make a plan that works for everyone, and check it is working for the whole family.

Professionals supporting individuals given a diagnosis of 'personality disorder' through crises describe feeling frustrated, inadequate, challenged, confused, uncertain, drained and personally distressed (Warrender *et al*, 2021). The negative impact on staff of supporting individuals with intellectual disabilities and behaviours that challenge has long been recognised (Hastings, 2002), including the risk of 'compassion fatigue' (see Box 11.12) and 'burnout' (see Box 13.7), high rates of sickness and high staff turnover. Teams that are well-designed and run will be more resilient to crises (see Box 7.6). In addition, a number of specific factors have been found to be important, including self-efficacy (belief in one's capacity to carry out the actions necessary to achieve positive results) and how staff are supported (Klaver *et al*, 2020). However, during a crisis is not the time to try to build skills or a sense of efficacy, or to reflect in-depth on what is going on; these need to be done once the situation has stabilised. Rather, in a crisis, staff need ready access to practical, emotional and physical support.

Take measures to ensure that staff do not become exhausted by the extra demands of the crisis. They still need breaks, both within a working day and over the longer time period. No one should be asked to support an individual in crisis for longer than two hours at a time; systems need to be in place for staff to swap roles and have short breaks within a shift. Staff should also still be able to take their usual number of rest days to enable them to 'recharge their batteries'. As a rule of thumb, no one should work more than five days without a rest day. If they do, their emotional health and ability to cope are likely to be compromised.

Time for day-to-day communication needs to be protected. The emotional reaction around a crisis can make this difficult to achieve; people may respond, 'how can we sit and talk, we've got a crisis to deal with?' However, brief and regular updates ensure that staff know the current situation, can share what they have learnt about how best to support the individual and can relay requests for anything needed to keep people safe. Space to talk about emotional reactions and concerns is also

 Intellectual Disabilities and 'Personality Disorder' © Pavilion Publishing and Media Ltd and its licensors 2023

important if the team is to pull together, provide the consistent approach needed and avoid splits occurring in the team (see Chapter 7).

Perhaps most importantly, staff need to know that their managers and the wider service 'have their back' during this difficult time. They need to know that they will be supported later to learn from the crisis and that their views will be valued and listened to. They need to know there is always a safe space where strong emotional responses can be explored without fear of seeming unprofessional or incapable (a secure base). This message can be conveyed through simple actions such as making sure supervision continues to take place, dropping by regularly to 'check in' with staff and addressing their concerns.

Learning from the crisis

Once the crisis has resolved, it is important not to simply go back to 'business as usual', however strong the emotional and practical pressures are to do this. Immediately after a crisis is the best time to build an understanding of what has happened and to work out how future crises might be contained more successfully or, hopefully, prevented. There are two parallel and interrelated strands to this process: insights that relate to a particular individual, and insights that relate to the team and wider service system.

The extent to which an individual can participate in exploring what happened in the crisis will be influenced by many factors (see Chapter 5). However, it is important that they understand that their views are respected and that the team are listening to them. The process described in Box 9.11 may help engage them as fully as possible; the more collaborative the work, the more valued and empowered the individual will feel.

Box 9.11: Exploring the crisis with the individual
Spending relaxed time with them e.g. going for a walk, kicking a ball around, sitting over a cup of tea or doing a puzzle together to build trust and creating space for them to talk if they want to.
Respect their wishes if they don't want to talk about what happened, but build bridges. *'It's OK not to talk about it, but what you think and feel matters to us.'*
Listen if they want to talk. Use active listening (Box 10.13) to follow up but do not press (shame about the crisis may trigger unconscious mechanisms, see Chapter 7).

→

Accept what they say as true for them, even if it seems incorrect, that they are 'blaming' others or misunderstood what happened. (Misunderstandings may be an important factor in the crisis.)
Validate their responses, don't trivialise or minimise. *'So, you were really upset about your mum forgetting your birthday, has she done that before?'* NOT: *'Surely all that fuss wasn't just about your mum forgetting to send a birthday card?'*
Resist giving advice or jumping in to how to do it differently.
Collaboratively build an understanding of the crisis and work together on what might help in the future (formulation see Chapter 4). Tailor intervention to the 3**R** stage the individual has reached.
If the individual is able to say what helped or didn't help them in the crisis, look at creating 'advanced directives' and include their wishes in their PBS plan and crisis relapse and contingency plan. Would a 'crisis card' (Box 9.18) and or a 'crisis box' (Box 9.17) help?
If they are in the **R**eason stage, it may be helpful to work on building skills that can help the individual cope better with triggers and regulate emotions (Box 9.16).

The staff team need to share and explore what they learnt during the crisis. Using both reflective case discussion and team reflection (see Boxes 7.7 and 9.12) helps ensure that learning applies to the individual and the wider service.

Box 9.12: Exploring the crisis with the team
Listen to your own feelings and to other staff. Seek and offer help if needed e.g. access to post-incident support. Recognise that it takes strength to accept help, and applaud each other for doing so.
Use **reflective case discussion** (see Chapter 7) to: ■ Reflect on what worked and didn't work to help the individual settle. Being non-judgmental and curious about what didn't work often gives most insight into what will work in future. ■ Reflect on how the crisis arose. Being non-judgmental and curious about vulnerabilities, warning signs and triggers that might have been missed can help prevent the crisis recurring. If there is confusion, try using a timeline to put events in order. ■ Explore worst case fears (see Pitonyak's questions Box 9.13). →

 Intellectual Disabilities and 'Personality Disorder' © Pavilion Publishing and Media Ltd and its licensors 2023

Feed insights about the individual into collaborative formulation, PBS plan and crisis relapse contingency plan. Feed insights about wider service issues into service improvement pathways for wider service issues.
Use **team reflection** (see Chapter 7) to: ■ Create space to safely explore emotional reactions to the crisis. ■ Reflect on what worked and didn't work from a wider service perspective. Being non-judgmental and curious about what didn't work often gives most insight into how staff and the service can develop for the future. ■ Be honest – are there things services are doing that mean certain needs are only met in a crisis? ■ Explore what needs to be done to improve future responses e.g. training needs, resources, communication, service model. ■ Explore what would need to happen for the right support to be activated at the right time to ensure a timely response to future warning signs and triggers. Feed insights into service improvement pathways.

It is important that the crisis is explored in a non-judgmental way. If staff feel this is about finding out what they did wrong, they are unlikely to share what may be vital information for fear of being reprimanded. It is important to use this time to explore the impact on the staff team and to think about what might help them cope better in the future. Often, it is the fear of what might happen, rather than the reality of an individual's behaviour, that causes a staff team to panic or lose confidence during a crisis. These might be fears about serious injury or death, of letting down the individual or colleagues, of doing something they know to be wrong (like shouting back), or losing their job. If these fears are not explored, they are unlikely to resolve naturally and will often mean that staff struggle to support the individual successfully in future crises. Some questions that may be helpful in exploring this are given in Box 9.13.

Box 9.13: Questions to identify what support staff will need at the height of a crisis

What is the worst-case scenario? What did you fear would happen in the darkest moments?

- To the individual?
- To other people?
- To yourself (individual staff member)?
- To your colleagues?
- To the public?

How could this be managed safely?

- What would you need if the individual had a terrible day and nothing you could do would make them calm down?
- What would you need to feel safe?
- What would you need so that you can go home at the end of a day without a knot in your stomach?
- What would you need to cope with X, Y and Z (feared outcomes)?

Adapted from Pitonyak D (2009)

Paradoxically, thinking about the worst-case scenario can help reduce the severity of any future crisis; staff who know what to do if things get really bad are more relaxed, calm and confident. These qualities help individuals feel contained and therefore help them settle more quickly.

The insights gained from exploring the crisis with the individual and the team then need to be translated into practice. Wider service issues need to feed into service-improvement processes.

For the individual, this should feed into reformulation. Interventions, including collaboratively developing a crisis relapse and contingency plan and updating PBS plans and care or hospital passports (see Chapter 17) need to be informed by the formulation. Interventions that are not informed by the formulation risk failing to address the needs underlying behaviours in crisis, and hence may make things worse rather than better. For example, the formulation for David (see Boxes 1.3 and 2.9) highlights the role of his insecure attachment, lack of a secure base and engagement with the staff team supporting him (see Box 9.14). Building trust, engagement and creating a secure base will widen his window of regulation (see Box 11.9), playing a central role in preventing further crises (see Box 9.15).

Intellectual Disabilities and 'Personality Disorder' © Pavilion Publishing and Media Ltd and its licensors 2023

Box 9.14: Formulation for David* following incident at the local pub

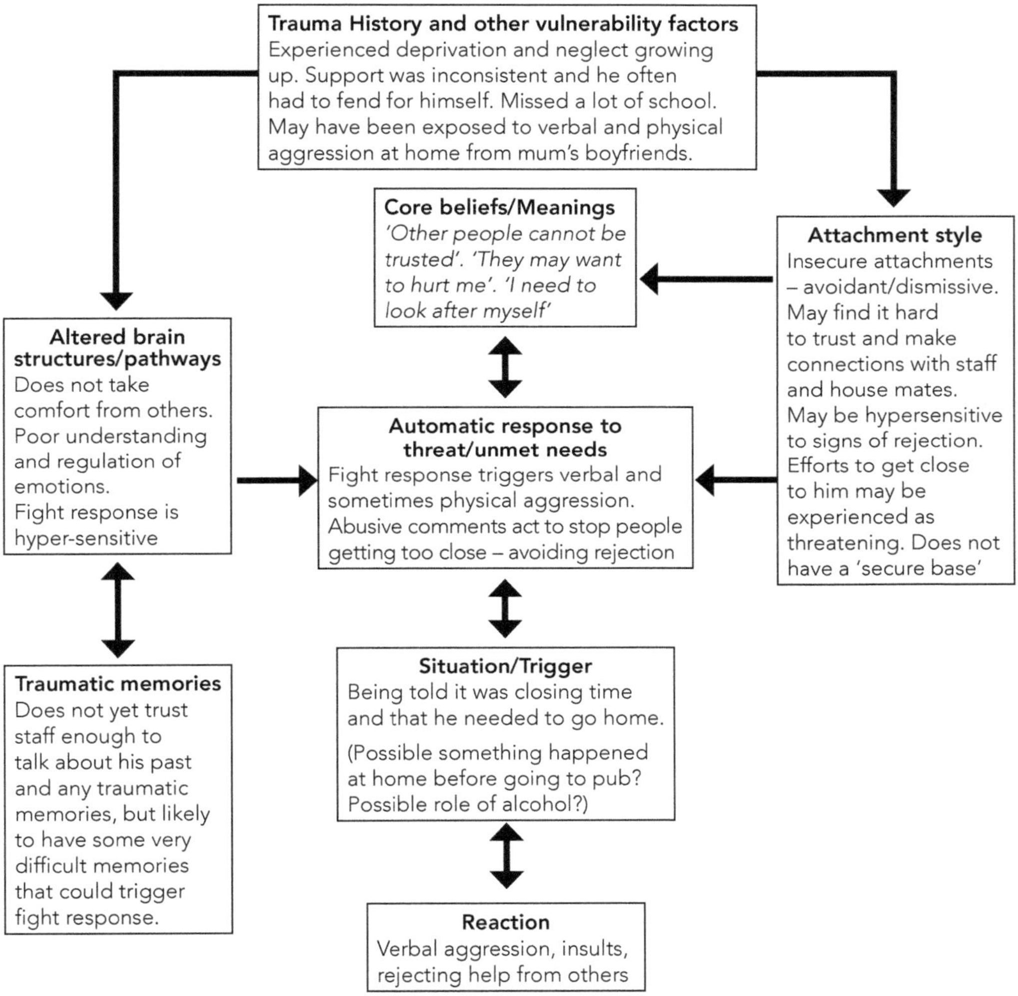

*David has been created from clinical experience and the literature. He is not based on a specific individual.

Box 9.15: Relapse crisis and contingency plan for David

Date reviewed: Date of Next Review: x/x/xx (one year from date of writing)

Persons Involved in Review: David, home manager, Keyworker, community nurse, clinical psychologist…

Has this Plan has been co-produced with the person who uses the Service?

No – We have not yet managed to engage David fully in this process. However, he knows what the plan is for and who has been involved in writing it and has told us some things he likes and doesn't like.

Briefly describe how your condition affects you: *I am fine. I just need other people to let me get on with my life. I don't know what all the fuss is about. I am only rude or aggressive if people are rude to me.*

List things people can do to help when you are in distress: *Give me space and time, don't ask too many questions. Do practical things like offering to make me a coffee or put on some music or going for a walk together. Just stay around so I can see you haven't left.*

List things that are not helpful when you are in distress: *Getting too close physically and talking a lot. Leaving me completely alone. Telling me to be more polite, getting into arguments about my behaviour. Telling me what to do.*

I do not give permission for you to talk to and work with: my mother

Who will be caring for any dependent children? I don't have any children

Any other people you care for: I am not a carer

List names and types of pets you are responsible for: I don't have any pets

Relapse Indicators/Warning Signs

Triggers – What acts as a trigger to a chain of events that may lead to crisis? e.g. significant anniversaries?

Not yet clear, but may be a build-up of tension in the house, perhaps others having visitors or birthday parties (things David missed out on and now finds very hard to enjoy? Memories?)

Early Warning – What are the signs of possible relapse?

Possibly being more withdrawn or an increase in negative comments at home?

Contingency Plan

How can you reduce the impact of these triggers?

I don't see this as my problem – others need to get their act together. Team need to find ways of engaging David and creating an secure base from which they can begin to work together.

Intellectual Disabilities and 'Personality Disorder' © Pavilion Publishing and Media Ltd and its licensors 2023

What activities tend to make you feel better? include strategies learned in the therapy programmes, note which are effective at different levels of distress. Going for long walks, making things at the men's shed, playing computer games. **Is there somewhere you could go to be with others and help reduce negative thoughts?** *I like going down the pub.* (Staff to build relationship with pub staff so leaving can be managed safely.) **Who are you going to call and what would be useful to you?** (What is their phone number?) There are people to call including___________ **Do these match your priorities in a crisis situation?** *I don't see this as my problem to sort out.*
Can you see yourself taking each of the actions identified? *Right now, I need others to manage these situations for me. I don't yet have the resources to do this myself. I need you to help me learn to trust you and engage with me first.*
Is there a Self Directed Support (SDS) Package in place? No
S**ervice actions to help prevent, identify early signs of relapse/crisis:** Regular contact, work with house staff to build trust and become a secure base for David. Liaise with pub and community policing. Referral to ISS if situation deteriorates. More detailed assessment and formulation needed to build PBS plan.
Date : Signed: Individual offered copy of Plan **YES** NO

It may be helpful for individuals who have reached the **R**eason stage to learn skills to help them regulate their emotions and behaviour to help prevent or more quickly resolve crises (see Box 9.16). However, this is not a 'quick fix' – learning skills takes time and remembering to use them in a crisis requires a lot of self-awareness and a degree of self-regulation. It can be helpful to compare learning coping skills with learning to play a musical instrument or a skilled game such as football. No one would expect someone to become a pianist or a footballer on the basis of being shown a piano or a football and being told to hit the keys or kick the ball in the goal. Rather, it takes practise, help from skilled coaches and persistence to become adept at a skill and then apply it in difficult circumstances.

<table>
<tr><th colspan="2">Box 9.16: Supporting an individual to learn and use skills that are helpful when experiencing a crisis</th></tr>
<tr><td>Identify</td><td>Collaboratively choose skills that appeal to/make sense to individual/address the underlying need, appear within their capabilities
Helpful skills might include:
Skill — Box
Relaxation — 11.16
Self-soothing — 11.17
Distraction — 15.15
Mindfulness — 15.16
Pain management — 17.10
Grounding techniques — 9.4
Alternatives to self-harm — 10.16</td></tr>
<tr><td>Learn</td><td>Use adaptations (Box 5.6) to maximise learning. Make learning fun – have short, regular sessions over a longer period of time. Adapt to changes in mood.</td></tr>
<tr><td>Create an accessible physical reminder</td><td>Be creative – make a book, put things on a phone, make a crisis card or crisis box; anything that works for the individual and reduces reliance on memory.</td></tr>
<tr><td>Practice</td><td>An individual's pattern of responding may be hard wired and over learnt. New skills need to be practiced over and over again for weeks or even months before they become familiar enough to be accessed when distressed.</td></tr>
<tr><td>Feedback and encouragement</td><td>Positive feedback about their performance and encouragement to continue with the learning process will greatly increase the chance of success.</td></tr>
<tr><td>Identify when to use</td><td>Individuals may be unaware of the subtle changes that indicate they are becoming upset. Help them identify warning signs, e.g. regular 'spot checks' during the day. (If they can't identify signs, it may help to build the skill into their person-centred daily routine so that they are used regularly). May need to learn vocabulary to talk about emotions and thoughts (see Chapter 11).</td></tr>
<tr><td>Use at early warning sign</td><td>May need help and prompting to do this at first (may never be able to do independently – and that is OK – build it into their PBS plan – AMBER)
'You look a little tense. Shall we to do something from your relaxation menu?'</td></tr>
</table>

 Intellectual Disabilities and 'Personality Disorder' © Pavilion Publishing and Media Ltd and its licensors 2023

It may be helpful to create a crisis box (Box 9.17) or a crisis card (Box 9.18) so that resources are at hand when needed. Developments in technology may also be helpful; increasingly, apps are being developed for use with smart phones that allow individuals to alert staff about their mental state, emotional or physical well-being, and facilitate access to skilled listeners.

Box 9.17: Crisis box
Is filled with fun, helpful, engaging and comforting things that can help us weather the storm of our emotions with compassion. They will help to get through a crisis.
Has lots of different names – Hope box, Happy box, Crisis kit. Call it what works best for you.
Can be a box, a bag, a backpack. Can have a big one that stays at home and a mini one that travels everywhere you go. Can be a collection of Apps on your phone.
Fill it with what works for you. If it doesn't work change it – it's your box.
This might include: **Comforts:** Things that make you feel safe, warm, loved. **Distractors:** Things that take your mind off the emotional storm, that make you smile or laugh. **Reminders:** Things that remind you of good times in the past and to come. **Ways to get help:** Contact numbers for people you can talk to (friends, family, professionals, organisations).
Examples: ■ Copy of your crisis (Box 9.15) or safety plan (Box 10.10). ■ Ear buds or headphones. ■ Essential oils, bubble bath, hand cream (check that these are not toxic if used to self-poison). ■ Favourite books, music and videos (ideally in format that is accessible but cannot be used to self-harm). ■ Relaxation guides/apps. ■ Photographs. ■ Letters from friends, letters to yourself from yourself. ■ Cuddly toys, fidget toys, stress balls. ■ Tub of Play-Doh. ■ Colouring books for adults and non-toxic felt-tips. ■ Sweets: favourite treat, popping candy, sour sweets (as a treat or as an alternative to swallowing pills, intense sensation).

Box 9.18: Crisis cards: Small cards carried in a wallet, purse or pocket. For use by individual OR to show to other people.
Prompts, reminders and key information for the individual to actively use*
Examples:
If you want to self-harm, **TALK** **T**ell someone what you are thinking and feeling. **A**sk for help. **L**isten to advice. **K**now who to call in a crisis. Ring Samaritans on **116 123**.
If you are feeling unwell or distressed **let us know what is going on**. Text Joe on _______ (key worker or care co-ordinator – text goes to a team number that will be picked up even if Joe is out of the office). **If you need to talk** Text or call X (friend or family member) Or: Ring Samaritans on **116 123** Or: Use the Y app If you need help or advice Ring 111 If you have self-harmed. Go to A&E.
Or: **Key information about how the individual wants to be supported if they experience a crisis that can be shown to others when in need.**
My name is _______ I'm feeling very distressed and out of control. Please talk to me calmly, use my name and tell me 'we can sort this together'. Contact this number (crisis team) and tell them I am unwell. They will be able to help us.
*Contents and presentation of information need to be tailored to individual's needs and preferences.

However, many individuals continue to be dependent on others to remind them when to use their coping skills. If this is the case, it is very important that this is recognised and that the individual is not blamed for failing to use the skill independently. Rather, their PBS plan and support package need to be adjusted

 Intellectual Disabilities and 'Personality Disorder' © Pavilion Publishing and Media Ltd and its licensors 2023

to build in external monitoring of their emotional state and to include sufficient support so that there are staff available to remind them to use their coping skills.

Preparation for the future

The insights gained from reflecting on a crisis can be used to build the resilience of staff teams for the future. Actions might include training, updating resources and information, networking with other services, thinking about qualities needed in crises when recruiting staff or developing procedures, and ensuring the provision of supervision and post-incident support.

Calmness, confidence and a sense of self-efficacy come from having the right knowledge, skills and back up. They can be built and maintained through preparation and practice. A crisis is not the time to be learning new skills. Hence, it is important that training is provided in anticipation of events that might happen. This would include learning about the survival cascade, the legal context, developing co-regulation and de-escalation skills, active listening and emotional validation as well as low-arousal reactive strategies. (Over emphasis on teaching reactive strategies is a characteristic of services that create and maintain behaviours that challenge – see Box 6.1).

Skills for use in crises need to be 'over-learnt'; that is, they need to be practised until the point that they become automatic, as there may be little time to think in a crisis. Over-learning also builds confidence. This is important because the more confident the staff team are that they can manage a crisis, the less likely it is to happen.

Is the approach working?

Successfully containing crises has significant benefits for the individual and those who support them. It can build stronger more trusting relationships, lead to a more helpful and individualised PBS plan and build the resilience and confidence to tackle difficult situations in the future. However, it is not always easy to tell if an approach is working.

If the approach taken to crisis management is totally effective, this is very obvious: there will be no more crises. In reality, some crises are likely to occur despite good preparation and implementation of primary and secondary preventative strategies. It may also take time for an approach to become fully effective. This can leave staff unclear as to whether the approach is working or not. However, there are a number of indicators that will show whether crises are becoming less frequent or less severe.

Where there is effective crisis management, individuals are likely to have fewer placement breakdowns, less frequent and shorter admissions, be on more effective medication regimens (and generally less medication overall), experience fewer and less-intrusive episodes of restrictive physical interventions, and have fewer contacts with emergency services. By monitoring variables chosen to reflect an individual's pattern of crises, a much clearer picture will emerge as to whether the plan is being effective. Individuals are also likely to be engaged in more positive and life-enriching activities and have more sources of fun and enjoyment in their lives.

If crises continue despite the plan, it may be that actions taken are unintentionally increasing the behaviours they are intended to reduce. For example, if an underlying need is regarded as unacceptable or unreasonable, the response sought may only be given to extreme behaviours that cannot be ignored. It may also be helpful to think about the message conveyed by the response to the behaviour. For example, it may be saying, 'We disapprove of this behaviour', 'Look, we are trying to do something' or 'We are too overwhelmed and exhausted to think', rather than actively addressing the underlying need.

When an individual has repeated crises, it is a message that the services being provided are not effectively meeting the individual's needs. It is then important to use reformulation (Chapter 4) and reflective practice (Chapter 7) to identify key issues that may have been overlooked in previous crises.

Complacency

If a crisis has been successfully resolved and an individual has been stable for a long period of time, it is easy to 'forget' about the crisis and the lessons learnt. Staff changes may mean that there is no one left who experienced the crisis. It is therefore important to have an approach that reviews the crisis relapse and contingency plan as part of the individual's annual review, checks that it is still accurate (for example, key personnel, services or phone numbers may have changed) and incorporates it into the most recent support plans (e.g. PBS plan and Health Action Plan). In this way it will remain available should a crisis occur.

Key learning points

- People may experience crises in the form of a sudden change, usually for the worse, in their social functioning, physical or mental health, triggered by events that lead to them being overwhelmed by internal or external stressors.

 Intellectual Disabilities and 'Personality Disorder' © Pavilion Publishing and Media Ltd and its licensors 2023

- Crises often seem to come out of the blue and can overwhelm both the individual and those who support them. However, it is possible to respond to crises proactively in a manner that can build stronger, more trusting relationships, lead to a more helpful and individualised PBS plan and build the resilience and confidence to tackle difficult situations in the future.
- Staff teams need to understand the changes that happen to the thoughts, emotions, physical sensations and behaviour of individuals experiencing a crisis and how to tailor their support to be most effective.
- Responses to crises that focus on achieving physical safety through restrictions are counterproductive and can prolong crises by increasing fear and distress. Individuals need to be supported to feel both physically and emotionally safe rather than be controlled.
- Maintaining a calm, confident and caring atmosphere is very helpful in resolving crises as quickly as possible. Individuals in crisis need staff to be warm, caring and compassionate towards them, but to remain cool, calm and containing towards their behaviour and emotions. This is often termed 'compassionate distance'.
- Once the situation has stabilised, a collaborative formulation of the crisis can be co-created. This information then feeds in to developing a PBS plan that includes primary, secondary and tertiary preventative strategies. This may be supported by a crisis relapse and contingency plan.
- Staff can only remain effective during a crisis if they themselves are supported. It is also important that they can access post-incident support and reflect on what has happened. This should include both reflective case discussion about the individual and a wider reflective review of the service's response to the crisis.
- Service-related issues identified when reflecting on the crisis should be fed into service-improvement pathways.
- Take care to ensure that the crisis relapse and contingency plan continues to be updated, does not get forgotten about, and that staff continue to have the skills, confidence and resources to follow it.

Intellectual Disabilities and 'Personality Disorder' © Pavilion Publishing and Media Ltd and its licensors 2023

Chapter 10: Self-harm, including suicide and self-injurious behaviour

This chapter looks at suicide, self-harm and self-injurious behaviour. It explores the similarities and differences between these behaviours and their motivations. This chapter follows the NICE (2022) recommendation for a unified approach to self-harm, rather than making decisions purely on the basis of whether or not behaviours were intended to end life. This includes suicide attempts but not self-injurious behaviour, which is primarily experienced by individuals with severe intellectual disabilities. The chapter explores person-centred risk formulation and how this can be integrated within a Positive Behavioural Support framework. It highlights the importance of staff holding positive attitudes and being able to talk about difficult issues. It identifies approaches that may be helpful for individuals with mild intellectual disabilities who self-harm.

Key topics

- Definitions, terminology and interrelationships
- Risk factors
- Self-harm and intellectual disabilities
- Developing positive attitudes
- Assessment and risk formulation
- Support during self-harm crises
- Talking about self-harm
- Alternatives to self-harm

The language chosen and the discussion of suicide and self-harm in this chapter seeks to comply with the recommendations of the Samaritans (2020). Thinking about people hurting themselves or attempting to end their lives can be worrying and distressing and can bring back painful memories. If this chapter raises any concerns, help is available (see Box 10.1).

Box 10.1: When life is difficult
Samaritans are here – day or night, 365 days a year.
You can call them for free on 116 123.
Email them at jo@samaritans.org.
Visit www.samaritans.org to find your nearest branch.

Definitions, terminology and interrelationships

NICE (2022) adopts a wide definition of self-harm:

> *'intentional self-poisoning or injury, irrespective of the apparent purpose.'*

This includes behaviours that are intended to end someone's life, usually described as suicide or suicide attempts, and those intended to make it possible to live with intense distress, usually referred to as self-harm. NICE advocates this definition because the approach to assessment and intervention they recommend is not defined by the intention of any particular episode (i.e. whether or not it was intended to end life). However, they position 'self-harm' as different from 'self-injurious behaviour' (SIB), which they define as:

> *'repetitive, stereotypical self-injurious behaviour (such as head banging).'*

NICE recommends that SIB is more appropriately supported following guidance for 'challenging behaviour' (NICE, 2015a).

The NICE definition of self-harm is used in this chapter when discussing assessment, formulation and interventions. However, understanding what is meant by the terms 'suicide', 'self-harm' and 'self-injurious behaviour' is useful as they are widely used and they may be helpful in understanding the wider picture of an individual's experiences, the service context – for example, the national suicide prevention strategy (HM Government, 2021) – and some of the barriers to receiving appropriate support.

Self-injurious behaviour

It is common for confusion to arise when discussing self-harm in individuals with intellectual disabilities. This is because some individuals with intellectual

 Intellectual Disabilities and 'Personality Disorder' © Pavilion Publishing and Media Ltd and its licensors 2023

disabilities experience SIB. This is different from what mental health services term 'self-harm' or 'self-injury' but, confusingly, is also often referred to as 'self-injury'. There are some similarities in the types of behaviour shown, but otherwise SIB and self-harm are different (see Box 10.2).

Box 10.2: Comparison of self-injurious behaviour and self-harm

Self-injurious behaviour	Self-harm
Occurs more often in less-able individuals (severe/profound intellectual disabilities).	Seen in individuals from moderate intellectual disabilities to those with superior intellectual abilities.
Associated with genetic syndromes e.g. Lesch-Nyhan, Fragile X, Cornelia de Lange, Prada Willi, Rett, Smith-Magenis.	No link to genetic syndromes. Associated with a range of risk factors e.g. deprivation, poor physical health, childhood adversity.
Not linked to impulsivity.	May be linked to impulsivity (risk increases with drug or alcohol use).
May be linked to underlying biochemical processes.	No biochemical links identified.
Associated with sensory difficulties e.g. blindness.	Not linked to sensory problems.
Associated with communication difficulties.	No link to communication difficulties – seen in individuals with excellent communication skills (although may struggle to talk about emotions).
May be associated with trauma, loss and attachment issues.	Well-established association with history of trauma and loss.
May function to get basic needs met, access interaction, manage pain or regulate arousal.	Complex psychological functions linked to emotions and mental state.
Not associated with suicide.	**At increased risk of suicide.**
Common behaviours include: poking or gouging ears, eyes, nose rectum or sexual organs, banging the head, head punching, biting or chewing self (usually arms or fingers) and picking at skin or wounds.	Common behaviours include: scratching or cutting self with objects, burning self, overdosing with medication. More rarely may include: banging or throwing head or body against something hard, sticking objects into the body or swallowing objects.

→

Associated with increased risk of residential care.	Compatible with successful life in community.
Difficult to change in adulthood – persistence rates around 70–80% over periods of up to 20 years (Biswas *et al*, 2022).	Many individuals cease to self-harm as they leave young adulthood. **Effective interventions available**.
NICE (2022) recommend consulting guideline for behaviours that challenge.	NICE (2022) recommends following guideline for self-harm, with adaptations to make this accessible.
Thinking about self-harm by individuals with mild intellectual disabilities as 'SIB' risks seeing it as intrinsic to the individual and as not likely to change, missing important functions and possible interventions.	

If individuals with mild intellectual disabilities hurt themselves, it is most helpful to understand this behaviour in the context of the NICE (2020) definition of 'self-harm': it unlikely that they are experiencing SIB. Hence, SIB will not be explored in the following sections.

Self-harm

Self-harm is the term used when a person hurts or damages themselves. This may be done in a number of ways, including self-poisoning with psychotropic medication (prescribed for mental health issues) or analgesics (pain killers), cutting or burning. Individuals may use different methods at different times. These behaviours may appear similar to those in an attempted suicide but differ in motivation: self-harm is not carried out in an attempt to end one's life. Rather, it can be seen as a way of trying to live one's life despite great distress. However, this does not make self-harm safe: it carries a number of risks (see Box 10.3).

Box 10.3: Issues with self-harm as a way of managing emotional stress.
May be followed by feelings of shame and guilt which add to emotional distress.
Brings short-term relief BUT does not address the causes of feelings so they often return.
Can add to the underlying issues e.g. other people taking more control over the individual's life.
Keeps the individual from learning more effective ways of managing emotions and meeting needs.

 Intellectual Disabilities and 'Personality Disorder' © Pavilion Publishing and Media Ltd and its licensors 2023

Intense relief brought by self-harm after a build-up of tension can be 'addictive' and making it hard to stop.
There is a risk of hurting themselves more than intended e.g. cuts may be deeper or may get infected, body may be damaged by medication (including risk of accidentally dying).

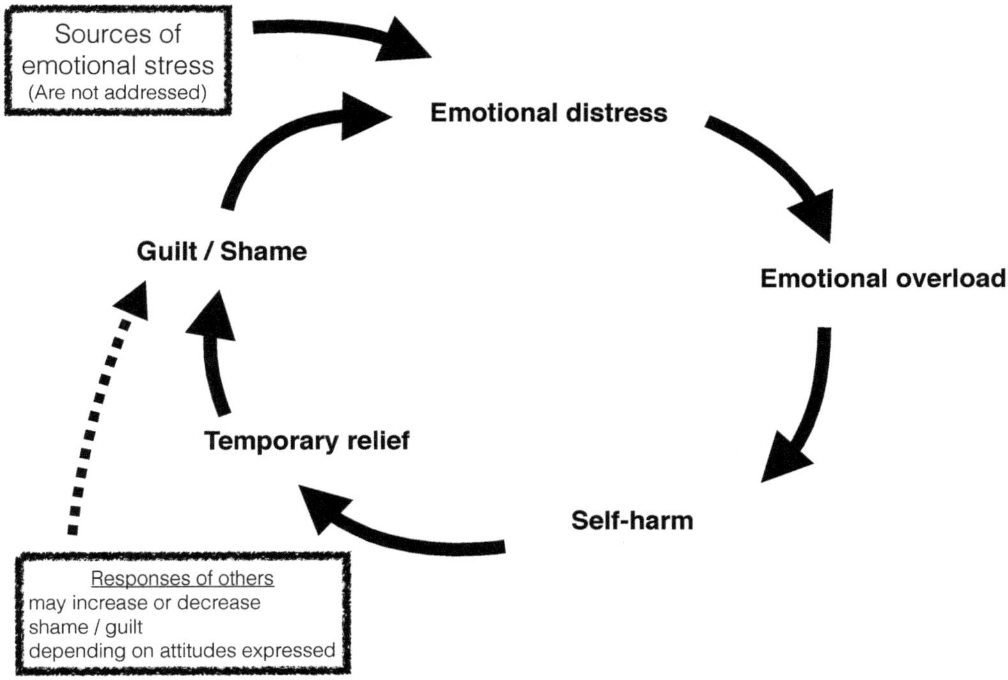

Self-harm can meet many different psychological needs (see Box 8.2) and may meet different needs for different individuals and on different occasions. For example, for one individual, it may act to reconnect with feelings after a period of dissociation, while for another it block outs emotional pain. On one occasion it may act to elicit care from others, but on another occasion be a means of self-punishment when experiencing feelings of inadequacy, self-hatred, guilt or shame. Self-harm can also sometimes be a source of comfort which enables an individual to continue to function despite intense emotional pain. Hence, it is important to recognise that each individual who self-harms does so for their own reasons and that the motivation for every episode of self-harm should be assessed in its own right (NICE, 2022).

Suicide

Suicide is the formal term for ending one's life. The Samaritans suggest that suicide should be considered 'an extreme and potentially preventable act'. It can be understood as something that an individual may do when painful circumstances exceed their resources for coping with that pain. While some people who end their lives may want to die, it is more likely they just wanted the pain they were suffering to end and could see no other way out. The most frequent methods of suicide in the UK are hanging and self-poisoning. The choice of method seems to be influenced by a number of factors including gender, culture and availability. For example, there was a significant fall in suicides by car exhaust gas inhalation in Scotland following the introduction of compulsory catalytic converters, although overall suicide rates did not change (Skilling *et al*, 2008).

There are sometimes, but not always, signs that indicate that a person is thinking about ending their life and these are explored in Box 10.4. It is important to be aware that thoughts of suicide (and risk) can vary across a relatively short time period (Royal College of Psychiatrists (RCP), 2020) and hence may easily be missed.

Box 10.4: Signs a person may be thinking about suicide: someone might show one, several or none of these	
Talking about death related topics	Dying, disappearing or going away, funerals, suicide methods or other types of self-harm: *'I'd be better off dead'*.
Looking at suicide related information	Searching for methods, seeking access to medication or objects that could be used.
Hopelessness	Saying things that suggest they believe that things will never get better; that they are trapped, or things in the future being irrelevant.
Change in mood or behaviour	A person might not seem themselves.
Depressed mood	Might seem distracted, sad, distant or lacking in concentration. Not wanting to do things they usually enjoy.
Expressions of self-loathing	Feelings of worthlessness or shame, feeling like a burden.
Sudden sense of calm:	Sometimes people feel that a solution has been found and they no longer appear depressed.
Putting things in order	Putting their affairs in order (like arranging wills, pet or childcare), or giving away their prized possessions.

Intellectual Disabilities and 'Personality Disorder' © Pavilion Publishing and Media Ltd and its licensors 2023

Saying goodbye	Unusual or unexpected visits or calls to family and friends. Saying goodbye to people as if they won't be seen again.
Seeming distant	Not wanting to talk, not replying to messages.
Self-destructive behaviour	Increased alcohol or drug use, reckless driving, unsafe sex. Taking unnecessary risks.
Samaritans (2023)	

Interrelationship between suicide and self-harm

There a number of difficulties in trying to distinguish 'suicide attempts' and 'self-harm' (see Box 10.5).

Box 10.5: Comparison of suicide and self-harm

	Suicide	Self-harm
Function	**To escape unbearable situation when there appears no hope or alternative.** To end one's life.	**Can be seen as finding ways to live with very difficult experiences.** Multiple possible functions, both managing internal processes e.g. physical and emotional pain and interpersonal functions such as accessing care.
Thoughts	Thoughts about ending one's life (suicidal ideation) and plans to do so (suicidal intent).	Multiple possible thoughts but not related to ending one's life.
History – progression	May or may not have a history of/also self-harm.	May or may not have a history of/go on to have suicidal thoughts and intent. May or may not act on these.
Outcome	May or may not result in intended death.	May result in unintended death. Are at greater risk of death by suicide than those who do not self-harm.
Perception by others	May be seen as '*deserving of sympathy*' as it was motivated by despair.	May be perceived as '*manipulative' or 'attention seeking*' and not worthy of sympathy and care.

Superficially, the major difference between attempted suicide and self-harm is motivation; a suicide attempt is intended to end life while self-harm is not. However, motivation cannot be assumed on the basis of the outcome of the behaviour. It is possible that a person may intend to self-harm but that this might accidentally lead to their death. Another person may intend to end their life but may unintentionally survive, making their behaviour look like self-harm. It is also possible that an individual may express a range of harmful behaviours that may have different motivations at different times. For example, on one occasion they may wish to end their life but on another occasion they may be trying to reconnect with their feelings.

Most importantly, there is a link between having engaged in self-harm and going on to die by suicide. In the year following an episode of self-harm, the rate of suicide increases by between 30 and 100-fold compared to the general population (RCP, 2020). For individuals who experience multiple episodes of self-harm, it is important to keep in mind that, despite this not being the motivation for previous episodes of self-harm, they are at increased risk of death by suicide (RCP, 2020).

Rather than trying to make distinctions, the focus needs to be understanding the individual's behaviour in context and finding ways of helping them keep themselves safe, finding alternative ways of regulating their emotions and on collaboratively solving problems.

Labelling a behaviour as 'non-suicidal self-harm', 'deliberate self-harm' or 'attempted suicide' without exploring its motivation is likely to lead to potentially unhelpful assumptions about what help should be given and the risks to the individual. It can increase the chances of individuals feeling misunderstood and be a barrier to engagement. Such distinctions can also trigger unhelpful attitudes, for example perceiving behaviour as 'manipulative' or as not deserving of care. Hence, when working with individuals who self-harm or attempt suicide, it is important to keep an open mind, to maintain curiosity about each incident and to listen to the individual. It is particularly important not to make the assumption that, as one act did not appear to be intended to end the individual's life, a future act will not be intended to do so.

Risk factors

Self-harm is extremely complex and can rarely, if ever, be attributed to a single cause. There are numerous risk factors (see Box 10.6), and individuals are often in more than one 'at-risk' group. On an individual basis, there are a number of

 Intellectual Disabilities and 'Personality Disorder' © Pavilion Publishing and Media Ltd and its licensors 2023

life events that may trigger an episode of self-harm (see Box 9.1). Risk can also be affected by exposure to media. Depending on how suicide and self-harm are presented, literature, news items and social media can act to increase or decrease these behaviours (Samaritans, 2020). However, it is not possible to predict who will die from suicide, and the absence of risk factors does not mean the absence of any risk of self-harm (Paris, 2019; NICE, 2022).

Box 10.6: Facts, figures and risk factors	
Rates (UK)	About 6,000 people die by suicide each year (3 times number that die in car accidents). The proportion of people aged 16–74 years who report having self-harmed is increasing (2.4% in 2000, to 3.8% 2007, to 6.4% in 2014) in both men and women and across age groups. An estimated 200,000 people are treated in hospital in England every year, the majority for self-poisoning.
Contact with services	Three-quarters of people who die by suicide have not been in contact with mental health services at all.
Risk factors	■ Age – self-harm rates peak in 16 to 24-year-old women and 25 to 34-year-old men. Suicide rates are highest in both men and women aged 45–49 years. ■ Gender – Men are 2-3 times more likely to die by suicide than women, but the rate of self-harm over all is twice as high for women as it is for men (men may choose more lethal methods). ■ Socio-economic disadvantage. ■ Social isolation. ■ Stressful life events, e.g. relationship difficulties, ■ Experiencing abuse as a child, domestic violence, trauma. ■ Loved one/family member died by suicide or exposure to self-harm (family, friends, social media). ■ Mental health problems, such as depression, psychosis or schizophrenia, bipolar disorder, post-traumatic stress disorder, or a 'personality disorder'. ■ Chronic physical health problems. ■ Alcohol and/or drug misuse. →

- Certain groups including: prisoners, asylum seekers, armed forces veterans, gay, lesbian, bisexual and transexual people (related to the stress of stigma and discrimination), individuals with autism, individual who experience epilepsy.

References: Cassidy *et al* (2022) Giambarberi and Munger Clary (2022) NICE (2020), Samaritans (2020)

Individuals given a diagnosis of 'personality disorder' are highly likely to self-harm: 50% to 80% may self-harm and, for many, this may occur frequently (Oumaya *et al*, 2008). About 10% will end their lives (Paris, 2019); this is about 400 times the rate for the general population (Oumaya *et al*, 2008).

Some may consider suicide on a daily basis for months or years, with these ideas varying in intensity over time, waxing when life events are stressful, and waning when they are not. For some individuals, years of unsuccessful interventions may precede their death by suicide (Paris, 2019).

The trauma and attachment issues experienced by individuals given a diagnosis of 'personality disorder' (see Chapter 2) mean that they may struggle to regulate intense emotions and may dissociate when stressed. Self-harm can function in different ways to help manage these feelings. When this is not understood by those supporting the individual, their responses can add to distress, making the behaviour more likely to occur. Endings (e.g. favourite staff leaving, stopping therapy, leaving hospital) may be particularly difficult for some individuals, increasing the risk of self-harm at such times (see Chapter 5).

Self-harm and intellectual disabilities

There is some suggestion that staff supporting individuals with intellectual disabilities underestimate the risk of suicide or minimise the seriousness of suicide attempts (Lunsky, 2004). Although information on rates of suicide for individuals with intellectual disabilities is not readily available, it is established that individuals with intellectual disabilities may attempt suicide and some will end their lives (DesNoyers-Hurley, 2002). The suicide risk factors identified in individuals with intellectual disabilities are very similar to those for the general population ((Lunsky *et al*, 2012; Merrick *et al*, 2006; Mollison *et al*, 2014). Additional risk factors for individuals with intellectual disabilities may be the increased incidence of autism and epilepsy.

Self-harm shown by individuals with intellectual disabilities follows the same pattern as that shown by more able individuals experiencing intense distress (James and Warner, 2005). Within inpatient settings for individuals with mild intellectual

 Intellectual Disabilities and 'Personality Disorder' © Pavilion Publishing and Media Ltd and its licensors 2023

disabilities, those who self-harmed were significantly more likely to be women, have been given a diagnosis of 'personality disorder' and had better communication skills than those who did not experience self-harm (van den Bogaard *et al*, 2018). Box 10.7 gives common triggers for self-harm experienced by individuals with intellectual disabilities with an example of one individual's experiences.

Box 10.7: Individuals with intellectual disabilities who self-harm

Most commonly mentioned triggers for self-harm:

External factors:
Being in disempowering circumstances.
Having a lack of control within their living environment.

Interpersonal factors:
Being bullied.
Arguments – either having an argument with someone else, or overhearing an argument, stress inducing interactions e.g. hearing bad news.

Individual factors:
Physical health issues. Having particular thoughts or memories, dissociation, flashbacks.

References: Heslop and Macaulay (2009), van den Bogaard *et al* (2018)

Example of the experience of self-harm

A 20-year-old woman with mild intellectual disabilities who had been given diagnoses including 'personality disorder' who experienced 55 incidents of self-harm in 41 weeks.

Staff comments on triggers:

'*Stress was the greatest trigger between not hurting and hurting herself.*'

'*Most of the time it was a longer course, during which you could see the tension rising. Conflicts with other clients, or trouble with support staff, when they had different opinions or when plans changed, disappointments, stuff with parents… eventually led to* [her] *hurting herself.*'

Individual's view: '*… I did it to get out of the traumatic flashbacks, it helped me to avoid thinking about the periods I have been through. Sometimes, I just walked up and down, did not know what to do, and then I took a knife and cut myself … I banged with my head. I often felt that a kind of ease came over me, which brought me to a normal level, so to say. Distractions helped me. Playing games, hitting a punching bag, sometimes just a hug and staying next to me, smoking cigarettes did help, but the best was just to offer closeness and seek distraction.*'

From: van den Bogaard *et al* (2018) individual 'M'

When individuals with mild intellectual disabilities self-harm, it is likely to have its origins in their experiences of adversity and trauma both in childhood and in their adult lives (see Chapters 2 and 6). It is therefore important to consider the relationship of self-harm to the individual's attachment strategies, early experiences, and the way they are currently being supported.

Developing positive attitudes

A core principle of supporting individuals who self-harm is to *'treat the person with respect, dignity and compassion, with an awareness of cultural sensitivity'* (NICE, 2022). **Every interaction aims to build a human connection, acknowledge distress, and leave the individual feeling more supported and hopeful about the future**. Central to achieving this is having positive attitudes towards individuals who self-harm and a compassionate understanding of their behaviour, rather than being judgmental or punitive. Promoting positive attitudes requires a whole-service approach covering a range of actions (see Box 10.8).

Box 10.8: Building a positive attitude to supporting individuals who self-harm	
Learn about self-harm.	Understanding self-harm helps promote compassion, keeping up to date promotes hope and positivity.
Acknowledge own emotional reaction to self-harm.	May feel shocked, confused or disgusted. May feel hopeless, powerless or helpless. May feel angry or frightened. *These are all natural human responses.* Recognise the frustration and pain of supporting someone who continues to self-harm despite everyone's best efforts.
Accept that it is natural to feel these responses.	Feeling responses are wrong or feeling guilty can make it difficult to acknowledge, accept and regulate these feelings.
Safely express these feelings.	Through peer support, supervision and reflection. Make use of post-incident support.
See the self-harm and the individual as separate. Self-harm is not who they are.	This helps to be both warm, caring and compassionate towards the individual and cool, calm and collected in the face of the self-harm. *'Staying warm and keeping your cool'* (see Chapter 9).

 Intellectual Disabilities and 'Personality Disorder' © Pavilion Publishing and Media Ltd and its licensors 2023

See self-harm as a survival strategy, that communicates unmet needs.	Seeing self-harm as conscious and planned is a barrier to compassion. Behaviours need to be understood in the context of insecure attachments, trauma, misplaced distrust and a history of needs not being met.
Learn about the individual, their past experiences and their needs, learn what helps them.	Understanding an individual better and seeing the world from their point of view, helps develop a person-centred, collaborative and constructive approach.
Learn about helpful approaches to self-harm.	Knowing there are potentially successful interventions helps promote hope and a positive, proactive approach.

Attitudes towards individuals who self-harm have become more positive (Day *et al*, 2018) although staff have been found to have different attitudes and understandings of self-harm depending on the client group they work with (Samways, 2022). However, some staff still hold unhelpful attitudes. For example, intellectual disabilities staff may see self-harm as 'part of who they are', and mental health staff may see it as 'deliberate'. The former view makes belief in the possibility of change less likely, while the latter is linked to unsympathetic and sometimes punitive responses, such as being kept waiting and being denied pain-minimising treatment (Weight and Kendal, 2013). Where negative attitudes and unhelpful responses are found, this has been attributed to lack of training, lack of staff support and limited resources (Akinola and Rayner, 2022).

To be confident and effective, staff need high-quality training and supervision. All staff need to have a good, regularly updated understanding of self-harm and helpful interventions, and to learn how to talk with individuals about their self-harm and how to keep themselves safe (NICE, 2022, recommendation 1.14). They also need supervision that takes into account the emotional impact of self-harm on staff and how best to support them, the need for reflection and the promotion of confidence and competence (NICE, 2022). Making reflective case discussions and team reflection (see Chapter 7) integral to practice will help promote positive attitudes and compassion.

Assessment and risk formulation

Assessments and interventions for individuals with mild intellectual disabilities experiencing self-harm are complex, and it is likely that most individuals will need specialist assessment. NICE (2022) recommend that assessment be carried out by 'a mental health professional experienced in assessing people with a learning disability who self-harm'. NICE (2022) also highlight the importance of making interventions accessible and taking a holistic approach that is integrated with NICE recommendations for supporting individuals with intellectual disabilities with mental health problems and behaviours that challenge (NICE, 2015a; 2016). This can be achieved by integrating effective interventions for self-harm with a trauma-informed Positive Behavioural Support (PBS) framework (see Chapter 8). Chapter 9 shows how this can be achieved if the individual first comes in to contact with services during a crisis.

Risk formulation

A priority when working with individuals who self-harm is keeping them safe. Until recently, generic risk assessment tools, allocating categories such as low, medium or high risk, were used to help make decisions about safety, support and interventions. However, this approach is not supported by current research evidence (NICE, 2022). Instead, it is recommended that assessment and support should be based on a person-centred risk formulation that considers an individual's needs and vulnerabilities, with the aim of promoting their immediate and long-term psychological and physical safety. A risk formulation is:

> *'A collaborative process between the person who has self-harmed and a mental health professional that aims to summarise the person's current risks and difficulties and understand why they are happening in order to inform a treatment plan. Formulation typically includes taking into consideration historical factors and experiences, more recent problems, and existing strengths and resources.'* (NICE, 2022)

In this process, risk factors are drawn together to construct a meaningful narrative that will inform an intervention plan. Pisani *et al* (2016) describe this as a 'preventative formulation' as the focus is on understanding what can be done to prevent, rather than just predict, future incidents. They highlight the importance of also considering foreseeable changes in an individual's life that could quickly increase risk status.

Risk formulation is very similar to the wider formulation approach described in Chapter 4, but with a specific focus on understanding the best way to keep the individual safe. The factors discussed in Chapter 4 for achieving effective formulations will equally apply to risk formulation. Box 10.9 gives an example risk formulation for 'Margaret'.

 Intellectual Disabilities and 'Personality Disorder' © Pavilion Publishing and Media Ltd and its licensors 2023

Box 10.9: Risk formulation for Margaret*

Context: Margaret was not in contact with services for mental health or people with intellectual disabilities.

General risk factors:

- Father died by suicide. Possible verbal abuse growing up. Says '*Dad shouted all the time*'.
- Experience of bullying at school and continued harassment on housing estate.
- Does not have a job, would like one but lacks confidence.
- Socially isolated – tensions in relationship with mother over father's death (feels she was to blame?).
- Self-harm has happened over a number of years, with most happening in the weeks leading up to the anniversary of father's death, but also after incidents of harassment – about 5-6 visits to A&E this year.

Triggers:

Margaret had been verbally abused by a group of teenagers.

Incident took place in the week of the anniversary of father's death.

Behaviours:

Took a whole packet of analgesics, also had deep scratches to her arms. Phoned her brother, John, who took her to A&E.

Margaret says:

'I got very upset about the things they called me and about my dad. I got confused and took too many headache pills. I wasn't paying attention and scratched myself with something.'

Resources:

- Margaret has formed a working relationship with her community nurse. Her brother is very supportive.
- Margaret likes visiting the local friendship cafe.
- Margaret has good verbal communication, can use a mobile phone, enjoys a number of activities.

Future:

- Risk persists as anniversary happens every year and continued vulnerability to harassment on estate.
- Can easily access pain killers when out – 6 shops sell them within walking distance of home.

→

- Lives with mother who is elderly and increasingly frail. Any sudden change in mother's health or her death would increase risk.
- Change in brother's circumstances making him less available would increase risk.

Risk formulation:

The recent episode of self-harm had a predictable trigger (anniversary of father's death), exacerbated by Margaret experiencing verbal abuse, her social isolation and lack of engaging activities. Margaret's self-harm appears to be helping her to manage intense emotions. If nothing changes, it is highly likely that Margaret will harm again. Margaret's current situation is fragile; it depends on the availability of her brother and her mother remaining in good health. There is a risk of a sudden reduction in her support and hence increased risk of self-harm. Margaret has easy access to items with which to harm herself and this would be difficult to change without being overly restrictive. Margaret understands that things happen when she is upset, but does not see the self-harm as under her control. However, she has asked her community nurse for help 'with my feelings' and to find a job.

As Margaret is engaging with services, it appears the risk of further self-harm can be reduced in the short-term by having regular contact with her community nurse. Longer-term risk can be reduced by supporting her to find more daytime activities and reducing her social isolation. It might be appropriate to explore options for Margaret to leave home or to set up a safety net in case the situation at home changes suddenly. Working with an experienced therapist to look at feelings and grief and guilt about her father's death could reduce risk in the longer term, but might make Margaret more vulnerable while the work is in progress. This risk could be managed by seeking Margaret's consent for the therapist to liaise with both John and the community nurse.

*Margaret has been created from clinical experience and the literature. She is not based on a specific individual.

Safety plan

If an individual frequently self-harms, NICE (2022) recommends collaboratively and compassionately carrying out a multidisciplinary, problem-solving review. This should include the individual, those involved in their care and support, and others who may need to be involved, to agree a joint plan and approach. This leads to a 'safety plan' held by the individual and shared with those they choose to include (see Box 10.10).

 Intellectual Disabilities and 'Personality Disorder' © Pavilion Publishing and Media Ltd and its licensors 2023

Box 10.10: Margaret's* safety plan: How to keep myself safe when I am upset

These are some of the things that I love in my life: My brother John, my hamster Rex, my new job.

These are some of the things that upset me, make me unwell: Being called names, thinking about my dad dying and it all being my fault. Having a row with my mum.

Signs I am getting unwell: Talking about headaches and needing pills, spending more time in my room.

These are the things that I have done when I am upset. I want to stop (description of behaviour): I want to stop getting in a muddle and taking too many pills and hurting myself.

These are the good things that help me to cope when I feel like this: Meeting up with John, talking to Rex (my hamster), snuggling up on my bed and watching cat videos on my phone.

These are the places I like to go to feel better: Going to the friendship cafe, going to the cinema.

These are the people (family/friends) who can help me when I am feeling very unwell:

Names and telephone number: John _______________

These are the professionals who can help me when I am feeling very unwell:

Names and telephone number: Lucy (community nurse), Sarah (therapist).

This is how I can make myself and my home safer: Carry my safety plan, don't have pills at home.

If I feel that I can no longer keep myself safe I will: Call or text someone who can help.

Useful contacts for me:

(local crisis line) xxxxxxxx

Medical Emergency: If I am seriously ill or my life is at risk. Call 999.

NHS helpline: When I need medical help fast, but it is not an emergency. Call 111.

Samaritans: When I need someone to talk to, call 116 123, 24 hours a day (everyday) or email jo@samaritans.org

If I can't face talking I can text Shout on 85258.

*Margaret has been created from clinical experience and the literature. She is not based on a specific individual.

The goal of a safety plan is to have a strategy in place for times when an individual is considering harming themselves or is in an emotional crisis. The safety plan will also consider the safe use of any medication prescribed to address possible underlying issues such as depression, or to help manage intense distress. Although medication can be helpful for some individuals it also carries the risk of being used to self-poison.

Having a plan in place for a time when it is difficult to think clearly can help an individual to regain a sense of control and calm. Accessible templates for safety plans are available, for example the Samaritans and Every Life Matters. However, it is important these are adapted to be meaningful for each individual and are in a form that is easily accessible when distressed. This might be on their phone or summarised as a card they can keep in a wallet (see Box 9.18).

A safety plan is very similar to a crisis relapse and contingency plan (see Box 9.15), however the emphasis is on the individual keeping themselves safe rather than the actions services should take. For individuals with intellectual disabilities, the recommendations and actions in a safety plan are more likely to be effective if they are also integrated into their PBS plan (see Chapter 8) and if the support they receive in day-to-day activities promotes emotional safety and regulation.

Support during self-harm crises

The way individuals are supported during episodes of self-harm is crucial to minimising the risk of harm and maximising the chances of building and maintaining positive working relationships. This is based on the same compassionate and containing support style used when supporting individuals who are experiencing crises and behaviours that challenge (see Chapters 8 and 9). Consequently, this section aims to provide additional, more specific information to facilitate (rather than replace) the application of trauma-informed PBS with individuals who hurt themselves.

Using this approach, staff respond to acts of self-harm calmly and kindly but with minimum fuss. Treatment of injuries is arranged promptly and given with appropriate pain relief. The individual is not criticised and their behaviour is not judged. Staff do not respond with threats ('If you self-harm again we will have to…'), punishment ('Now you've self-harmed we won't be able to…'), ultimatums ('You've got to make a choice, give up self-harm or…') or emotional outbursts (How could you? You could have died'). The focus is on actively addressing the individual's emotional needs, building a collaborative working relationship and creating a positive view of their future.

 Intellectual Disabilities and 'Personality Disorder' © Pavilion Publishing and Media Ltd and its licensors 2023

Maintaining a collaborative and compassionate support style can, however, be challenged by the need to keep individuals safe. The anxiety created by suicide attempts and self-harm and a determination to prevent physical harm can lead to a restrictive approach, relying on the use of restrictive practices (see Boxes 9.5 and 9.8). Although the need to prioritise physical safety can appear obvious, an overly restrictive approach increases emotional distress and hence intensifies the need to self-harm. For example, compulsory admission has been found to increase self-harm (Lundahl *et al*, 2023) and restrictive physical interventions intensify feelings of hopelessness (Bush and Griffith, 2017). Physical containment may still need to be used within a compassionate and containing approach (see Chapter 9). However, as a result of the principles embedded in the approach, these will be the least restrictive option and will form the smallest part of a PBS plan that focuses on primary and secondary prevention and is based on a formulation of the needs driving self-harm.

Once an individual has been supported compassionately through a crisis, it is time explore the behaviour further and to understand how it may be made less likely to occur in the future. The happier, healthier, more engaged and more hopeful an individual is, the less they will need to self-harm. Some ideas for doing this are given in Box 10.11, and the suggestions given in Box 8.12 may also be helpful.

Box 10.11: Proactive strategies to reduce the need to self-harm that can be used with individuals not yet ready to engage in interventions focused on giving up self-harm (also see Box 8.12)	
Collaboration	'*Nothing about me without me.*' The more involved the individual is, the more empowered they are likely to feel, hence they have less need to find control through self-harm.
Healthy lifestyle	Leading a healthy lifestyle builds resilience and can give the individual the energy to address their self-harm. Build a person-centred daily routine, encourage health promoting behaviours and meaningful activities – even tiny changes add up (see Boxes 17.1 and 17.10).
Sleep	Build a relaxing, personalised night-time routine to promote sleep. (Be vigilant for signs of nightmares, flashbacks or intrusive thoughts). Create a sense of safety in bedroom e.g. night light, soft toys, cuddly blankets, balance privacy with knowing help is at hand. Being well-rested increases an individual's resilience.

➔

Activities	Engaging in enjoyed, meaningful activities promotes well-being. Include activities offering different benefits: **Physical:** Walking, jogging, dancing or swimming can be used to reduce the build-up of physical tension and may also be soothing through their rhythmic, repetitive nature. **Mentally absorbing:** Computer games, word search and handicrafts need active focus and can be totally absorbing. These can be highly effective distractions from emotional distress. **Passive:** Watching TV or listening to music can provide distraction at times when an individual is too distressed to engage more actively.
Things to look forward to	Advanced planning of small treats and enjoyable activities. Include short term e.g. this afternoon, tomorrow, and longer term e.g. next week, next month. Helps to build a more positive outlook and foster hope for the future. Record in a way that helps the individual remember they are coming e.g. in a diary, on a timetable, pictures on a wall or a photo in their wallet.
Things to look back on	With consent, activities can be recorded e.g. by photos or notes in a journal. These might be added to a memory book (box 16.8) to look back on when things get tough.
Co-regulating intense emotions	Strategies for managing intense emotions before they build up can be very helpful (see Chapter 11).
Plan ahead	Identify events that may trigger strong emotions and decide how best to address these e.g. staff changes, anniversaries.
Managing triggers	Endings see Chapter 5. Anniversaries – build a constructive ritual around the event, write a survival story (Box 16.8).

Talking about self-harm

Individuals who self-harm, including those with intellectual disabilities, largely agree that they want to talk about their feelings regarding self-harm or suicide attempts and that being encouraged to do so by staff de-stigmatises sensitive topics and allows engagement with staff and their own care (NICE, 2022; Heslop and Macaulay, 2009). However, staff may be reluctant to start such conversations for fear that it may increase the risk of the behaviour occurring. In fact, thoughtfully talking

Intellectual Disabilities and 'Personality Disorder' © Pavilion Publishing and Media Ltd and its licensors 2023

about self-harm and suicide does not create or increase risk and it may it reduce it (Blades *et al*, 2018; NICE, 2022).

Staff may need to be proactive in laying the foundations and creating opportunities for such conversations (see Box 10.12).

Box 10.12: Talking about self-harm, suicide attempts and thoughts about suicide or self-harm

'I just spat it out ... there was a big ton weight coming off my body to make me feel better that somebody knew... Aye, I was glad, I was very happy with myself that I told somebody'

Individuals with intellectual disabilities who self-harm said they found it easier to talk about self-harm if staff were:

- Easy to talk to and a good listener.
- Non-judgemental, accepting and respectful.
- Trustworthy and honest.
- Caring, generally kind and nice.
- Understanding and perceptive.
- Calm and having the ability to help others calm down.

(Heslop and Macaulay 2009)

Take the time to get to know them and for them to know you: individuals are more likely to talk to people they know, who have shown that they are non-judgemental and trustworthy e.g. listening to and responding with kindness to everyday concerns (Heslop and Macaulay, 2009).

Getting conversations about self-harm started

Remember: Thoughtfully talking about suicide does not create or increase risk and it may it reduce it (Blades *et al*, 2018).

Share information: Some individuals find reading accessible information about self-harm a good starting point. A leaflet can also be handed to staff as a non-verbal way of starting a conversation.

Time and place: Think about where and when to have the conversation before you start. Choose a time when the individual appears calm and relatively relaxed and you know you will not be interrupted or have to rush off. Individuals may prefer to talk while they are doing something e.g. chatting over coffee, walking.

→

Approach: Take a gentle approach, be understanding, tactful and non-judgmental. Use 'open ended' questions (see below). Possible opening comments and questions might be: *How are things going? I'd like to help.'* *How about a cup of coffee and a talk about things?'*
Gentle prompting: Encourage the individual to express whatever they are feeling, even if it is uncomfortable. If the individual hasn't mentioned self-harm, bring up the subject in a non-confrontational way: *'I've seen scratches on your arms. I want to understand what you are going through.'*
Let individual set their own agenda: Let the discussion to go at the individual's own pace, don't ask lots of questions.
Dealing with rebuffs: If the individual does not want to talk, do not push. Just express calm concern for them and let them know you're available whenever they do want to talk or need support.
Respond to approaches: When an individual is ready to talk, they may approach staff but may not express the reason they want to talk. Make space to discuss minor concerns the individual brings and then ask questions such as *'Is there anything else bothering you?'*
Confidentiality: Explain how confidentiality works in your setting e.g. shared notes. Make it clear that you cannot promise to keep information private e.g. *'If I am worried about your safety (or that of someone around you or that of a child), I may need to share information and seek advice. I will tell you of any actions I feel I need to take.'*

Paradoxically, when individuals spontaneously talk about attempting suicide it is sometimes, disrespectfully, dismissed as 'attention seeking' and hence unlikely to be acted upon. There is no evidence that anyone who discloses suicidal plans is at lower risk of acting on them. A disclosure of a suicidal plan should always be taken seriously. By talking about suicide, an individual may be seeking help to stay alive or to solve insoluble problems, eliciting care or trying to let you know how really terrible they feel in the only way they know.

Conversations about self-harm and suicide need to occur within the context of the approach to building positive, collaborative working relationships explored in Chapter 5, and be tailored to the needs and communication abilities of each individual. It is important to help the individual express their concerns as fully as possible, without feeling pressurised or judged. An approach that is particularly

 Intellectual Disabilities and 'Personality Disorder' © Pavilion Publishing and Media Ltd and its licensors 2023

helpful when trying to talk about difficult topics is that of 'active listening'. Active listening uses verbal and non-verbal techniques to help the other person open up and put their thoughts into words and explore issues for themselves. These techniques are explained more fully in Box 10.13.

Box 10.13: Active listening

Active listening is an approach that helps the individual to open up and share thoughts and feelings. Rather than passively leaving the individual to talk, it uses sensitive questions to help the individual express themselves more fully and clarify their thoughts. It does not make assumptions about what the individual is experiencing (e.g. '*I know just how you feel*'), does not give glib solutions (e.g. '*There's nothing to worry about*') and is not judgmental (e.g. '*How could you!?*') Useful techniques to achieve this include:

Body language: Sit in a relaxed but not totally laid-back position. Turn towards the person. Look at them (but don't stare). Use gestures and facial expression.

Pace and silences: Let the individual set the pace of the conversation. Don't rush them. Allow some silences, don't jump straight in; it can take time to find the words to express difficult thoughts and feelings. Most people find silence difficult and want to fill it. Resist this temptation. Use the techniques below to gently keep the conversation flowing.

Open questions: Questions that cannot be answered '*yes*' or '*no*'. This opens the conversation up and encourages the person to give more information. For example: '*How are you feeling?*' (answer 'angry') vs '*Are you feeling sad?*' (answer 'no'), '*What's worrying you?* vs '*Are you feeling worried?*'

Small questions: Big questions such as '*How can I help?*' or '*What's wrong?*' can be overwhelming, the person may not know where to start to answer them.

It is more helpful to ask smaller questions such as '*I can hear you're upset, how long have you been feeling like this, what lead to you feeling like this?*'

Summarising: This pulls together what the person has been saying, '*So you want your independence but you get lonely in your flat?*' This shows that you have been listening and have understood what has been said.

Reflecting: Repeating back a word or phrase can encourage people to go on. If someone says, '*It's been really difficult recently,*' but then stops talking, you can keep the conversation going by repeating, '*So, it's been difficult*'. This helps them keep track of what they were saying.

Clarifying: Individuals often avoid talking fully about the most difficult things and will just give a hint of what they are thinking. If the individual mentions something important but does not elaborate, it can be helpful to use questions such as, '*Tell me more about…*'. Sometimes just a '*Yes*', '*Go on*', or '*I see*' can help.

→

Reacting: It is important to have an emotional balance. An individual may not want to talk if they think what they are saying is upsetting the listener. However, if the listener seems completely unmoved this may stop the person because they think they are boring the listener or the listener does not care. Phrases such as '*That must have been difficult*', or '*You've had an awful time*', show that the listener is aware of but not overcome by the feelings.

It is important to think beyond encouraging an individual to open up, and to consider what they might say once they start talking. Staff need to be prepared, emotionally, to cope with whatever they might hear, however distressing. By taking up a position of 'compassionate distance' (see Chapter 9) staff will be able to respond with warmth and concern but not be overwhelmed by the distressing nature of the conversation. It is also important to understand the limitations of confidentiality in preparation for hearing things that might impact on the individual's safety (See Box 10.14).

Box 10.14: Confidentiality: protecting personal and sensitive information about individuals, unless there is significant risk to the individual, the public or children.

Sharing confidential information: When a significant risk to safety is imminent and not sharing information would be likely to result in death or serious injury, then relevant information can and should be shared with those people for whom consent has been given to share.

Individuals are safer if essential information is shared between services and with key people in the individual's life.

If consent to share information is not given, staff face the choice of breaching confidentiality (with risks to the working relationship) or withholding information that might make the individual safer.

Guidance has been developed to help with these difficult decisions (Department of Health and Social Care, 2021; Zero Suicide Alliance undated) within the context of the current legal framework.

If information needs to be shared against the individual's wishes, they need to be told what information will be shared and with whom and why, to minimise their sense of betrayal. This can be discussed openly and the individual can be given choices. For example, staff might say, '*Your doctor needs to know you aren't taking your medication. Do you want us to tell her together or would you rather I speak to her? Or would you like to write it down for her?*' This approach gives some choice and control to the individual while ensuring the important information is shared.

NICE (2022) stress the importance of continuing to involve the individual in decisions about their support, even when staff have had to go against their wishes.

 Intellectual Disabilities and 'Personality Disorder' © Pavilion Publishing and Media Ltd and its licensors 2023

For individuals who do not want to think about or talk about self-harm, the tree of life (Ncube 2006, see Box 4.7) might offer a more engaging approach. Collaboratively creating a tree of life can help put self-harm in the wider context of someone's life and can help identify strengths and positive relationships.

Understanding self-harm

Once an individual is able to talk about how they are feeling it may be possible for them to start to understand and potentially engage in trying to find ways of reducing and regulating their emotional distress and meeting psychological needs without self-harm. Specialist, CBT-informed psychological interventions to reduce self-harm recommended by NICE (2022) will be delivered by appropriately trained professionals. However, if support staff have a good knowledge of self-harm and ways of regulating intense emotions (see Chapter 11) they can work with the individual to reinforce and generalise the work in therapy sessions. Individuals are more likely to use techniques they have learnt if given the encouragement of those who support them in everyday activities.

It is helpful if individuals understand why people might self-harm, know that they are not alone, and that there are things that they can do when they feel able to try to change their behaviour. There are a range of accessible resources available from organisations such as Mind and the Samaritans that can be tailored to an individual's needs. These discussions can be recorded in a format that is helpful for the individual. For example, staff can work with the individual to decide on words, pictures, drawing or paintings that summarise what the individual does and why they do it. Conversations should also be optimistic about the possibilities of replacing self-harm and consider some of the options open to the individual. Where an individual is not yet in a position to resist the urge to self-harm, work should follow NICE (2022) recommendations on 'harm minimisation' (see Box 10.15)

Box 10.15: Harm minimisation

An approach that accepts the individual's continued urge to self-harm while aiming to keep long-term damage and frequency of injury to a minimum. It can include suggestions to avoid, delay or reduce self-harm.

If an individual is engaged in on-going care and intervention but is not yet in a position to resist the urge to self-harm, only consider harm minimisation strategies:

- In the spirit of hope and optimism, and to reduce the severity and/or recurrence of injury.

→

- As part of an overall approach to the individual's ongoing recovery-focused care and support, and not as a standalone intervention.
- After being discussed and agreed in a collaborative way with the individual and their family members or carers (as appropriate), and the wider multidisciplinary team.

May include: distraction techniques and coping strategies, approaches to self-care, wound hygiene and aftercare, factual information about the potential complications of self-harm and the impact of alcohol and recreational drugs on self-harm.

Although 'safer' self-harm strategies are often considered a harm minimisation strategy, NICE (2022) neither recommends, nor recommends against them.

Harm minimisation may not be appropriate for all individuals .

NICE (2022) recommendations 1.11.11-13.

Alternatives to self-harm

Alternatives to self-harm are generally secondary prevention (amber), that is, actions taken in the escalation phase of the time-intensity model (see Box 8.9), as levels of arousal or distress are increasing. Some are tertiary prevention (red) intended to replace more harmful behaviours at the point of crisis. It is therefore important that these are not standalone interventions but form part of a PBS plan that has primary prevention as its main component (see Chapter 8).

Alternatives to self-harm aim to meet the psychological needs underlying self-harm. Hence, it is important to have a clear hypothesis of what function self-harm is serving for an individual before choosing alternatives. For example, running flat out may be helpful if the individual needs to release physical tension and anger. However, if the individual needs to feel cared for, running is unlikely to help. Instead, it may be helpful to have a pampering session such as a warm bath with scented oil followed by massaging in body lotion. Some alternatives, grouped by the needs they might meet, are given in Box 10.16.

Box 10.16: Alternatives to self-harm

To communicate, express pain or intense feelings:

- Call or text a friend or listening organisation such as the Samaritans.
- Paint, draw, or scribble on a big piece of paper with red ink or paint.
- Write feelings in a journal, story or poem.
- Play music that expresses the emotion.

Intellectual Disabilities and 'Personality Disorder' © Pavilion Publishing and Media Ltd and its licensors 2023

To regulate emotions – calming down:

- Take a warm bath or shower.
- Stroke or cuddle with a dog or cat.
- Wrap up in a warm blanket, drink a mug of hot chocolate.
- Massage own neck, hands, and feet, rub in scented body lotion.
- Listen to calming music, smell something nice like lavender oil.
- Go for a walk in the park or a garden.
- Breathing exercises, mindfulness exercises.

To release tension or vent anger:

- Exercise vigorously – run, dance, skip, do press-ups or sit-ups.
- Play something that involves hitting/kicking/throwing a ball – squash, swing-ball.
- Punch a cushion or mattress or scream into a pillow, use pillow to hit a wall.
- Squeeze a stress ball, Play-Doh or clay.
- Rip something up (sheets of paper, a magazine, phone book), pop bubble wrap.
- Make some noise (play an instrument, bang on pots and pans, shout loudly).

To reconnect with life and feelings

- Take a cold shower or bath.
- Hold an ice cube in the crook of an arm or leg, squeeze it hard in a hand or press it firmly on the place that would otherwise be burned*, stick sellotape or a plaster on skin then peel it off*.
- Chew something with a very strong taste e.g. sour sweets, (mild) chilli pepper, root ginger, peppermint, a lemon or grapefruit peel*.
- Rub liniment on area that would be burned or cut*.
- Put a elasticated bracelet on wrists, arms, or legs and snap it*.

To escape:

- Go through the ritual but don't actually do the injury.
- Use mindfulness techniques.

To feel cared for:

- Put on bandages/dressings without the injury.
- Have a manicure, pedicure or other pampering beauty treatment.
- Make a favourite meal/food.

To focus:

- Do a puzzle of some kind – word search, Rubrik's cube, cross out all the 'o's in a newspaper.

→

To see blood or make marks:

- Draw on self with a red felt-tip pen, use red food colouring on places that would have been cut.

To replace self-poisoning:

- Swallow sweets such as Smarties or Tic Tacs.
- Drink something bitter such as tonic water, or pure lemon juice*.

To feel in control:

- Write lists, tidy up, declutter, weed the garden, clench and relax muscles.

To delay self-harm:

- Sit on hands, count for as long as possible.

* be thoughtful about the message these techniques convey, they are aiming for a strong sensation, not to cause physical pain or to punish the individual.

This list is not exhaustive and, with support, individuals may be able to create their own personal alternatives. It is also important to recognise that these alternatives are unlikely to give the same intensity of experience as acts of self-harm. However, they are all devoid of the negative effects of self-harm and, combined with efforts to improve the individual's quality of life, physical and mental well-being and regulate intense emotions, may greatly reduce the frequency or intensity of harm.

It is important to plan in advance what alternatives might be helpful as some may require particular items to be available, for example bracelets, felt-tip pens and food colouring. It can be helpful to add these items to the individual's crisis Box (see Box 9.17). It is also important to think about whether there is a risk of the alternative being used to self-harm. For example, aromatherapy oils are great for providing intense smells and helping an individual reconnect with their senses or to evoke pleasant memories. However, some may be harmful if they are drunk. Where this might be a risk, it is better to add the oil to a few tissues and keep it in an airtight pot.

Overall, support for individuals who self-harm will be most effective when these behaviours are seen in the context of the individual's life experiences and are part of a wider therapeutic endeavour to improve their overall quality of life.

 Intellectual Disabilities and 'Personality Disorder' © Pavilion Publishing and Media Ltd and its licensors 2023

Key learning points

- The inclusive definition of self-harm given by NICE (2022) – '*intentional self-poisoning or injury, irrespective of the apparent purpose*' – avoids making complex distinctions and the associated risk of making unhelpful and potentially harmful assumptions about the motivation of behaviours.
- The term 'self-harm' more accurately characterises the experiences of individuals with mild intellectual disabilities, including the range of underlying psychological needs and the associated increased risk of death by suicide. This is different from the SIB experienced by individuals with more severe intellectual disabilities.
- Self-harm is extremely complex and can rarely, if ever, be attributed to a single cause. There are numerous risk factors and individuals are often in more than one 'at-risk' group. When individuals with mild intellectual disabilities self-harm, it is likely to have its origins in their experiences of adversity and trauma both in childhood and in their adult lives.
- Supporting individuals who self-harm with respect, dignity and compassion, must be central to all interactions to promote engagement with services and reduce the risk of further self-harm. Positive, hopeful attitudes can be promoted through training, supervision, reflection and support.
- Individuals who attempt suicide or self-harm should have a multidisciplinary, collaborative risk formulation and safety plan.
- Individuals with mild intellectual disabilities who self-harm can be supported by integrating self-harm-specific recommendations within an attachment and trauma-informed BPS approach offering the right support at the right time.
- Approaches to keeping individuals safe need to proactively address the psychological needs that lead to self-harm as well as keeping individuals safe. An emphasis on physical safety can lead to overly restrictive practices that may act to increase the risk of self-harm.
- All staff need to be aware of the benefits of talking about self-harm and to be able to use active listening to help individuals explore their experiences.
- Alternatives to self-harm can be helpful within a wider PBS plan that promotes well-being and engagement but should not be used in isolation.

Chapter 11: Emotional distress – containing and regulating emotions

This chapter explores emotions, the functions they serve and how they relate to other areas of functioning. It looks at how emotions are regulated and what is meant by validating emotions. It considers how the experience of emotions and emotional distress may be influenced by factors such as developmental trauma. It looks at how emotions may be experienced by individuals given a diagnosis of 'personality disorder' and individuals with intellectual disabilities, and the difficulties they may experience. It looks at how individuals experiencing these difficulties can be supported and helped to understand, accept, tolerate and regulate their emotions.

Key topics

- Emotions
- The interrelationship of emotions with thoughts, behaviour and physical sensations
- Regulating emotions
- Understanding and accepting emotions
- Emotions and 'personality disorder'
- Emotions and intellectual disabilities
- Assessment and formulation
- Supporting individuals to regulate their emotions
- Promoting understanding and acceptance of emotions
- Promoting self-regulation

Emotions

For something that is a universal part of human experience, emotions are remarkably difficult to define (Mulligan and Scherer, 2012) and there are many different theories about what happens when an emotion is experienced. An emotion may be described as a state of mind that arises in response to internal events (such as thoughts or physical sensations) or external events (such as other people's behaviour). An emotion is usually a short-term experience. When an emotional state persists for any length of time it is usually referred to as a 'mood'.

There is debate about how many emotions there are. Ekman (1999) suggested there are six basic (hard wired) emotions: anger, disgust, fear, sadness, happiness and surprise. These hard-wired emotions are the first instinctive response and are directly connected to the stimulus or event. They have a wide variety of expressions, from mild to intense, and there is an extensive vocabulary to reflect these differences (for example, 'sadness': melancholy, low, down, depressed, grief-stricken). These hard-wired emotions can also be combined and influenced by social experience to create many different, recognisable emotions (Cowen and Keltner, 2017). Secondary emotions are learnt, habitual reactions to hard-wired emotions, which may have an evaluative component or act to replace an emotion someone finds painful with a less painful one (Evans, 2023). For example, someone's instinctive reaction to an exam result might be happiness followed by pride in their achievement, or guilt that they have done better than their studying partner. The meaning an individual gives to an emotion (subjective truth) will also be shaped by their past experiences of that emotion (de Bruiji *et al*, 2021).

The process by which emotions are built, come to be understood, regulated and expressed is part of a process termed 'emotional development'. Emotional development is an evolving concept with many different meanings (de Bruijn *et al*, 2021) which is closely interrelated with, and overlaps, other aspects of development, particularly social development and attachment (see Chapter 2). Building on the work of people such as Mahler (1979), a number of stages have been suggested (see Box 11.1).

Box 11.1: Stages of emotional development

Adaptation (birth–6 months)	Early awareness of self as separate from parent. Distress from intense stimuli, unmet physical needs. Balanced through rhythm and regularity.
Socialisation (7-18 months)	Building trust and attachment to parents. Early two-way communication and wanting interaction. Basic emotions expressed. Need to be together/connected, wants parent to be around and always available. Fear of separation and loss of parent.
Individuation or 'give and take' (19 –36 months)	Exploring, finding own will and expressing this, in context of secure attachment. Own self is central. Need for autonomy, fear of loss of control but looks for boundaries. Quick temper, anger, jealousy. Impulsive and has trouble sharing.

 Intellectual Disabilities and 'Personality Disorder' © Pavilion Publishing and Media Ltd and its licensors 2023

Identification (3-7 years)	Sense of self as separate. Security comes from care giver being there at recurring moments rather than always present. Interest in peer group, developing identity. Fear of exclusion and letting caregiver down. Emotions include love, shyness and fear of failure.
Reality awareness 7+ years	Parent has a coaching role. Shame, insecurity, rapid mood swings. Increasing ability to inhibit and self-regulate emotions and behaviour. Aware of and seeks social acceptance.
References: Frankish (2019; 2021), Sappok and Conty (2021), Vonk (2021)	

It is sometimes suggested that emotions serve no useful function for modern humans; that they disrupt and disorganise behaviour and that they are illogical. While it is true that emotions can be messy, they do in fact serve a range of useful functions. Some of the most frequently suggested functions are given in Box 11.2.

Box 11.2: Functions of emotions
Maintain social systems e.g. form attachments, maintain co-operative relations.
Communicate with or influence others: tell others how someone is feeling and hence how to interact with them – comfort someone who is sad, avoid someone who is angry.
Communicate information about the situation to the individual experiencing the emotions e.g. awareness of danger, 'gut feeling'.
Prepare for action/keep safe through the survival cascade (see Box 9.3).
Avoid physical threats and danger.
Motivate to act e.g. overcome obstacles.
Prioritise actions: help people decide what they want to do and what is most important to them.
Help encode key information about a situation – events may be remembered more clearly if linked to emotions.
Enrich the experience of life.
Protection from emotional pain. Secondary emotions may act as protection from instinctive reaction, covering them with something experienced as less painful e.g. anger replacing sadness, or as a judgemental response to the emotion, such as guilt for feeling angry. However, these may get in the way of addressing the needs indicated by the instinctive emotion.

There is general agreement that emotions comprise a number of different components, although every theory has a slightly different view of what the components are and how they interact. The most commonly suggested components are given in Box 11.3.

Box 11.3: Commonly suggested components of emotions

Expression	External signs of emotion e.g. facial expression, changes to voice, posture and body language.
Subjective experience	How an individual experiences the emotion (in contrast to what they may show to others through the expression of emotion).
Action tendencies or motivation	The desire to act e.g. run away, attack, approach.
Physical reaction	Physiological changes e.g. heart rate, breathing, circulation, sweating.
Interpretation or thoughts	Appraisal and interpretation of the events, situation and physical reactions.

Some approaches include physical reactions and thoughts about the situation as part of emotion, while others view these as separate, but closely involved. Whichever view is taken, emotions, thoughts and physical sensations are all interrelated and shape the way individuals behave.

The interrelationship of emotions with thoughts, behaviour and physical sensations

As a result of the way information is processed by the brain, emotions are closely interwoven with thoughts, behaviour and physical sensations (see Box 15.8). Neurologically, cognition and emotion are not independent functions (Wijnroks, 2021). Emotional distress is partly caused by external events but also by how those events are interpreted. Two people may respond to the same situation with completely different emotions because of differences in the way that situation was interpreted. Interpretation also influences responses to the physical sensations that accompany emotional reactions. For example, a racing heartbeat might be interpreted as a sign of excitement or as being a heart attack. The first interpretation will add to enjoyment while the latter might spiral into a distressing panic attack. How a situation is perceived can also influence the physical response to emotions. For example, one person may perceive a situation as threatening and their

 Intellectual Disabilities and 'Personality Disorder' © Pavilion Publishing and Media Ltd and its licensors 2023

resulting fear triggers their survival cascade. Another, who does not perceive the situation as threatening, will remain calm and relaxed (see Box 9.3).

The relationship between thoughts and emotions can also work the other way. An individual's mood or emotional state influences what they pay attention to, how events are interpreted, what is laid down as a memory and what memories can most easily be recalled. For example, when someone is feeling unhappy, they are more likely to notice 'put downs' than when they are feeling cheerful. Events linked with strong emotions are more likely to be encoded in memory. Once an event is encoded in memory, a person will be most likely to remember that event when in a mood similar to the mood they were in at the time the memory was laid down (state-dependent memory) (Mcleod, 2023a). Whatever mood a person is in, or emotion they are experiencing, they are more likely to recall events that have a similar emotional content. Hence, when happy a person will find it easiest to recall happy events from their past, but if they are feeling depressed they will recall sad events, and, if angry, will recall past annoyances.

The relationship between emotions and behaviour is complex. Emotions can create a drive, motivation or impulse to behave in a certain way (see Chapter 14). However, people may or may not act on that drive. Behaviour that is driven purely by emotion is often an 'instinctive', rapid response to an immediate situation (see Box 9.3 and Box 15.10). This is often helpful in an emergency, but it is less helpful in everyday life. Mostly, reactions are more thought through, with the emotion felt being only one of the issues that a person considers as they choose to act.

These complex interrelationships can be explored using the Cognitive Behaviour Therapy (CBT) hot cross bun diagram (see Box 15.9).

Individual differences

There are considerable differences in the patterns and intensity of people's emotional experiences. These differences are influenced by the individual's biology (such as genes, brain pathways and hormones), their personality, their experiences growing up, and their present circumstances. There are differences in the ease with which emotions are triggered and resolved, the time they are experienced for, the strength of emotions, how much they fluctuate and what is the predominant emotion or mood. People also differ in their ability to tolerate and regulate unpleasant emotional states and the extent to which this has a negative impact on their quality of life. Some will have a broad arousal range in which they are able to function comfortably, others will have a much narrower band and may quickly become over or under-aroused. This is referred to as their window of tolerance (Siegel, 1999) or window of regulation (see Box 11.4). When a person is operating within this window, they can effectively contain and cope with their emotions: they experience a range of emotions, but these do not get in the way of their everyday functioning.

11.4: Windows of regulation

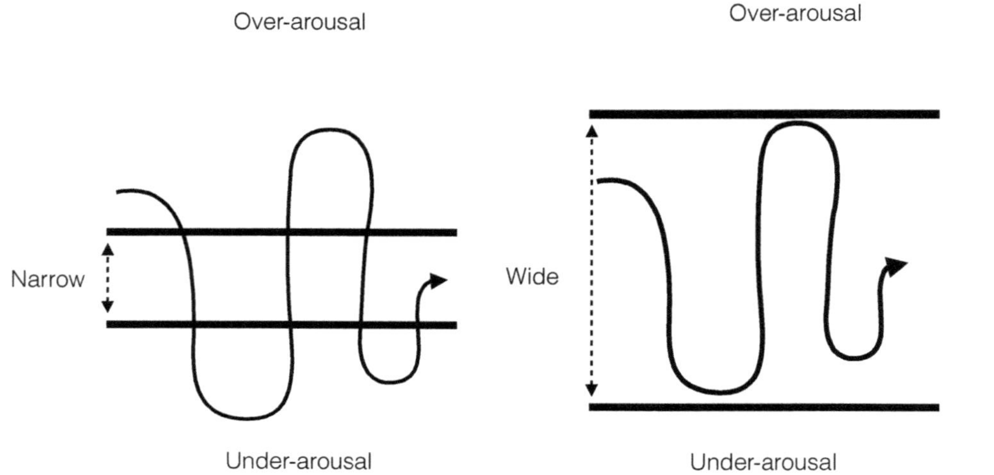

Narrow window of regulation
Limited ability to regulate emotional arousal

Wide window of regulation
Greater ability to regulate emotional arousal

(Siegel 1999)

When someone's level of emotional arousal is outside the window of regulation, it is referred to as being 'dysregulated'. Emotion dysregulation is defined as patterns of emotional experience or expression that interfere with goal-directed activity (Thompson, 2019). When someone is 'dysregulated', they are overwhelmed by their emotions and struggle to return to 'normal'. They might be so angry that they smash their belongings and assault someone, or be so down that they cannot get out of bed and have thoughts of, or attempt, suicide. Some individuals are easily pushed into dysregulation by happy excitement as well as emotional distress.

Regulating emotions

Emotional regulation is the process by which emotions are moderated, managed and contained using a wide range of regulatory strategies (Turnbull and Salas,

 Intellectual Disabilities and 'Personality Disorder' © Pavilion Publishing and Media Ltd and its licensors 2023

2021). This may be automatic, happening without deliberate thought. It may also be explicit: consciously monitoring emotions and using techniques to manage emotions in order to achieve goals, such as keeping one's temper. Conscious regulation may be used in anticipation of an emotion occurring. For example, actively managing nerves before giving a performance or speech. It may also be used reactively when the first signs of an emotion are triggered by an unexpected situation.

The wider an individual's window of regulation, the less actively they have to work to regulate emotions. To stay regulated, someone with a narrow window of regulation may need to actively manage their emotions for much of the time. This can be exhausting and difficult to maintain.

The ability to regulate emotions is closely related to the ability to regulate impulses (see Chapter 14) and relies on the healthy development and functioning of complex neurological systems involving many different areas of the brain. If an individual is unable to regulate their emotions, it will have repercussions for their relationships and their ability to regulate their behaviour (Paterson *et al*, 2017).

From co-regulation to regulation

Developing the ability to regulate emotions is one of many strands in the wider developmental process described in Chapter 2. Initially, babies are unable to regulate their emotions and physiological arousal. They are totally dependent on their parents to restore their emotional balance. The process by which this is achieved is called co-regulation.

A baby's biology is designed to detect and synchronise with the emotional and physiological state of those around them (Morgan *et al*, 2023). Hence, they are able to respond to soothing interactions with parents by calming but become distressed if their parent is agitated. The parent's state is transmitted nonverbally, through facial expression, body tone, posture and voice. Initially, parents respond to the baby's emotional cues by providing physical and emotional comfort though touch (e.g. hugging, stroking), proprioception (e.g. rhythmic rocking), and voice (e.g. soft tone of voice, singing a lullaby). They may also create a soothing setting, for example reducing noise, softening lighting and providing cosy blankets and cuddly toys. As the child develops, these remain important but additional strategies are brought into play to reflect and further develop the child's growing ability to self-regulate (see Box 11.5).

Box 11.5: Developmentally appropriate sequence of co-regulation strategies and learning about emotions

Infancy	Self-regulation by adult – relaxed breathing, low heart rate, relaxed posture and facial expression, slow movements. (Resolve source of distress e.g. feed, change nappy.) Provides physical comfort e.g. holding, hugging, stroking. Provides soothing proprioceptive stimuli e.g. rocking, bouncing. Provides emotional comfort e.g. soft voice, soothing music or songs. Changes environment e.g. moving to less stimulating/stressful setting. Creating a sense of safety e.g. soft toys, warm cosy blankets.
↓	Reassuring words in calm voice. Distraction, shift focus on to something else. Name emotions.
↓	Use simple calming techniques together e.g. long breaths while counting to 3. Help child label their feelings and express them in words. Help child identify sensations that signal dysregulation so they can use techniques before they become upset. Teach child simple problem-solving techniques by suggesting options. Tell stories to help child see things from someone else's perspective.
↓	Anticipatory coaching, helping the child prepare to handle a potentially dysregulating situation (e.g. talking through how to address a disagreement with a friend). 'Debriefing' after an emotionally distressing event, helping child to understand what happened from everyone's perspectives and think what might be done in the future. Encourage child to use more problem-solving and emotional-management skills.
15+	As self-regulation emerges, provide adolescent with guidance for complex problems and emotional support in dealing with significant stressors. Serve as the adolescent's secure base and safe haven while the adolescent handles the rest.

Adapted from Li (2023)

The presence of this external support, or 'scaffolding', is essential for the child to successfully navigate their emotional experiences (Paley *et al*, 2022). The process of co-regulation has been likened to learning to ride a bike (Li, 2023). Initially, a child sits on the saddle and the parent does the rest. Gradually, they are able to take a

Intellectual Disabilities and 'Personality Disorder' © Pavilion Publishing and Media Ltd and its licensors 2023

more active role until they can ride independently. However, if they never get any help from an adult, they will struggle to teach themselves and may never manage to ride alone. Without co-regulation, a child struggles to achieve regulation and may experience periods of dysregulation (for example, emotional outbursts) or develop maladaptive and ineffective coping strategies.

A parent's ability to co-regulate is influenced by many factors, including their physical and mental well-being (see Chapter 17) and the support available to them. When parents are highly dysregulated, whether in response to their child's distress or to some other stressor, they may have more difficulty accessing the parenting practices that would typically help their child navigate strong emotions. In contrast, well-regulated parents who are not overwhelmed by their own emotions may be more able to think flexibly and try different co-regulation strategies. Children of well-regulated parents may be better able to avail themselves of the emotion scaffolding provided because their attention is not being diverted to concerns about their parent's current emotional state (Paley *et al*, 2022).

Effective co-regulation is dependent on the parent being able to regulate their own emotional responses. A dysregulated adult can never regulate a dysregulated child (Perry, 2020).

Understanding and accepting emotions

As children develop, parents may also provide guidance in identifying and understanding emotions by narrating children's experiences. For example, '*I think you got scared when the dog ran up to you*'. They also model emotion regulation strategies and convey what is expected in their family with respect to how emotions are expressed and managed (Paley *et al*, 2022).

Validating emotions

Children learn about emotions through what their parents say and do in response to the child's emotions and the emotional tone of that response. For example, if a child is upset, a parent may ask them why they are unhappy and try to comfort them. This gives the child a name for the emotion and makes it clear that the feeling belongs to the child. It also tells the child that their parent thinks the feeling is real (subjectively true) and that they will help the child to manage it. As similar experiences are repeated, the child gradually learns to recognise their own emotions and regulate them independently of their parents. This process is called 'validating' (see Box 11.6).

Box 11.6: Emotional validation

Validating parental response:

- Acknowledges the child's emotion.
- Names the emotion for the child.
- Responds to the child's emotion as a real and genuine response to the situation.
- Accepts that the emotion must run its course.
- Calmly gives support and comfort until the emotion has run its course.
- Shows that the emotion expressed does not change the way they view the child (unconditional positive regard).

Growing up in a **validating environment** means that a child learns:

- To recognise their emotions.
- The names or labels for those emotions.
- That distress can be tolerated.
- To trust their own understanding of their emotions – will not need to look to others to tell them what they are feeling.
- To distinguish their own emotions from those of others around them.
- To sooth themselves until the strong emotion has passed.

Growing up in **an invalidating environment** means that a child may:

- Not learn about their emotions or how to tolerate and regulate them.
- Experience emotions as confusing, overwhelming and be unable to tolerable them.
- Be unable to recognise or actively regulate their emotions.
- Learn that only extreme reactions will get them the care that they need.
- Learn that they are only lovable when they express the emotions other people want them to show.

However, in some families, the child's emotions are not validated. This may occur in different ways. In some families, the child's experiences are not acknowledged. The child may then receive the message that their feelings are not real. For example, a parent may be unable to cope with the pain of knowing that their child is unhappy and may therefore continue to behave as if nothing is going on. The child then has no name for the feeling and gets the message that they should be feeling differently. Some parents may judge a child's responses as overreactions and meet them with disbelief (*'Don't be so silly'*) or punishment (*'Stop that or I'll give you something real to cry about'*). Families may impose their interpretation

 Intellectual Disabilities and 'Personality Disorder' © Pavilion Publishing and Media Ltd and its licensors 2023

on the child (*'He's not really upset, he's just playing up'*), sending the message that the child's experience is not real.

Some families are unable to separate themselves from their child's emotions; if the child is upset, they become upset, if something upsets a parent, they behave as if it has also upset the child. This leaves the frightened and overwhelmed child confused about whom the emotions belong to. Some families respond positively to the child only when they show acceptable emotions and reject them if they are unhappy, angry or fearful. In this situation, the child comes to see strong emotions as unacceptable.

As well as validating the child's experience of emotion, the family plays an important part in shaping appropriate responses to emotions. If family members listen to and take action to help when the child asks for help, or notice and respond to early signs of distress and ask what is wrong, the child will learn that help will be given when they need it. However, if family members ignore or do not notice the need for help, the child's response will escalate until it cannot be ignored. In this way, a child is taught that only extreme responses to emotions will get them the help they need. Some families run on an even keel, sharing feelings and expressing their emotions in a contained way. Others are highly volatile; emotions are easily triggered and are given free rein. This is termed 'high expressed emotion'. Families where there are high expressed emotions may be less able to help children learn to regulate and tolerate emotions.

Where emotions are consistently validated and co-regulated, the child will come to understand their emotions and will gradually be able to self-regulate. However, growing up in an invalidating, unresponsive or chaotic environment leaves children without the skills to understand or regulate their emotions.

Impact of adversity and trauma

Chapter 2 explored the profound effects of adversity and trauma on all aspects of an individual's development. Adversity and trauma reduce positive emotional experiences but lead to over-exposure to intense, distressing emotional experiences. Disruption to the parent-child bond means the child is less likely to experience co-regulation and more likely to have invalidating experiences. Exposure to difficult situations means they may be hypersensitive to threat and to other people's emotions. This can lead to experiencing intense emotions with few automatic or conscious strategies to regulate those emotions. Individuals are likely to have a narrow window of regulation, meaning that they are easily overwhelmed by their emotions and will struggle to empathise, reflect, learn and remember (Paterson *et al*, 2017). This may lead to experiencing mental health problems such as depression or showing behaviours that challenge. Some individuals who have experienced severe trauma may come to automatically dissociate in response to emotional distress, mentally leaving a situation that they cannot cope with (see Box 9.4). Cumulatively, these factors are reflected in delayed and disrupted emotional development such that individuals may not have the ability to understand or regulate their emotions.

Emotions and 'personality disorder'

Individuals given a diagnosis of 'personality disorder' often experience dysregulation. Patterns of emotional experience that are 'maladaptive' or poorly regulated form part of the diagnostic criteria for 'personality disorder' (see Box 1.9). These are thought to arise from multiple factors including biological vulnerabilities and experiences such as trauma (see Chapter 2). Many individuals given a diagnosis of 'personality disorder' experience highly volatile emotions: their emotions are easily triggered, reach a high level of intensity and may be slow to calm down. Individuals may swing rapidly from elation to depression or from boredom to anger. They may often feel anxious, ill at ease or irritable. Mood changes are often short-lived, rarely lasting more than a few days, and often happen several times in one day. Changes may be triggered by small events or may seem to arise out of the blue. These moods are intense, giving the impression that the person lives on an emotional roller-coaster. Individuals may experience more sadness, anxiety, anger and jealousy but less happiness than people not given this diagnosis.

Individuals given a diagnosis of 'personality disorder' may not understand their emotions and struggle to tolerate and regulate them (Matthies and Philipsen, 2014). Some individuals may lack awareness of their emotions to the extent that they may not recognise a particular emotion despite their behaviour clearly acting out that emotion. For example, an individual might say they are not angry while they are shouting and swearing with their face contorted with emotion. Individuals may struggle to tolerate uncomfortable emotions and rapidly feel overwhelmed. These intense feelings mean that individuals are often in their emotional mind (see Box 15.10) and struggle to see situations clearly. They may accept their emotional interpretation of events as reality and may then act in ways that seem extreme or inappropriate to others who are looking at the situation in a more objective manner. They may use unconscious mechanisms in response to their emotional distress which distort their communications and relationships (see Chapter 7).

Some individuals may also experience the 'empathy paradox' (see Box 12.4) leading to an excessive and inappropriate awareness of others' emotions which can lead to intense personal distress and emotional instability.

 Intellectual Disabilities and 'Personality Disorder' © Pavilion Publishing and Media Ltd and its licensors 2023

Emotions and intellectual disabilities

Individuals with intellectual disabilities experience the same range of emotions as neurotypical people. Like other people, individuals with intellectual disabilities also vary in the intensity and volatility of their emotions and their ability to regulate them. How individuals with intellectual disabilities experience and express emotions will also be influenced by their biological make-up, the level of their intellectual functioning and their experiences while growing up. This will be reflected in the level of emotional development they achieve (Frankish, 2019; 2021; Sappok and Conty, 2021). For individuals whose emotional development has not progressed beyond the early stages, it is unrealistic to expect them to achieve emotional regulation. They will remain dependent on others to co-regulate. The more severe an individual's intellectual disabilities, the more they will struggle to understand emotions, and the more likely they are to express their emotions through their behaviour rather than being able to put them into words (see Chapter 8). Some individuals with intellectual disabilities are also more reactive in terms of their physiology, meaning that their emotional responses are likely to be stronger and also take longer to resolve. The impact of social factors such as stereotypes can mean that the emotional reactions of individuals with intellectual disabilities are misunderstood or ignored and they do not receive the support and comfort that they need. This may lead them to show behaviours that challenge as the only way to express their feelings.

Individuals with intellectual disabilities who might be given a diagnosis of 'personality disorder' will have been shaped by these factors. They may also have a biological predisposition to experience intense and volatile emotions. They are likely to have grown up in an environment where parents struggled to co-regulate or validate their emotions. They may also be hypersensitive to other people's emotions. The combination of these factors means that they are likely to experience intense distress that they have great difficulty understanding and are unable to regulate (see Box 11.7).

Box 11.7: Difficulties with emotions and issues that may arise from them	
Emotions	Intense and volatile: easily triggered, high levels of arousal, slow to calm down, rapid changes of mood state. Frequently experiencing intense anger, jealousy, despair, fear or hatred, guilt or shame. Low tolerance for frustration, quick to anger. Difficulty distinguishing their own emotions from those around them e.g. becoming acutely distressed because other people are upset.

→

Memories	Being swamped with negative memories when experiencing strong emotions, which increases distress.
Understanding	Experiencing emotions as confusing, overwhelming and intolerable. Difficulty recognising, naming and talking about emotions. Inability to 'explain' their emotions and actions. Seeing strong emotions as wrong and punishing themselves for having such feelings.
Expression	Expressed in socially unacceptable ways e.g. shouting abuse, fighting. Experiencing a dissociative state when experiencing strong emotions. Having repeated emotional crises that can lead to relationship breakdowns, placement breakdowns and hospital admissions (see Chapter 9).
Regulation	Dysregulation. Inability to self-soothe or distract themselves when distressed. This leads them to use strategies that bring short-term relief but cause damage in the long term to the individual and their relationships with family, friends and services e.g. repeated phone calls, visits to A&E, use of drugs and alcohol, behaviours such as self-harm and suicide attempts (see Chapter 10).
Health risk behaviours	Living a chaotic and confusing lifestyle as behaviour is driven by emotional needs and reactions rather than rational thought. Impulsivity (see Chapter 14).
Impact on others	Others are likely to be confused, upset or frightened by the unpredictability and intensity of reactions. May dislike or avoid individual, relationships may breakdown. Reactions may appear disproportionate leading to invalidation by friends, family and staff which in turn increases emotional distress. Those around them also being overwhelmed by the individual's emotions and consequently being unable to help them regulate their emotions. Leading to a spiralling 'whirlpool of distress'.

Individuals are likely to have a narrow window of regulation and easily become dysregulated. Hence, their reactions may seem to come from nowhere and to be out of all proportion to any possible triggers. This can lead those around them to challenge the validity of the emotion. The individual may be seen as 'overreacting',

 Intellectual Disabilities and 'Personality Disorder' © Pavilion Publishing and Media Ltd and its licensors 2023

'attention seeking', being 'manipulative' or using 'emotional blackmail'. If this occurs, the individual's reaction is not validated and they do not get the support they need. As a result of this, the individual's distress is intensified and their behaviour becomes even more extreme, trapping them in a cycle of invalidation.

The experience of intense emotions and the inability to understand or regulate them can contribute to individuals leading chaotic lives. Their behaviour is driven by the emotion of the moment, meaning they are disorganised, important tasks are forgotten or neglected, and they may act in ways that are harmful to themselves or other people. The resulting chaos has the effect of triggering more distress, which in turn increases the chaos.

Many individuals with intellectual disabilities who might be given a diagnosis of 'personality disorder' have practical and cognitive skills that are more developed than their emotional abilities. Assumptions that they can tolerate being alone, or 'should' be able to manage their own emotional states with little support, commonly lead to a poor fit between the person's support package and their emotional needs. This may lead to them both being left to struggle and being seen as the cause of the resulting intense distress.

Assessment and formulation

Assessment and formulation of emotions and emotional regulation should take place as part of a holistic attachment and trauma-informed PBS assessment (see Box 8.6).

Assessment

Box 11.8 gives some suggestions for areas to explore.

Box 11.8: Exploring emotions	
Understanding emotions	Own: Do they know the names of emotions and can they describe what they feel like? Can they use emojis? How do they feel about emotions? Do they feel ashamed, guilty or a failure for experiencing certain emotions? Do they see some emotions as 'good' and others as 'bad'? Other people's: Do they recognise that other people have emotions? How do they respond?
Expressing emotions	How easy is it to make a best guess what they are feeling? Is it easy or difficult to work out when they are happy/sad/angry? ➔

	How does the individual respond to events which would be expected to be highly distressing for them – do they communicate an emotional response or appear outwardly unaffected? Do their words, actions and body language reflect the emotional state they report feeling? Do they express feelings indirectly using unconscious mechanisms (see Box 7.5)? Can they answer questions about how they feel or what might have made them feel that way?
Window of regulation	How wide is their window of regulation? Are they upset many times a day, or rarely? How quickly do they calm down? Are they more regulated in some settings than others? With some people but not others? Do they become distressed in situations that others remain calm in? How sensitive are they to emotional atmospheres? Do they quickly 'catch' emotions from others?
Emotional regulation	Are there any situations in which they can self-regulate? Are they able to use relaxation or self-soothing? Transition objects? Do they use unhealthy strategies to regulate? Self-harm? Drugs or alcohol? What co-regulation and de-escalation techniques help?
Comforting	When an individual is really upset, do they prefer space to work things out alone, or do they prefer to be with someone? Do they need that person to sit quietly, give them a hug, hold their hand, say certain things, help them solve the problem? (also see seeking comfort in box 12.7).
Sense of self and cognitive distortions	How do they see themselves? Does this impact on their emotions e.g. sensitive to criticism? (See Chapter 16) Do they experience cognitive distortions? How do these influence their emotions? (See Chapter 15).
Relationships	Does the individual seek support from others during times of distress, anxiety or discomfort? How do they do this? Is distress triggered by interactions with others? Is this related to interpersonal conflict?
Relationship to behaviours	Does the individual experience behaviours that challenge or have health-risk behaviours? Are these expressions of emotions? What is the relationship?
Impact on others	Do others find it easy to understand and co-regulate the individual? Or are they confused, frightened, overwhelmed?

 Intellectual Disabilities and 'Personality Disorder' © Pavilion Publishing and Media Ltd and its licensors 2023

History	Have they experienced things that might impact on emotions and regulation? Abuse? Trauma? Invalidation?
Hard wiring	Is there a mismatch between an individual's intellectual abilities and their abilities to understand and regulate emotions? Could they have a developmental disorder that impacts on understanding or regulating emotions e.g. ASD or ADHD?
Level of emotional development	What level of emotional development best reflects the picture of the individual's abilities and behaviours gained from the assessment? What implications does this have for the way they should be supported and their potential to achieve self-regulation?
Adapted from BPS (2017) section 5 Assessment, including Perry and Flood (2016)	

It may be helpful to think of assessing emotions as needing to explore three main aspects (Hammann *et al*, 2022): understanding emotions (both own and other people's), expressing emotions (being able to appropriately convey to others their emotional state), and emotional regulation. It may be possible to identify patterns of responding relating to different settings, activities, social groups or support styles, that may help clarify the specific issues that an individual struggles with. It is also important to try to establish an individual's midway level of arousal. Being in this zone creates the maximum 'buffer' to cope with unexpected stressors. If this is identified, it is then possible to balance exciting and relaxing activities to help them stay regulated.

It can be helpful to explore an individual's level of emotional development both in terms of understanding the most effective ways of comforting them and offering appropriate co-regulation, and also to gain some indications of their potential to move towards self-regulation. Tools such as the Frankish Assessment of the Impact of Trauma in Intellectual Disability (Frankish, 2019) and the Scale of Emotional Development (Sappok *et al*, 2016) may be helpful in this process.

Formulation

The CBT hot cross bun diagram (Box 15.9) can be very helpful in formulating the interrelationships between emotions and thoughts, sensations and behaviour.

Within a wider formulation of an individual's experiences, particularly the impact of trauma, it may be helpful to generate hypotheses about an individual's window of regulation and the extent to which they are currently dependent on others for co-regulation rather than being able to self-regulate. This will help identify the most effective way of supporting them to stay regulated, their potential to improve self-regulation and potential ways of achieving this. It may also highlight gaps between what an individual can do and what is expected of them within their support structure, with the resulting need to adapt the support to create a better 'fit'. (Such conversations often need to include those commissioning care packages.)

Box 11.9: Formulation of window of regulation for 'David'*

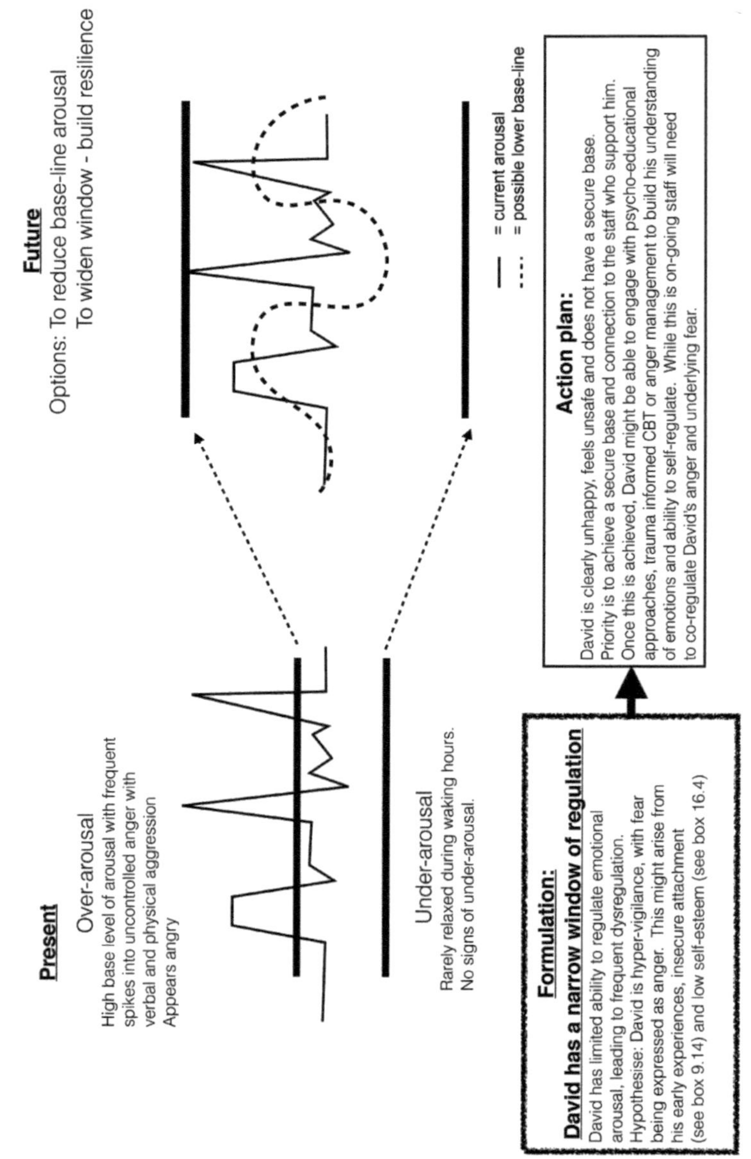

*David has been created from clinical experience & the literature. He is not based on a specific individual.

Intellectual Disabilities and 'Personality Disorder' © Pavilion Publishing and Media Ltd and its licensors 2023

It is also important to be hold in mind that emotional development levels reflect an individual's presentation at the time of assessment, and levels can change, for example an emotionally aware interpersonal environment with consistent caregivers may help the person develop skills, or an especially difficult experience (for example, significant bereavement) might lead to loss of skills.

Supporting individuals to regulate their emotions

For individuals in the **R**egulate phase (see Box 3.1), the priority is to develop a PBS plan that will help an individual to feel safe and enable them to stay within their window of regulation for long enough to start to develop the connections and relationships with others that form the basis of future emotional and behavioural regulation (Paterson *et al*, 2017). It is important that their PBS plan has the wider aim of helping the individual enjoy their life. Contented individuals are less likely to become dysregulated. For individuals at the **R**eason stage, there are a number of approaches to building understanding, tolerance and regulation of emotions. Interventions that build a positive sense of self or address cognitive distortions can also help widen an individual's window of regulation.

Whatever stage they have reached, all individuals will benefit from living in an emotionally competent environment.

An emotionally competent environment

Emotions are contagious. Humans are programmed to synchronise with the emotional climate around them: it is hard to stay calm if other people are angry, excited or frightened. There is a risk that family, friends and staff may be sucked into the individual's intense experience and also become overwhelmed by the emotion. In such situations, those around the individual also experience the situation as unbearable, hopeless and impossible to manage. They are then unable to help the individual contain their emotions. A negative cycle or 'whirlpool of distress' develops, with the individual's distress intensifying as they realise others are also overwhelmed by emotions.

To avoid this, it is important to create an emotionally competent environment around the individual. Emotions are understood and accepted and all aspects of the setting promote a sense of calm, acceptance and containment (see Box 11.10). It aims to create a safe haven, which provides comfort and hope, and helps individuals stay in and quickly return to their window of regulation. It is able to provide co-regulation and compassionate containment when individuals are acutely distressed.

Intellectual Disabilities and 'Personality Disorder' © Pavilion Publishing and Media Ltd and its licensors 2023

Box 11.10: Emotionally competent environment	
Support style.	Proactive, compassionate and containing (see Box 13.4).
Low expressed emotion.	Strong emotions are accepted as part of life, they are acknowledged, expressed and resolved with the minimum of fuss. Those around an individual who is distressed do not join in the shouting or charge about, but react to events in a calm, kind and matter of fact way.
Emotionally competent staff.	Confident staff who understand their own and others' emotions (Box 11.11)
A safe haven.	There is a sense of emotional and physical safety (Boxes 5.8 and 6.4). Staff create a safe haven, where individuals can go to seek comfort and hope when they are distressed. Balances the need for privacy with the need to be aware of what individual is doing/access in an emergency e.g. doors that lock but can be opened by staff if necessary. Safe places for personal possessions e.g. safe or locker. (Availability of de-escalation room and safety pod™ see Chapter 6).
Predictability and structure.	A predictable, person-centred routine creates a sense of calm, order and being cared for and about. (Lack of routine can recreate childhood chaos, triggering memories of neglect and feeling out of control and uncared for. It can also undermine physical and mental well-being and make it harder to engage in positive mood-enhancing activities.) Creating a (fairly) tidy living area is a good first step to reducing stress and creating calm. Clutter can be a great source of stress; nothing can be found and cleaning becomes a daunting task. Just looking at the mess can induce feelings of anger or despair.
Managing transitions and ending.	Support is structured to successfully manage difficult times that can trigger dysregulation such as transitions and endings (see Chapter 5).
Boundaries are maintained.	Maintaining boundaries that respect everyone's needs gives the message that the place is safe and that people care (see Box 13.12).
Healthy lifestyle	Promote regular and healthy daily routines e.g. healthy eating, regular exercise, consistent sleep, waking routines. Physical exercise releases tension and promotes positive moods. Rhythmic movement promotes regulation e.g. walking, dancing, drumming. ➔

 Intellectual Disabilities and 'Personality Disorder' © Pavilion Publishing and Media Ltd and its licensors 2023

	Erratic eating patterns, especially high consumption of sugary snacks and drinks that are high in caffeine (such as colas, sports drinks and special coffees) can create physical highs and lows that feed into wildly fluctuating emotions. Erratic sleep patterns undermine mental well-being.
Responding to individual's distress.	Skilled at co-regulation, de-escalation, able to use least restrictive appropriate reactive techniques to contain emotional outbursts (Box 8.14).
Supporting staff.	Have an effective support system including, supervision, reflection, post-incident support and staff counselling to maintain emotional health and prevent compassion fatigue and burnout (see Box 13.7).

Supporting individuals who are dysregulated can be stressful and challenging; staff need to be skilled at recognising and regulating their own emotions as well as those of the individuals they support (see Box 11.11).

Box 11.11: Staff emotional competencies*:	
Personal qualities:	Calm, confident, unshockable and unflappable (also see Box 9.9), compassionate, consistent mood – behaviour and responses are predictable.
Own emotions	Recognise, accept and understand their own emotions. Able to express emotions appropriately (low expressed emotion). Able to regulate own emotions. Skilled at remaining relaxed and calm in the presence of intense emotions. Self-aware, thoughtful, reflective, able to seek, accept and use help and supervision. Know when it is time to 'swap out' of supporting a particular situation or accepts this when it is suggested to them. Take actions to prevent 'compassion fatigue' (see Box 11.12) – good self-care.
Other's emotions	Recognise, accept and understand a wide range of emotions in others. Able to validate others' emotions. Skilled at co-regulating emotions – respond sensitively to cues of the individual's changing emotional state while remaining warm and calm themselves. →

Other's emotions	Able to remain calm despite others around them being distressed. *'I see you are afraid/upset/angry, that's OK, I will help you, but they are your feelings not mine, they won't overwhelm me.'* Remain positive about an individual whatever their emotional state.
*No one is perfect – this list looks a bit daunting: it is something to aspire to and to support people to work towards, not to judge staff against.	

Staff will also need to be well supported (see Chapters 7 and 9). Without appropriate support, staff are at risk of experiencing secondary or vicarious trauma (see Box 2.3), burnout (see Box 13.7) and compassion or empathy fatigue (see Box 11.12).

Box 11.12: Compassion fatigue

The loss of the ability to nurture, to care for and empathise with the individual supported. It includes the loss of active efforts to attune to an individual and the loss of the connection arising from a shared humanity. Also called 'empathy fatigue'.

Compassion fatigue has many features in common with burnout including reduced ability to cope and physical and emotional exhaustion (see Box 13.7).

Early warning signs of compassion fatigue:

- Distancing: detaching or disengaging with individuals as people e.g. referring to someone by their diagnosis.
- Losing or not being curious about the connection between an individual's experiences and the challenges they present to staff.
- Feeling irritated by or angry about an individual seeking interaction or engagement.
- Losing the ability to enjoy interacting with individual.
- Losing the ability to see things from the individual's perspective.
- Blaming individuals for the difficulties they experience, for not engaging or not making progress.
- Feeling hopeless or powerless.
- Ceasing to care about what happens to individuals.

Reference: Cocker and Joss (2016)

Validating emotions

Many well-meaning responses to emotional distress can, unintentionally, intensify distress because of the message they convey to the individual about their emotions (see Box 11.13).

 Intellectual Disabilities and 'Personality Disorder' © Pavilion Publishing and Media Ltd and its licensors 2023

Box 11.13: Common, well-intentioned, comments that are likely to be experienced as invalidating	
What is said	What is heard
'Calm down', 'Don't worry', 'Cheer up' 'Everything is fine'	'You should not be feeling this way' 'You are only acceptable if you're are happy'
'It's not the end of the world', 'It was only…' 'At least it's not…' 'It could be worse'	'You are over-reacting' 'It's wrong to show your feelings'
'It will be fine' 'Nothing's going to happen'	'You are worrying about nothing, you are wrong to worry'
'You've got the wrong end of the stick'	'It's your fault you feel this way'
'If I was you, I would…'	'You are doing it wrong, it's your fault'
'You're just tired', 'You don't really mean that' 'You don't want to kill yourself really, you had a good day'	'Your feelings aren't real'
'I'm sorry you feel that way about it'	'I don't care how you feel, your reality is wrong'
'Don't think about it, just get on with it'	'What you feel is trivial and unimportant' 'I don't want to listen to how you feel'
'I'm not having this discussion'	'Your emotion does not exist, how you feel does not matter'
'Why are you angry/sad/upset?'	'You should not be angry/sad/ upset about this'

It is helpful if staff understand the importance of avoiding such comments and instead learn strategies for validating emotions (see Box 11.14).

Box 11.14: Validating emotions	
Validating emotions. It says: *'I hear you. I see you. I get it. I care about your feelings.'* *'I can see you are angry/sad/upset/scared and this is understandable.'*	
Listen with an open mind – don't judge.	Be curious and thoughtful.

→

Identify and acknowledge the emotion.	*'You are feeling really angry'* (if they have said they are angry). *'You seem really angry'* (if they haven't named the emotion). *'Have I got that right?' 'I wonder if you are feeling sad?'*
Identify the source of the emotion.	*'Can you tell me what upset you?'* *'What made you feel like this?'* *'Something made you angry, can you tell me what happened?'* Use *'what'* not *'why'* in questions to avoid them sounding like accusations.
Accepting the emotional reaction as real.	*'You're feeling angry because your mum kept you waiting. I can understand that waiting would make you angry.'*
Empathise.	Show that you can see things from their perspective and recognise how they are feeling. *'I can see you are really upset right now, that must be awful for you.'*
Timing.	Some individuals respond to having feelings validated immediately, others need to hear this once they are regulated. Silence is more helpful at the time of extreme distress.
Patience.	If someone is used to their feelings not being validated, they may find validation difficult to accept or be confused by your reaction.
Disbelief.	An individual who has experienced difficult relationships may think you are lying or trying to trick them. If they don't accept what you say validate their lack of trust. *'At the moment you can't believe me, that's OK.'*
Recognise emotions are complicated.	Reactions are often mixed and this is complicated for everyone to understand. *'I can see you are excited about… but I wonder if you are a bit anxious, too?'*

Reference: Anderson *et al* (2020)

Validating emotions is important as it creates a situation in which an individual is able to move towards being able to name and accept their own emotional reactions. This replicates the pattern of developmental interactions between a parent and child (see Box 11.6). Validating emotions does not make them go away. However, it avoids adding the distress of feeling alone and misunderstood to the original upset. It may still be necessary to use other techniques to help the individual return to their window of regulation.

 Intellectual Disabilities and 'Personality Disorder' © Pavilion Publishing and Media Ltd and its licensors 2023

It can be uncomfortable to validate emotions when an individual's interpretation of the situation seems biased or unfair, or their emotional reaction appears unwarranted or excessive. Using validation may feel like reinforcing the individual's inappropriate behaviour or giving the message that such behaviour is acceptable. However, validation does not mean agreeing with or approving the thinking behind the emotion or its behavioural expression. It is simply the recognition that the individual is feeling in a particular way and that you recognise that the emotion underlying the response is genuine. Making the effort to identify what an individual is feeling and to accept that feeling as real, can also be the starting point for staff beginning to explore why the individual might react so strongly to certain situations. This, in turn, can lead to information that can help identify better ways of helping the individual.

Co-regulation and de-escalation

Even in a calm and stable setting, with skilled staff, there are still likely to be many occasions when individuals become dysregulated. Many individuals, once their arousal level is raised, will need the help of others to return to their window of regulation. Being left alone in a distressed state is likely to prolong their negative experience. When an individual is dysregulated, one staff member should lead the interaction with the individual but with others nearby in case the situation escalates. Ideally, staff should be familiar and trusted. Box 11.15 gives a number of techniques that can be helpful, based on the developmental sequence of parental co-regulation behaviours and recognised de-escalation techniques (see also Box 9.10 for supporting individuals in crisis and 9.4 for individuals who dissociate). The techniques used are adjusted to the individual's receptive and expressive language skills and arousal state. However, co-regulation is always based on the member of staff remaining calm and warm and using non-verbal communication to convey this to the individual. This signals that the situation is safe and draws the individual towards automatically mirroring that calm.

Box 11.15: Co-regulation and de-escalation techniques	
Foundation ↓	**Self-regulation by staff –** relaxed breathing, low heart rate. Use calm, attentive, non-threatening body language e.g. relaxed eye-contact, turn towards them, soft, open hand gestures, relaxed body posture. Move slowly and gently. Respectful and polite at all times. Resolve source of distress e.g. interpersonal conflict, unmet physical needs. Change environment e.g. moving to less stimulating/stressful setting, remove on-lookers. →

	Creating a sense of safety e.g. warm, cosy blankets. Provide soothing proprioceptive stimuli e.g. rocking, bouncing, swinging. Use soft voice, soothing music or songs. [If agreed by team and part of PBS plan, provide comfort through professional touch e.g. one armed hug, see Box 13.3].
	Reassuring words in calm voice: '*Everyone gets upset sometimes, you'll get through this*'. Distraction (see Box 15.15) e.g. talk about a favourite topic, offer a calm fun activity. Use positive and help focused statements e.g. '*I'm here to help, tell me about it*'. Use active listening, give undivided attention, be non-judgmental. Focus on feelings not facts, use restatement to clarify facts (see Box 10.13) tolerate silence. Validate emotions. Accept that the content of what an individual says is true for them at that time, even if you feel it is inaccurate e.g. '*You feel that everyone else is being treated better than you*'. Re-focus on positive aspects e.g. if they are distressed by lack of progress, remind them of gains they have made. If it is known that they respond well to it, use gentle humour to lighten the mood.
	Give simple choices e.g. '*I know you are upset at your family not visiting but we could go for a walk or play a computer game*'. Use simple calming techniques together e.g. long breaths while counting to 3, shake out the tension.
More sophisticated	Encourage use of familiar relaxation, mindfulness or self-soothing strategies.

For some individuals, medication may have a limited but important role in managing acute distress. Where medication is used on an 'as required' basis, this should be supported by guidelines and reviewed after every use. Its use should be integrated into the PBS plan.

Co-regulation highlights the importance of non-verbal rather than verbal behaviours in helping an individual become regulated. As a result of the way information flows through the brain (see Box 15.8), the majority of information is conveyed nonverbally. A rough guide is the 7-38-55 rule (Mehrabian, 1972): 7% of meaning is communicated through spoken word, 38% through tone of voice, and 55% through body language. Reassuring words will only be effective if they are supported by a calm and confident voice and relaxed body language.

 Intellectual Disabilities and 'Personality Disorder' © Pavilion Publishing and Media Ltd and its licensors 2023

Co-regulating strategies will form part of the amber section of an individual's PBS plan (see Box 8.13). Despite everyone's best efforts, it will not always be possible to prevent situations from escalating; distressed individuals may try to harm themselves, others or staff. In these situations, staff need to be able to respond quickly, calmly and effectively (see Box 8.14). Chapter 9 explores what to do if the situation escalates into a crisis and Chapter 10 explores self-harm.

Promoting understanding and acceptance of emotions

Validating emotions at the time they are experienced lays the foundation for individuals to begin understanding their emotional reactions. However, this is just the starting point. It is also important to create an environment in which it is seen as healthy and safe to talk about emotions. At a time when the individual is calm, it may be helpful to talk gently about recent incidents and speculate with the individual about what they may have been feeling. Staff will need to use their knowledge of the individual and their own skills at mentalising to best guess what emotions might lie behind the individual's behaviour.

Some individuals may be able to cope with questions such as '*I wondered if you were feeling angry when you shouted at X?*' For others, this will be too direct and may be taken as criticism. If this is the case, it can be helpful to explore how some other person might feel in a similar situation, chat about a (not too personal – see Box 13.10) time you have felt similar feelings or take examples from a TV programme they enjoy watching.

It can be helpful to have lots of pictures of people showing different facial expressions and to talk about what emotions they may be feeling and what might have caused these. This makes a neutral starting point and creates the opportunity for the individual to talk about their own reactions if they feel comfortable doing so.

As an individual becomes more comfortable talking about emotions, it may be possible to work with them to spot what situations trigger these difficult feelings. It may help to keep a feelings diary – noting the emotion and what they were doing at the time. Most individuals will not manage to do this alone. It can be helpful to create a quiet, relaxed time in the evening, perhaps over a cup of chamomile tea, to chat and fill the diary out together. Then, once a week, make time to go over the diary entries and explore more about the situations; who was there, what was happening, did it go as planned?

Some of the situations will be ones which the individual cannot do much to change; for example, a planned fun outing being cancelled or a much-loved but unreliable family member failing to call at the promised time. It can help to work with the individual to find ways in which they can care for themselves at these times.

Promoting self-regulation

Developing the ability to regulate their physiological and emotional arousal can have many benefits for individuals: it can build self-esteem and self-efficacy, create a feeling of being more in control and reduce the fear of being alone, helping individuals feel comfortable in their own company. Paradoxically, by helping individuals to be comfortable in their own company, their relationships are also likely to improve. This is because they are more able to give other people space and are likely to reduce the frustrating and sometimes harmful behaviours they are driven to in order to avoid being alone.

Relaxation and self-soothing are closely related and overlap. For example, breathing techniques can be described by either term. Relaxation focuses primarily on reducing physiological arousal while self-soothing focuses on being kind to oneself. As emotional and physiological arousal are so closely related, they have similar effects. It is more important to have a range of enjoyable options to help someone regulate themselves rather than worrying about what a particular technique is called.

Relaxation

Relaxation techniques help individuals to begin to regulate their level of physiological arousal (see Box 11.16).

Box 11.16: Relaxation techniques – reducing physiological arousal
Breathing exercises e.g. 'elephant breathing', belly breathing, calm breath or square breathing, bubble breathing.
Adapted progressive muscle relaxation – tensing and relaxing different muscle groups.
Behavioural relaxation – similar to progressive muscle relaxation but does not tense muscles first.
Visualisation and guided imagery e.g. imagining lying on a beach in the sunshine.
Multi-sensory rooms e.g. 'Snoezelen' rooms.

 Intellectual Disabilities and 'Personality Disorder' © Pavilion Publishing and Media Ltd and its licensors 2023

Meditation and mindfulness e.g. 'grounding', 'mindfulness of an object' and 'mindfulness of sounds' and 'body scan'.
References: Dagnan *et al* (2018), ecl (2023) PELICAN, Williams and Jones (2022)

If someone is also having difficulties with worrying thoughts, it is important to avoid approaches to relaxation that involve clearing the mind. Such approaches just make more room for worrying thoughts and can trigger 'psychotic' experiences. Rather, choose an approach that gives the individual something to focus on such as mindfulness and distraction techniques (see Boxes 15.15 and 15.16).

Self-soothing

Self-soothing means finding ways to comfort, care for and calm oneself to help tolerate emotions until they pass. This usually involves physical, sensual activities that are pleasant and calming for the body and mind. An example might be going for a walk in a garden, listening to the birds and smelling the flowers. Each person will find different things that work for them. Some suggestions are given in Box 11.17.

Box 11.17: Self-soothing techniques – caring for self until the emotional storm has passed

- A warm scented bath or shower.
- Listening to classical music, a relaxation tape, sounds from nature – birds singing, water flowing.
- Doing yoga exercises.
- Going for a walk in the park, feeding the ducks, looking at things as you pass them.
- Smelling flowers, fresh coffee, bread baking, cooking.
- Watching a favourite film.
- Singing.
- A cup of tea, coffee or hot chocolate.
- Eating a favourite treat.
- Looking at pictures or paintings.
- Curling up with a hot water bottle or favourite soft toy and a duvet or throw.
- Making a fuss of a pet or taking a dog for a walk.
- Stroking a silk scarf or furry cushion.
- Rubbing in body lotion or hand cream especially with a favourite scent.
- Saying a prayer, singing a hymn or reading a favourite verse.

→

- Hold a religious symbol or book.
- Saying positive statements e.g. *'I can survive this' 'I'm worth caring about'*.
- Look at photos of a special time or person.
- Rocking in a rocking chair or swing.
- Dancing slowly.
- Take 10 deep breaths.

Dialectical behaviour therapy (DBT – see Chapter 2) suggests thinking about the five senses; choosing activities that stimulate vision, hearing, smell, taste and touch. Another sense, that is often important for individuals with intellectual disabilities, is proprioception, or feeling movement. Many people find rhythmic motion very soothing.

Individuals may also be able to soothe themselves by drawing on religious or spiritual beliefs and positive memories or relationships. Where an individual has religious beliefs, it may be helpful to work with someone of that faith to find prayers, texts or other symbols that might be helpful for them in times of distress. Such work should always be driven by the individual's beliefs; staff should not try to influence or impose religion on the individual.

It can be very helpful to have a portable 'self-soother'. This might take the form of a necklace (cross, crucifix, locket with photographs), a keyring with photos, a cue card with special phrases, a scented handkerchief, music on a portable player or an app on a mobile phone. This means that whenever difficult feelings occur, the individual has something to hold on to, look at, read, listen to or smell.

It is important to remember that the individual will initially find it difficult to use these techniques; they may not recognise that they are becoming upset, and, once upset, may find it difficult not to fall into their unhelpful response pattern. It is therefore important to practice these approaches when the individual is not upset, and it is helpful if practise is built into the individual's daily routine.

Staff also need to be vigilant for early signs of distress. They can then gently prompt the individual to try their chosen approaches. This needs to be done sensitively, in a way that validates the emotional response and respects individual choice. For example, staff might say *'It looks like you're a bit upset? Have I got that right? Would a cup of tea or a warm bath help? We could do elephant breathing together?'* The goal-setting approach explored in Chapter 16 can be used for teaching new coping skills and embedding them in the individual's behavioural repertoire.

 Intellectual Disabilities and 'Personality Disorder' © Pavilion Publishing and Media Ltd and its licensors 2023

Therapeutic activities

Some individuals may be able to engage in therapy to help them further understand and regulate their emotions. Regulating emotions is addressed, directly or indirectly, in therapy approaches developed for individuals with a diagnosis of 'personality disorder' (see Chapter 3). It is also addressed in CBT and there are more specific approaches aimed at particular emotions, for example anxiety management (Dagnan *et al*, 2018) and anger management (Nicoll *et al*, 2013). Trauma-specific approaches may be appropriate for individuals who have survived very difficult experiences, particularly where these memories pervade their everyday lives and cause significant distress.

If individuals struggle with the cognitive demands of these therapy approaches, it may be helpful to attend groups that teach relaxation or healthy living skills.

Individuals gain much more benefit from such interventions if they feel safe and are supported by family carers or staff who understand, validate and co-regulate their emotional reactions. If cycles of invalidation and whirlpools of distress are not recognised and addressed, they will undermine the positive effects of therapy. Even with positive support, change is likely to be slow and may take much longer than the usual length of interventions. It is important to remember that the difficulties individuals are experiencing have taken a lifetime to develop and that the individual is likely to lack even the most basic skills such as naming their emotions. Many individuals will continue to need ongoing support or additional support at stressful times in order to be able to remain within their window of regulation.

Overall, understanding an individual's level of emotional development gives useful pointers about how staff can help them function as well as possible in everyday life. It also maximises the opportunities for individuals to achieve further emotional development, better regulation of emotional states, and more stable relationships. Progress will depend on the individual having a stable home, consistent caregivers and an emotionally competent environment.

Key learning points

- Emotions are spontaneous, short-lived states of mind that arise in response to internal or external events. They both shape and are shaped by an individual's thoughts, physical sensations and behaviours.
- There are huge individual differences in the way individuals experience, perceive and tolerate emotions. These differences are shaped by their biology, personal

history and learning opportunities, including the experience of adversity and trauma.

- Emotional regulation is the process by which emotions are moderated, managed and contained using a wide range of automatic and conscious strategies. Conscious regulation may be used in anticipation of an emotion occurring or reactively, at the first signs of an emotion triggered by an unexpected situation.
- The window of regulation is the range of fluctuation in arousal that an individual can tolerate without becoming dysregulated. A narrow window of regulation means an individual is vulnerable to becoming dysregulated and experiencing extreme distress that may seem out of proportion to others.
- Regulating emotions is very difficult for many individuals with intellectual disabilities, particularly those who might be given a diagnosis of 'personality disorder'. Many individuals develop worrying ways of coping with intense emotions, such as self-harm.
- Some individuals are hyper-sensitive to other people's emotional states, which can lead to them quickly becoming dysregulated if others around them are not calm.
- Co-regulation is the process by which a regulated person helps someone who is dysregulated to achieve emotional balance. They respond sensitively to cues of an individual's changing emotional state while remaining warm and calm themselves. Co-regulation occurs between parents and children and can also occur between staff and the individuals they support.
- It is important to understand and accept that, however extreme a response may seem, it is real for that individual (validation). If responses are not validated, an individual will not get the support they need, their distress will be intensified and their behaviour may become more extreme.
- Assessment and formulation are used to understand which aspects of emotional regulation an individual struggles with and how this may have arisen from their biology and experiences.
- Interventions can help individuals stay within their window of regulation by creating an emotionally capable environment and using co-regulation strategies. Some individuals may be helped to widen their window of regulation by learning about emotions and learning skills such as relaxation, mindfulness or self-soothing.
- Some individuals at the **R**eason stage will benefit from therapy approaches that directly or indirectly develop their understanding of and ability to tolerate and regulate emotions.

 Intellectual Disabilities and 'Personality Disorder' © Pavilion Publishing and Media Ltd and its licensors 2023

Chapter 12: Interpersonal relationships

This chapter explores the nature of relationships and families. It looks at the importance of relationships for well-being and at factors that influence the number and quality of relationships an individual has. It explores how attachments, social cognition, social capital, social skills and social learning shape relationships. It considers how relationships may be influenced by having intellectual disabilities and experiencing developmental trauma. It explores how difficulties in any one of these areas can contribute to individuals experiencing difficulties in relating to friends, family members and those they live with. It explores how these difficulties may be addressed within a trauma-informed Positive Behavioural Support framework and interventions.

Key topics

- Relationships
- Factors influencing relationships
- 'Personality disorder' and interpersonal relationships
- Intellectual disabilities and interpersonal relationships
- Assessment and formulation
- Reducing and resolving conflict
- Promoting positive interpersonal behaviour and positive relationships

Relationships

Humans are, by nature, social beings, and have a drive to seek others and form relationships. People live in complex social networks and are biologically designed to work together for survival. Some relationships are close and intimate, such as those between partners. Others are very superficial, such as between a shopper and the cashier at a supermarket.

The number and, more importantly, the quality of relationships an adult has, are important factors in their well-being (Block *et al*, 2020; Mental Health Foundation, 2023). Positive, supportive relationships give a sense of purpose and belonging, reduce stress and help people cope with trauma. They also increase happiness, contribute to a healthy sense of self and positive self-esteem. Positive relationships can create helpful pressure to change unhealthy behaviour patterns. Those with positive relationships have better physical and mental health, recover more quickly from illness and live longer.

Factors influencing relationships

Human relationships are immensely complicated. An individual's ability to relate to others develops throughout their lives and is shaped by the interaction of many different factors including economic and social status and personality. Relationships are underpinned by complex neurological pathways that are built through the developmental period and sophisticated learnt behaviours. Hence, they are very vulnerable to the effects of adversity and trauma, exposure to inappropriate models and reduced learning opportunities (see Chapter 2). The importance of these factors for the development of healthy relationships are explored in the following sections.

Families

An individual's first experience of relationships is usually within their family. A family may be defined as a group of people linked by blood or co-residence. Families may take many forms.

Whatever form it takes, a healthy family has a number of characteristics. Family members care for each other and spend time together, working together to achieve family goals (such as getting the chores done), having fun and celebrating (for example, birthdays, festivals, milestones and achievements). They have good communication and can talk about emotions, fears and wishes. There is trust that they will meet each other's needs and help each other in times of crisis.

Healthy families protect children and keep them safe, making them feel secure and loved. They create a secure base to explore from and a safe haven to retreat to. Families create appropriate boundaries (see Box 12.1) which perform many important functions, including making life predictable, learning the difference between self and others, and how to respect oneself.

 Intellectual Disabilities and 'Personality Disorder' © Pavilion Publishing and Media Ltd and its licensors 2023

Box 12.1: The importance of boundaries in parent-child relationships	
Boundaries: **appropriate limits** which respect everyone's needs and feelings	
Predictable	Know what will happen in a situation. This creates a sense of safety and comfort which builds into trust.
Expectations	Know what behaviour is expected.
Consequences	Know what will happen if boundaries are not respected, helps learn to make healthy choices.
Sense of self	Help differentiate self from parent.
Sense of others, respect	Helps create an awareness of others as people with their own needs rather than objects that exist to meet the child's needs. A foundation of empathy.
Sense of the adult being in charge	Makes clear the balance of power, that the adult is looking after the child. Creates a sense of being cared for. Avoids prolonged struggles as to who is in charge.
Containment	Contains intense emotions, supports child while they learn to do this for themselves. Contains impulsive behaviour while child learns to do this for themselves. Creates sense of emotional and physical safety – a secure base.
Learn to set own boundaries	Child learns by example that it is possible to say 'no' to things that are harmful.

Families help children to understand and manage their own emotions (see Chapter 11), to think about their own behaviour, and to understand the thoughts and feelings of others. They build a child's image of themselves and the world, providing the basis for self-esteem and core beliefs (see Chapters 15 and 16). Families foster skills and build healthy interdependence, giving children a range of responses to situations that will arise and helping them build a social network outside the family. Families also promote children's moral development (see Box 12.2), teaching them social and religious values. These provide them with a context within which to evaluate their conduct and make choices about how to act.

Box 12.2: Kohlberg's stages of moral development:

The process by which people develop the distinction between right and wrong (morality) and engage in reasoning between the two (moral reasoning).

Levels	Stages	Individual view
Pre-conventional 3-7 Years	AVOIDING PUNISHMENT Right = reward Wrong = prohibited/punished	Can I avoid being punished?
Reasoning based on reward and punishment	SELF-INTEREST Right = what is good for me Wrong = what is bad for me	What is in it for me?
Conventional 8-13 Years	GOOD GIRL/BOY ATTITUDE Right = what others say is right Wrong = what others say is wrong	I am a good citizen (Seeking approval of others)
Reasoning based on external ethics (also ethics of care)	LAW and ORDER MORALITY Right = what law says is right Wrong = what law says is wrong	I collaborate to maintain law and order
Post-conventional Reasoning based on personal ethics	SOCIAL CONTRACT Right = what I think is right Wrong = what I think is wrong	I disobey wrong rules and act consistently with my own principles (individual rights)
Not achieved by all adults as requires abstract reasoning	PRINCIPLE Right /wrong = my judgement based on universal ethical principles, mutual respect	I have an obligation to disobey unjust laws and commit myself to follow the ones that are grounded in justice and well-being

Understanding these stages offer helpful insights into the ways that both children and adults make moral choices and how moral thinking may influence decisions and behaviours. However, the way moral reasoning is expressed is also influenced by other factors such as habits and competing motives such as peer pressure.

References: Kohlberg (1984), Cherry (2022a), Mcleod (2023b)

Families may be seen as having a lifecycle, moving through different stages, with the exact sequence varying depending on the type of family. At each stage, the family needs to successfully achieve certain tasks. People need to adapt to their changing circumstances, first as independent adults, then as part of a relationship, and then as parents. Parents then need to create a safe and healthy environment

Intellectual Disabilities and 'Personality Disorder' © Pavilion Publishing and Media Ltd and its licensors 2023

in which their children can develop. They need to adapt their parenting style to meet the needs of babies, toddlers, young children and adolescents. Parents need to successfully launch their children into the world.

Families also need to adapt and respond to life events such as moves, separations, disabilities, illnesses and deaths. They will need to respond to external factors such as economic changes (for example, unemployment) and widespread events (such as flooding or wars).

Most families successfully negotiate these changes. However, problems can arise when families become stuck at a particular stage and cannot adapt or move on. For example, a family may successfully parent small children but struggle to give them the increasing freedom they need in adolescence. This is particularly difficult if that child has needed extra care because of a disability or illness. When this happens, it can lead to difficulties within family relationships.

Attachment

Chapter 2 explored the impact of early experiences, particularly parenting, on the nature of a child's attachments. Subsequent relationships can entrench or ameliorate the impact of these early relationships. Depending on the nature of their experience, adults develop either secure or insecure attachments (see Box 2.6). Adults who make secure attachments tend both to view themselves as being worthy of love and to view other people as potentially loving. Individuals with insecure attachments may hold negative beliefs about themselves and others. They may anxiously hold others close, keep others at a distance, or switch between these two extremes. They are less able to draw emotional comfort from their relationships and may not be able to support their partner in return.

Attachment strategies are not fixed, and people may at times show behaviours characteristic of different attachments. However, an individual's relationships will tend to be characterised more by some attachment strategies than the others. Where an individual has very unstable views of themselves and others, they may fluctuate frequently between different attachment strategies.

Social cognition

Social cognition is a broad concept encompassing information processing about the self, others, and the social world (Salgado *et al*, 2020). It encompasses processes such as emotion recognition, empathy, theory of mind (ToM), and mentalising (see Box 12.3). It contributes to the ability of an individual to understand and effectively respond to other people's perspectives and to use this information to interact appropriately.

Box 12.3: Concepts relating to understanding own and other's perspectives and emotions	
Social cognition	Information processing about others, the self, and the social world. A broad concept encompassing processes such as emotion recognition, empathy, ToM, and mentalising. It contributes to the ability of an individual to understand and effectively respond to the perspectives of 'others', enabling them to establish and maintain interpersonal relationships.
Empathy	The capacity to 'put yourself in someone else's shoes.' To see things from their perspective. The ability to sense other people's emotions, coupled with the ability to imagine what someone else might be thinking or feeling.
Emotional recognition	The identification of emotions from e.g. body language, facial expressions. This enables an individual to infer emotional states in others. This information is a prerequisite for empathy and mentalising.
Theory of mind (ToM)	The ability to attribute significance to mental states (e.g. beliefs, desires, feelings, intentions, needs, thoughts, and reasons) of self and others in order to understand, explain, and predict behaviours. It enables individuals to predict the next move of a social interaction partner and thus adapt the own behaviour to respond appropriately.
Mentalising	The ability to understand and interpret the mental states of oneself and others, particularly when understanding behaviour. To see one's own behaviour as coherently organised by mental states and to differentiate oneself from others (Bateman *et al*, 2020).
Emotional intelligence	Emotional intelligence is the 'ability to monitor one's own and other people's emotions, to discriminate between different emotions and label them appropriately, and to use emotional information to guide thinking and behaviour' (Salovey and Mayer, 1990).
References: Frothingham (2023) Salgado *et al* (2020)	

Understanding the different elements of social cognition has developed from a number of different theoretical perspectives and work with different groups of

 Intellectual Disabilities and 'Personality Disorder' © Pavilion Publishing and Media Ltd and its licensors 2023

individuals. This has led to a number of similar but not identical terms. For example, the term 'mentalising' was developed within the context of understanding the experiences of individuals given the diagnosis 'personality disorder', while ToM grew out of work with individuals with an Autism Spectrum Disorder (ASD).

The development of the ability to mentalise is discussed in Chapter 2. In adults, the ability to understand what other people may be thinking and feeling is important for healthy relationships. If a person cannot mentalise, they struggle to understand their own behaviour and are unable to imagine the impact their behaviour has on other people. They are unable to imagine how events or experiences might make someone feel or make a best guess as to the motivation for another's behaviour. Hence, they are less likely to be able to offer emotional support or to experience sympathy or empathy and their behaviour may be perceived as inappropriate or inconsiderate.

Depending on each individual's unique biology and experiences, different elements of social cognition may be compromised. This can lead to different patterns of challenges. One example is the 'empathy paradox' or 'borderline empathy paradox' (Krohn, 1974) which has been found in some (but not all) individuals given a diagnosis of 'borderline personality disorder ' (see Box 12.4). Despite being able to recognise subtle emotional states in others, they are unable to use this to facilitate interpersonal relationships.

Box 12.4: The empathy paradox

Having impaired interpersonal functioning despite having **enhanced empathy**. Being able to recognise subtle emotional states in others but not be able to use this to facilitate interpersonal relationships.

Found in **some but not all individuals** given a diagnosis of 'borderline personality disorder' (BPD).

Better and quicker discrimination of mental states by individuals with 'BPD' was reflected at a neurophysiological level by stronger activation of different areas of the brain.

Individuals appear to be highly vigilant to social stimuli and resonate intuitively with mental states of others.

A combination of increased attention to social stimuli and dysfunctional social information processing may account in part for the specific empathic enhancements and reduced overall social functioning.

Enhanced empathy may be characterised as an 'excessive and inappropriate awareness' which might lead to intense personal distress and emotional instability.

→

It has been proposed that a child may develop enhanced empathic sensitivity in response to confusing or neglectful parenting, which motivates the child toward increased empathic functioning.

References: Dinsdale and Crespi (2012), Frick *et al* (2012), Krohn (1974), Salgado *et al* (2020).

Social capital

> *'Social capital is the goodwill available to individuals or groups. Its source lies in the structure and content of the* [individual's] *social relations. Its effects flow from the information, influence, and solidarity it makes available to the* [individual].*'* (Nahapiet and Ghoshal, 1998, p.243)

Social capital arises from the human capacity to consider others, to think and act generously and cooperatively (Ehsan *et al*, 2019) and is dependent on the levels of trust and reciprocity within social networks which create obligations and expectations (Hoffman *et al*, 2005).

Healthy social relationships tend to be reciprocal; there is give and take on both sides. Sometimes, a person will give more than they take and at other times take more than they give. However, over time, these will tend to balance out. The giving can take many forms such as spending time, listening, giving emotional support, sharing helpful information, lending money or possessions. When a person gives more than they take it, can be thought of as building up 'social capital'. When they take more than they give, this may be seen as using up this social capital. While it is over simplistic to think of these interactions as if money was changing hands, it is possible for someone to reach the end of their 'emotional credit limit'. Other people will become reluctant to help them because they know that person cannot be trusted to return favours.

People may fail to build up social capital or go over their 'emotional credit limit' for a number of reasons. Some people may lack the skills needed to recognise other people's feelings and needs (social cognition). Often people may be too preoccupied by their own needs to think about others. Some people may also feel a sense of entitlement; that others should look after them. Many will have grown up in dysfunctional settings where caring and sharing were not part of everyday behaviour and hence will not have had the opportunity to learn that it is important to give as well as take. This may also have influenced their moral development, making it unlikely that they have progressed beyond the pre-conventional level where decisions are made on the basis of reward or punishment and self-interests (see Box 12.3).

Intellectual Disabilities and 'Personality Disorder' © Pavilion Publishing and Media Ltd and its licensors 2023

Social skills

Whatever a person's social opportunities, social skills play a significant factor in making and maintaining relationships. Social skills are a set of learnt abilities that enable an individual to interact competently and appropriately in a given social context (American Psychological Association, 2023a). Social skills comprise a variety of verbal and non-verbal skills including eye contact, body language, tone of voice and the words spoken. They also include such skills as being able to initiate and maintain a conversation, take turns and make requests. There is a robust negative correlation between social skills and behavioural difficulties (Hukkelberg *et al*, 2019).

Most people acquire these skills naturally through their life experiences as part of the social learning process. However, social skills can be formally taught and improved, although the skills learnt may not always generalise to other settings. Someone who is unable to mentalise will struggle to know which is the right social skill for a particular situation.

Social learning and reciprocal roles

The foundations for relationships and social behaviour are laid down in parent-child interactions. As the child moves through life, they gradually acquire a repertoire of social behaviour. This is mostly learnt informally; it is rarely taught specifically.

The social learning model developed by Bandura (1977) is a useful way of understanding this informal learning process. This approach suggests that people learn new ways of behaving by observing the behaviour of others. Individuals are more likely to copy or imitate behaviours if they are modelled by people they admire, or they see the person being rewarded for those behaviours. Social learning theory suggests that, for an individual to adopt a new behaviour, certain factors must occur (see Box 12.5).

Box 12.5: Social learning model	
Model	The person showing the behaviour imitated e.g. parents, characters on TV, friends, peer group, teachers, people who are admired.
What needs to happen for a behaviour to be imitated:	
Attention	The behaviour has to grab attention as being worth imitating.
Retention	Behaviour has to be remembered to be imitated, particularly at a later time.

→

Reproduction	Have the ability to do it, e.g. may lack physical skills, strengths or developmental milestones needed to carry out the behaviour.
Motivation	Have a reason for behaving that way. More likely to imitate if perceived benefits outweigh perceived costs.
Reference: Mcleod (2023c)	

This model is useful as it directs attention to *what a person sees happening around them*, not just at the consequences applied to their own behaviour. It highlights that people can absorb very different behaviours depending on what is modelled and rewarded around them.

The ways in which parents interact with their children are absorbed to form reciprocal roles (Box 7.2). Children exposed to positive role models will internalise a range of healthy, flexible reciprocal roles, giving them options to constructively interact in different settings and to add to or adjust these depending on later experiences. For others, their exposure to positive reciprocal roles may be restricted by negative life experiences such as loss, deprivation or abuse. Such experiences make individuals vulnerable to absorbing and rigidly enacting roles that are unhelpful or harmful outside of the survival situation in which the role was learnt (Jenaway, 2019) and which may be less likely to evolve with later experiences.

'Personality disorder' and interpersonal relationships

Pervasive interpersonal difficulties are one of the issues that can contribute to someone being given a diagnosis of 'personality disorder' (see Box 1.9). Their developmental experiences shape all aspects of their functioning (see Chapter 2) leaving them without the resources to regulate intense emotions (Chapter 11) and impulses (Chapter 14). They struggle to understand their own and other people's thoughts and feelings. Their experiences may lead them to see the world in a distorted way (Chapter 15) and to find it difficult to take responsibility for their behaviour (external locus of control, lack of self-efficacy). Insecure attachments (Box 2.6) mean that relationships are a source of anxiety, such as fear of being abandoned or rejected. They may be overly dependent on others (ambivalent attachment) or overly independent (avoidant attachment) or switch between these extremes (disorganised attachment). Their limited and skewed learning experiences mean that they may not have had the opportunities to develop a sophisticated moral compass

 Intellectual Disabilities and 'Personality Disorder' © Pavilion Publishing and Media Ltd and its licensors 2023

(Gupta, 2023), and that appropriate behaviour will have neither been modelled nor rewarded. Hence, they lack the sophisticated social skills that most people automatically use to meet their needs through social interaction. Without these sophisticated skills, they are unable to shape interactions in ways that are mutually beneficial and leave both parties feeling good about the other person and the interaction. Relationships may lack reciprocity (feel one-sided) or unconsciously draw people into repeating unhelpful patterns from the past (see Chapter 7).

Individuals often unconsciously respond to a misperception of a situation that is distorted by their own emotions, thoughts and past relationships. Consequently, family, friends and partners may feel confused or unfairly treated. Individuals may engage in a range of interpersonal behaviours that other people find difficult or distressing. They may also fail to respect the usual boundaries in relationships, becoming overly involved and having unrealistic expectations of what a relationship can offer. For some, the empathy paradox (Box 12.4) can create an excessive and inappropriate awareness of others' emotions, which can lead to intense personal distress which they lack the ability to regulate.

Individuals who have been given a diagnosis of 'personality disorder' are also often vulnerable to abuse. They may stay in difficult or abusive relationships for fear that being alone is worse. They may also be unable to protect themselves from people who exploit them emotionally (including coercive control) or financially. Some individuals may put themselves at risk, for example, by self-harming from fear that someone may leave them or to elicit the care and contact they desperately need.

Intellectual disabilities and interpersonal relationships

Having intellectual disabilities shapes an individual's ability to form relationships, both directly and through the impact of the support systems around them. Limited intellectual skills impede the development of social skills and make it harder for individuals to understand the subtle distinctions between different types of relationships. In addition, healthy brain development underpins the ability to mentalise. For some individuals with atypical brain development, learning to mentalise may be next to impossible.

Intellectual disabilities can restrict an individual's social circle both directly (for example, by having limited ability to travel independently or struggling to use the internet), and indirectly (for example, attending a special school that is far away means fewer friends near home). Individuals are likely to have poorer formal and informal social networks and less social support than those without disabilities (Mithen *et al*, 2015). Relationships with support staff are often their closest and most significant relationships (Giesbers *et al*, 2019). Communication difficulties or behaviours that challenge also impact on friendship patterns (McCausland *et al*, 2021). Mainstream dating options rarely work out well for individuals with intellectual disabilities, often costing them a great deal of money and risking their dignity and safety (McCarthy et al, 2020).

Having complex needs may mean that individuals may be surrounded by highly complex systems that may include family, friends, partners and paid carers. The disempowerment that arises from the way services for individuals with intellectual disabilities are organised can have a significant impact on relationships. For example, individuals may have very little choice about the people they live with or whether friends can stay the night. They may be heavily dependent on parents or staff who may 'gate-keep' relationships. Their social life may be curtailed by factors such as events finishing too late for day staff to accompany them (Coleman and Sharrock, 2022; McCarthy *et al*, 2021).

Individuals' relationships with their families may also be complicated as a result of factors such as parents' emotional responses to having a child with disabilities, disrupted attachments, moving more slowly through the family lifecycle and living at home long after siblings have left home. Where personal or family relationships are abusive, levels of dependence may make it more difficult for individuals with intellectual disabilities to step away from them. It is also difficult for individuals with intellectual disabilities to form their own families. Mothers with intellectual disabilities are more likely to experience several risk factors during pregnancy, are more at risk of having a child taken into care and may lack the support needed to successfully promote child development (Llewellyn et al, 2015).

Sexual relationships

Disappointingly, despite the issues being raised several decades ago (Booth and Booth, 1992; Brown, 1994; Leyin, 1992), lack of knowledge still impacts on the abilities of individuals to form healthy intimate relationships. The staff around them still often lack the knowledge and clear guidance to support them effectively (Brown and McCann, 2018; Coleman and Sharrock, 2022; Bates *et al*, 2020). Concerns about the risks of relationships and consequent over-protection are particularly apparent for women with intellectual disabilities, contributing to men greatly outnumbering women in specialist dating services (McCarthy *et al*, 2020). They note that:

 Intellectual Disabilities and 'Personality Disorder' © Pavilion Publishing and Media Ltd and its licensors 2023

'While people with intellectual disabilities, like everyone else, have the right to be protected from actual abuse as far as is reasonably possible, there is no logical, moral or ethical reason why they should be protected from the 'everyday' highs and lows of relationships.'

Impact of trauma

When individuals with intellectual disabilities also experience the effects of adversity and trauma during the developmental period, this can lead to them experiencing pervasive difficulties that impact on their interactions with their families, friends and partners, professionals and members of the public (see Box 12.6).

Box 12.6: Difficulties with relationships

Inappropriate interpersonal behaviours:

- Appearing to be rude and inconsiderate.
- Appearing selfish '*me, me, me*'.
- Being impatient, struggle to wait.
- Not taking turns or sharing, 'hogging' certain people's time.
- Making comments that appear rude or hurtful, swearing and other unacceptable language.

Difficulties with relationships and interpersonal conflict:

- Unstable friendship patterns, frequently changing patterns of friendship.
- Intense distress when relationships break down.
- Impulsive relationships e.g. instantly falling in love.
- Arguments.
- Personality clashes.
- Jealousies and resentments e.g. thinking someone else gets better treatment than they do.
- Repeated conflicts over everyday things e.g. TV programs, what activities to do.
- Bullying/being bullied, physical assaults/being assaulted.
- Fear of being alone, abandonment, rejection.
- 'Over-dependence', 'Clingy'.
- Remaining in abusive relationships, having relationships with partners who do not treat them well.

→

- Being abused, physically, emotionally, sexually or financially by 'friends', partners or family.
- Placement breakdowns because of interpersonal behaviour, or seeking to leave behind difficult relationships.

Relationships distorted by unconscious mechanisms: For example, getting trapped in a negative cycles (see chapter 7).

Lack of skills, knowledge and opportunities to practice appropriate behaviour:

- Over protection.
- Restrictive policies, lack of positive risk taking and risk formulation.
- Attitudes and stereotypes.
- Practical restrictions, staff shift patterns, struggling with technology.

Assessment and formulation

Safety first

Individuals with intellectual disabilities who might be given a diagnosis of 'personality disorder' may show patterns of relating that make them very vulnerable to abuse, but, at the same time, make it difficult for them to perceive those relationships as abusive and also to trust services to do a better job of keeping them safe. Hence, it is important to be vigilant for signs of possible abuse (Solace, 2022). Where there are concerns that patterns of relating put individuals at risk, that they are being or have been bullied or abused, or that they are bullying or abusing others, it is important to follow safeguarding procedures. The Care Act (2014) sets out a clear legal framework for how local authorities and other parts of the system should protect adults at risk of abuse or neglect.

Moving to a more supportive setting that is able to provide a secure base can significantly reduce risks but can be particularly challenging (and, at times, highly resisted) for individuals whose early experience of care has taught them that it increases risk and reduces safety (Jones, 2021). Chapter 5 highlights the steps services need to take to facilitate engagement at such difficult times.

Where concerns relate to intimate relationships, it is important to have a good understanding of the legal issues that impact on sexuality and individuals with intellectual disabilities (Thompson, 2018). Thoughtful and facilitative guidelines for supporting individuals with personal and sexual relationships are an essential

 Intellectual Disabilities and 'Personality Disorder' © Pavilion Publishing and Media Ltd and its licensors 2023

prerequisite to keeping individuals and staff safe, while facilitating healthy relationships and positive risk-taking.

Assessment

The multiplicity of factors that can influence how individuals relate to other people means that it is important to look at the whole person, including their physical, emotional and social well-being (Coleman and Sharrock, 2022). This can be achieved following the trauma-informed Positive Behavioural Support (PBS) assessment suggestions in Box 8.6.

As similar issues can arise from very different underlying factors, it is important to try to build a picture both of an individual's pattern of relating and the factors that might be contributing to that pattern. Box 12.7 gives some suggestions for exploring the pattern of an individual's current relationships.

Box 12.7: Exploring current relationships	
Responses to familiar **others**	How does the individual interact with the people around them? Friends? Family? Co-residents? Staff? People visiting them? People visiting others? What expectations do they appear to have of those interactions? Do they approach or withdraw? Do they initiate interactions? Do they respond to greetings? Facial expressions? Body language? If supported by paid carers, how does the individual respond to: ■ Beginning and ending of shifts? ■ Staff taking absences from work, having sick leave, or leaving the job? Does this vary with different staff members? If so, how? ■ Does the person show a strong preference for a particular caregiver? How do they show this? Does this cause any difficulties or concerns? What are the characteristics of the preferred person? If supported by unpaid carers/family members, how do they respond to separating from and being reunited with them?
Responses to new people	How does the individual react to new people? Instantly or overly friendly? Distant, anxious or avoiding or aggressive? How do these initial reactions evolve over time? Do they build trust?

→

Seeking comfort	Does the individual seek support from others during times of distress, anxiety or discomfort? How do they do this? Do the people around them recognise these as support-seeking behaviours? How does the individual respond to reassurance in unfamiliar situations? Do they appear more confident and relaxed in the presence of certain people? How does the individual respond to events which would be expected to be highly distressing for them – do they communicate an emotional response or appear outwardly unaffected?
Considering others and reciprocity	Does the individual show signs of considering others? E.g. social graces, asking before doing things that impact on others, ask how someone is feeling, doing a kindness? Do they take turns, wait in queues, respect others' property, say hurtful comments? Do they do nice things for anyone else? If so, who? Do they listen to anyone? If so, who?
Stability	How predictable/consistent are the individual's responses? Do they fluctuate? Is this their usual pattern of interaction or is it in response to a particular event?
Adapted from BPS (2017) section 5 Assessment including Perry and Flood (2016)	

Box 12.8 gives some areas to explore in order to build an understanding of factors that might have shaped the development of an individual's abilities to interact with others and what might be driving their current patterns of interacting.

Box 12.8: Exploring factors that might impact on relationships	
Learning history and past learning experiences	What have they experienced, what did they do to survive? What behaviours were modelled? What behaviours were successful in getting needs met/keeping safe? What attachments did their early experiences shape? Were they able to form secure attachments? Was their development shaped by trauma, separation or loss?
Current situation	What are they experiencing? Is abuse occurring? What are they doing to survive? What behaviour is being modelled? What behaviour results in their needs being met? What learning opportunities do they have? Are they being over-protected or exposed to unnecessary risk? Are they abusing others e.g. bullying, physical assaults.

Intellectual Disabilities and 'Personality Disorder' © Pavilion Publishing and Media Ltd and its licensors 2023

Emotional reactivity and regulation	Do they experience intense overwhelming emotions? Are they hyper-sensitive to the emotions of others (the empathy paradox)? Have their neurological pathways been shaped by neurodiversity or trauma making them hyper-reactive to threat?
Thoughts	Do they have a sense of agency and belief that they might be able to control/are responsible for their behaviour? Do they have a sense of entitlement/being special? Do they have an immature sense of 'fairness' (Box 15.11)?
Moral compass	Have their experiences/divergent development left them at the pre-conventional level of moral development? Are decisions made only on the basis of self-interest? Do they understand that others have rights that should be respected? That each individual has both rights and responsibilities? Is '*they started it*' an acceptable reason for inappropriate behaviour towards another person? Are they driven to seek revenge or to punish others for perceived slights or injustices?
Attitudes and prejudice	Are inappropriate behaviours targeted towards people with particular characteristics? Is this related to race, gender, age, sexuality?
Self-esteem	Do they need to put others down? Do they feel they are worthy of a partner who is good to them? Do they need to appear big/powerful or need the admiration of others? Do they need to fit in with a crowd?
Social cognition	Do they show empathy? Do they show any understanding of others' thoughts and feelings? Can they see things from another's perspective? Is this understanding a best guess or distorted?
Response to being alone	Do they spend a lot/very little time alone? Does being alone make them feel safe or anxious? Are they relaxed or absorbed in activities? Do they use objects to give comfort and security (transitional objects) such as a blanket, cushion or soft toy? Do they avoid being alone or actively seek it?
Response to others	Do they need to keep people close or push them away? Are they overly trusting, trust no one, slow to build trust?
Social skills	Do they show skilled behaviours in some situations/states of mind but not others? What skills do they have? What skills do they lack?
Service issues	Do the services that support the individual have policies that facilitate the formation of healthy relationships? Are policies being followed? What are the attitudes towards relationships and sexuality? Are all staff following the same approach? Are there effective systems to support positive risk taking? Do their family and support services hold different views on facilitating relationships, levels of risk and protection?

Some of these factors can also be explored using formal assessments such as the Manchester Attachment Scale – Third party observational measure (Penketh *et al*, 2013) and the Adult Attachment Projective Picture System (Gallichan and George, 2014). However, these should be used with caution to help generate hypotheses about patterns of interaction and the purposes they serve, rather than making a 'diagnosis' of an attachment category which may be inaccurate and lead to unhelpful assumptions (British Psychological Society (BPS), 2017).

When interpreting the results of assessments, it is particularly important to consider the impact of any stressful life events. At times of high stress, individuals are likely to use adaptive and functional attachment behaviours and show patterns of interacting that do not characterise their behaviour in less stressful circumstances (BPS, 2017). Patterns of relating may change as an individual moves through the 3 Rs of **R**egulate, **R**elate, **R**eason (see Box 3.1). The stage an individual has reached and the extent to which they can actively engage will also shape the choice of assessments.

For individuals at the **R**eason stage, Cognitive Analytic Therapy (CAT) approaches might be used by a trained therapist to identify and explore unhealthy reciprocal roles. Understanding of relationships and social conventions can be explored using tools such as *Sex and the 3 Rs* (Thompson and McCarthy, 2016) and the Social and Moral Awareness Test (SMAT) (Dodd *et al*, 2010).

Unconscious mechanisms (Chapter 7) and cognitive distortions (see Box 15.4) may have a significant impact on an individual's interpersonal behaviour. Individuals cannot always articulate their thoughts. In such situations it can be helpful for teams to reflect on what thoughts might be behind certain behaviours (see Box 16.4).

It is also important to consider the role of divergent neurodevelopment in an individual's pattern of relationships, particularly on mentalising, moral reasoning and social skills, as some difficulties may be 'hard wired'. Such deficits will be less amenable to intervention and may require thoughtful supportive strategies. Individuals with unrecognised ASD may come into contact with services as a result of difficulties with relationships, and this may be mistaken for 'personality disorder'. The possibility of ASD should be considered where it appears an individual's issues may relate to underlying difficulties with information processing. Although developed for children, the Coventry Grid (Moran, 2010) may be helpful in such situations as it contrasts the differences between ASD and attachment issues across a number of areas of functioning.

 Intellectual Disabilities and 'Personality Disorder' © Pavilion Publishing and Media Ltd and its licensors 2023

Finally, given the significant impact of the approach taken by carers on individuals' relationships, it is important to explore the impact of the formal and informal policies of the systems around an individual and the attitudes of their carers and family, as these may be shaping their opportunities and experiences.

Formulation

The complexity of relationship difficulties means that formulation may need to identify themes and patterns linking the past and present from a wide range of different sources about different aspects of functioning. It will need to consider attachment and social cognition, learning and opportunities within the context of an individual's current support system. It may need to explore sensitive issues such as past and present abuse that could re-traumatise individuals. Hence, it may be helpful to include a reflective case discussion before proceeding to create a collaborative formulation.

Formulation can be a powerful tool in challenging the all-too-frequent assumption that individuals choose to interact with others in inappropriate ways (see Chapter 13 for a discussion of 'manipulative' behaviour). Focusing attention on their developmental experiences and current opportunities can promote empathy and suggest a positive way forward (see Box 12.9).

Where issues relate to sexual relationships, it may be helpful to use team reflections to explore a service's policies with regard to promoting safe and healthy interpersonal and sexual relationships, including support to safely access social media and internet dating. This may give helpful insights into how organisational constraints may be contributing to an individual's difficulties or might impact on potential interventions.

This chapter explores reducing and resolving conflict and gives some strategies for promoting positive interpersonal behaviour and positive relationships. See Chapter 5 for approaches to engage individuals, Chapter 7 for more details about unconscious mechanisms that can distort communication, and Chapter 13 for information about maintaining professional relationships.

Box 12.9: Formulation for 'Elizabeth'*

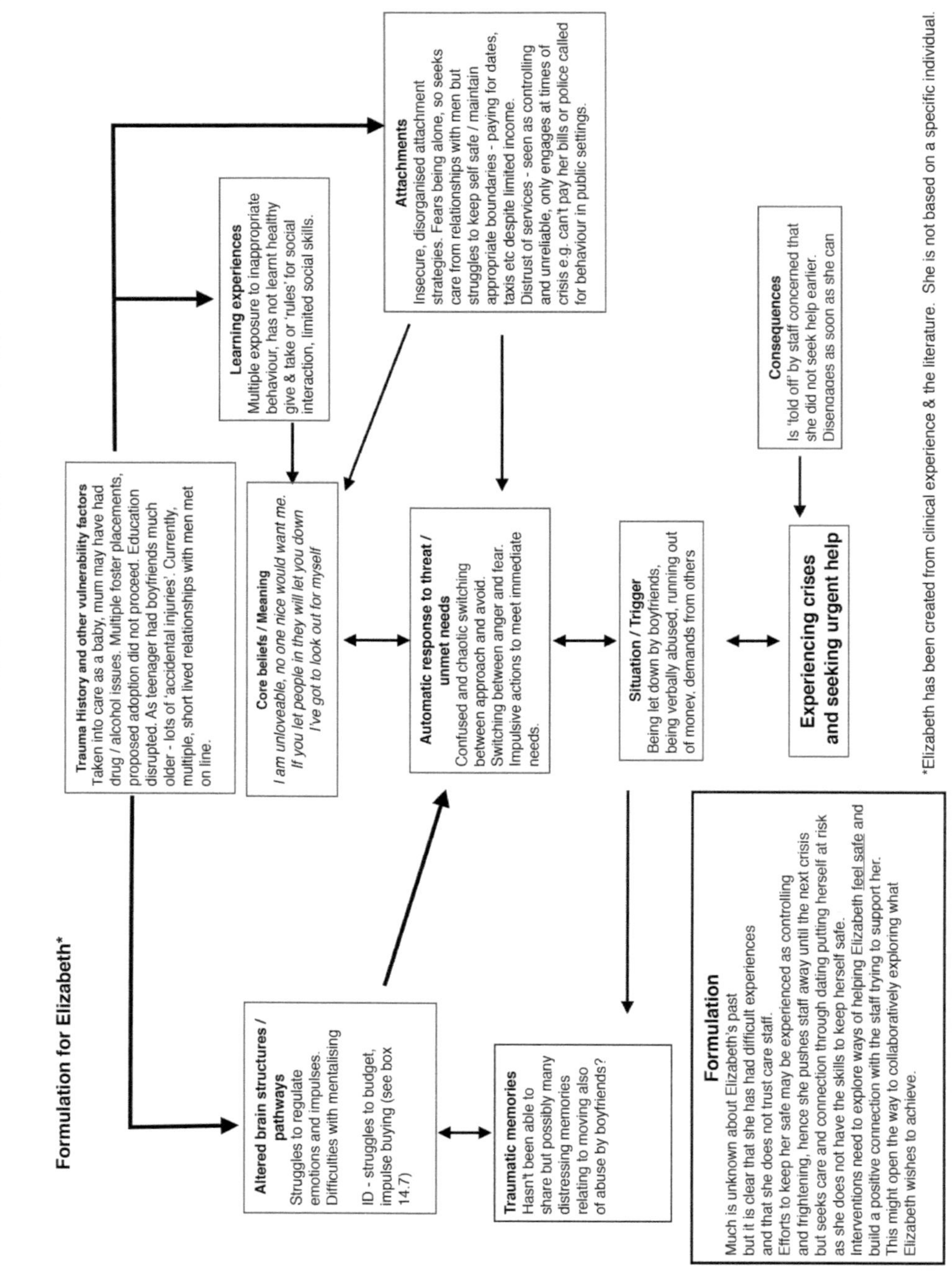

*Elizabeth has been created from clinical experience & the literature. She is not based on a specific individual.

 Intellectual Disabilities and 'Personality Disorder' © Pavilion Publishing and Media Ltd and its licensors 2023

Reducing and resolving conflict

Conflict can arise in many different interactions: with co-residents, friends and partners or family members. Sometimes, it seems like an individual cannot get on with anyone for more than a short period of time; no sooner is one situation resolved than another arises. Conflict causes a lot of distress, hurtful things are said, and it can sometimes result in physical aggression. It is important to explore the issues underlying why an individual becomes involved in conflict and ensure that their PBS plan supports and addresses these issues. This will also include the least restrictive responses to safely and compassionately containing aggression (see Chapter 8). However, there are also a number of more general strategies that can minimise and safely contain conflict.

When working to reduce conflict, it is important to take a longer-term view. In the short term, it can feel easier to separate an individual and keep them away from those they do not get on with. It can feel easier to allow one individual to impose their wishes on others rather than cope with the outburst that would be triggered by a more balanced response. In this way, an individual can become totally isolated or can come to totally dominate all decisions. Working within a proactive, compassionate and containing support style can help maintain the balance between being flexible and failing to maintain appropriate limits (see Box 13.4). Within this framework, conflict can be addressed using a problem-solving approach (see Box 12.10).

Box 12.10: Problem-solving approach to interpersonal conflict
No-blame: The aim is to find out what happened and how it could be done differently. It is not about deciding 'who is to blame'.
Define the problem: Seek information from everyone involved or who saw what happened to find out what caused the tension and conflict.
Generate alternatives: Ideas about what could be done differently. Ask both individuals involved what could have been done differently (they are each likely to have ideas about what the other could have done, although they may struggle to think how they could do things differently).
Evaluated alternatives and select potential solution: Be as collaborative as possible, involve both individuals in creating an action plan.
Implement chosen solution
Evaluate outcome: Is it working? Remember, it may take time for changes to become apparent. Look for small differences.

If it appears that everyone is clashing with everyone else in a setting, it may be helpful to look at the support approaches used. It may be that the way support is structured does not meet an individual's needs for engagement, interaction or time alone. Responses may inadvertently be reinforcing inappropriate behaviour. For example, arguing individuals may be split up, with each being offered a fun activity that would not otherwise have been offered. There may also be too much emphasis on shared activities and becoming a 'family'. Individuals may need more time to themselves and to have a break from the people they live with.

Bullying

Sometimes, it will become apparent that an individual's pattern of interacting may be characterised as 'bullying' (see Box 12.11).

Box 12.11: What is bullying?
Bullying occurs when an individual or group of individuals use their power to distress, hurt or exploit less powerful individuals. It is targeted, repeated and the perpetrators have more power than the victims.
It may take the form of: ■ Name calling. ■ Ignoring or excluding a person. ■ Physical aggression e.g. pushing, hitting. ■ Taking money or possessions. ■ Damaging someone's possessions. ■ Using technology such as text messaging and social networks to distress and intimidate someone (cyber bulling). ■ Spreading gossip or rumours about someone (indirect bullying).
Motivations may include: to impress others or keep in with a crowd, to boost self-esteem, an outlet for jealousy, a response to perceived rejection, to punish someone or as an expression of prejudice.
One part of a pair or reciprocal roles: bully vs bullied, that may be learnt as a result of experiencing bullying or abuse.

Bullying is serious and needs to be addressed on both an individual and service level as a safeguarding issue and to address offences that may have been committed. Once actions have been taken to ensure safeguarding, bullying can be explored and addressed through the creation of a PBS plan (see Chapter 8) and approaches to promoting positive interpersonal behaviours.

 Intellectual Disabilities and 'Personality Disorder' © Pavilion Publishing and Media Ltd and its licensors 2023

However, it is important to be thoughtful about how this label is used. Being labelled a bully may lead to an individual being judged, perceived negatively and their behaviour seen as conscious and planned. While the behaviour is unacceptable, recognising that the individual may be a survivor using the only means they know to protect themselves or meet their intense needs, may facilitate a more positive and constructive approach.

Creating a collaborative and kind culture that contains inappropriate interactions, openly talking about what bullying is, sharing accessible information and supporting individuals to access skills training (Stannis *et al*, 2019) can all help reduce the risks of bullying.

Promoting positive interpersonal behaviour and positive relationships

Promoting positive interpersonal behaviour and relationships needs to take place within a framework that validates emotions, supports individuals to regulate their emotions (Chapter 11) and promotes a positive sense of self and self-efficacy (Chapter 15). It is very hard to think about other people if you are overwhelmed by your own feelings, feel worthless and believe that you have no control over your behaviour. It is also important to identify and address the needs that lead to inappropriate behaviour through a PBS plan (see Chapter 8).

Standards

Where the individual lives in a shared residential setting or accesses day services, it is important to ensure that they are made aware of the behaviours expected and are supported to show these behaviours. Box 12.12 suggests some positive actions that can be taken to create a capable environment (see Chapter 6) that promotes positive interactions and minimises inappropriate interactions.

Box 12.12: Creating an environment which promotes positive interpersonal behaviour	
Support style	Use a proactive, compassionate and containing support style that creates a secure base (see Box 13.4). Emotionally competent (see Box 11.10) Use PACE (see Box 5.10).
Goals	Clear, specific, visible statements of the behaviours that are expected. These should be positive and give clear examples e.g.: →

	■ Be respectful – use polite language to everyone. ■ Be considerate – think about others when you play music or loud games, take turns. ■ Be kind to others – say nice things, share things, do things for others. ■ Respect other people's belongings. ■ Talk it out – use words when there are things that bug you. ■ Listen to others. ■ Look after your room. ■ Do your chores on the cleaning schedule.
Personal agency	Individuals are expected to take responsibility for their actions but in a context which is non-blaming, non-judgmental, and compassionate towards the difficulties they have in doing this. This can be expressed as Rights and Responsibilities e.g. *You have a right to be heard and a responsibility to listen.*
Boundaries	Set **appropriate limits** which respect everyone's needs and feelings (Box 13.12). Maintain these boundaries thoughtfully – reactive strategies in PBS plan (Boxes 8.13 and 8.14).
Model	Show the expected behaviour. Use SET (Box 13.13) to make the reasons for your actions clear.
Put in words	Give names to appropriate behaviours: ■ *'Thank you, it was kind of you to hold the door open for me.'* ■ *'It was considerate of you to turn your music down when Fred came home.'* ■ *'I noticed you shared your sweets with Lucy, that was generous of you.'* ■ *'I noticed you thanked George for helping you. That was polite.'*
Reward	Ensure appropriate behaviour results in praise, smiles, interaction and spending time with someone, appropriate requests being met or positive alternatives offered. Respond calmly to inappropriate behaviour, minimising interaction and responses.
Explore	Create opportunities to discuss behaviour and interactions including constructive peer-group discussions and peer feedback. Tailor this to the 3 **R**s.

 Intellectual Disabilities and 'Personality Disorder' © Pavilion Publishing and Media Ltd and its licensors 2023

Constructive criticism	Individuals need to know when and why their behaviour had not been at the standard expected – this needs to be done in a way that they can hear and that builds rather than undermines their self-efficacy (Box 16.6).

The ability to regulate behaviour depends on many factors (see Chapter 14). The extent to which an individual is able to regulate their behaviour is influenced both by their abilities and their beliefs about their abilities and their responsibilities. If someone does not understand or accept that they have a responsibility to behave appropriately towards others, they will not use the abilities they have. It is therefore important to create an environment in which individuals are expected to take responsibility for their actions but in a context which is non-blaming, non-judgmental, and compassionate towards the difficulties they have in doing this (Bolton *et al*, 2011). Inappropriate behaviour is never acceptable and always needs to be addressed. Standards should not be lowered because 'they can't help it'. Instead, the question should be what help and support does an individual need to use the abilities they have to achieve the standards?

It is important to apply the standards to all individuals in a particular setting. If some individuals are perceived as being allowed to behave inappropriately, or as 'getting away with it', others are likely to copy those behaviours rather than show the behaviours staff are trying to promote. This may present challenges when some individuals are more unwell or significantly less able than others and are therefore unable to reach a higher standard of behaviour. In these situations, it is helpful to give a clear and consistent explanation to the individual. For example, '*Fred is very unwell at the moment and that makes him very grumpy. He's having a hard time being polite. You're well, so we need to work together on you being polite to other people.*'

House meetings

Standards of behaviour and whether they are being met can be a helpful item for discussion in house meetings. This provides the opportunity to collaboratively explore standards and rules, why they are needed, and if they can be improved in any way. It can also provide an opportunity to explore problems that have been encountered during the week. Meetings need to be skillfully supported to take a problem-solving approach in which everyone has a chance to speak and to listen to others. A structured agenda can be very helpful. For example, ask people to share times they have seen others behaving appropriately and giving praise to each other before exploring any problems. Hearing directly from peers about the impact of behaviour is often much more powerful than being told by staff and can motivate individuals to change their behaviour.

Understanding social behaviour

Many individuals will have had little experience of appropriate interactions and may not know what many of the expected behaviours look like. Modelling behaviours and giving them names helps an individual build an understanding of what is and is not acceptable and gives them words to describe those behaviours. Where an individual struggles to understand an expected behaviour, it can be helpful to use Social Stories™ or Social Articles™.

Social Stories™

Social Stories™ were developed by Carol Gray (2015) as a way of explaining the social world. Originally designed for children with ASD, they have been extended to help adolescents and young adults (Timmins, 2018), when they are sometimes called Social Articles™. A patient, respectful and unassuming quality is the hallmark of the approach (Gray, 2014). This tone, which is neither directive nor critical, makes Social Stories™ a non-threatening and sensitive way to help individuals to understand situations and explore different ways of behaving and interacting. They are written to strictly defined criteria (see Box 12.13), which have been developed and refined since the original version.

Box 12.13: Creating stories in the spirit of the principles of Social Stories™	
Goal:	To share accurate information using a content, format, and voice that is descriptive, meaningful, and physically, socially, and emotionally safe for the reader.
Discovery	Gather information to 1) improve individual's understanding in relation to a situation, skill, or concept and 2) identify the topic and focus of each story or article. Involve those around the individual and where possible the individual themselves.
Parts and a title	The title and introduction clearly identify the topic, a body adds detail, and a conclusion reinforces and summarises the information. **Each story should address only one issue**. Make a new story for other issues.
Format	Tailored to the individual's abilities, attention span, learning style and – whenever possible – talents and/or interests. Illustrated in way that helps engagement and understanding.
Voice and vocabulary	A patient and supportive 'voice', vocabulary that is literally accurate. Uses the first person (I…) except for any negative information which should be third person (He, she, they…). Avoid words the individual does not like.

 Intellectual Disabilities and 'Personality Disorder' © Pavilion Publishing and Media Ltd and its licensors 2023

Six questions	Answers questions that describe context, including place (WHERE), time-related information (WHEN), relevant people (WHO), important cues (WHAT), basic activities, behaviours, or statements (HOW), and the reasons or rationale behind them (WHY).
Sentences	Descriptive Sentence (D): Descriptive Sentences accurately describe relevant aspects of context, including external and/or internal factors. They are free of assumption or bias, judgment, devaluation, or unidentified opinion. Perspective Sentence (P): Describe the individual's experience/viewpoint. Coaching Sentence (C): Convey something the individual could do differently. Affirmative Sentence (A): Convey the benefits of doing things differently.
Formula	Describes more than directs. At least two descriptive sentences for each coaching sentence.
Review and revise	Stories always need checking and refining – they evolve.
Using the story first time	Work through the story in a relaxed and supportive way. Encourage and answer questions about the story. Check it is understood, jointly re-write any confusing sentences. Choose illustrations. Make a final version.
Going forward	Re-read the story regularly to remind individual of the information, create space to talk and to celebrate progress.
Adapted from: Social Stories 10.2 (2014)	

When using this approach with individuals who do not have ASD, it may be helpful to be more flexible in tailoring them to meet individual needs and particularly in working more collaboratively with the individual in generating alternative behaviours (see Box 12.14). However, maintaining the positive tone and balance of descriptive and coaching sentences is important in avoiding becoming too directive or critical, as this is likely to lead to the story being rejected.

Box 12.14: Example story text based on Social Stories™ principles	
Title	Things I can say when I am angry
Introduction	
(D)	Swear words are words that are rude or insulting.
(D)	Swearing is when someone says these rude words.
(C)	There are other things I can say when I am angry.
Body	
(D)	Most people swear sometimes.
(D)	Sometimes my dad swears.
(D)	Sometimes my brother swears.
(D)	People may swear when something goes wrong.
(D)	People may swear when they are angry.
(D)	People may swear when they have an argument.
(D)	These are some of the swear words I use: F***, S***, P*** off, W*****
(P)	Sometimes I swear when I am angry with other people.
(P)	I swear when my laptop doesn't work.
(P)	Swearing makes me feel better. It gets my anger out.
(D)	People do not like to hear swear words. It makes them feel uncomfortable.
(D)	People do not like it when someone swears at them. It hurts their feelings and makes them upset.
(C)	It is important to be kind to other people.
(A)	People like it when I am polite to them.
(C)	There are other words I can use to get my anger out: Fudge, Sugar, go away, nitwit.
(D)	They are not swear words and will not upset other people.
(A)	Saying these words will help me be kind to people.
(A)	Saying these things can get my anger out.
Conclusion	I can be polite when I am angry by using words like Fudge!!! and Sugar!!!
Formular	D 12 + P 3 + A 3 = 18 ÷ C 3 = 6 > 2. The ratio of description to coaching in this story is 6:1 which is better than the minimum standard of 2:1.

For individuals at the **R**eason stage, psycho-educational approaches are helpful for developing an individual's understanding of relationships, how to keep safe and how to get help.

Intellectual Disabilities and 'Personality Disorder' © Pavilion Publishing and Media Ltd and its licensors 2023

Social cognition

Development of compassion and empathy may be very challenging. However, Social Stories™ may be used to help individuals to understand that other people have rights and that it is important to respect these. Modelling appropriate behaviour and talking about why it was done can help build understanding. Many individuals will not understand their own thoughts or emotions, hence the starting point may be helping them recognise and name their own feelings (see Chapter 11).

Where individuals have great difficulty in understanding other people's feelings, it may be helpful to adapt some of the materials developed to help people with ASD understand theory of mind. These resources explain concepts, break the process into steps and identify the specific skills that are needed, often using helpful visual aids such as thought bubbles and cartoon strips (Howlin *et al*,1999; Ordetx, 2018; Wareham and Kelly, 2020).

Families

Some families may be a great source of support to their adult child. However, for other individuals, their relationship with their family may be a source of great distress. An individual may still crave the love, attention and approval of their family, despite many years of experiencing that this is unlikely to be given. Others may be distraught when promised visits do not occur, trips home are cancelled, or phone calls missed. These situations are complex and may need intervention by therapists skilled in systemic approaches that focus on relationships between a group of people, rather than solely on an individuals' thoughts and feelings. However, thoughtful reflection and compassionate changes to ways of interacting with family members can sometimes draw them into a more collaborative pattern of interactions. It is helpful to understand systemic approaches and ways of working that do not require the member of staff to be a qualified therapist (Jones and Haydon-Laurelut, 2019, section III).

Therapeutic activities

Some individuals at the **R**eason stage may be able to engage in therapy to help them improve their relationships. Potentially helpful approaches were discussed in Chapter 3 and include Dyadic Developmental Psychotherapy (Jones, 2021), DBT and DBT skills groups, and Cognitive Analytic Therapy.

This work needs to take place within a proactive, compassionate and containing support style to promote positive interactions while the individual develops new understanding and is supported to try out new ways of interacting.

Key learning points

- An individual's first experience of relationships is usually within their family. Healthy families provide a secure base and safe haven in which to learn about relationships and appropriate behaviour.
- Positive, supportive relationships promote physical and mental well-being. They give a sense of purpose and belonging, reduce stress and help people cope with trauma. They also increase happiness, contribute to a healthy identity and boost self-esteem.
- Human relationships are immensely complicated. They are underpinned by a wide range of learnt behaviours and complex neurological pathways that are built through the developmental period. Hence, they are very vulnerable to the effects of adversity and trauma, exposure to inappropriate models and reduced learning opportunities.
- Individuals with intellectual disabilities who might be given a diagnosis of 'personality disorder' are likely to have wide-ranging difficulties in their relationships. Relationships may be unstable, overly intense and sometimes abusive.
- These difficulties are the result of a range of biological and social factors associated with their intellectual disabilities and their experiences, including trauma.
- Individuals can be supported to show more appropriate interpersonal behaviour through several approaches, including setting and maintaining standards, constructively managing conflict and resolving bullying within the context of a PBS plan that addresses underlying needs.
- Individuals can be supported to have more positive relationships through a number of approaches by working collaboratively with the systems around them. This might include developing or updating policies and procedures, staff training and support, and relationship and sexuality education for individuals. Systemic approaches may be helpful when there are complex issues within family relationships.
- Individuals at the **R**eason stage may also benefit from interventions to address some of the issues that underlie their difficulties with relationships including lack of skills, distorted thinking and insecure attachment styles.

 Intellectual Disabilities and 'Personality Disorder' © Pavilion Publishing and Media Ltd and its licensors 2023

Chapter 13: Building and maintaining professional, compassionate and containing relationships in everyday interactions

This chapter explores professional relationships and the importance of boundaries. It shows how clear, well-maintained boundaries can combine with a hopeful, compassionate and collaborative interest in each individual, to create an effective support style. It looks at challenges to maintaining professional relationships and boundaries and the factors that can lead to these challenges. It explores how to co-create appropriate limits which respect everyone's needs and maintain these through a compassionate and containing team approach.

Key topics

- Professional relationships
- Professional boundaries
- Challenges to professional relationships
- Assessment and formulation
- Practical approaches to everyday interactions

Professional relationships

Health and social care staff have a wide range of roles and undertake many different tasks, ranging from complex medical treatments and intimate personal care, to helping an individual with activities of daily living. However diverse their responsibilities, all staff share the characteristic of being in a professional relationship with the people they support. Professional relationships can often feel very similar to personal relationships. For example, staff may chat, joke and have fun with the individuals they support. Despite some surface similarities, professional and personal relationships differ in many dimensions (see Box 13.1).

Box 13.1: Comparison of professional and personal relationships

Characteristic	Professional	Personal
Purpose	Goal directed – intervention/ support. To achieve specific objectives of the service.	Pleasure, interest directed, connection and interaction.
Behaviour	Regulated by professional and ethical codes.	Guided by personal values and beliefs.
Sharing information	No or very limited sharing of own personal information. Work/ family life are separate. Maintains individual's confidentiality within professional limits.	Free sharing of information, including both work and private life. Interaction on social media. Nothing is confidential.
Financial		
Payment	Is paid to provide therapy/ intervention/support.	No payment for being in the relationship.
Money	Does not lend or borrow money.	May lend or borrow money.
Gifts	Does not give or accept gifts/only token gifts e.g. card/chocolates.	Give/receive depending on choice.
Relationship		
Length	Time limited e.g. duration needed for intervention/time the individual lives in that service/ time staff member works for that organisation.	No time limits – depends on decisions of those in the relationship.
Location	Defined by the nature of the intervention/support.	Places unlimited and undefined.
Structure	Defined by the nature of the intervention.	Spontaneous, unstructured.
Boundaries	Consistent – defined by intervention/codes of conduct.	Continually evolving by mutual agreement, flexible, inconsistent.
Power balance	Unequal – professional has more power through authority, knowledge, law.	Generally equal in healthy relationships.

 Intellectual Disabilities and 'Personality Disorder' © Pavilion Publishing and Media Ltd and its licensors 2023

Responsibility for relationship	Professional leads in starting, maintaining and ending relationship within consent.	Shared/equal responsibility.
Preparation for relationship	Requires training and induction to the role.	No formal training or preparation.
Time spent in relationship	Dictated by contractual agreements and intervention requirements, only in working hours.	Personal choice, mutually agreed.
Intimate contact	Dictated by intervention requirements, regulated by codes of conduct, given only with consent/in best interests	Negotiated by individuals for mutual pleasure.
Emotions	Empathy, compassion, compassionate distance. No 'special' connections	Love, affection, best friends, special connections.

Personal relationships are highly varied, flexible and wide ranging. In contrast, professional relationships seek to achieve mutually agreed goals through the appropriate use of professional power, from a basis of trust and respect, within a clearly defined framework. Staff are employed by organisations to achieve certain objectives. These can be described as their 'primary tasks'. A primary task is the 'what' and is the purpose of an interaction. For example, a support worker's primary task may be helping an individual with activities such as shopping and cooking. Other characteristics of professional relationships aim to accomplish the primary task, and these comprise the 'how'. For example, codes of conduct aim to keep everyone safe and promote high standards. Practical considerations, for example whether individuals are seen in their own homes or in a clinical setting, are determined by the policies and practices of the parent organisation. Certain ways of interacting within a professional relationship, such as showing warmth and empathy, help to engage individuals (see Chapter 5) and create a reparative relationship (see Chapter 3).

> *'We want to establish a relationship that is warm, friendly, compassionate and non-judgmental. At the same time, the relationship has a purpose and a time-frame, which is the achievement of the primary task within a defined period of time.'* (Bolton *et al*, 2011).

Professional boundaries

Professional boundaries create a formal structure for achieving the primary task and set standards for the relationships between an individual and staff. They are a specific form of interpersonal boundaries (see Chapter 12) and serve many important functions for both the individual and the staff who support them (see Box 13.2).

Box 13.2: Functions of professional boundaries: achieving the primary task safely and effectively	
Boundaries: appropriate limits which respect everyone's needs and feelings	
For the individual	
Protection	From the abuse of professional power. From the risk of risks of physical, emotional, sexual and financial abuse by members of staff.
Quality of care	Ensure staff have the necessary skills for their job and that these are kept up to date. That care is delivered in the right way at the right time.
Building a reparative relationship	Help individual to build trust and feel cared for.
Emotional and physical containment	Create a **secure base** (Skelly, 2017) and a **safe haven** (Hughes, 2007) in which behaviour, emotions and impulses can be co-regulated and new ways of being can be explored. Help build a sense of self and recognise the needs of others.
Foster healthy inter-dependence	Promote engagement but avoid creating over-dependence. Adjusting boundaries allows for healthy growth.
For staff	
Protection	Shield staff's privacy and time, guard them against entering into unprofessional relationships with individuals. Promote mutual respect and help protect staff from verbal and physical aggression and other forms of abuse from the individuals they support. Provide some protection from misunderstandings or unfounded allegations of misconduct.
Structure	Provide a secure framework in which staff can use their professional power (skills and knowledge) to benefit individuals.

 Intellectual Disabilities and 'Personality Disorder' © Pavilion Publishing and Media Ltd and its licensors 2023

Emotional containment	Help staff stay in their wise and reasonable states of mind (see Box 15.10) while working, hence promote planned and thoughtful actions.
Compassionate distance	Help staff stay warm and keep their cool.

The *creation, monitoring and maintaining of these boundaries is the responsibility of staff*, within the context of the law, guidance from professional bodies and local policies and procedures. The need for professional boundaries is taught as part of formal training for professions such as nursing, medicine and psychology, and promoted and enforced by professional bodies such as the Royal College of Nursing. The voluntary code of conduct for support workers and minimum standards for training (Skills for Care, 2013a; 2013b) highlight the need to learn how 'your relationship with individuals must be different from your personal relationships outside work' (1.2.2) and the need to establish and maintain appropriate professional boundaries. However, learning about professional boundaries may not form part of the training of other staff who come into contact with individuals using a service. For example, receptionists, cleaners or cooks may have no guidance on where to draw the limits of their role. This is important to address within a trauma-informed model where everyone has a role to play in healing and all staff are expected to interact in a more 'therapeutic' way (see Chapter 3).

Boundaries help ensure that professional relationships are consistent and respectful, allowing a real sense of partnership to develop (the Personality Disorder Commission, 2018). Appropriate boundaries also have important therapeutic benefits such as containing emotions and behaviour. These therapeutic boundaries are more flexible, within the limits of the formal professional structure, and may be collaboratively developed between staff and the individuals they support to meet each individual's needs.

Physical contact

An example of the importance of professional boundaries being tailored to individual need is the approach taken to physical contact. Human touch is essential for healthy development and ongoing well-being (Christensen *et al*, 2022; McNichols, 2021; While, 2021). Expressive touch conveys emotion, support and compassion, generates trust and provides comfort. However, strict boundaries intended to protect individuals from abuse can mean that individuals rarely, if ever, experience the positive, healthy touching that characterises close relationships: their only experiences of touch may be clinical holding in response to behaviours that challenge, and the contact necessary for medical procedures. Consequently, some individuals may be driven to show behaviours that challenge in order to experience the safety of being held or adopt a 'sick role' to experience touch through physical care (see Chapter 17). However, it is possible to delineate clear boundaries that distinguish appropriate professional touch from that which is unprofessional (see Box 13.3). This can be used to facilitate expressive touch safely within a professional relationship. Where identified as a need, by assessment and formulation, appropriate physical contact can be built into an individual's support plans.

Box 13.3: Differences between professional and non-professional physical contact

Types of physical contact between staff and individual:

Instrumental touch: as a result of performing procedures or direct care.

Protective touch: prevent someone from endangering themselves or others.

Expressive touch: conveys emotion, support and compassion, generates trust, care and comfort.

Professional	Unprofessional
Driven by individual's needs and preferences.	Driven by needs of staff member.
Based on a team decision.	Isolated decision of staff member or unofficial sub-group.
Based on consent or best interest discussion for individuals without capacity.	No consideration of capacity.
Use described in care plan.	Not in care plan.
Use recorded in notes.	Not recorded in notes.
Impact monitored and reviewed.	No formal monitoring or review.
Complies with local policies e.g. intimate care.	Based on views of individual staff member or unofficial subgroup.
Whole team, including manager and any professionals involved are aware of what contact is being made.	Contact is known only to the staff member or to a sub-group of staff.
Visible – takes place in shared areas or with other staff/chaperone present, or for intimate care, occurs in private areas at specific times.	May occur when others are not present, in private place, not timetabled.

 Intellectual Disabilities and 'Personality Disorder' © Pavilion Publishing and Media Ltd and its licensors 2023

Contact initiated by individual or in response to a specific need.	Contact lead by staff member.
Type of contact is related to the need it is to fulfil: **Comfort or greetings:** handshake, high fives, holding hand, hand on shoulder, arm round shoulder. **Support with learning tasks:** hand over hand, hand on shoulders. **Restrictive physical intervention:** hand on arm, hand on shoulder. **Intimate care:** contact minimum necessary for effective care.	Contact related to perceptions of member of staff. May include contact unlikely to be agreed by team e.g. full body hug, sitting on lap, cuddling on sofa, touching intimate areas when not involved in agreed intimate care, allowing individual to touch more intimate areas e.g. head resting on staff member's lap or chest.
Staff have opportunity to discuss their views and reactions to the physical contact in supervision.	Unofficial nature means it is unlikely to be discussed in supervision.
Individual has the opportunity to express their views on the contact with staff not involved in the contact.	Individual has no channel to express their views.

Proactive compassionate and containing support style

Some staff are uncomfortable with the concepts of boundaries, rules and power. Boundaries are often associated with concepts such as 'control', 'domination' and 'force'. There are many examples of professional power being misused (see Chapter 6). However, the absence of boundaries also carries risks: creating insecurity and anxiety and, in extreme cases, leading to chaos, disorder and avoidable harm. Rather than trying to 'control' individuals, boundaries set appropriate limits, which respect everyone's needs and feelings. Recognising the importance of boundaries is essential to their effectiveness. They need to be implemented with conviction, and in the expectation that they will be both helpful and followed. This conveys the message that staff believe individuals are capable of interacting in the expected, positive and appropriate manner.

The way therapeutic boundaries are created, implemented and maintained within a wider approach to the individuals supported, can combine to make four different support styles (see Box 13.4).

Box 13.4: Support styles

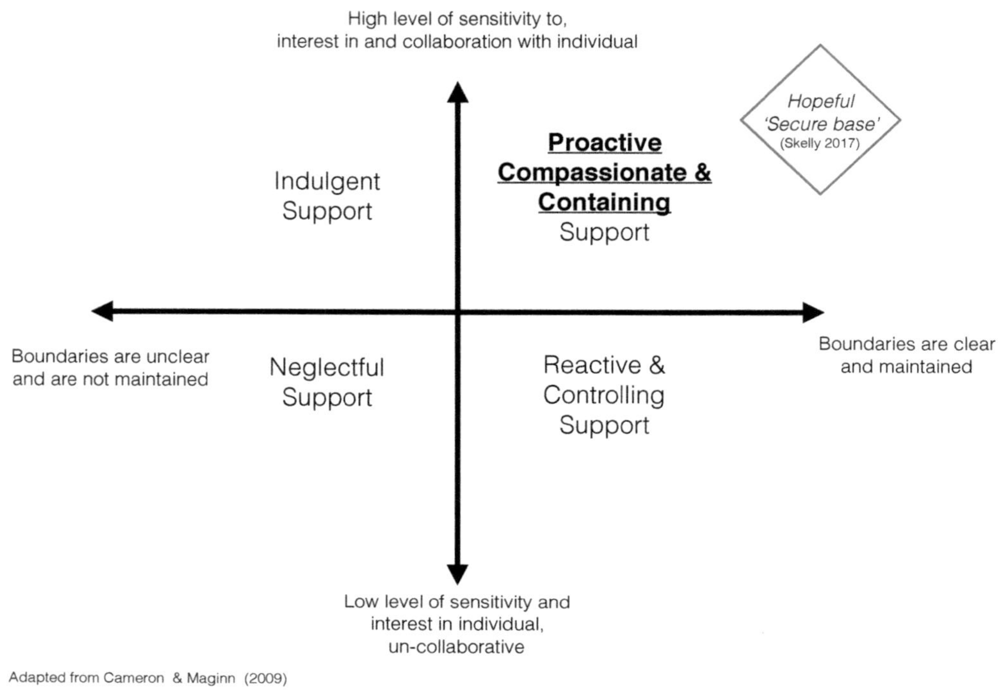

Different support styles

Proactive Compassionate and Containing	Found in the most effective services. Staff are very interested in and empathetic towards the individuals they support and are sensitive to their individual needs. They are positive and have hopeful, but realistic expectations for the individuals they support. They also recognise the need for clear and well-maintained, co-developed boundaries to promote positive behaviour and contain intense emotions and harmful or risky behaviours. This approach is active (see box 5.7) and confident, caring and predictable, without being over-controlling.
Indulgent	Sometimes seen in new, enthusiastic, but inexperienced services. Staff are kind, caring and hopeful but overly friendly, avoid confrontation and have difficulty saying 'no'. An over-emphasis on 'rights', choice and freedom, but under-recognition of responsibilities and the limitations of capacity to make choices. Intense emotions and risky behaviour may be uncontained, leading to crises or placement breakdown.

 Intellectual Disabilities and 'Personality Disorder' © Pavilion Publishing and Media Ltd and its licensors 2023

Neglectful	Over-stretched, exhausted services. Staff are too busy and tired to take an interest in the individuals they support and lack the energy to maintain boundaries. Focus on delivering basic care and leave the rest to chance. The lack of care and support may place individuals at risk of harm.
Reactive and controlling	Services that are isolated (geographically or socially) from outside scrutiny. Here staff have little interest in the individual, the focus becomes controlling the individual's behaviour. This support style is abusive and traumatises the individuals it is intended to help (see Chapters 6 and 9).

A proactive, compassionate and containing support style helps individuals to feel accepted, valued and cared for. Individuals are able to build trust because staff are consistent and predictable. It provides the supportive structure needed by individuals with insecure attachments, who struggle to form appropriate relationships and contain their own emotions and behaviour.

Challenges to professional relationships

Most adults recognise and respect professional relationships automatically. Healthy developmental experiences teach them that they are separate from others, that other people also have needs and that there are boundaries to behaviour and interactions. The difference between professional and personal relationships is absorbed as the result of multiple interactions while growing up, and appropriate patterns of behaviour are adopted automatically when interacting with professionals (healthy reciprocal roles – see Box 7.2).

However, a number of factors can leave individuals struggling to differentiate between personal and professional relationships. These make it difficult for individuals to recognise and accept that staff are not friends. Some factors may lead individuals to seek things from professional relationships that are inappropriate or to hold staff to impossibly high standards. These challenges can arise from an individual's intellectual disabilities, the nature of the supporting role, the activation of unconscious mechanisms (see Chapter 7) and the impact of experiences, including trauma, on an individual's ability to form healthy relationships. The characteristics of staff members may also interact with those of specific individuals to create challenges.

The nature of certain situations can also blur boundaries. Pitonyak (2008) draws parallels between supporting individuals in crisis and the intensity of the relationship of someone being rescued from the sea towards the person rescuing them. He notes that an individual who is in crisis may form strong feelings towards a particular member of staff, sometimes becoming obsessed with their comings and goings. He says that:

'This is natural:

A person being rescued at sea does not tell their rescuer that they appreciate the help but would like other rescuers to have a shot at helping. A person near drowning grabs on to the first helpful person that shows up. And so it is true that we can expect people in crisis to over-identify with one caregiver from time to time.'

Intellectual disabilities and professional relationships

Many individuals with intellectual disabilities have life-long contact with professionals to promote their well-being and provide support with activities of daily living. For many, this will include the need for intimate personal care such as help with washing and managing continence. It may also include supporting an individual to access a range of social and leisure activities. Sometimes, an individual will be supported by the same members of staff for many hours a day, with the professional relationships continuing over long periods of time.

The nature of the support role, wherein staff are friendly, kind, considerate and responsive to the individual's needs, and the amount of time spent with the individual, mean that individuals are likely to form strong emotional connections to their support staff. The nature of interactions can make it difficult for individuals with intellectual disabilities to understand that their valued supporters are not friends. When asked who their friends are, many individuals name one of their support workers (Callus, 2017; McCausland *et al*, 2021). Some individuals may 'fall in love' with staff members and sometimes seek to form intimate relationships with them.

The social isolation and loneliness of many individuals with intellectual disabilities can make staff feel sorry for the individuals they support. This can draw staff to try to compensate, by letting an individual into their life. Staff may share information about their own lives, let the individual meet their family, include them in special events and outings. Staff may be distressed that the individual never receives a hug or cuddle from another person and may therefore allow these behaviours to occur. Where staff support individuals over longer periods of time, they may form

 Intellectual Disabilities and 'Personality Disorder' © Pavilion Publishing and Media Ltd and its licensors 2023

strong emotional bonds with the individuals they support, which may gradually erode professional boundaries. In such situations, staff risk losing their professional perspective, for example making decisions on the basis of emotional connections rather than the thoughtful application of their professional skills.

Impact of developmental trauma

For some individuals, the combination of their unique biology and developmental experiences (see Chapter 2) mean that they struggle to form healthy relationships and to respect interpersonal boundaries (see Chapter 12). These difficulties are likely to shape all their interactions with staff and it can sometimes feel that individuals are, unconsciously, 'destruction testing' a team's professional boundaries. Lacking a sophisticated moral compass (Gupta, 2023), individuals may only consider the immediate outcome for themselves, not what is 'right' or 'wrong' or the impact on other people, and treat boundaries as obstacles to be overcome. Patterns of interaction may be shaped by unhealthy reciprocal roles, for example 'bullying' staff or perceiving staff as 'bullying' them (see Box 7.2). They may switch suddenly between these extremes. Individuals may view staff as friends, sharing 'secrets' and confidences and looking to connect on social media. They may see other members of staff as enemies to be avoided at all costs. These patterns put unconscious pressure on staff to blur or cross their usual boundaries, to make exceptions and go the extra mile.

If an individual is able to make a connection with someone, they may then want that person to provide all their support, regardless of the skills required, and to be available whenever they are needed regardless of other commitments. They may be drawn towards staff who appear 'softer' and more likely to bend the rules. In contrast, they may avoid or reject staff who attempt to maintain boundaries. Any misstep or refusal by staff may lead the individual to reject them completely. Insecurity and lack of trust may lead individuals to view all offers of help with great suspicion. They may need to check things and test out staff behaviour over and over again; seeking reassurance repeatedly but not being reassured by it. Experience may have taught them that being open and direct about what they need is unlikely to succeed and that they may need to exaggerate or disguise what they are seeking. Limited and skewed learning experiences may mean they lack the sophisticated social skills that allow people to shape interactions in ways that are mutually beneficial and leave both parties feeling good about the other person and the interaction. Box 13.5 gives some examples of these challenging everyday interactions.

Box 13.5: Examples of everyday interactions using survival strategies to meet intense needs
Following a member of staff around all shift. Refusing to do something until that person is present. Becoming angry or jealous if they talk to other individuals or staff.
'Sacking' key workers or named nurses, requesting frequent changes to the staff who support them.
Making unfounded allegations about staff members.
Chatting and flirting with staff, wanting to go on social outings with them.
Repeatedly asking the same question despite staff providing answers.
Requesting help and support with things they have the skills to do independently, reluctant to do things alone.
Making the same request to sequential members of staff until given the answer they were seeking.
Giving partial information e.g. '*X swore at me*' [after I turned the TV over in the middle of Eastenders]
'*The GP says I need painkillers*' [and I need to take more exercise].
Giving information/urgent requests at the point a session is about to end or a shift is coming to an end.
Using phrases that overstate the situation: '*I have never…, no one has ever…*'
Creating false permission: '*The doctor says I must… X said that I could*' (when that person is not present to check with)
Misquoting other people: '*X said you didn't do it right last time.*'
Sharing with others information that was shared as private or in confidence: '*Mary doesn't like you either.*'
Psychological pressure: '*If you don't then I will… If I can't, then I will. No one cares about me so I'll…*'
Doing something when another individual is the focus of attention e.g. self-harming during someone else's birthday party.

These patterns of interaction can leave staff feeling overwhelmed, confused, exhausted and frustrated. They can also lead to unprofessional behaviour such as taking on roles and responsibilities beyond the primary task at the expense of other responsibilities, or sharing unwise confidences such as their own current difficulties.

 Intellectual Disabilities and 'Personality Disorder' © Pavilion Publishing and Media Ltd and its licensors 2023

Some interactions will leave staff feeling they have been misled, tricked or exploited in some way. They may trigger strong emotional reactions (see Box 13.6) and can attract the judgmental label of being 'manipulative'.

Box 13.6: Feelings in staff arising from interactions with individuals, that might lead to the individual being labelled 'manipulative'

Feel:

- Used and taken in.
- Tricked into doing something.
- Sympathy and kindness have been exploited.
- Embarrassed and humiliated when full situation becomes clear.
- Powerless, controlled by the individual, that the individual is 'getting their own way'.
- Fearful for reputation, fear of losing job.

Staff characteristics and behaviour

How staff respond to challenges to their professional boundaries will be influenced by a number of factors. Chapter 7 explored how unconscious mechanisms used by staff can influence their thoughts, feelings and behaviour in relation to the individuals they support. Their behaviour will also be shaped by their own attachment strategies and 'hot buttons', and their responses to individuals adopting unhealthy reciprocal roles.

Every member of staff will have their own pattern of attachment strategies that they use in everyday interactions and when under stress (Beacon House, 2020a). Whatever attachment strategies they use, staff who understand and can regulate their own emotions are able to build positive working relationships with the people they support (Ruiz-Aranda *et al*, 2021). However, staff attachment strategies may interact with those of the individuals they support. For example, staff using ambivalent strategies may struggle to maintain boundaries for fear of being rejected. This may lead to an overly supportive relationship (doing a lot for the individual) which undermines the individual's self-efficacy and encourages dependence (Bolton *et al*, 2011). In contrast, staff using avoidant strategies might not actively follow up when an individual does not engage or might push an individual too hard in their efforts to promote independence, leading to hostility or disengagement.

Staff are only human, and, like everyone else, they will have 'hot buttons'. Hot buttons are strong reactions that occur when an interaction in the present causes someone to re-experience an old emotional wound ('emotional baggage'), triggering their automatic survival cascade, fight-flight response to threat (see Chapter 9). Hot buttons may arise from experiences such as self-doubt, fear of failure or rejection or feeling out of control (Taylor, 2022). They may also arise if someone else's behaviour violates a person's expectations about how people should behave. Consequently, certain behaviours in others, usually unintentionally, press hot buttons causing upset, irritation or anger. If someone is not aware of their hot buttons, this can lead to being thrown off balance and failing to regulate automatic threat behaviours. The patterns and intensity of interacting that some individuals use to meet their overwhelming needs are highly likely to hit staff's hot buttons and can trigger unprofessional responses. This might include enacting unhealthy reciprocal roles (see Box 7.2). For example, a member of staff who has a need to rescue people may be vulnerable to becoming over-involved in trying to keep an individual safe. A staff member who needs to feel in control may be drawn to over-restrictive practices in an effort to contain an individual who appears out of control.

Burnout

If staff are not supported with challenges to their professional boundaries, this can potentially lead to exhaustion, compassion fatigue (see Box 11.12) and burnout (see Box 13.7).

Box 13.7: Burnout	
Burnout: is a state of long-term exhaustion, diminished interest and loss of sense of achievement. Some of the signs of burnout are:	
Emotional	Feeling overwhelmed, ineffective, a sense of failure, self-doubt, helpless, trapped, defeated, empty, unhappy, dissatisfied. Lacking motivation, everything is too much effort. Being 'beyond caring', feeling mentally drained. Experiencing depression.
Thoughts	Negative outlook – nothing will change, nothing will make a difference. Cynical attitudes – people deserve the problems they have, blaming the victim.
Physical	Feeling physically drained, tired all the time. Headaches/back ache. Changes to appetite, problems sleeping. Increased vulnerability to physical illness, stress related illnesses.

 Intellectual Disabilities and 'Personality Disorder' © Pavilion Publishing and Media Ltd and its licensors 2023

Behavioural	Reduced job performance, coming in late, going home early. Putting things off, not getting things done. Detachment, not engaging with others. Taking frustrations out on others, shouting, criticising, undermining. Use of food, alcohol, drugs to cope.

Burnout was identified by Freudenberger (1974) and the concept further developed by Maslach (1999)
Reference: Dall'Ora *et al* (2020)

Chapter 7 explored how to build positive, collaborative working relationships within and between teams, by developing an understanding of key psychological processes and using reflective practices. These same processes can be applied to understanding the factors influencing professional relationships between individuals and members of staff.

Staff need to be supported to develop their awareness of their own attachment strategies (Beacon House, 2020a), hot buttons and the automatic thoughts they trigger. This allows them to explore how an individual's motivations and the underlying reasons for their behaviour might be very different from the automatic assumptions triggered. The interactions may still not be pleasant, but their interpretation and the response to them can remain professional.

Assessment and formulation

Developing an understanding of, and a way forward from, patterns of interacting with staff will form part of the wider assessment of an individual's abilities to form relationships (see Chapter 12). For example, it is helpful to have an understanding of an individual's attachment strategies.

> *'Understanding attachment strategies, starting with our own, helps us to make sense of why people can't always connect and be open to support.'*
> (Beacon House, 2020a)

Within this wider context, it may be helpful to explore certain patterns of interactions more fully. This might be achieved by collating information about challenging interactions and exploring these in a team reflective case discussion (see Box 7.9). If issues are identified in supporting more than one individual, a wider team reflection may be helpful (see Box 7.7).

Box 13.8 explores some of the examples from Box 13.5. It looks at the automatic assumptions and reactions these might trigger and gives some ideas of how these interactions might be more constructively understood by considering underlying needs and skills deficits.

Box 13.8: Everyday examples: What might be driving the behaviour and how interpretation of the behaviour can influence responses	
Individual 1	*I really need to do … They won't do it if I ask, they always do what the doctor says.* Experience has taught them their needs are not important or will be used against them. Do not trust staff to listen to them. Cannot manage the urge or wait until later. Do what they think will work, without considering the implications for the staff member.
Comment:	*The doctor says I must…* (when the doctor is not present to check with).
Staff thought:	That doctor is always changing things without checking, what a muddle.
Staff response:	*'It would be good if they would let me know, but if they say so, I guess it's OK.'* Find out later that was not what was said. Feel angry and used. They tricked me.
Staff alternative thought:	What's going on here? That doesn't fit the guidelines. I know (individual) really wants to do this, it must be tough sticking to the guidelines, I guess they are desperate.
Staff alternative response	*'OK, I'll just check if the guidelines have been updated. I really want to help you (achieve what the guidelines are working for). I guess you really want to do …* *The guidelines haven't changed yet, so I can't do that today. How about we do …*
Individual 2	*I really need them to stick around, it's so scary right now. I can't think straight, is that the same answer they said last time? Will it really happen?* Insecure attachment, struggle to be alone, can't trust that anyone will do what they say, asks but can't hold on to or believe the answer.
Issue:	Asks the same question despite staff providing answers.
Staff thought:	If I answer this again, I'll go bonkers. They never listen to me.

 Intellectual Disabilities and 'Personality Disorder' © Pavilion Publishing and Media Ltd and its licensors 2023

Staff response:	*'I've answered that already. What did I say?'* Feel exasperated and rejected.
Staff alternative thought:	I've already answered this several times. What is going on here? What is stopping them from hearing me? Are they anxious? Can I do anything to help them?
Staff alternative response:	*'I really want to help you understand what is going on. I wonder if something is worrying you? Can I write it down for you? What about we put some music on?'*
Individual 3	*I hate it when she goes home. I can't cope without her. She's the only one who helps me.* Fear being abandoned.
Issue:	Giving information/urgent requests at the point a shift is coming to an end.
Staff thought:	What now? I'm never going to catch that bus, but I better deal with it as its urgent.
Staff response:	*'OK, let's talk about it and see if I can sort it out.'* Feel annoyed but also special.
Staff alternative thought:	Why now? they've had a whole shift to tell me this. Handover is always a stressful time, I wonder if they are worried about me leaving?
Staff alternative response:	*'Gosh, that sounds important. I have to go now, it's the end of my shift, but I'll tell … what you said and he will sort things out, you know you get on with him. I'll check that it's sorted when I am in tomorrow.'*

Professional relationships run through all the intervention stages identified in Chapter 3 (see Box 3.1). They are the vehicle that allows staff to help individuals contain and regulate their distress and behaviour in the **R**egulate stage. Building collaborative, trusting working relationships is the primary focus of the **R**elate stage. This enables staff to co-regulate emotions, establish person-centred routines and build the connections that might allow progression to the **R**eason stage. In the **R**eason stage, professional relationships help achieve therapeutic gains.

Chapter 9 explored how to relate to individuals in the **R**egulate stage (crisis) and Chapter 5 explored how to build positive working relationships in the **R**elate stage. Chapter 3 explored the importance of the 'how' of relationships for effective interventions in the **R**eason stage. The following section explores how to create and maintain professional and therapeutic boundaries and respond constructively to challenging everyday interactions.

Practical approaches to everyday interactions

It is common sense to set up patterns of support that reduce the likelihood of problematic interactions occurring. While strategies can also be put in place after problems have developed, it can take much longer to resolve issues.

Team support

A helpful approach is to think in terms of 'team support' (see Box 13.9). Staff work as part of a cohesive team within a team, ideally consisting of three or four members, rather than individually (Wong, 2020). It may need to be a little larger to allow for certain shift patterns.

Box 13.9: The team support approach	
Training:	Understand and recognise the emotional needs and interpersonal issues that arise from having intellectual disabilities and experiencing developmental trauma. Know about the importance of professional relationships, how these might be challenged and what action to take if this occurs.
Expectations:	There is an expectation, supported by boundaries, that staff and individuals will be treated with respect and kindness. These are explicit and available in accessible formats. There is a clear and accessible statement of what is and is not offered by the service/individual staff members. Emotional bonds are expected and accepted with support to keep them within appropriate boundaries. Individuals are expected to work with a 'core team within a team' rather than one special person. Rotas and diaries are managed to ensure all staff work regularly with the individual.
Roles:	Named nurse, key-worker and other roles are defined by tasks not in terms of special relationships. Tasks may be spread across several people rather than one individual. Changes are made on the basis of practical issues not whether the staff member is liked or disliked.
Clarity and honesty:	Accessible information shows who will be working when. Staff say hello and goodbye at the start and end of shifts. New staff are introduced gradually so that trust can develop. Endings are marked by cards or a party to make them concrete. Start and end of staff leave is clear.

 Intellectual Disabilities and 'Personality Disorder' © Pavilion Publishing and Media Ltd and its licensors 2023

Preferences:	If patterns of preferences emerge, preferred staff are allocated to support necessary but not fun activities. Favourite activities are supported by less preferred staff.
Openness:	Staff are supported to be open with each other, about their emotional responses to individuals and there are regular opportunities to explore these in team reflections and supervision.
Post-incident support:	Staff are supported to when there have been incidents of verbal and physical aggression. There is learning from incidents and changes are made to reduce likelihood of further incidents.
Quality control:	The nature and quality of professional relationships is monitored and proactive measures taken if there are signs of difficulties. Complaints are investigated promptly and thoroughly. There are robust procedures for supporting individuals and staff while allegations are investigated.

The team approach aims to facilitate the building of trust and emotional connections with a small, consistent team of staff. The team within a team work together, sharing the responsibilities of key worker or named nurse roles, meaning there is always someone available who knows the individual well and can resolve day-to-day issues. This aims to reduce the intensity of the connection formed when there is only one special relationship, and minimise the likelihood of over-dependence on one or two members of staff. The smaller team also makes it easier for staff to adhere to agreed boundaries in a predictable but flexible manner. This approach also makes the support system more resilient to planned and unplanned staff absences and turnover (Wong, 2020).

Creating and maintaining boundaries

Professional boundaries

When working with individuals who struggle to accept the structure of professional relationships or to engage with professionals, it is important to make explicit a team's implicit professional boundaries and agree where there is flexibility. This promotes consistency, reduces the risk of splitting (see Chapter 7) and defines the parameters within which boundaries can be tailored to meet individual needs. For example, how much flexibility is there in appointment times, staying late or coming in especially for one individual? Staff need to be confident of the limits to confidentiality (see Box 10.14) to help them respond appropriately to requests to keep information secret: open lines of communication are important to keep everyone safe.

Discussions about grey areas such as self-disclosure are also important. Deciding how much personal information to share with an individual is difficult. If no personal information is shared, this can lead to distrust or to the gaps being filled by an individual's own ideas, which may be inaccurate and unhelpful. However, sharing too much information strengthens the perception that staff are friends and may be a gateway to disclosing inappropriate information about experiences and views. Such disclosures are likely to create tensions within the team as the individual is unlikely to 'respect confidentiality' and will share such information with others. Sharing inappropriate information also tells the individual that the member of staff is not to be trusted (*'If they say this to me, what are they saying about me to other people?'*). There are no fixed rules on what can be shared, but some suggestions are given in Box 13.10. A balanced approach will let the individual feel that they know staff and can trust what they say, but not risk crossing boundaries.

Box 13.10: Suggestions for boundaries around self-disclosure
Don't volunteer information.
Do not share anything that your co-workers and manager do not already know about you.
Only share positive comments about other individuals, staff or services e.g. *'I like Justin too, he's got a great sense of humour'*.
Consider questions carefully before answering honestly but with minimal information e.g. *'Where were you last week?' 'I took some leave'* vs *'I was on holiday, in Spain with my boyfriend, celebrating our engagement.'*
NEVER share on-going personal issues e.g. *'Yes I know how you feel, I just split up with my girlfriend and I can't stop thinking about her.'*
It may sometimes be helpful to share in relation to a successfully resolved personal issue that relates to what an individual is experiencing e.g. *'I used to have a problem with alcohol but going to AA helped me get back on track. It's really worth giving AA a try.'* Discuss in supervision and with colleagues BEFORE sharing.
Don't talk specifically about where you go when not at work e.g. *'Yes, I love eating out, too'* vs *'My favourite restaurant is that Thai place on the London Road'*.
Be confident about not sharing information that feels uncomfortable. Humour may take the sting out of this e.g. *'I can't answer that, I might get fired'*.
'…it is usually okay to talk to the person about your day and your interests, or spend time making small talk about local news for example (assuming these are not particularly sensitive topics for them). Lots of conversations are not really about what is said, but the fact that one person had chosen to interact with another, shown an interest in them and shared a bit about themselves in return' (Williams and Jones, 2022, p39)

 Intellectual Disabilities and 'Personality Disorder' © Pavilion Publishing and Media Ltd and its licensors 2023

Once agreed, it is helpful if these professional boundaries are collated in an accessible form, shared, and regularly revisited, to ensure everyone, including the individuals supported, are aware of them.

Staff may find it helpful to have a buddy system (pairs or trios) who monitor and check in with each other to ensure boundaries are maintained (Wong, 2020).

Therapeutic boundaries

Staff also need to proactively facilitate the creation and maintenance of therapeutic boundaries. Individuals will not recognise this need themselves: they are unlikely to have experienced of appropriate boundaries (Wong, 2020) and struggle to, or cannot, regulate the impulses and emotions that are driving their behaviour. They will have a narrow focus on their own survival and will not be thinking about the effects of their behaviour on others.

To be effective, boundaries need to be created and flexibly maintained within an approach that is sensitive and responsive to individual needs. One way to minimise the need for individuals to 'push boundaries' is to ensure that they have as much control as possible over other areas of their lives (Anderson *et al*, 2020).

Rigid, one-size-fits-all boundaries are likely to be counterproductive, making individuals feel controlled and uncared for (see Chapter 9). However, too much flexibility will lead to insecurity and confusion. It is important to occupy the middle ground between these two extremes. Boundaries may also need to be looser or tighter depending on an individual's needs. For example, breathing room is an approach that changes the parameters of therapy in a thought-out way, to help engage individuals who find conventional settings too threatening (see Box 13.11). However, such an approach would be unhelpful for an individual struggling to understand that the therapist was not a friend.

Box 13.11: Breathing room

Taking some moments to think or do something unrelated to talking about problems/doing interventions. Anything the individual enjoys doing, as long as it ensures their health and safety, the person supporting them is comfortable with it and it is supported by a team decision.

Aim: Create a comfortable space, build trust and comfort for someone who struggles to engage.

Activities e.g. going to a coffee shop (or just having coffee), going for a walk, listening to their favourite song together at the beginning of each session or when they need a break, looking at cat pictures on Instagram, kicking a ball around.

→

Step 1:	Acknowledge the fact that it is hard to get to know a stranger. Be empathetic to their struggles.
Step 2:	Explain that the intervention doesn't have to be in a therapy room. Ask about what they love to do, or try to learn about their general interests in life. Normalise the need to take a moment in a different context to get ready to do the work, or take a break from work
Step 3:	Explain what a breathing room is. Let the individual choose one (or more). Offer multiple options. Only offer options you are comfortable with and which are safe.
Step 4:	Interact with the individual, keeping it light, do not ask any questions that might make them uncomfortable. Once the client feels free and ready in the breathing room, come back to the conventional setting for the rest of the session. For individuals who find engagement very hard, this step might be omitted until a good connection has built in the breathing room.
Step 5	Check with individual how they found the experience of breathing room and how it could be improved for next time.

Adapted from Chowdhury (2019) and Bennett *et al* (2017)

An individual should always be given the reason for the boundary. It is important that, wherever possible, boundaries are created collaboratively. However, initial parameters should be set in a team discussion without the individual being present. This allows team members to express honest concerns about the issues involved without the risk that the individual will see staff as taking different 'sides' on the issue, and to consider factors such as the individual's attachment strategies (see Box 5.10). Box 13.12 gives some suggestions as to how boundaries can be created and maintained.

Box 13.12: Creating and maintaining boundaries	
Think it through first	What is the reason for this boundary? Will it work? Is it the best solution? Does it consider everyone's needs? Does it have the right balance of containment and freedom? If others are involved, make sure it is a joint decision. What would someone from outside the situation think of the boundary?
Attachments	Does it fit the individual's attachment style? Clear, firm boundaries may be needed for ambivalent attachments while a creative, more flexible approach may help those with avoidant attachments to engage.

 Intellectual Disabilities and 'Personality Disorder' © Pavilion Publishing and Media Ltd and its licensors 2023

Frame of mind	Be confident that the boundary is fair and the best thing for everyone involved. If you don't believe in it, you won't convey conviction. Remember boundaries help people feel safe and cared for.
Use a calm but confident tone of voice	Using too soft a tone will lack conviction, but too firm is likely to be interpreted as being angry.
Clear and specific with reason	Conversations about boundaries should be respectful, empathic and based on a specific reason. *'The latest I can take a phone call is 4.30pm. After that it will go straight to voicemail. This is so I can write up my notes leave before the office locks up. If you leave a message, I'll phone next time I am in the office.'*
Validate their experience and emotions	*'I know this is hard for you, you really want to talk to me at the time you are upset.'*
Offer a compromise if appropriate or provide an alternative	*Remember the crisis card we made. If you need to talk, you can ring the Samaritans, or text SHOUT. I remember they have really helped you in the past.'*
Where there is no choice about something	Give two choices about the way it is done so that individual still has a sense of control. e.g. finger-prick test. *'Do you want to put your headphones on and listen to some music, or shall we chat about last night's Eastenders?'*
Explain what else they can do.	*'If it's a health worry, ring 111, they will be able to help you. If it's an emergency ring 999.'*
Make clear you are not rejecting them	*'This is the same rule for everyone. Remember, I will see you once a week and I will reply if you leave a message'* [this may need a follow up of how many messages a week you can reply to].
Do not apologise for the boundary	Fair boundaries are good for everyone. You are doing the right thing by yourself and the individual and the other people you support.
If boundary is challenged or crossed	Respond calmly. Use 'SET' see Box 13.12. *'I really want to sort this out. I can see you are really upset that your call went to voicemail. Remember, I can't answer calls after 4.30, but I will reply to your messages.'*

→

Being told you don't care	Do not apologise. Do not take it personally. Staying calm and sticking to the boundary **shows that you keep your word** (even if it isn't what they wanted) and **can be trusted to do what you say you will**.
Problem-solve	*'Let's think about the best way for you to get support when I am not available, who else can you call? What about us making a crisis box?'*

Creating and maintaining boundaries often involves conversations about limits and behaviours of concern that may be unwelcome to the individual. It is therefore important to use a means of communication that maximises the chances of them hearing the key information. The acronym SET has been used to summarise an approach to effective communication. It identifies both the tone of the interaction and the order in which things should be said to best convey the message (see Box 13.13).

Box 13.13: SET – Effective communication should include three steps:		
1	**S**upport:	*'People don't care what you know unless they know that you care.'* Reassurance that the relationship is a safe one and that their needs matter. *'I am worried about how you are feeling.'* *'I want to try to help you feel better.'* *'I hope we can work this out.'* *'Your opinion is important.'* *'Thank you for letting me know how you feel.'*
2	**E**mpathy:	Convey understanding of the uncomfortable feelings the individual is having and that it is OK to have such feelings. Without a statement of empathy, they may feel that their feelings are not understood. *'I see you are angry, and I understand how you can get mad at me.'* *'How frustrating this must be for you.'* *'You probably wish I'd stop bothering you.'* *'Seeing that text message really hurt you'.*
3	**T**ruth:	A realistic and honest assessment of the situation and each person's role in the intervention/solving the problem. It is an objective statement that focuses on the 'it', not on the subjective experience of either, given without judgement or anger. Sharing of your point of view of the facts of the situation. →

 Intellectual Disabilities and 'Personality Disorder' © Pavilion Publishing and Media Ltd and its licensors 2023

	'This is what I can do…' 'This is what will happen…' 'Either this… or that' Beware of withholding the truth out of kindness or to avoid upset, trust will be lost and in the end there will be more distress or upset.
Adapted from: Kreisman and Straus (1991), Herring (2009), Johnston (2020)	

SET acts to help the individual both feel heard themselves, and to listen to what staff need to say to them. It starts with explicitly stating that the member of staff wishes to help. Next, it recognises and empathises with the individual's feelings (see Chapter 11). It then honestly states the facts of the situation.

When appropriate boundaries are challenged, it is important to remember that a carefully considered boundary is not the problem: it is an important part of the solution. An individual's response to boundaries is driven by powerful underlying factors such as fear of rejection and abandonment or feeling controlled. Their reaction is the result of all that has happened to them and how they interpret staff actions. Giving in (as opposed to thought-through changes) creates dependence and proves staff are untrustworthy.

Facilitating healthy interdependence

It is important to work in ways that do not create 'over dependence'. 'Helping' can sometimes inadvertently lead to helplessness and disempowerment (Gregson and Delaney, 2021). An overly supportive relationship undermines self-efficacy and risks encouraging dependence. It may also invite an overly strong attachment, leading to very intense emotions (Bolton *et al*, 2011). The approach needs to be balanced, as an overly demanding relationship is likely to lead to hostility or disengagement. Box 13.14 gives some examples of helpful and less helpful interactions.

Box 13.14: Examples of interactions that might or might not promote healthy interdependence

Helpful	Unhelpful
What help do you need to do this for yourself?	Leave it with me and I'll sort it out.
At what point do you get stuck? How about you do it up to there, then I'll help you finish it?	Is there someone you can get to do that for you?
I don't know anything about that either – shall we look it up together?	I was planning to take leave that day, but if you really need me to go with you, I could cancel it.

→

Do you remember when you did X? I think you handled that well. This is a bit like X. I think maybe you could do it if you give it a try.	You know sometimes you just need to push yourself to do things you don't want to bother with.
Is there something about this that makes you think you can't do it? Is there another way round that?	You can't always expect other people to do this for you, I think it's time you did it yourself.
Adapted from: Bolton *et al* (2011)	

The term 'over-dependent' is sometimes used to describe individuals who require more support than appears necessary on the basis of their abilities, and there may be pressure for them to become more 'independent'. Individuals may be perceived as lacking motivation or judged to be 'lazy'. However, this is an oversimplification of a more complex experience. Where an individual does not use skills at the expected level, this may be due to a lack of confidence, lack of learning opportunities (overprotection) or their abilities being overestimated. Where this is the case, building an individual's sense of safety and self-efficacy (Box 16.6) may help them be better able to work towards reaching their potential (Gregson and Delaney, 2021).

However, this often has much less to do with skills and much more to do with relationships. Supporting an individual with activities of daily living can be seen as having two components: the task and the process. Usually, the focus is on the task, for example buying food items. However, the process involves the enjoyable company and support of a valued staff member who creates an atmosphere of confidence, safety and, often, fun. If an individual becomes 'independent', they will lose this valued social interaction from a life that may otherwise have limited opportunities for positive interactions. For individuals with insecure attachments, being alone may also be a frightening experience, triggering fear of abandonment or the intrusion of unpleasant thoughts and memories. Hence, it may be loneliness, anxiety or a need to feel cherished that stops an individual from realising their potential.

It is therefore important to ensure that underlying needs are addressed independently from the help an individual needs with activities of daily living. This might include learning self-soothing skills, joining a support group, having regular pampering sessions or following independent activities with a social one, for example, '*I'll pop to the chemists while you get the bits for tea, then we can meet in the cafe for a coffee before we go home*'. Sometimes, 'over-dependent' is used to describe individuals who simply seek a lot of contact and social interaction. Consciously scheduling brief interactions throughout an individual's day and staff

 Intellectual Disabilities and 'Personality Disorder' © Pavilion Publishing and Media Ltd and its licensors 2023

learning techniques to end interactions in a respectful but timely manner without causing upset, are also helpful in ensuring the need for interaction is met, while also allowing staff to complete their primary tasks (see Box 13.15).

Box 13.15: Respectfully ending interactions in a timely manner
Schedule the next interaction at the beginning of the conversation/appointment so the individual knows when they will speak to you again e.g. *'I know you have lots to talk to me about, let's book another date now, in case we can't do it all today'. 'I'm very busy now, we may need to talk again after supper when I've got a bit more time.'*
Structure the interaction: ■ State how long the interaction can be e.g. I've got 10 minutes/this appointment is for 1 hour. ■ Make an agenda/tick list of items to discuss. e.g. *'Let's make a list of what we need to talk about…'* ■ Use the agenda to keep track e.g. tick items off or say *'We haven't talked about X'*. ■ If new issues come up, put them on an agenda for the next conversation or negotiate a swap: *'We haven't time to talk about that as well, which of these shall we leave for next time?'* ■ Give a 5-minute warning that the conversation is about to end: *'We've got 5 minutes left, let's round this up and make sure everything is on the list for next time.'* ■ End on time, saying, *'We need to stop now, I have to do Y. We can talk about the other things next time we meet.'* ■ Remind the individual of something pleasant they can do now the interaction has finished. ■ Use SET (Box 13.13). *'I really want to help you with this. I know you want to talk about it now. However, I need to go now, I've made a note of it and we will talk about it next time.'*
Thank them for co-operating. *'Thank you, it really helps me when we finish on time.'*

Positive responses to behaviours that can make staff feel 'manipulated'

Truly 'manipulative' behaviour is intended to exploit, control, or otherwise influence others to one's advantage. It is often carried out in a conscious and planned manner and sustained over periods of time. In contrast, many of the behaviours shown by individuals who might be given a diagnosis of 'personality disorder' are more likely to be spontaneous responses to situations in which they are trying to address intense needs or cope with overwhelming emotions. Their behaviour needs to be understood in the context of their adverse experiences, limited and distorted learning opportunities and repeated experiences of their needs being neither recognised nor met (Paterson *et al*, 2017). Staff are likely to find this much easier if they have been given the opportunity to explore these issues and their own emotional reactions in a supportive setting, for example participating in CaPDID training (Anderson *et al*, 2020).

Responding constructively to behaviours that can make staff feel manipulated involves a number of steps. The factors contributing to these patterns of interacting need to be understood, the underlying needs and healthy ways of addressing them need to be identified and worked towards. Consistent boundaries can then be put in place so that the inappropriate means of meeting the needs are no longer effective. If the individual is viewed as struggling to survive in the only way they know, it is much easier to respond to these behaviours in a calm and compassionate way. Thinking of these behaviours in this way also recognises that the individual may continue to behave in such ways until new ways of meeting their needs become established. Once staff achieve this calm and positive mindset, most of these behaviours are relatively straightforward to contain within a team approach (see Box 13.16).

Box 13.16: Constructive, respectful approaches to survival behaviours	
Acceptance	There are things you can't do, things you can't change, people you don't like, people who don't like you. That is reality, not the end of the world. Don't let it get to you. The individual you are supporting will not have got to acceptance yet, but you can model how it is done.
Commitment	Continue to care and compassionately do what is right whatever is thrown at you.
Unmet needs	Recognise these interactions are trying to meet important needs. Identify and address them.
Clear boundaries	Co-create realistic limits that respect everyone's needs and stick to them.
Write it down	Keep good, timely, notes, write down agreements, guidelines, contracts etc. These avoid confusion at the time and allow things to be checked, help reduce conflict and can highlight even very small positive changes.

Intellectual Disabilities and 'Personality Disorder' © Pavilion Publishing and Media Ltd and its licensors 2023

Share it	Make sure everyone knows what has been agreed. Ensure individual has an accessible version.
Review and update	Check regularly – are approaches working, do they need to be changed to reflect progress?
Stay cool	Take a deep breath, everything will work out OK if you keep your head.
Make time to think	Remember, nothing is so urgent, important or special that it justifies breaking professional boundaries. There is always a solution that will support an individual in a professional manner. It may just take some thought to find it.
Check and double check	Don't jump to conclusions. What you are told someone said or did may not be accurate. Look for the evidence to support it. Maintain a questioning, neutral approach e.g. Individual: *'X said I can…'* Staff: *'Did they? I'll just check if the guidelines have been changed… It's not in the guidelines, so I can't do it today, but I'll check and get the guidelines updated if things have changed.'*
Get both sides	Remember, there are two sides to every story. Get the other side before taking action. Wires may have got crossed – someone may not have said or done what you have been told they did.
Get the wider picture	Keep a sense of proportion. Remember that no one is perfect (even if someone is telling you so!) Are things really as dark as they are painted? Step back and look at the wider picture. Everything looks huge and terrifying when looked at through a microscope.
Don't argue	Avoid arguments about the guidelines/boundaries. Use SET: Support: *We drew up these guidelines together because we want to help you…* Empathy: *I can see it upsets you that I can't do…* Fact: *The guidelines say we can do… I will make a note that you are unhappy and we can look at this on Friday when the team review the guidelines.*
Use Social Stories™	Social stories can be an effective way of helping individuals understand the reason for boundaries – and the options that are still available to meet their needs (see Chapter 12).

It is important to talk to the individual about what is being done, how the team will meet their needs and to negotiate some aspects of the boundaries with them. Ironically, if this is not done sensitively, the process may make the individual feel tricked, powerless, controlled and 'manipulated' by staff. This in turn will lead to an intensification of the behaviours the staff team was trying to reduce.

Unfounded allegations of abuse

Individuals with intellectual disabilities and individuals given a diagnosis of 'personality disorder' are vulnerable to being abused, including by the staff supporting them (see Chapters 2 and 6). All allegations need to be properly investigated. However, investigation sometimes shows that the allegations were unfounded. There are many different circumstances that can lead to an unfounded allegation, including experiencing flashbacks and the triggering of unconscious mechanisms. For individuals who split staff into 'loved' or 'hated', allegations may be a way to escape from the presence of someone they experience as unbearable or terrifying (despite their appropriate professional behaviour). It may also be a way of finding some control over a frightening situation or removing someone experienced as over-controlling. Rather than being seen as malicious, unfounded allegations can be seen as another survival strategy in response to a situation experienced as threatening or unbearable. Where an individual makes repeated unfounded allegations, it is possible to work with the safeguarding process to find ways of keeping everyone safe while the factors driving the need to avoid certain members of staff are understood and a way forward identified.

Thoughtfully building and maintaining professional behaviours and boundaries in everyday interactions is an important part of a compassionate and containing support style, creating a secure base from which an individual can live their best life and a safe haven in which to seek comfort when things are difficult.

Key learning points

- Professional and personal relationships are superficially similar but, in reality, they differ in every dimension. These differences are essential to protect both the individual and the staff member and to achieve the service's primary task.
- Boundaries are appropriate limits that respect everyone's needs and feelings. They perform a range of important functions within parent-child interactions and within professional relationships, helping to create a secure base.
- Individuals with intellectual disabilities who have experienced developmental trauma are likely to have wide-ranging difficulties in their relationships with the staff supporting them. They may use survival strategies that challenge professional boundaries, some of which can make staff feel 'manipulated'.

 Intellectual Disabilities and 'Personality Disorder' © Pavilion Publishing and Media Ltd and its licensors 2023

- It is important to understand that individuals have developed these survival strategies to meet their needs in situations where the usual, acceptable approaches did not work and that they did not experience many of the positive interactions that develop healthy social skills. To cope with overwhelming needs, they have learnt to do whatever helps them get through.
- To address these issues, it is important that staff have a good understanding of the difference between professional and personal relationships and have the confidence to create and maintain professional boundaries.
- As individual staff members are easily overwhelmed by the needs of individuals who might be given a diagnosis of 'personality disorder', a team approach to support is essential.
- The team needs to work in a proactive, containing support style. This style provides the high expectations, clear and maintained boundaries, high sensitivity to needs and interest in the individual that are necessary for positive relationships to develop and be maintained. This creates a secure base in which individuals can thrive.

Chapter 14: Understanding impulsivity and regulating impulses

This chapter explores impulses, impulsive behaviour and how impulses are regulated. It explores some of the factors that affect the ability to regulate impulses and the difficulties individuals may experience regulating impulses. It looks at the issues staff may face in supporting individuals who behave impulsively and how these may be addressed within a compassionate, containing support style and a trauma-informed Positive Behavioural Support framework.

Key topics

- Impulses and impulsive behaviour
- Development of impulse control
- Impulsivity
- Impulsivity and individuals with intellectual disabilities
- Impulsive behaviour, choices and unwise decisions
- Assessment and formulation
- Supporting individuals with impulsive behaviours
- Practical strategies for supporting individuals to regulate impulses
- Promoting the development of impulse regulation

Impulses and impulsive behaviour

An impulse is a sudden and compelling urge to act, often resulting in action without deliberation (American Psychological Association, 2023). Impulses often come from basic drives, such as the need for food, comfort, safety, affection, possessions, amusement and sexual gratification. Impulses may also arise from strong emotions, such as anger or jealousy. Impulsive behaviours are not thought through or planned; rather, they focus on the immediate satisfaction of the urge without considering later consequences (Heshmat, 2022). Impulsive behaviours are often ones that stimulate the 'reward pathway' in the brain, creating feelings of intense pleasure (Mcleod,

2023d). Everyone acts on impulse at times; acting spontaneously brings fun and excitement to life. However, life would become totally chaotic if this were the only way people behaved.

Regulating impulses

Regulating an impulse can be understood as a process of deciding to behave in a particular way in response to a situation, rather than simply reacting to it. This ability has been given a variety of other names including self-control, impulse control, will power and delayed gratification (missing out on an immediate reward to achieve a more valued reward later). Regulating impulses can be understood as an individual's reasoning mind (see Box 15.10) taking priority over their emotional mind (Heshmat, 2022). It is a complex process with multiple steps (see Box 14.1). It is achieved by many different neurological mechanisms working together and is shaped by learning and experience. It is also dependent on the ability to hold things in mind (working memory) and to focus on the important issues (selective attention) (Mirabella, 2021). Regulating impulses is one of a group of abilities called 'executive functions'. These abilities help people behave in organised and purposeful ways.

Box 14.1: Regulating impulses

Processes involved in regulating impulses:

- Inhibit action long enough to think about how best to respond (inhibition).
- Manage sensations caused by the underlying urge e.g. hunger, anger (regulation).
- Resist temptation of intense pleasure from immediate action (delay gratification).
- Think through the possible consequences of various actions (logical thinking).
- Recall what has happened in similar situations in the past (memory).
- Think what might happen in the future (sense of time).
- Link causes to consequences that might not be immediate (logical thinking).
- Work out how others might react to the behaviour (mentalise, moral compass).
- Weigh up the options and make a plan for how they will satisfy or manage the underlying impulse (reasoning and problem solving).
- Pay attention, concentrate and stay focused long enough to consider all these issues (attention).
- Wish to stop the impulsive behaviour (motivation).
- Be positive, believe that controlling the impulse will achieve the more positive outcome imagined (internal locus of control – optimistic).

 Intellectual Disabilities and 'Personality Disorder' © Pavilion Publishing and Media Ltd and its licensors 2023

Importance of regulating impulses:

- Allows the inhibition of behaviours that are not compatible with long-term goals e.g. resisting the temptation of an expensive holiday when saving for a deposit on a house.
- Contributes to maintaining relationships e.g. not saying what first comes to mind hence avoiding comments that might antagonise, shock or hurt other people.
- Reduces conflict and aggressive behaviour.
- Allows the inhibition of behaviours that would be damaging to intimate relationships e.g. someone in a relationship saying 'no' to an invitation from an attractive colleague.
- Helps to keep individuals safe and healthy e.g. resisting the highly enjoyable but short-term 'fix' of a cigarette.
- Protects individuals from engaging in risky behaviour e.g. gambling away savings or having unprotected sex with strangers.
- Helps individuals comply with the rules of society e.g. not pushing to the front of a queue, resisting the urge to commit crimes.

The ability to regulate impulses is influenced by internal factors such as emotional arousal and external stimuli, pressures and demands (Heshmat, 2022). Some of these factors are given in Box 14.2.

Box 14.2: Factors that influence impulse regulation

Temptation	Presence/absence of tempting sights, sounds or smells.
Intensity of need	Deprivation/satiation e.g. being hungry vs having just eaten.
Intensity of emotion	Experiencing intense emotions makes it harder to regulate impulses.
Physical state	E.g. being tired vs well rested/healthy.
Mental state	E.g. being sad or angry vs being happy or content.
Attitudes and values	Condone/condemn the action, recognise or minimise the potential consequences, that rationalise risk taking e.g. '*all my family die young*'. Attribution style (see Chapter 15) particularly external locus of control which reduces an individual's belief in their ability to regulate their thoughts, emotions and behaviour.

→

Perceptions	The perception of the likelihood of punishment, perception of others' efforts to keep them safe as being helpful vs controlling.
Learning history	Opportunities to practice and develop needed skills, exposure to helpful and unhelpful modelling of impulse control. History of consequences or lack of consequences for impulsive behaviour.
Experiences	Experiencing developmental trauma, trauma as an adult, symptoms of PTSD, being exposed to stigma, having repeated experiences of failure.
Disinhibiting substances	Using/abstaining from disinhibiting substances e.g. drugs or alcohol.
Social factors	Social/peer pressure vs social/peer support. Mixing with peers who engage in risky behaviour normalises the risk, creates opportunities and increases temptation.

For example, the likelihood of someone speeding might be increased by holding the belief that speed limits are overly restrictive, having had an alcoholic drink, driving a Maserati, seeing a clear straight road without a speed camera and being encouraged by a passenger.

Maintaining the motoring analogy, regulating impulses may be likened to the braking system on a truck (Elliott and Smith, 2009). Whether or not the truck stops in time will depend on the weight of the truck (the intensity of the drive), the steepness of the descent (external influences) and the quality of the braking system (how well an individual can control impulses). Brakes may be good enough in some situations but may fail in others.

Impulsivity

When an individual struggles to regulate impulses, this may be referred to as impulsivity, impulsiveness or disinhibition. Impulsivity is the tendency to act rapidly, without thinking something through or considering the consequences. It results in behaviours that are unnecessarily risky or inappropriate to the situation and which often result in undesirable outcomes. Impulsivity can take a number of forms (see Box 14.3).

Box 14.3: Types of impulsivity (the five factor model)	
Positive urgency	The tendency to behave impulsively while in a positive mood.
Negative urgency	The tendency to behave impulsively while in a negative mood.

 Intellectual Disabilities and 'Personality Disorder' © Pavilion Publishing and Media Ltd and its licensors 2023

Lack of premeditation	The inability to anticipate the likely consequences of an action.
Lack of perseverance	The inability to see a task through to the end.
Sensation seeking	Being attracted to risky behaviours, looking for thrills.
References: Miller *et al* (2003); Teese *et al* (2021)	

Being very impulsive has a negative impact on well-being and exposes individuals to risks (Salters-Pedneault, 2023). It can lead them to behave in socially unacceptable ways. For example, impulsivity increases the likelihood of violent behaviour (Alford *et al*, 2020). Some of the most frequent issues arising from poor impulse control are given in Box 14.4.

Box 14.4: Issues that can arise as a result of impulsive behaviour:	
Lifestyle	Spur of the moment, unplanned, disorganised, chaotic. Joining and quitting a lot of groups. Quitting jobs suddenly. Abruptly changing or cancelling plans, not seeing things through. Not doing what has been agreed to or being where they said they would be. Clearing out belongings to 'start anew'. Constantly 'turning over a new leaf'. Difficulty completing actions that do not lead to an immediate reward.
Thoughts and emotions	Changing mind, goals and priorities. Jumping to conclusions. Impatient, low threshold for frustration, anger and verbal abuse. Quickly bored, seeking excitement. Disregard of norms, rules, conventions, laws. Not considering long-term consequences of behaviour. Not learning from experience/making the same mistakes despite the negative consequences.
Relationships	Changing friendship patterns and short-lived relationships. Frequent outbursts, arguments, escalating confrontations, verbal and physical aggression.
Behaviours	Inappropriate – 'over-sharing', getting too close, inappropriate touching, urinating in public. Risky – running across roads, jumping off things, risky sex. Gambling.
Health	Binge eating, over-eating unhealthy foods, unhealthy choices driven by immediate rewards over long-term health e.g. smoking, not exercising.
Finances	Over-spending, impulse spending, 'shopaholic' behaviour. Taking out loans, multiple credit cards.

→

Substance use	Drug and alcohol misuse, misuse of prescription and over-the-counter medication, binge drinking, heavy regular drinking.
Law	Breaking law e.g. shop lifting, speeding, public behaviour, damaging property.

Impulsivity is one of the criteria for a number of mental health diagnoses including bi-polar disorder, Attention Deficit Hyperactivity Disorder (ADHD) and 'personality disorder' (particularly the categories 'borderline' and 'antisocial') and is associated with substance misuse. However, different patterns of impulsive behaviour are associated with different diagnoses. For example, individuals given a diagnosis of ADHD tend to show generalised difficulties with impulse control arising from their struggles with attention and cognitive processing. In contrast, individuals given a diagnosis of 'personality disorder' have more specific difficulties which may fluctuate depending on the situation and their emotional state. They may find it difficult to delay gratification (McHugh and Balaratnasingam, 2018). They are more likely to behave impulsively in response to emotions or interpersonal factors (Matthies and Philipsen, 2014) and this is worsened by stress (McHugh and Balaratnasingam, 2018). In these situations, the ability of individuals given a diagnosis of 'personality disorder' to control impulses has been described as being like *'having a golf-cart braking system on a five-tonne truck'* (Elliott and Smith, 2009).

Development of impulse control

The ability to regulate impulses takes place within the wider developmental process described in Chapter 2. It begins to develop in early childhood but is not complete until the full development of the frontal cortex in early adulthood. Many parts of the brain are needed for these skills to develop successfully including the limbic system and the prefrontal cortex. Regulatory processes are not well-developed under three years of age, meaning that young children are dependent on adults to help them regulate both impulses and emotions (see Chapter 11). Impulse control develops significantly between the ages of four to seven years. Adolescents may engage in more risky behaviour than younger children. This is thought to arise from their increased freedom and difficulties making decisions in social situations, including the impact of peer pressure.

Interactions between a child and their parents are important in the development of impulse control. Initially, parents need to contain the child's impulsive behaviour. For example, grabbing a child to stop them running in front of a car.

 Intellectual Disabilities and 'Personality Disorder' © Pavilion Publishing and Media Ltd and its licensors 2023

However, as the child grows, parents need to give the child increasing freedom in which to regulate themselves. This is a balancing act; too much parental control and the child will not have the opportunity to practice these skills, too little parental containment and the child will not understand that it is necessary to regulate impulses (and might come to serious harm).

Parents also help the child learn to regulate the intense emotions that can trigger impulsive behaviour (see Chapter 11) and the emotional distress caused by resisting an impulse. Again, initially, the parent will comfort the child, often by giving cuddles and then offering fun distractions, soothing them with their own calm response to the situation (co-regulation – see Chapter 11). Gradually, the child needs to be supported to regulate their reactions alone. If parents continue to jump in at the first sign of distress, the child never has the opportunity to learn to regulate their own emotions. If parents never offer comfort, the child cannot learn that such feelings can be contained.

Parents also provide examples of how to respond to temptations. If parents have a healthy balance between indulging harmless, fun impulses and resisting more harmful ones, children will see first-hand how such situations may be managed.

However, not all children react to situations in the same way. Some are naturally more impulsive and drawn to excitement, while others are naturally more cautious. Boys tend to be more impulsive than girls. These differences in temperament interact with parenting style and life experiences to create a range of patterns of responding to impulses (see Box 2.1). By adulthood, these different patterns develop into a characteristic approach to situations where impulse regulation might be required. This forms part of 'Conscientiousness', one of the 'big five' personality traits (see Chapter 1). Characteristic approaches to impulses will range from being highly planned and organised, through easygoing and careless, to disinhibited or impulsive.

Disrupted development

The complexity of the mechanisms underpinning the regulation of impulses and the level of learning involved means that this ability is vulnerable to disruption in several ways. Factors may alter the development of underlying neurological systems, shape what is learnt, create more intense drives, or make an individual more vulnerable to external factors such as stress or peer influences.

Developmental trauma (see Chapter 2) may adversely impact the development of the cognitive systems and brain circuits that support inhibitory aspects of executive functioning (Marshall *et al*, 2016). PTSD symptoms arising from that trauma may also impair some aspects of impulse control (Kim and Choi, 2020). Young adults with a history of trauma have a strong disposition toward urgency (predisposition to act rashly in intense emotional contexts) and tend to use fewer appropriate cognitive emotion regulation strategies than other individuals (Ceschi *et al*, 2014). Trauma may also affect impulse regulation indirectly, through its impact on self-esteem and self-efficacy (see Chapter 16). Anticipating failure, individuals with low self-efficacy may not try to regulate impulses. Trauma in adulthood may also lead to an increase in impulsive behaviour (Bountress *et al*, 2017) possibly related to emotional distress and symptoms of PTSD.

Previously well-regulated individuals may also become impulsive as the result of accident or injury. Traumatic brain injury, neurodegenerative diseases, infections such as meningitis and chemical poisoning can all damage the neurological systems that are necessary for impulse regulation.

Impulse regulation and individuals with intellectual disabilities

Having intellectual disabilities does not necessarily mean that an individual will behave impulsively. However, by definition, individuals, with intellectual disabilities have incomplete or divergent neurological development. Hence, the neurological processes that underpin impulse control may be compromised. Higher rates of impulsivity are associated with a number of conditions that can cause intellectual disabilities, including; foetal alcohol syndrome, Smith-Magenis syndrome, Fragile X syndrome and William's syndrome (Royal College of Psychiatry, 2021). ASD may also be associated with higher impulsivity (Freeman *et al*, 2016). Individuals with intellectual disabilities are also more likely to be given a diagnosis of ADHD than the general population. In addition, for the many individuals who have experienced trauma, either in the developmental period or as an adult, this will shape their ability to regulate impulses. At best, an individual's ability to regulate impulses will be at a stage that reflects their overall level of intellectual functioning.

Low self-esteem and self-efficacy arising from the experience of growing up with multiple experiences of failure and being stigmatised (see Chapter 16) will also have a negative impact on the ability to control impulses. Having fewer resources and finding life more challenging also contribute to individuals with intellectual disabilities being more easily overwhelmed by impulses.

 Intellectual Disabilities and 'Personality Disorder' © Pavilion Publishing and Media Ltd and its licensors 2023

Overall, the more severe an individual's intellectual disabilities, the more support they will need from others, to help them regulate impulses. Depending on their experiences, learning opportunities, the nature of their intellectual disabilities and their biology, each individual will have a unique profile of impulse regulation or impulsivity. For some, this will be generalised across multiple situations and emotional states. For others, it may be more patterned depending on internal and external factors. Individuals may experience many of the difficulties associated with impulsivity (Box 14.4), but these will be shaped by the opportunities available to them. Many of these difficulties will meet the definition for behaviours that challenge (see Box 8.1). Like all behaviours that challenge, impulsive behaviours may be meeting important needs for the individual (see Box 8.2). These might include the need for pleasure and excitement, to connect with others and to feel part of a group, to express or escape from intense emotions or to assert their independence from people perceived as trying to control them.

Impulsive behaviour, choice and unwise decisions

By definition, an impulsive act is unpremeditated and carried out without consideration of the long-term consequences. An individual acting impulsively is likely to be in their 'emotional mind' and will therefore be making an unconscious decision driven only by factors in the present. Impulsive behaviour is not an active, thought-through choice. Rather, it is an automatic response to a situation. This is very different from making a decision, however unwise, to behave in this way.

Making a decision requires that an individual can understand and retain information relevant to the decision and use that information to decide how to act at a particular time. Where a decision has been thought through, the law respects an individual's right to make 'unwise' choices. Decisions tend to be considered as 'unwise' when the option an individual chooses is different to and less cautious than the one the person judging would choose for themselves, having evaluated the available evidence (Farmer, 2016). For example, an individual who weighs the evidence that links smoking to cancer against their enjoyment of cigarettes, and decides to continue smoking, may be thought to be acting 'unwisely' by more cautious individuals. In contrast, someone who has decided not to smoke but is unable to resist the offer of a cigarette may be acting impulsively.

The right to make our own decisions runs through a number of human rights (Equality and Human Rights Commission, 2018). All adults are presumed to have

Intellectual Disabilities and 'Personality Disorder' © Pavilion Publishing and Media Ltd and its licensors 2023

sufficient capacity to make choices and decisions, unless there's significant evidence to suggest otherwise (Mental Capacity Act MCA,2005, see Box 14.5).

Box 14.5: Presumption of capacity and test of capacity	
Presumption of capacity	A person is not to be treated as unable to make a decision merely because this decision is considered 'unwise'.
Capacity	People can lack capacity to make some decisions, but have capacity to make others. Mental capacity can fluctuate. Someone may lack capacity at one point in time, but may be able to make the same decision at a later point in time.
Lack of capacity	A person may be found to lack capacity to make a decision if they have 'an impairment or disturbance' that affects the way their mind or brain works, and that the impairment or disturbance means that they are unable to make a specific decision at a specific time. A person is unable to make a decision if they cannot: ■ Understand the information relevant to the decision. ■ Retain that information. ■ Use or weigh up that information as part of the process of making the decision.
Two stage test of capacity	1) Does the person have an impairment of their mind or brain, whether as a result of an illness, or external factors such as alcohol or drug use? 2) Does the impairment mean the person is unable to make a specific decision when they need to?

The presumption of capacity and knowing that capacity should not be questioned on the basis of 'unwise' decisions alone, can lead staff to feel they must accept risky actions made by an individual, particularly when they say this is what they 'choose' to do. However, impulsive acts are different from unwise decisions and lack the important thinking processes behind the decision. Simply wanting or 'needing' to do something, however strong the urge, is not an unwise decision. Individuals acting impulsively are likely to lack capacity at the point where they are 'choosing' to act in a risky manner and may need the protection of the MCA.

Even if an individual's decisions are unwise rather than lacking capacity, there is still a duty of care (see Chapter 8) that supports staff needing to create safe boundaries around impulsive behaviours.

 Intellectual Disabilities and 'Personality Disorder' © Pavilion Publishing and Media Ltd and its licensors 2023

Assessment and formulation

Safety first

Impulsive behaviours are inherently risky and it is important to consider the immediate and longer-term safety of the individual, those who live with or support them and the general public. Decisions need to balance the risks to all involved, considering both physical and emotional safety, to decide on the best course of action for each individual. How to achieve this is explored in Chapters 8 and, if the situation has reached crisis point, in Chapter 9. If there are serious risks, the approach to risk formulation in Chapter 10 should be used.

Once an individual's impulsive behaviour is contained within a stable setting, assessment and formulation of impulsive behaviour follow the trauma-informed Positive Behavioural Support (PBS) framework for behaviours that challenge (see Chapter 8). However, there are a few things to consider when thinking about impulsive behaviour (see Box 14.6).

Box 14.6: What makes the brakes fail? Factors to consider when assessing and formulating impulsive behaviours	
Conditions/ diagnoses linked to impulsivity	Does the individual have a condition that may be associated with impulsivity? E.g. foetal alcohol syndrome, Smith-Magenis syndrome, Fragile X syndrome and William's syndrome, ASD, ADHD, Bi-polar disorder. What patterns of impulsivity are associated with that condition?
Intellectual abilities	Is the individual able to reason at a concrete/abstract level (see Box 15.7)? Does the individual have deficits in executive functioning? Are these at a level expected for their overall level of intellectual functioning? Can they plan or inhibit behaviours under some conditions? E.g. when calm but not when angry. Do they have a concept of time? Are they able to recall the past and think about the future?
Pattern of impulsive behaviours	Is it generalised across multiple situations and emotional states? Or is it more patterned depending on internal and external factors? Mood state: Positive? Negative? Angry? Distressed? Stressed? Bored (sensation seeking)? Physical state: Hungry? Thirsty? Tired? Excited? Under the influence of drugs or alcohol? Activities: doing something challenging/easy? Nothing to do? Giving up quickly? →

	Social factors: crowds, presence of attractive individuals, presence of people who are disliked, presence of a particular peer group? Temptations/opportunities: do behaviours occur when there are tempting sights, sounds, smells? Consequences: do behaviours intensify if strenuous efforts are made by others to control them?
Attitudes, values and beliefs	Do they hold beliefs/attitudes that support the impulsive behaviour? Do they hold beliefs about the consequences of the behaviour? E.g. it is safe, they won't get caught or prosecuted?
Experiences	How have an individual's experiences shaped their ability to regulate impulses? Head injuries? Illnesses? Trauma? Learning opportunities? Consequences?

Exploring these questions will generate helpful working hypotheses about the possible factors driving an individual's impulsive behaviours. To use Elliott and Smith's (2009) analogy of the braking system:

> *How heavy is the truck? How steep is the descent? How good are the brakes?*

Thoughtfully exploring when and where impulsive behaviours occur can sometimes identify situations in which small changes to an individual's routine can make a huge difference to their ability to regulate impulses.

Where doubts remain about the role of underlying processing issues, it may be helpful to arrange a comprehensive assessment of the individual's intellectual abilities including executive functioning and understanding of time concepts. This will help identify what aspects will need long-term support and those that might be amenable to interventions.

Box 14.7 gives a formulation for Elizabeth's difficulties with overspending and queue jumping, focusing on the factors influencing her impulsive behaviours.

 Intellectual Disabilities and 'Personality Disorder' © Pavilion Publishing and Media Ltd and its licensors 2023

14.7 Formulation for 'Elizabeth'*

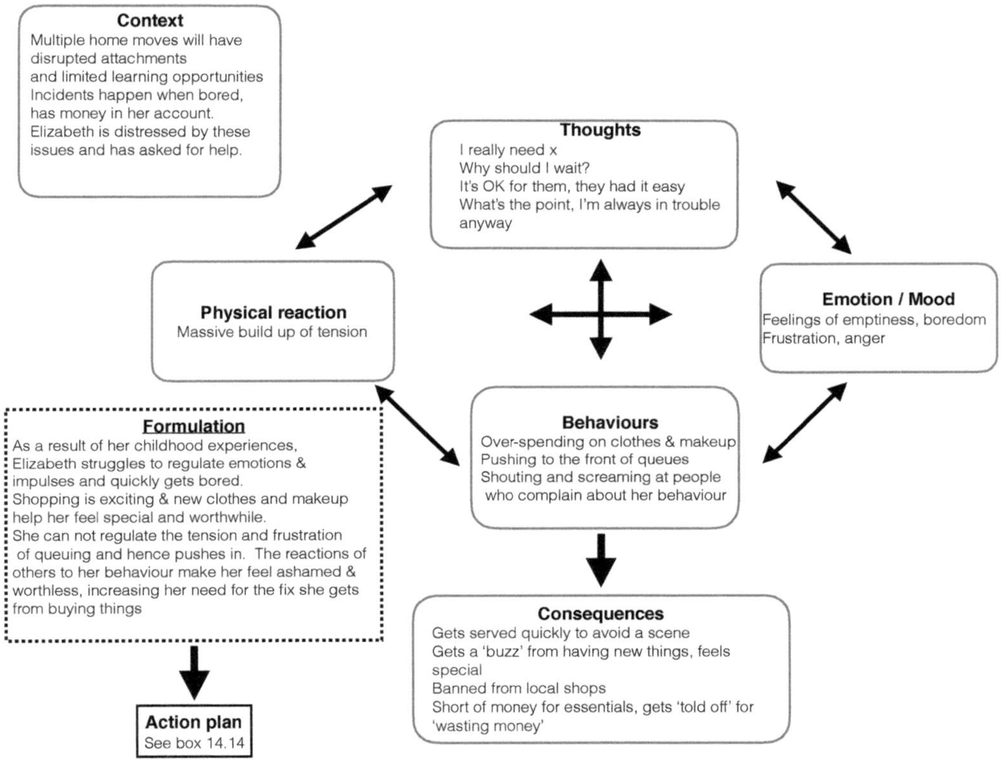

*Elizabeth has been created from clinical experience & the literature. She is not based on a specific individual.

For all individuals, whatever intervention stage they have reached (see Box 3.1), the formulation can then be used to identify preventative strategies to be included in their PBS plan (see Chapter 8). In addition to the strategies given in Chapter 8, there are some strategies that are particularly relevant when intervening with impulsive behaviours. These will include primary prevention strategies that 'lighten the load' and reduce 'the steepness of the descent', and secondary strategies to 'improve the breaks'. The approach to supporting individuals during incidents of impulsive behaviour will follow the tertiary strategies in Chapter 8.

Where an individual has reached the **R**eason stage and chooses to work on improving their impulse control, primary prevention is still very important as it maximises the chances of them successfully using newly learnt strategies.

Supporting individuals with impulsive behaviours

Supporting individuals who behave impulsively can be worrying, distressing and frustrating. Staff may find that some behaviours conflict with their own moral code and may find it hard not to be judgmental. Other behaviours can create fears for the safety of the individual, those they live with or the staff supporting them. Such fears can push staff to behave in controlling ways (see Boxes 9.5 and 9.8) which undermine relationships and, paradoxically, may intensify the behaviours of concern. Conversely, anxiety about not infringing the individual's human rights may leave staff feeling unable to take action, exposing individuals to avoidable risks. It can be particularly challenging to support individuals who appear able to regulate impulses in some situations. This is vulnerable to misinterpretation as making an active choice (unwise decision) to behave in risky ways.

It is important that staff are helped to understand such emotional reactions and explore the impact that these reactions may have on the way they are able to support individuals with impulsive behaviours (see Chapter 7). As with many of the other issues explored in this book, staff will only be able to support individuals successfully if they are able to approach the issues individuals experience in a balanced and compassionate manner.

Boundaries

Clear boundaries (see Chapter 13) that are developed and maintained within a proactive, collaborative and compassionate support style are particularly important when supporting individuals with impulsive behaviour.

Boundaries are most helpful when they are explicit and transparent. This is best achieved by recording them in the format that is most accessible for each individual (NHS England, 2018) and keeping them readily to hand. Boundaries should be created collaboratively with some room for the individual to negotiate if they feel the boundaries are overly restrictive. It is also important that the agreed boundaries are accepted and consistently maintained by the whole team. Otherwise, the individual will be given conflicting messages and splits may emerge within the team (see Chapter 7). Good teamwork is essential.

Boundaries need to be reviewed regularly and revised to take into account changes to the formulation and the impact the boundaries are having on the impulsive behaviour. The extent to which boundaries can be loosened will depend on the relative

 Intellectual Disabilities and 'Personality Disorder' © Pavilion Publishing and Media Ltd and its licensors 2023

contribution of 'hardware' and 'software'. Where difficulties are hard wired, successful containment may be misinterpreted as an improvement in an individual's ability to regulate impulses. Relaxing boundaries is likely to lead to difficulties re-emerging. However, if an individual has worked hard at changing how they respond to tempting situations they may be justifiably angry if boundaries are not expanded to reward their hard work. For such individuals, a process of positive risk assessment (Sellars, 2011) can be used to manage the risks to the individual and others.

Least restrictive alternative

Give some thought to making changes to the environment. For example, if an individual is driven to eat all the food in the kitchen, stopping them from doing this may involve unacceptably frequent use of restrictive physical interventions. Locking the kitchen door might prevent this but at the cost of stopping the individual helping themselves to drinks when they are thirsty. However, if the food cupboard and the fridge have locks, the food would be protected but the kitchen would still be accessible. Locking things should never be undertaken lightly. It should always take place within the appropriate protections of the legal framework, for example the Mental Capacity Act (2005) and the Mental Health Act (1983, amended 1995 and 2007), and duty of care (Royal College of Nursing, 2023). There needs to be a full consultation; discussion with the local ethics committee might be helpful and it may be appropriate to seek a legal opinion. The decision needs to be recorded in writing and should be reviewed regularly. Any restrictions imposed should be the least restrictive alternative.

Practical strategies for supporting individuals to regulate impulses

There are a range of strategies that help reduce urges and manage trigger situations. The RCP (2021) recommend that individuals with intellectual disabilities and ADHD should have access to regular outdoor activities to manage their arousal level. It is likely that regular physical activities will also benefit individuals with impulsivity arising from other issues. Practising controlled movement patterns may also improve impulsivity (Farrokhian *et al*, 2020).

A number of other practical strategies that can be used to help individuals avoid behaving impulsively are given in Box 14.8. An effective PBS plan is likely to contain both strategies that help reduce urges and those that manage trigger situations, chosen to meet the needs identified in the individual's formulation.

Box 14.8: Practical strategies for supporting individuals to regulate impulses	
Primary prevention 'Lightening the load' or 'flattening the descent'	**Reduce intensity of urges:** Ensure basic needs (food, drink, sleep, exercise, social interaction) are met regularly and predictably e.g. hunger – healthy eating plan with small meals, regular snacks and small treats, having a small snack before going to tempting situations. Interaction – schedule regular social activities, phone calls, text messages. Being part of a group – find alternative positive groups to join. Excitement – find a legal, safer activity that meets the same need e.g. involvement in stock car racing rather than 'joy riding'. Timetable of alternative, enjoyable but not tempting, activities. **Co-regulate emotions:** see Box 11.15 **Manage temptations:** Put things out of sight, choose routes to avoid tempting places, choose times of day that avoid temptations/reduce drives, put limits on cards, use a jam jar bank account. Unsubscribe from tempting emails, block access to websites, delete apps. Break things into smaller chunks, small, frequent rewards – goal planning (see Box 16.6). Structure time to reduce opportunities and regulate arousal.
Secondary prevention 'Strengthening the brakes'	**Use distractions** when temptations cannot be avoided (see Box 15.15). For additional active strategies that individuals can be supported to use if they are in the **R**eason stage, see Box 14.13.

Peer pressure

It can be difficult to manage temptation if an individual's impulsive behaviour is linked to being in the company of certain people. In such situations, it is usually counterproductive to try to separate the individual from their 'friends'. Rather, they need to be supported to develop a wider social network and take up different activities so that they spend less time with the 'bad influences'. It may be helpful to look in more depth at their ability to form relationships (Chapter 12). It is also important to build their self-esteem, because when people feel better about

 Intellectual Disabilities and 'Personality Disorder' © Pavilion Publishing and Media Ltd and its licensors 2023

themselves, they will often choose friends who are more supportive of them (see Chapter 16). Where 'friendships' are damaging to the individual, safeguarding procedures must be followed (see Chapter 12).

Managing trigger activities

Frequently, the activities that trigger impulsive behaviour cannot be avoided. Where this is the case, the activity needs to be carefully planned with the individual. A problem-solving approach can be used to work out how the activity can best be managed (see Box 12.10).

Providing immediate rewards

Many individuals have great difficulty in making connections between immediate actions and delayed benefits. It can be helpful for them to have a small immediate reward for behaving appropriately. One approach that had been developed to facilitate this is the use of a reward system (token program or token economy). Reward systems give a 'token' (sticker, counter, button in a jar) immediately after the desired action. Once a number of tokens have been collected, they can be exchanged for an agreed reward. The token provides immediate, tangible evidence of success and helps to bridge the delay until the final reward is given.

There is evidence that reward systems can be effective and that their effectiveness can be enhanced through the use of computer-based systems and wearable technology (Beahm *et al*, 2023; Evmenova *et al*, 2018). However, their complexity means that reward systems can be time-consuming and challenging to implement (Beahm *et al*, 2023). Reward systems can feel like 'bribery' and often make staff feel uncomfortable. These systems are also vulnerable to becoming punitive: there is a great temptation to take away tokens for 'bad' behaviour. They can raise difficult ethical issues about what an individual is entitled to by right and what has to be earned. If use of a reward system is considered, discussing this with the service's ethics committee will help avoid these pitfalls.

Medication

Medication may be useful if impulsivity is linked to ADHD (RCP, 2021). It is also possible that medication may be helpful where impulsive behaviour is linked to periods of emotional distress. Medication should always be combined with other practical interventions; it is unlikely to be effective if used alone. (See Chapter 9, Safety first, for a discussion about the risk of over-medication.)

Promoting the development of impulse regulation

In addition, for individuals who have reached the **R**eason stage, it may be appropriate to explore ways of helping them develop and improve their ability to regulate impulses and underlying urges.

Positive risk-taking

This work needs to be carried out collaboratively within the framework of positive risk-taking (Sellars, 2011) to minimise the risks to the individual and to others. There needs to be a shared willingness to take positive risks and to see the inevitable slip-ups and lapses as learning opportunities, not disasters. It is totally unrealistic to expect that an individual will never give in to temptation or behave impulsively. For example, after working with an individual on issues relating to their spending patterns, an individual might be supported to test this on a trip alone to the local shop. With their agreement, staff might shadow them so that support is available if things do not go to plan. The individual might take twice the amount of money needed for their shopping list but leave their bank card at home.

As part of the positive risk-taking process, the team can explore, with the individual, how they will respond to the inevitable lapses. It is very important that lapses are not punished; if an individual is anxious about how staff will react to their impulsive behaviour, they will be reluctant to talk about it and may try to hide lapses from staff. The anxiety will also increase the risk of a lapse occurring.

Each time the individual engages in the impulsive behaviour, it should be viewed as a chance to learn. In a calm and non-judgmental way, staff can explore why the person was not able to resist on this occasion. Box 14.9 shows how this might be done using the example of managing spending and behaviour during a shopping trip.

Box 14.9: Collaboratively learning lapses To take place once lapse has been resolved and individual is calm and in temptation-free setting.	
Reassurance:	*'It's OK, we knew it would be hard to resist the temptation to buy extra stuff. We're not angry, so don't be so hard on yourself.'*
Highlight what went well:	*'You did great queuing to pay for your shopping.'*

Intellectual Disabilities and 'Personality Disorder' © Pavilion Publishing and Media Ltd and its licensors 2023

Remember past successes:	*'You have come so far, look how well you have been doing, you have saved £50 already.'*
Remember what they are working towards:	*'If we stick to this plan, you will soon have enough money for that trip to Spain.'*
Check they are willing to talk about what happened:	*Is now a good time to think about what happened?'*
Explore what happened (active listening):	*'What happened?' 'Did something upset you?' 'What went through your mind?' 'How were you feeling?' 'Did you try the distraction techniques?'*
Explore what they might do differently next time:	*'What do you think might have helped you?' 'What about a picture of Spain in your wallet?' 'Would it help to have support in the chemists until you are more confident?'*

The information gathered can be used to refine the support they are giving the individual, to update risk-management strategies and identify learning needs.

Support

Whichever interventions are used to promote impulse regulation, it will be difficult for an individual to implement strategies on their own. Wherever possible, staff should try to work with the individual to practise using the skills. This could include role-playing situations in which the skills might be needed. Practice builds up new patterns of responding at times when the urge is not overpowering. For some issues, it may be possible to join a support group such as Alcoholics Anonymous or Gamblers Anonymous. For those who use computers and smartphones, there is a lot of support available online. However, it is important to work with the individual to find appropriate sites as internet sites are not always regulated and may have content or contacts that will make the problem worse.

Increasing motivation

Individuals may appear to not want to change their impulsive behaviour. If this seems to be the case, it may be helpful to explore where they are in the cycle of change (Prochaska and DiClemente, 1983). This may show that the individual does not see that they have an issue, holds very different views of the issue from staff or does not see the benefits of change. Where this is the case, it may be helpful to encourage the individual to think about the impact of their impulsive behaviour in a way that is not judgmental, damaging to their self-esteem or frightening. If the approach is judgmental or critical, it will be self-defeating. The individual's emotional reaction (for example, fear, shame or guilt) will increase the strength of the impulse and make them respond to staff as enemies rather than allies.

An approach called 'motivational interviewing', originally developed by (Miller, 1983), can be helpful in this situation. Motivational interviewing is a person-centred, collaborative approach that aims to strengthen an individual's motivation for and commitment to change. This approach recognises that the individual and the staff supporting them may have very different views about the pros and cons of a behaviour and the need for change. These differences can make the individual feel staff are trying to control them rather than trying to help them and can lead to resistance. To address this, motivational interviewing aims to help the individual identify their own goals, to define the problem for themselves and to find solutions that will work for them. The process of motivational interviewing is given in more detail in Box 14.10.

Box 14.10: Motivational interviewing	
Express empathy	*'It must be very hard for you…' 'It sounds like…'*
Help self-reflection	Open questions – *'How do you feel?' 'What do you think of that?'*
Explore goals	*'What do you want to do?' 'How do you want to feel?'*
Develop discrepancy	Between the present and goals: *'What would need to change for that to happen?' 'Is there anything about (behaviour) that bothers you?' 'What's the worst that could happen if you carried on…?'*
Elicit motivation	*'What concerns do you have?'*
Roll with resistance	Don't confront, don't challenge, avoid arguments, de-escalate, dance together don't wrestle. *'So, it sounds like (behaviour) is a good thing to do?' 'So, maybe it's OK if you never change/stop (behaviour)?'*
Invite exploration of new points of view	*'What about…?' 'What if….?'*
Reflect ambivalence	*'On the one hand you… On the other you…'*
Can-do approach	Support individual's belief that they can change. *'What could work for you if you decided to change?' 'When have you succeeded in doing something you wanted to achieve?'*
Cost-benefit analysis	Listing the pros and cons of the behaviour, see example below.
References: Hartney (2023), Miller and Rose (2009)	

 Intellectual Disabilities and 'Personality Disorder' © Pavilion Publishing and Media Ltd and its licensors 2023

Using this approach, staff need to work with the individual to identify their wishes and aims. They can then explore what gets in the way of achieving those aims and how these difficulties might be overcome. In this way, staff and the individual can be on the same side; trying to achieve the individual's own goal by overcoming the negative consequences of the impulsive behaviour.

It is also important to explore the positive side of the impulsive behaviour as this will often explain why the individual finds the behaviour so difficult to control. Box 14.11 gives an example of the consequences an individual might identify for continuing or stopping smoking.

Box 14.11: Example of a conversation about an individual's perceptions of the costs and benefits of smoking or giving up smoking

Smoking	Give up smoking
Pros: I enjoy smoking, it makes me feel great. I look cool and tough when I smoke. Smoking helps me calm down when I am angry. Smoking helps me concentrate. Smoking helps when I am worried about things.	**Pros:** Smoking is expensive – I will be able to afford the new clothes I want. I might cough less. I have been told that smoking is damaging my heart and lungs (but I can't feel anything wrong with them!)
Cons: Sometimes I cough.	**Cons:** I will be left out when my friends smoke. My friends will laugh at me. I feel terrible when I want a cigarette and don't have one. I will lose my temper more often and get in more trouble.

Some of the issues identified might surprise staff supporting the individual; it certainly makes clear why this particular individual would find it very hard to give up smoking. However, by making explicit what the individual really thinks and feels, this process also creates opportunities. Staff can work creatively with the individual to find other ways of achieving the positive consequences of the behaviour and to enhance the perceived benefits of change. For the example given above, actions such as teaching strategies for managing anger and anxiety, building self-esteem, developing a wider social network, exploring nicotine substitutes (such as patches or gum) and a full health check might help shift the balance in favour of giving up smoking. Once the balance has shifted in favour of changing the behaviour, these discussions can be turned into a book or poster that the individual can use to motivate themselves when they are feeling discouraged. Some other strategies for increasing the motivation to change are given in Box 14.12.

Box 14.12: Strategies for increasing motivation	
Increasing knowledge	Provide accessible information, education, personal feedback.
Increasing awareness of emotions	Identify and recognise emotions relating to impulsive behaviour.
Inspiration and hope	Learning how others have changed their behaviour.
Changing self-image	Realising that changing their behaviour helps them become who they want to be.
Building self-efficacy	Building belief in their ability to change (see Chapter 16).
Exploring impact on others	Social stories can be used to help individuals understand the impact behaviour has on others and how changing behaviour might have a more positive effect.
Helping relationships	Finding people who are supportive of the changes.
Social impact	Looking at how society views the changes, what options do they open?
Goal planning	Breaking a goal into a series of achievable steps working towards the final goal (see Box 16.6).

Changing behaviour

If an individual decides they want to try to change their behaviour, a number of approaches can be helpful. It can be helpful to explore with them the relationship between urges, emotions and actions. Many individuals do not realise that urges and emotions are not a good basis for action – most people don't do things just because they feel like it. It may be helpful for them to learn strategies for regulating emotions (see Chapter 11). For some individuals, distorted thinking seems to play a significant role in their impulsive behaviour. If this is the case, it may be helpful to explore this more fully, taking the approaches given in Chapter 15.

 Intellectual Disabilities and 'Personality Disorder' © Pavilion Publishing and Media Ltd and its licensors 2023

There are a number of practical things an individual can do at the point of feeling an impulse that can help them avoid behaving impulsively. Some examples are given in Box 14.13.

Box 14.13: Avoiding behaving impulsively in trigger situations:	
Make time to think	■ Take three deep breaths. ■ Count to 10.
Interrupt the physical sequence of the behaviour	■ Put own hand over mouth e.g. to stop impulsive comments. ■ Clasp own hands or sit on them e.g. to stop self-harm or hitting others. ■ Put own hands pockets e.g. to stop smoking.
Take physical exercise	■ Walk, jog, swim, dance.
Do something different	■ Jump up and down on the spot. ■ Tear up cardboard.
Do something incompatible with the behaviour	■ Rub lotion on body part that would have been harmed. ■ Post money in piggybank. ■ Suck on cigarette replacement.

These actions work in a number of different ways. Some interrupt the sequence of behaviour long enough for the individual to remember they are trying to stop behaving in that way. Others channel and disperse the buildup of physical tension and energy that often accompany impulsive behaviour. Others satisfy the urge to act but direct it in a way that is not harmful for the individual. Individuals should be supported to try a number of these approaches and to practise using them at times when they are not experiencing an impulse. They are likely to struggle at first to remember to use the strategies or may not be able to implement them successfully. The approaches suggested in Chapter 16 for setting goals and evaluating progress may be very helpful in encouraging individuals to persist in their efforts to use new approaches.

Box 14.14 gives an action plan for supporting Elizabeth in her goal to reduce overspending and learn how to queue based on the formulation in Box 14.7.

Box 14.14: Action plan to help 'Elizabeth'* regulate her impulsive shopping and queue-jumping behaviours	
Boredom	Building a timetable of fun and varied activities including Zumba sessions and helping at a local charity shop that has lots of vintage fashion.
Emotions	Learning about emotions and ways of regulating them. Create a crisis box (see Box 9.17).
Physical tension	Building mindfulness exercises into daily routine. Practicing shaking out the tension to use in queues.
Worthlessness and emptiness	Creating a life story with support staff. Learning about self-compassion.
Awareness of others	Creating social stories about the impact of her behaviour on others in the queue and the shop assistants.
Alternatives	Fun pampering and fashion sessions with existing purchases. Creating new looks with existing clothes.
Practical actions	Shop at quieter times, shop from a list. Don't take all money out at once.
Social support	Praise and encouragement from staff. A safe space to talk about lapses without being judged, joining a local self-advocacy group. Create a 'crisis' card (see Box 9.18) with actions when Elizabeth feels particularly low and vulnerable to temptation so she can call someone.

*Elizabeth has been created from clinical experience and the literature. She is not based on a specific individual.

Specialist therapeutic interventions

Some individuals may have complex problems arising from issues with impulse control such as serious drug or alcohol misuse, other addictive behaviours or eating disorders. In these situations, it is important to support them to seek specialist help for these difficulties. Specialist services can be accessed through the individual's GP or psychiatrist.

Supporting individuals with impulsive behaviours within a proactive, compassionate and containing support style, will help keep everyone safe while promoting positive interactions and building self-esteem.

Intellectual Disabilities and 'Personality Disorder' © Pavilion Publishing and Media Ltd and its licensors 2023

Key learning points

- Impulses are sudden thoughts that urge immediate action and often come from basic drives or intense emotions. Impulsive behaviours seek the immediate satisfaction of the urge without consideration of later consequences.
- Regulating impulses requires the motivation and ability to choose to behave in a particular way rather than simply reacting to a situation. Regulating impulses is part of a group of abilities called executive functions that help people behave in organised and purposeful ways.
- Below the age of three years, children are heavily dependent on their parents to regulate impulses. Their ability to self-regulate develops as a result of the interaction between neurological development and experience, but is not complete until early adulthood.
- Impulsivity describes the tendency to react rapidly in an unplanned way without considering the negative consequences of the action across a wide range of situations.
- The picture is more complex where the individual also has intellectual disabilities, as a number of conditions that cause intellectual disabilities also influence the ability to control impulses. It is therefore important not to make assumptions about the causes of impulsivity and the ability to control impulses; rather, these should be carefully assessed.
- When trying to manage an individual's impulsive behaviour, staff need to work closely together to contain risks and create a safe environment with clear boundaries.
- Staff members may also need the space to explore their emotional reactions to behaviours that they find upsetting.
- Once the individual is safe, their impulse control and the functions of their impulsive behaviours can be assessed. This information can then be used to address the underlying needs and to develop a PBS plan.
- For individuals with the potential to improve their impulse control, work can then begin on increasing motivation and developing skills.
- For individuals with complex problems such as addictive behaviour, it may be necessary to support them in seeking specialist help.

Chapter 15: Understanding patterns of thinking

This chapter looks at what thoughts are and how thinking develops. It explores how much 'thinking' is automatic or unconscious, and looks at core beliefs, automatic thoughts and attribution styles. It looks at the interrelationship between thoughts, emotions and behaviour, and how different states of mind can occur. This chapter looks at how thinking can be shaped by factors such as having intellectual disabilities and having experienced trauma. It considers how these processes mean that no two individuals will experience and understand a situation in the same way. It explores the importance of understanding each individual's different ways of thinking and the implications of this for person-centred support and intervention.

Key topics

- Thoughts and thinking
- Core beliefs, automatic thoughts and attribution styles
- Development of thinking
- Interrelationships between thoughts, emotions and behaviour
- States of mind
- Thinking and intellectual disabilities
- Assessment and formulation
- Practical and social support
- Building a positive relationship with thoughts

Thoughts and thinking

Thoughts comprise symbolic responses within the brain to stimuli that originate from within the body and from the external environment. Thoughts are usually short-lived events that can take different forms including words and images (see Box 15.1) and allow people to make sense of themselves, other people and the world, to solve problems and make plans.

Box 15.1: Thoughts and thinking:
Words or pictures inside our heads. Thoughts include: ideas, beliefs, notions, mental pictures, views, visualisations. Thoughts are used to solve problems, think about ourselves, other people and the world, think about the past the present and the future, to learn, to make choices, decisions and plans.
Important things to understand about thoughts:
■ Other people cannot see or hear our thoughts, but they may guess them (mentalise) from our behaviour, what we say, our body language and facial expressions. ■ Everyone has thoughts. ■ These include pleasant and unpleasant thoughts. ■ It is natural to think about things we may think of as 'wrong' or 'bad'. ■ Thoughts cannot hurt anyone. ■ Thoughts alone cannot make things happen in the world. ■ For thoughts to have an effect in the world, someone needs to act upon them.
Some people cannot think in or create mental images. This is called *aphantasia* and is a healthy variation of thought.
Metacognition* – Thoughts about thoughts and thinking – awareness of one's own cognitive processes, sometimes involving a conscious attempt to alter them e.g. thinking '*What is a thought?*' '*Why did I think that?*'
Processes that support and influence thinking: ■ Attention helps us focus on the things we want to do or think about. ■ Memory helps us hold on to information and events or remember to do things planned in the future. ■ Motivation is the drive that helps us turn thoughts into actions. ■ Executive functions enable us to plan, focus, follow instructions, juggle multiple tasks and inhibit responses.
Thoughts are different from: Behaviours – what we say and do. Emotions – feelings such as happiness or sadness. Bodily sensations – pain, tiredness, feeling hot or cold, awareness of heart rate, breathing or sweating.
Reference: *American Psychological Association (2023c)

 Intellectual Disabilities and 'Personality Disorder' © Pavilion Publishing and Media Ltd and its licensors 2023

The thinking process by which individuals make a 'best guess' at the thoughts and motivations of others is called 'mentalising' or 'social cognition' (see Box 12.3). The thinking processes by which individuals regulate impulses and organise activity are called executive functions (see Chapter 14).

At times, people are very aware of the thinking process, for example when struggling to learn something new and difficult. However, much of the time thinking is automatic and people rarely question why they viewed a situation as they did or chose to act in a certain way. Even when we are aware of thoughts, preconscious brain processes work behind the scenes to generate those thoughts. During these opaque processes, unconscious representations and calculations seem to be involved (Morsella, 2012). These mechanisms rapidly assess threats, making decisions about safety and triggering instinctive responses. They simplify the world and provide mental shortcuts that reduce how much time is expended thinking about new people and different situations. They can also act to protect individuals from ideas and feelings that they find frightening or unacceptable (see Chapter 7). Unconscious mechanisms lead to beliefs and thinking styles that characterise the way an individual understands themselves, other people and the world.

Thoughts are not easy to control. It is common to have difficulty focusing on something, to find it difficult to stop thinking about a problem or to struggle to avoid daydreaming. Random thoughts may pop into someone's head or wanted thoughts vanish unexpectedly. It has been said that if bodies were as difficult to control as thoughts, no one would ever get down a flight of stairs without falling. Sometimes, out of control thoughts can cause anxiety and distress (see Box 15.2).

Box 15.2: Distressing and out of control thoughts	
Worries	Concerns about things that might happen in the future. Often focus on '*what if…*'
Intrusive thoughts	Unwelcome, unpleasant, involuntary thoughts, images or ideas which are difficult to get rid of.
■ Obsessions	Repeated thoughts, urges, or mental images that cause anxiety e.g. fear of germs or contamination. Unwanted forbidden or taboo thoughts involving sex, religion, or harm. Aggressive thoughts towards others or self.
■ Flashbacks*	A vivid experience in which some aspects of a past traumatic event is re-experienced as if it is happening in the present. This might include: →

	■ seeing full or partial images of what happened. ■ noticing sounds, smells or tastes connected to the trauma. ■ feeling physical sensations, such as pain or pressure. ■ experiencing emotions felt during the trauma.
■ Ruminations	'Over thinking' situations, life events or abstract questions such as '*Why do these things happen to me?*' or '*Why am I like this?*' Endless cycles of thoughts about possible causes and consequences.
Hallucinations	Sensing things that are not really present. This may include seeing, feeling, smelling or hearing things. Hearing things is the most common experience.
■ Auditory	Hearing voices – these are experienced as if they occurred outside the person – as if spoken by someone not visibly present and beyond the control of the person hearing them.
Delusions	Fixed, false beliefs that do not match the reality as experienced by other people. For example: Paranoia – an individual suspects, without sufficient evidence, that others are deceiving, exploiting or harming them. Always on their guard, staying vigilant to protect themselves from others. Unable to trust others and see threatening intentions behind innocent behaviours or comments. Ordinary situations are seen as menacing and may trigger anger or aggression. Unforgiving of perceived insults or slights, holding grudges and seeking revenge. Reluctant to talk to others for fear that what they say will be used against them.
Reference* Mind (2023)	

The more worried a person is about a thought and the harder they try to stop it, the more persistent it becomes. Trying not to think about something can make people think about that topic more. This has been called the 'rebound effect of thought suppression' (Wegner *et al*, 1987) or, more memorably, the 'pink elephant paradox'. This effect can be induced by giving the instruction '*Do not think about a pink elephant*'. For most people, this instruction results in a vivid picture of a pink elephant. The harder someone tries to block out the image of the elephant, the bigger and more vivid the image becomes. This is why it is usually not helpful to tell someone in distress to 'think about something else'. When people are caught

 Intellectual Disabilities and 'Personality Disorder' © Pavilion Publishing and Media Ltd and its licensors 2023

up in distressing thoughts, they are unlikely to be able to 'think their way out' of the cycle. Rather, they may need help to shift their thinking and break out of the negative cycle. Actions that may achieve this are discussed later in this chapter.

Core beliefs, automatic thoughts and attribution styles

Psychological theories have suggested a number of preconscious and unconscious mechanisms that shape individuals' perceptions. Similar mechanisms have been given different names or slightly different roles within different theories. The following examples are helpful in understanding the world view of individuals who have intellectual disabilities, have experienced trauma or might be given a diagnosis of 'personality disorder' (see also Box 7.4).

Core beliefs

The brain organises information (experiences, knowledge and assumptions) about particular aspects of the world and uses this to provide shortcuts for interpreting events and making decisions about how to behave in any particular situation. The organised information on any aspect of the world is called a 'core belief' (Beck, 1979) within CBT or a 'schema' in other approaches. Core beliefs effectively provide a guide to, and make sense of the world (see Box 15.3). Core beliefs can be seen as positive, neutral, or negative, depending on how much they help or hinder an individual's functioning (Dibdin, 2022). Core beliefs shape attitudes, assumptions and rules for living.

Box 15.3: Core beliefs	
An individual's most central ideas about themselves, others, and the world. These beliefs act like a lens through which every situation and life experience is seen. They may be flexible and developing or rigid and unchanging. They may be positive and optimistic or negative and pessimistic.	
Activation: Negative core beliefs can lie dormant and only become active when a situation triggers them e.g. a relationship break down may trigger an individual's core belief that they are unlovable; despairing of finding another partner, they may become depressed.	
Self	I am … kind, strong, helpless, unlovable, worthless (also see Box 16.3).
Other people	Other people are kind, untrustworthy.

→

Relationships	I can't attract/keep a good person. Even if I try to explain, I won't be heard. I have to take what I can get. People I depend on will let me down, women/men can't be trusted/are tough, scary, angry…
The world	The world is… hostile, an unhappy place, is/isn't a safe place, owes me a living.
The future	Things will improve. Nothing will work out, get better, change. There is no hope.
Reference: Villines (2022)	

Automatic thoughts

Automatic thoughts are specific to the situation in which they are generated and are shaped by an individual's underlying core beliefs, attitudes and rules for living. If an individual's core beliefs are biased, this will shape the nature of their automatic thoughts. '*You can think of automatic thoughts as the plants that grow: which plants grow will depend on the kind of soil that we give them*' (Whalley, 2019).

Biased automatic thoughts that lead individuals to perceive reality inaccurately are called cognitive distortions (thinking errors). For example, people may exaggerate, jump to conclusions or take things personally (see Box 15.4).

Box 15.4: Cognitive distortions Thoughts that cause individuals to perceive reality inaccurately. They are inaccurate, biased, extreme or false and have the potential to increase distress and damage relationships.	
Black and white thinking Also called 'all-or-nothing' thinking or 'splitting' (see Box 7.2)	Allows no shades of grey or degrees. Something is good or bad, right or wrong, a total success or utter failure. A person is either a hero or a villain. '*There are no prizes for second place.*' '*My partner is an angel.*'
Catastrophising	Magnifies the likely negative outcomes of situations, '*It will be a total disaster*', '*I'll never find another lover if they leave*'.
Exaggerating/ over-generalising	One instance is treated as if it is always the case. For example: One person is rude = '*people ALWAYS treat me badly*'. Girlfriend fails to reply to one text = '*she NEVER calls me back*'. One person ignores you = '*NO ONE EVER listens to me*'.

 Intellectual Disabilities and 'Personality Disorder' © Pavilion Publishing and Media Ltd and its licensors 2023

Jumping to conclusions	Making assumptions about other people's thoughts and motives without any evidence. *'He did that to wind me up'*, *'There's no point getting up, it's going to be a bad day'*.
Taking things personally	Assuming general comments are aimed specifically at the person or taking the blame for things that had nothing to do with the person. *'It's my fault, if I had stayed at home, it wouldn't have happened.'*
Focusing on the negative, discounting the positive	If something nice is said or happens it is not noticed or invalidated in some way. For example: *'She's just saying that to make me feel better, she doesn't mean it'*. If something negative occurs, it is noticed and remembered.
Fixed rules	Has rigid rules and harsh judgement for breaking them. These thoughts create feelings of failure, disappointment and guilt. *'I SHOULD be happy,' 'I OUGHT to be better by now'*, *'I MUST survive on my own'*, *'I CAN'T be the first one to call back'*.
Emotional reasoning	Being unaware of the difference between fact and feeling. *'I feel … (angry/upset /empty) so I must … (hit them/cut myself/get drunk)'*. (This way of thinking can increase impulsive behaviour.)

Everyone experiences cognitive distortions at times, particularly when stressed or distressed. However, when an individual routinely thinks in these ways, it can contribute to a range of difficulties in everyday life and may have a negative impact on their well-being and relationships. For example, thinking in an 'all-or-nothing' way can contribute to extreme behaviours. If an individual thinks they are either totally in control or totally out of control, they are likely to despair of regulating themselves at the first small signs of distress or anger as they see total loss of control as inevitable.

Attribution styles

Attribution style, or explanatory style, refers to the way people make sense of their own actions and explain things that happen in their lives. Events may be appraised on three important dimensions: stability, specificity and locus (location) of control. These dimensions are explored more fully in Box 15.5.

Box 15.5: Attribution styles: how individuals seek to explain events	
Attribution styles help explain why some individuals seem to give up and accept their fate in the face of adversity while others remain upbeat despite a string of 'failures'.	
Stability	Stable vs unstable/long term vs short term. Will it change over time? *'I aways mess this up'* or *'I learn from my mistakes'*.

→

Specificity	Global vs specific. Impact on whole of life or only part of it. *'I can't get anything right'* or *'I'm useless at …'*
Locus of control	Internal (under own control) vs external (not under own control) to the individual. Internal locus of control associated with resilience, problem solving, higher motivation, belief that the individual can change things *'I wonder what I did to upset them?'* or *'They are out to get me'*.
Optimism	Ascribe negative events as unstable, specific and external, but positive events as stable, global or internal e.g. *'I passed the exam because I always put in the work'* vs *'I failed the exam because I had a cold and the room was very noisy.'* Associated with higher levels of motivation, achievement and well-being.
Pessimism	Will tend to ascribe negative events as stable, global and internal but positive events as unstable, specific and internal e.g. *'I passed the exam because it was an easy paper'* vs *'I failed the exam because I am a useless'*. Associated with passivity, poor problem solving, low self-esteem and depression.
Reference: Huston (2019)	

Attribution style is an important aspect of thinking as it influences factors such as how much responsibility an individual takes for their behaviour, their beliefs about whether they can change and whether they take an optimistic or pessimistic view of the future. Locus of control appears to be related to control of behaviour and responsibility. Individuals who believe that they are able to influence events (internal locus of control) are more likely to exhibit control of their behaviour, take responsibility for their actions and may be more motivated to try to change their behaviour.

Self-reinforcing cycles and resistance to change

Unconscious mechanisms are resistant to change, even when there is evidence that they are no longer accurate or helpful. These processes are automatic and make sense in the context of the person's life experiences. Hence, they are unlikely to be questioned; individuals are likely to think that this is just the way the world is. The mechanisms also act as filters for interpreting and responding to information. Individuals are more likely to notice things that fit with their beliefs and disregard contradictory information. Where a contradiction is noticed it will tend to be interpreted as the exception to the rule rather than evidence that the rule is wrong. These mechanisms are also self-reinforcing; they lead people to act and react in ways that make their expectations come true (see Box 15.6).

 Intellectual Disabilities and 'Personality Disorder' © Pavilion Publishing and Media Ltd and its licensors 2023

Box 15.6: How core beliefs and cognitive distortions can become a self-reinforcing cycle		
Core beliefs	*I am likeable.* *People are trustworthy.*	*I am not likeable.* *People cannot be trusted.*
Trigger situation: Friend cancels an outing saying she has a hospital appointment		
Thoughts	*Poor X, I hope she's OK. She must be worried. I'll make sure I give her time to talk next time we get together.*	Jumps to conclusion: *What a lame excuse, I always thought she didn't like me. I bet she found someone more fun to go out with.*
Emotion	Calm but worried for friend.	Upset, sad, rejected or angry.
Behaviour	Sends friend a sympathetic text suggesting coffee next week, goes for a walk in the park.	Cries, sends an unsympathetic text saying she feels let down. Remembers other times people have 'let her down'.
Consequences	Friend feels valued, agrees to meet up, says thank you for the support. Confirms beliefs: *I am likeable.* *People are trustworthy.*	Friend is upset and does not reply. Confirms beliefs: *I am not likeable.* *People cannot be trusted.*

Individuals may be drawn to other people or situations that confirm their beliefs. They may also make faulty assumptions about other people's motives or thoughts and respond as if these were true. *Individuals may also, unconsciously, behave towards others in ways that are likely to trigger the behaviour they expect.* The reaction will be seen as proof that the belief is true rather than a natural human reaction to the triggering behaviour. In this way, individuals can become trapped in patterns of thinking that have a negative impact on their well-being. For example, if an individual expects to be 'told off' for a mistake, they may become defensive or even lash out before the other person has made any comment. The other person feels unfairly attacked and therefore responds negatively. This negative response confirms the individual's belief that they are disliked, or unsupported, or not understood by others.

Development of thinking

The wider developmental process and how development may be delayed or disrupted is described in Chapter 2. Within this wider process, the ability to think develops from birth to adulthood as a result of the complex interaction of multiple factors from

Intellectual Disabilities and 'Personality Disorder' © Pavilion Publishing and Media Ltd and its licensors 2023

genes to culture. The development of thinking can be considered to have two closely interrelated strands, which can be likened (at the risk of being overly simplistic) to a computer having hardware and software (Brette, 2022). Neurological development builds increasingly sophisticated processing abilities (hardware) and experiences shape the building of conscious and unconscious thinking styles and mechanisms (software). The brain 'hardware' is relatively fixed once the developmental period is over. However, the 'software' of thinking may have more potential to change depending on how strongly pathways are built up during development.

Thinking begins with discovering the world through the senses, followed by the development of language, logical thinking, abstract reasoning and increasing abilities to control and plan behaviour. A number of stages in this process have been identified (see Box 15.7).

Box 15.7: Developmental stages in thinking

Sensorimotor	birth–2 years	Experience the world though senses and movement. Thoughts derive from senses and what is going on in the world. Child gradually learns that they are separate from the world.
Pre-operational	2–7 years	Thinking is not logical (magical thinking), imagination is strong. Child has difficulty understanding time. Child can solve problems by manipulating objects. Language and symbols allow thinking about things that are not present. World centres around them.
Concrete operational	7–11 years	Developing logical thinking and problem solving in relation to real life. Understands time and quantities. Greater understanding of their position in the wider world.
Formal operational	11–adulthood	Abstract thought develops. Able to think about multiple possibilities and take different perspectives. Concepts learnt in one setting can be applied in another. Develop ability to plan and use strategies.

References: Piaget (1971); Nortje (2021)

Some cognitive distortions are characteristic of particular stages of development. For example, 'splitting' characterises the thinking of very young children (18–36 months). At this age, children find it hard to cope with ambiguity. When someone meets the child's needs, they are all-good or perfect. When someone frustrates those needs, or is

 Intellectual Disabilities and 'Personality Disorder' © Pavilion Publishing and Media Ltd and its licensors 2023

not there when needed, they are all bad. The process of splitting protects the child from the painful anxiety experienced when trying to make sense of contradictory feelings such as how can you love someone yet also hate them at the same time? If, as the child develops, they learn to cope with this anxiety, they no longer need to use splitting. However, if that development is compromised the use of splitting may continue.

The foundations of core beliefs and attribution styles are laid down in a child's interactions with their parents and are shaped by major life events, adversity and trauma. Beliefs may change and new beliefs develop as an individual's world experiences expand with the move through adolescence to adulthood. Chapter 16 explores how these experiences shape an individual's sense of self. In a similar way, experiences shape a person's view of other people, the world and the future (Nowicki *et al*, 2018). The more difficult someone's life has been, the more likely they are to hold negative beliefs. These beliefs may be helpful when they accurately reflect the world the person lives in. For example, growing up in a war zone might create the core belief that the world is a dangerous place. This belief is helpful all the time that the war continues but, once peace is achieved, it might cause the person to be unnecessarily anxious, cautious and mistrustful.

Experiencing developmental trauma will impact on the growth of thinking in multiple ways, including shaping neurological pathways, limiting learning opportunities and making individuals hypersensitive to threats (see Chapter 2). It also disrupts learning to mentalise. This can result in some individuals lacking any ability to mentalise; they are unable to take another person's perspective or guess what their thoughts, emotions or motivations might be. Some treat their beliefs about the other person's mind as a rigid reality (as if they could really 'mind read'), rather than a 'best-guess-that-could-be-wrong'. Others may be hyper-vigilant to other people's minds, for example always on the lookout for signs of anger and so misinterpret neutral responses for aggression, disagreement or criticism.

Interrelationships between thoughts, emotions and behaviour

The way the brain is wired means that thoughts, emotions and behaviour are closely interwoven. Small areas of the brain are responsible for specific functions such as processing sensory information or controlling movement. Other parts of the brain, such as the prefrontal cortex integrate and act upon information relayed from multiple specialised areas, across different parts of the brain.

> '*… our thoughts,* [emotions]*, and actions are determined by the complex, long-distance integration of localised processes, which are created by specialised populations of cells connected to other regions that each perform different functions.*' (Badcock, 2019)

The way the brain is structured means that information coming into the brain passes through areas that screen for threat, trigger memories, respond emotionally and control automatic physical responses *before* reaching the areas involved in conscious thought (see Box 15.8). Unconscious reactions to potential threats would have helped our ancestors to survive before the development of complex human languages took place. This helps explain the importance of non-verbal communication in conveying messages. Mehrabian (1972) proposed a rule of 7% (words) – 38% (tone of voice) – 55% (body language) when there is conflicting information. Although the actual proportions may vary depending on the circumstances (Thompson, 2011), this rule of thumb acts to highlight the risks of relying on words to convey what is meant and the importance of multi-modal communication of important messages. For example, information can be shared more effectively by ensuring that the verbal message is supported by appropriate tone of voice, facial expressions and gestures.

Box 15.8. The flow of information through the brain

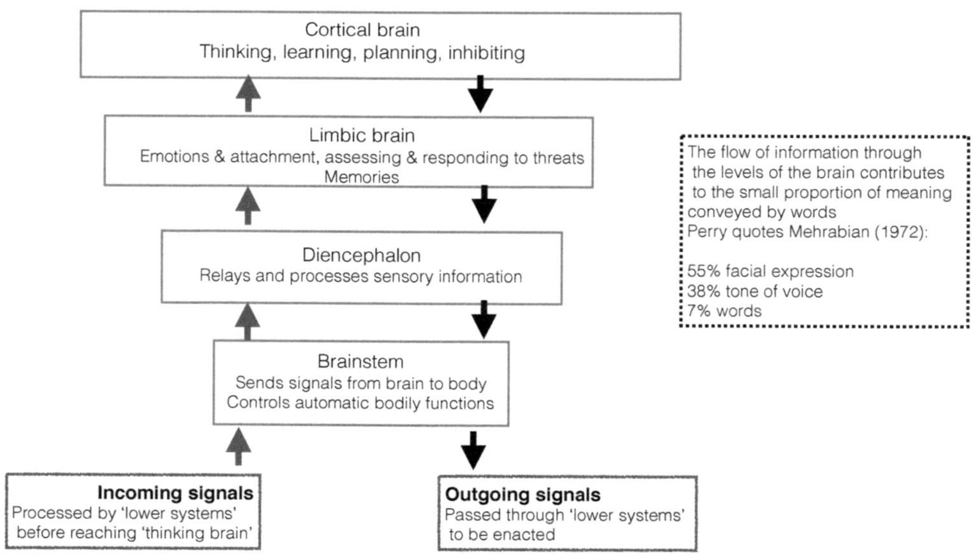

Adapted from Perry (2020) Neurosequential model

 Intellectual Disabilities and 'Personality Disorder' © Pavilion Publishing and Media Ltd and its licensors 2023

Instructions from the 'thinking' brain pass back through these areas to be acted on. Hence, thinking is both shaped by and shapes emotions, physical responses and behaviour. For example, thoughts play a key role in creating the experience of complex emotions such as guilt and shame from the six 'basic emotions' that humans appear to be 'hard wired' to experience (see Chapter 11). Guilt and shame may be the result of thoughts that start *'I should have...'*, *'I shouldn't have...'*, *'If only I had/hadn't...'*.

One way of thinking about the complex interaction between thoughts, emotions, behaviour and bodily sensations is the 'five aspects of experience' diagram (see Box 15.9).

15.9 The hot cross bun

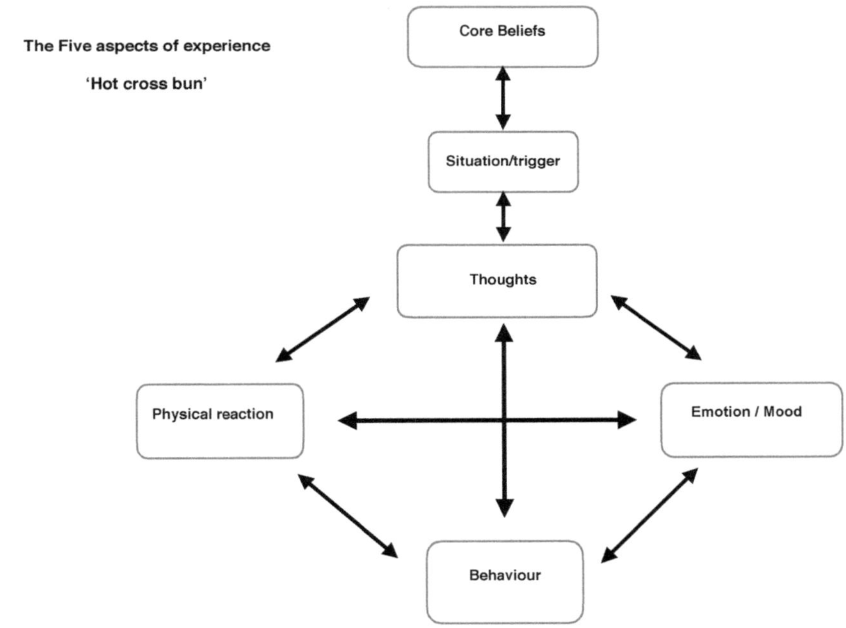

Adapted from Padesky (1986) in Beck et al (1995)

Affectionately referred to as the 'hot cross bun' because of the pattern it makes, this diagram is used in CBT to make sense of troubling patterns of thinking, feeling and behaving. The structure of this diagram privileges 'thoughts' because of the primary role they are given in CBT, but it is useful for highlighting the direct and indirect ways that all elements interact. It shows the potential for the development of negative cycles that may trigger a change in an individual's state of mind.

Thoughts are often the part of this system that is most inaccessible. The automatic nature of thoughts means it will be difficult for the individual to identify their own thoughts. Other people can see behaviour, and emotions can be guessed from facial expressions and body language. However, to make a good and useful guess at another person's thoughts needs careful consideration, taking into account their life experiences and their different perspective on events.

States of mind

The evolution of the brain to help survival in very different situations has led to it being able to adopt different ways of processing information or states of mind to best meet those demands (see Box 15.10).

Box 15.10: States of mind	
Emotional mind	**'This is what I want to/need to/must do.'** *Hot, impulsive and over-involved, feeling not thinking.* ■ Uses structures in the base of the brain (e.g.brain stem, limbic system). ■ Uses energy level, feelings and psychological needs to guide choices and behaviour: ■ Facts are distorted to fit emotional reality. ■ Thinking is illogical, based on attitudes, prejudices and preconceptions. ■ Responses and actions are immediate, uncontrolled, automatic, based on habit/instinct. ■ Considers only the immediate impact.
Reasonable (logical/rational) mind	**'This is what I should do.'** *Cool, considered, thinking not feeling.* ■ Uses front of the brain (neocortex) to process information. ■ Plans, looks at the long-term. ■ Narrow focus on the issues. ■ Uses cause and effect reasoning to guide the choices and behaviour. ■ Thinks objectively, looks at the facts. →

 Intellectual Disabilities and 'Personality Disorder' © Pavilion Publishing and Media Ltd and its licensors 2023

	■ Problem solves, tests things out (scientific), attempts new approaches. ■ Acting, doing, achieving, striving. ■ Judging – this is right/wrong, good/bad.
Wise/intuitive mind	**'This is what is right for me.'** *Warm, involved, engaged, balanced.* ■ The reasonable and emotional mind join forces – the neocortex and base of brain work together. ■ Takes both logic and emotion into account when making decisions. ■ Attempts to integrate and find compromises between the logical and emotional perspective. ■ Looks at the bigger picture. ■ Being, flowing, calming, soothing. ■ Knowing what is right. ■ Accepting – this is how it is.

Depending on the pathways built up during development, an individual's stress level and skills at managing their thoughts, they can switch between reasoning, intuitive and emotional ways of thinking. The change may be a conscious choice, for example engaging in mindfulness exercises to promote the wise/intuitive mind. For some individuals, their day-to-day thinking stays in the emotional mind; their behaviour is directly linked to their emotional state via unconscious 'rules' such as '*I feel angry so I must…*'. This can make it difficult for them to respond in a planned and conscious way rather than acting impulsively (see Chapter 14).

Impact of stress on thinking

Most often, the change of state of mind is an automatic reaction to the situation the individual is in. The more stressed or distressed an individual becomes, the more likely it is that their emotional mind will take over: switching off rational thought (see Chapter 9). The emotional mind is important for survival; logical thinking takes too long in a dangerous situation. However, it causes difficulties in modern life where stressful situations are rarely life-threatening and often require problem-solving skills (reasonable mind).

When in their emotional mind, individuals cease to think logically and struggle to solve problems or see beyond the immediate situation. Their behaviour becomes driven by instinct and emotion and feels out of conscious control. They are unlikely to hear, let alone respond to, reason. They will, however, be hypersensitive to threat signals and the emotional climate around them. For example, they will become more fearful if those around them are anxious but may be soothed by a calm voice and non-threatening body language (see Chapter 11).

Stress can also activate dormant core beliefs, triggering cognitive distortions and distressing, out-of-control thoughts (see Box 15.2). It can lead to individuals experiencing a breakdown of thinking including experiencing hallucinations, delusions or dissociation (Box 9.4). These experiences are usually short-lived and resolve as stress levels reduce. If this is not the case, an assessment by a psychiatrist may be needed to ensure the appropriate support is given.

Thinking and intellectual disabilities

By definition (see Chapter 1), all individuals with intellectual disabilities will have a significantly reduced ability to understand new or complex information and to learn new skills, as a result of their incomplete or divergent neurological development ('hardware'). Their thinking patterns will also have been shaped by their experience ('software'). For any given concern about their thinking, there is always the question: is this hard wired because of their intellectual disabilities, or a 'software' issue arising because of their experiences or an interaction of the two?

Most individuals with intellectual disabilities will not have developed the ability to think abstractly; they are able to problem-solve in a logical way but only in relation to real-life problems impacting on them at the present time. Some individuals may not have achieved the ability to think logically even about concrete things. They may make sense of the world by how things are associated together, for example, '*It hurt when I went to the dentist; the dentist is bad and I don't want to go there again*'. This misses out the logical thoughts that the dentist was trying to help them, tried her best to hurt as little as possible and that bad teeth hurt much more if they are not treated. These thinking styles are hard wired and not amenable to change.

The thinking styles of individuals with intellectual disabilities are also shaped by their experiences. These aspects of thinking may have more potential to change depending on how strongly pathways are built up during development. Individuals are vulnerable to developing unhelpful attribution styles as a result of experiencing dependence on others, disempowerment and discrimination. This can lead to an external locus of control, a sense of pervading personal powerlessness and an acceptance that things

 Intellectual Disabilities and 'Personality Disorder' © Pavilion Publishing and Media Ltd and its licensors 2023

cannot be changed. For some, over-protection can create a sense of entitlement, with the expectation that they will be given special treatment and that rules will not apply to them. Having an external locus of control can make it hard for individuals to see the part they play in the difficulties they experience and makes it less likely that they will take responsibility for their behaviour. The combination of intellectual disabilities and negative life experiences often leads individuals to have an immature concept of 'fairness', which can contribute to tensions and interpersonal conflict (see Box 15.11).

Box 15.11: Concept of 'fairness'

Immature	Mature
■ Fairness = everyone treated the same. Perceives 'different' treatment as being given more or less than others. ■ Leads to anger and frustration shown in comments such as: *'It's not fair – no one else has to...'* *'X is allowed to.../everyone else is...'* ■ Reinforced by selective attention: notice occasions when fair but different treatment gives them a 'worse deal' but not when it gives them a 'better deal' – leads to belief that it is always them that 'misses out'.	■ Fairness includes considering individual differences in needs and abilities e.g. a baby and a teenager require different things but can still be treated 'fairly'. ■ Much of life is fundamentally unfair and there is very little that can be done about it (acceptance) – met calmly. ■ Some unfairness is unjust and so generates 'righteous anger' that is channeled into challenging injustice e.g. racism, stigma.

Developmental trauma (see Chapter 2) and the experience of being stigmatised (see Chapter 16) have a profound impact on an individual's core beliefs about themselves, other people and the world. Where individuals have become hyper-sensitive to threat cues, they will switch rapidly to their emotional mind in situations others would not find threatening. The impact that growing up with intellectual disabilities and experiencing trauma has on thinking can affect multiple aspects of an individual's functioning (see Box 15.12).

Box 15.12: Issues with thinking contribute to in a wide range of difficulties:

- Being misunderstood or disbelieved by those supporting them.
- Low or high (unrealistic) self-esteem.
- Intense emotional reactions particularly to apparently neutral comments or situations.

→

- Difficulties regulating intense emotions such as anger.
- Difficulty trusting other people.
- Difficulties with mentalising – understanding own thoughts and feelings and those of other people.
- Interpersonal conflict and relationship breakdown.
- Impulsive behaviour.
- Verbal and physical aggression.
- Experiencing low mood and mental health problems such as depression.
- Lower expectations and reduced motivation for change.
- Low adherence to interventions to promote physical and mental well-being.
- Poor fit between their needs and how conventional services are designed.

They are likely to behave in ways that seem irrational, erratic and incomprehensible to people who have the ability to use abstract reasoning and see who do not see the world through a lens distorted by negative experiences.

Where individuals with intellectual disabilities have been given (formally or informally) a diagnosis of 'personality disorder', awareness of that intellectual disability can be lost (Lee and Kiemle, 2015). Essential information about their abilities to process information and understand the world around them may not be taken into consideration.

Understanding thoughts

Individuals with intellectual disabilities often do not have a clear understanding of what thoughts are and may have difficulty distinguishing thoughts from emotions. Even if they are able to understand the idea of thoughts, they may have difficulty recognising and explaining what they are thinking. Some individuals will experience thoughts as if hearing voices speaking to them. Their responses, when asked questions about 'hearing voices', can be mistaken for auditory hallucinations and may lead to the misdiagnosis of 'psychosis' or 'schizophrenia'.

Assessment and formulation

Assessment of an individual's thinking will have two components. First, working out their thinking styles and the contribution they make to the difficulties the individual is experiencing. Second, building working hypotheses about the roles of

Intellectual Disabilities and 'Personality Disorder' © Pavilion Publishing and Media Ltd and its licensors 2023

'hardware' and 'software' in their thinking patterns to inform plans for intervention. Given the inaccessibility of thoughts and the difficulties of accurately assessing cognitive abilities when individuals are very distressed, this is a challenging process. Consequently, it is important to remain curious as to the mechanisms underlying an individual's thinking and to review the formulation regularly, as work with the individual progresses and more information becomes available.

Informal assessment

Useful insights into the extent of an individual's intellectual disabilities can be gained by looking at how well an individual copes with everyday practical tasks. Can they handle money, work out a bus timetable, use a mobile phone or use a computer? Individuals who can successfully do such tasks are likely to have relatively mild intellectual disabilities. Most individuals with mild intellectual disabilities will have reached the concrete operational stage of thinking. This means that they have the capacity for logical thinking in relation to practical situations and can have some understanding of their relationship to the wider world. Cognitive distortions may be more a reflection of their experiences than their underlying intellectual deficits. If their performance fluctuates widely, this may indicate they are switching between their reasonable mind and emotional mind, perhaps as a result of hyper-sensitivity to threat. Contrasting direct observations with an individual's account of their abilities and difficulties may also give insight into the extent to which they accept and understand their strengths and needs.

If an individual is having difficulties in all areas of their life, it may be that they have more severe intellectual disabilities. They may have only reached the pre-operational stage of thinking. At this stage, an individual cannot think logically but rather their understanding is based on association of events. Individuals at this stage have little awareness of the wider world, rather, they are the centre of their own small universe and will struggle to consider other people's needs. Much of their thinking style will be hard wired.

Giving an individual space to talk about what is going on in their life can give helpful insights into how they see themselves, other people and the world. It can also give insights into attribution styles and cognitive distortions. By regularly chatting with an individual, using the active listening approach (see Box 10.13), it may be possible to identify themes in the individual's thinking and to explore these with gentle questions, for example, *'It seems to me you think no one likes you?'* or *'You seem to worry a lot, what do you think might happen to your mum?'* This will help in understanding their core beliefs and cognitive distortions. In turn, this is likely to help explain patterns of behaviour that on the surface may seem self-defeating.

Where an individual is not able to express their thoughts, it can be helpful to consider:

> *'What would I be thinking and feeling for [unexplained behaviour] to seem like my only / best option?' How would [individual's experience] make me see myself / other people / the world / the future?'*

Such thoughtful, reflective questioning can generate helpful working hypotheses. In essence, this is person-centred practice: putting yourself in the shoes of an individual with support needs. If we can remain compassionate and stay curious about why they may be struggling to develop adaptive coping strategies, even as we observe (or are directly affected by) their behaviours that challenge, this becomes trauma-informed practice.

Formal assessment

If there is any remaining confusion about an individual's abilities, it would be helpful for them to be offered a referral to a psychologist for an intellectual assessment and detailed profile of their intellectual strengths and needs, including executive functioning. However, assessment will be difficult if an individual is very distressed and their distress would make results difficult to interpret. Formal assessment is most likely to give helpful results once an individual is in a stable situation.

Formulation

Understanding the impact of an individual's intellectual disabilities, thinking styles and cognitive distortions will form a part of the formulation of all difficulties experienced by individuals (see Chapter 4). More detailed exploration of the impact of an individual's thinking is most likely to happen within the context of individual intervention. Box 15.13 gives a formulation for 'Margaret', that explores how her thoughts and feelings of grief and guilt around her father's death by suicide might relate to her self-harm. This builds on the initial risk formulation (Box 10.9) carried out to create her safety plan (Box 10.10) following her initial contact with services for self-harm.

 Intellectual Disabilities and 'Personality Disorder' © Pavilion Publishing and Media Ltd and its licensors 2023

Box 15.13: Formulation for 'Margaret'*

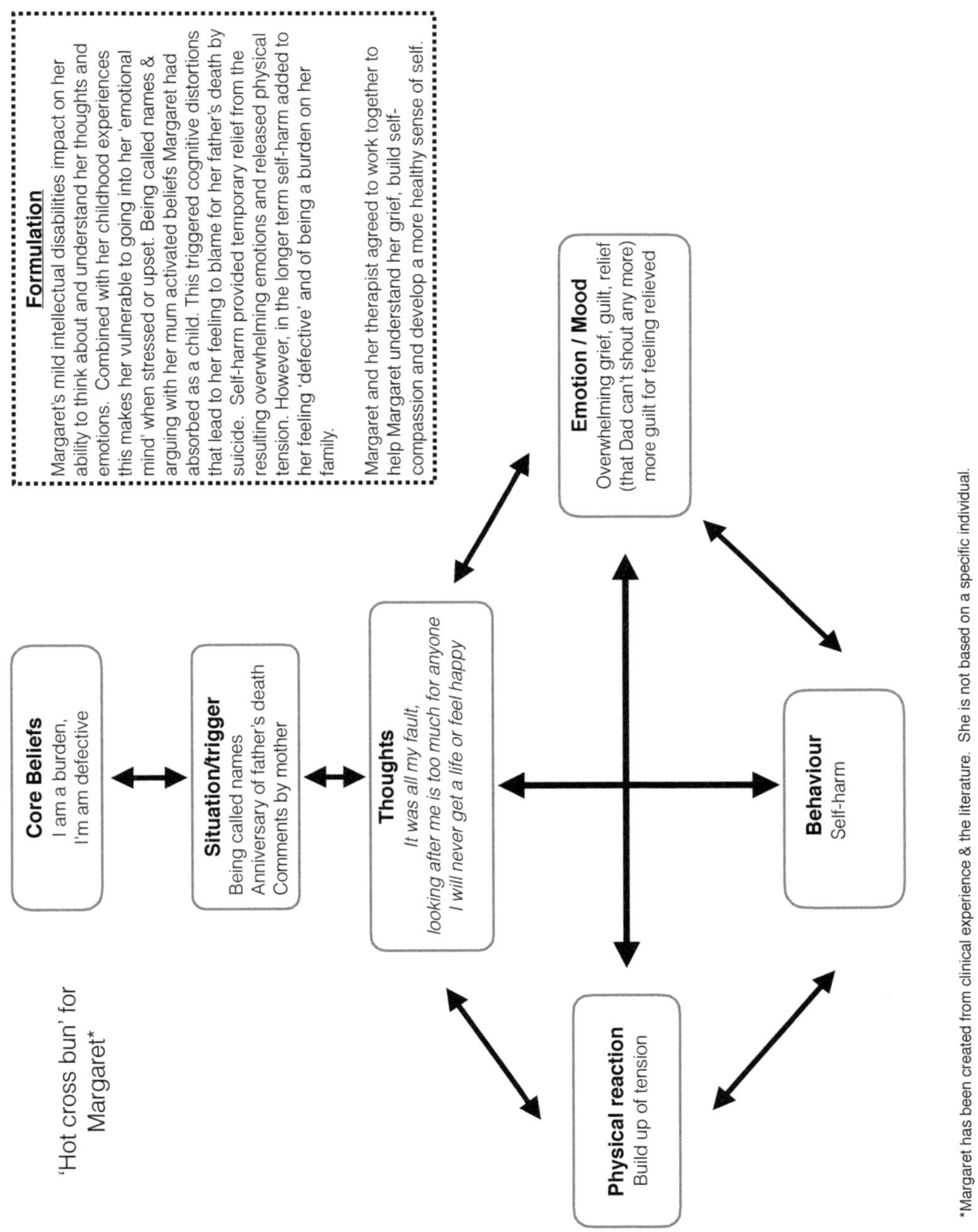

Practical and social support

The first step to take when addressing issues related to thinking is to ensure that an individual has the right level of practical and social support. This is because inadequate support increases the demands on the individual and results in high levels of stress. High levels of stress cause mental exhaustion, reduce an individual's capacity to think clearly and can activate unhelpful core beliefs. It is surprising how many problems related to unhelpful thinking can be resolved simply by reducing stress to more manageable levels and by providing support tailored to the individual's abilities. Where an individual's thinking might be amenable to change, being well-supported and stable is a prerequisite for successful intervention.

Once the individual is well supported, their remaining issues relating to thinking can be addressed. For individuals at the **R**egulate and **R**elate stages (see Box 3.1), issues with thinking will be addressed through the way they are supported and will be incorporated into their PBS plan (see Chapter 8). Specialist interventions that may be considered for individuals at the **R**eason stage are mentioned later in this chapter. However, all individuals will benefit from a support style that keeps thinking in mind, in everyday interactions and aims to promote positive thinking.

Keeping thinking in mind in everyday interactions

When supporting individuals with intellectual disabilities with issues arising from unhelpful core beliefs, attribution styles and cognitive distortions, it is essential to have a good understanding of how these arise and how they may influence behaviour.

It is also important that staff understand their own thinking styles and how these might lead to them jumping to conclusions about why individuals might behave in a particular way. For example, someone who places great value on intellectual abilities may be more comfortable perceiving an individual's behaviour as planned and conscious or due to 'lacking motivation', rather than arising from their intellectual disabilities (and hence devaluing). Developing and maintaining an open, curious, non-judgmental mindset that is always asking 'why?', helps minimise the risk of interactions being distorted by unconscious mechanisms (see Chapter 7). Without this, there is a risk that individuals' 'survival strategies' (see Chapter 8) will be perceived in negative and unhelpful ways. If an individual is described using terms such as 'self-destructive', 'self-centred', 'ungrateful', 'inconsiderate', or 'manipulative', it is a sign that important underlying mechanisms have not been recognised and that reflective practices are needed.

 Intellectual Disabilities and 'Personality Disorder' © Pavilion Publishing and Media Ltd and its licensors 2023

Chapter 16 explores the importance of valuing and validating everyday interactions in creating a positive sense of self. Adopting this approach will also help promote positive views of other people and the wider world. Again, 'how' things are done is as important as 'what' is done (see Chapter 3). However, there are some practical steps that can be taken to reduce the occurrence of unhelpful thinking and to resolve it as quickly as possible when it does occur.

Box 15.14: Supporting individuals with unhelpful thinking patterns and frightening thoughts	
Primary prevention (see Box 8.12)	Look for ways of avoiding triggering unhelpful thoughts.
Reduce misunderstandings	Never assume an individual understands your reasons for doing something, always give a brief explanation. For example: *'I'm writing that down so I don't forget to tell your doctor'*. *'I need to answer the phone then I'll come straight back'* (may avoid paranoid interpretation, or triggering thoughts of dislike or abandonment).
View everyday events and practices through the individual's lens	Staff talking in the office or kitchen, a meeting about someone else, a meter reader visiting, may all be seen very differently by someone feeling unsafe who believes that people don't like them or actively want to hurt them. Change practices and or provide regular accessible explanations.
Promote positive emotions	Negative thoughts and thinking errors are often related to emotional states. Using the approaches in Chapter 11 to promote positive emotions is likely to reduce the impact of unhelpful thinking.
Reduce stress	Build in regular soothing/tension releasing activities. Try mindfulness exercises such as the birthday cake (see Box 15.16).
Secondary prevention (see Box 8.13)	Respond to unhelpful thinking and frightening thoughts (e.g. hallucinations) in ways that help it resolve quickly and safely.
Reassurance	If someone is extremely distressed and appears frightened of things that are unreal to staff: Reassure them that they are safe. Use relaxed body language and calm voice. Validate what they are experiencing. Let them know you believe it is real to them but that they are in a safe place. (If prescribed, use of as required medication* may be helpful.)

→

Active listening	Listen to the individual and help them express their concerns (see Box 10.13).
Do not challenge or confront their thinking	Challenging an individual's thoughts in everyday interactions will make them feel misunderstood, frightened or angry. This is likely to intensify the worrying thoughts or experiences. (The appropriate place to 'challenge' thoughts is to do so compassionately and thoughtfully in a therapeutic interaction when the individual feels safe and supported.)
Acceptance	Accept that the content of anything they say is true for the individual at that time even if you feel it is inaccurate. '*You think that everyone hates you.*' '*You can hear your dad calling you names.*'
Remind the individual of facts they may have forgotten	For example, if an individual is worried about hearing from their family, remind them, '*Mum usually rings on Friday and it is Thursday today*'.
Distraction	Engage the individual; chat to them about their favourite topic, offer a fun activity, put on some calming music, offer a cup of tea (see Box 15.15).

* For some individuals, medication may have a limited but important role in managing acute distress. Where medication is used on an 'as required' basis this should be supported by guidelines and reviewed after every use. Its use should be integrated into the PBS plan.

Using distraction is one of the easiest and most effective ways of gaining respite from unpleasant or worrying thoughts. It is also highly effective at breaking the vicious cycles that can develop between emotions, physical sensations and thoughts (see Box 7.14).

Box 15.15: Distracting activities

Temporarily shift focus from the thought/emotions of concern. Gives a 'breather', a chance for the intensity of the intrusion to reduce.

Mentally active tasks: require a degree of concentration that is helpful for dislodging unwanted thoughts.

Physically active tasks: are helpful when there is also a build up of physical tension. Some activities combine physical and mental activity e.g. a dance routine.

Social activities: choose these when an individual finds company enjoyable.

Solo activities: choose these when an individual finds interaction stressful.

 Intellectual Disabilities and 'Personality Disorder' © Pavilion Publishing and Media Ltd and its licensors 2023

Mental exercises:	Counting, counting backwards, reciting poetry, listing objects that are red/yellow, listing animals, naming all the items in a room.
Absorbing activities:	Reading, word search, picture search e.g. 'Where's Wally?', spot the difference, crossing out the letter 'o' in a newspaper, crossword puzzles, knitting, cross-stitch, doodling, colouring.
Games:	Noughts and crosses, Jenga, computer games, phone apps, draughts/ checkers, dominos.
Physical activities:	Badminton, swing ball, shooting hoops, exercise class, exercise video/ DVD, line dancing, dance DVD or YouTube Zumba.
Repetitive chores:	Weeding, vacuuming, sorting laundry, pairing socks, cleaning windows.

Mindfulness

The term 'mindfulness' is used to refer to developing a state of mind in which the individual is able, purposefully, to pay attention to their current experience on a moment-to-moment basis. This state of mind promotes awareness of thoughts, emotions and sensations in a non-judgmental and accepting way. Mindfulness has its origins in religion and is created through exercises based on meditation. Mindfulness techniques form part of several modern therapies including DBT and Acceptance and Commitment Therapy (ACT), discussed later in this chapter. Mindfulness exercises can help individuals to remain in the present moment (manage their attention), reduce stress and build tolerance of distressing thoughts, emotions and physical sensations. Mindfulness approaches have been adapted for individuals with intellectual disabilities (Currie *et al*, 2019; Griffith and Hastings, undated; Singh and Hwang, 2020). Mindfulness-based programmes constitute a specialist approach and require skilled practitioners (Griffith and Hastings, undated).

However, it has been found that a full understanding of what mindfulness is, or its purpose, is not required in order to lead to therapeutic gains (Currie *et al*, 2019). Hence, regular mindfulness exercises as part of a daily routine are potentially beneficial. Box 15.16 gives one example of a mindfulness exercise that was created to help individuals understand how to breathe in and out slowly. Mindfulness exercises are easily built into an individual's daily routine and act both as a distraction and a means of promoting a positive mood.

Intellectual Disabilities and 'Personality Disorder' © Pavilion Publishing and Media Ltd and its licensors 2023

Box 15.16: The birthday cake mindfulness exercise

Most individuals have experienced blowing out candles and birthdays are usually (but not always) positive experiences. Blowing out candles is a concrete experience of controlling breathing that makes sense to many individuals who otherwise struggle with focusing on their breathing.

Help them to imagine and act out the process of blowing out candles on a birthday cake. As they do this, encourage them to focus on their breathing and to feel the air moving in and out of their body. The appearance of the cake is adjusted to appeal to the individual and the number of candles is adjusted to promote a long, slow breath. Once the most helpful appearance of the cake and the number of candles has been worked out, this is made into a personalised visual prompt for the individual to use at times when their thoughts are distressing them or at any time they want to reduce stress.

Outline of prompts to be tailored to each individual:

- Think about a (colour) birthday cake [picture of cake].
- Blow the candles out gently and smoothly [picture of someone blowing out candles].
- Blow out the candles one at a time [picture of a row of candles].
- Try doing that three more times 1, 2, 3, [each showing picture of someone blowing out candles].
- If you start thinking about other things, think about the cake again and gently and smoothly blow out the candles [picture of cake].
- As you are thinking about the birthday cake, think about your breathing.
- There are two parts to breathing.
- Before you blow the candles out you breathe in.
- Air comes in your nose and mouth, goes down your throat to your lungs and your tummy moves out [pictures of where the air goes].
- Now think about breathing in.
- Can you feel the air going in your nose and mouth?
- Can you feel it going down your throat?
- Can you feel it fill your lungs?
- Can you feel your tummy move out?
- Try thinking about breathing in three times.
- The second part of breathing is breathing out.
- Your tummy moves inwards.

→

 Intellectual Disabilities and 'Personality Disorder' © Pavilion Publishing and Media Ltd and its licensors 2023

- Your breath goes out of your lungs, up your throat and goes out of your nose and mouth [picture of where the air goes].
- Can you feel your breath leaving your body?
- Can you feel your tummy move in?
- Can you feel your breath going up your throat?
- Can you feel your breath come out of your nose and mouth?
- Now think about the (colour) birthday cake [picture of cake].
- You breathe in before you blow the candles out.
- You breathe out to blow the candles out [picture of candles].
- Try thinking about breathing in and out as you blow the candles out.

Rose and Webb (2012)

Other examples of mindfulness activities adapted for individuals with intellectual disabilities include 'grounding', 'mindfulness of an object' and 'mindfulness of sounds' (Williams and Jones, 2022) and 'body scan' (PELICAN, undated).

Building a positive relationship with thoughts

Some individuals who have reached the **R**eason stage (see Box 3.1) may wish to engage in exploring how to develop new ways of thinking. There are a range of specialist therapies that may be beneficial. Some approaches such as CBT and schema therapy (Jacob and Arntz, 2013) focus on the *content* of thoughts and internal experiences and changing what is thought and done (Churchill *et al*, 2013; Hayes and Hofmann, 2021). These can be intellectually demanding but have been successfully adapted for individuals with mild intellectual disabilities (de Klerk *et al*, 2022).

In contrast, 'third wave' therapies focus on the *process* of thoughts, helping individuals to become aware of their thoughts and accept them in a non-judgmental way. This includes ACT and Compassion Focused Therapy. These approaches have evolved from and extend traditional CBT to be more holistic and to include concepts such as acceptance and mindfulness. Although there is growing evidence that these approaches can be adapted for individuals with intellectual disabilities (Patterson *et al*, 2019; Patterson and Golightly, 2022), some of the concepts involved can be intellectually demanding. A review of the use of ACT with individuals with intellectual disabilities concluded that, while it was found to reduce stress and improve adaptive skills, there was a need for further adaptations (Byrne and O'Mahony, 2020).

Where specialist approaches are not available or are too intellectually demanding for an individual, resources such as that developed by Williams and Jones (2022) may be helpful. This offers a range of worksheets based on the concepts of ACT and is designed to be accessible for individuals with different levels of intellectual disabilities. Everyday conversations also present multiple opportunities to share information about thoughts and how the world works (see Box 15.17).

Box 15.17: Everyday conversations that can act to build helpful core beliefs: putting things into words	
Thoughts	Share facts about thoughts (see Box 15.1).
Self	
Helpless dependent	Explain that no one can do everything, everyone needs help sometimes. Feedback small steps towards independence that the individual has already made, remind them of times they have achieved things.
Unlovable	Explain that no one gets on with everyone. Feedback likeable qualities: '*You've got such a good sense of humour*', '*People love your smile*'.
Worthless	Separate the behaviour from the person. Explain that everyone does bad things sometimes but that does not make them a bad person. Explore forgiving and making new starts.
Undeserving	Explain that everyone deserves to be treated well and have their rights respected. People don't have to be perfect to have rights and making a mistake does not take away someone's rights (although certain behaviours may incur legal penalties).
Entitlement	Explain that rules apply to everyone – even princes get speeding tickets. Rights are balanced by responsibilities. We all depend on each other and must share and contribute.
Relationships	Build trust, be reliable. Explain that other people are only human and will make mistakes. Explain reasons: '*Sorry I was late, I had to take an urgent phone call, I will stay until we get things done.*'
The world	Check if there is anything in the environment that is making them feel unsafe (see it through their eyes not yours). Explain some people and places are hostile, others are safe, welcoming and kind. There are things that can be done to make it safer.
The future	Explain that nothing stays the same, change is inevitable. If you try you might be surprised what can be achieved.

 Intellectual Disabilities and 'Personality Disorder' © Pavilion Publishing and Media Ltd and its licensors 2023

Taking the time to think about situations, what an individual might be thinking, and sharing helpful comments can gradually help individuals understand what thoughts are and that there are different ways of seeing the world.

Key learning points

- Thoughts are symbolic responses within the brain to internal and external stimuli. Thinking allows individuals to make sense of themselves, other people, and the world, to solve problems and to make plans.
- Much thought is automatic, and people are unaware of how their core beliefs and patterns of thinking shape how they understand and respond to the world.
- The way someone thinks is influenced by both the development of their brain and by their life experiences, including developmental trauma.
- Thoughts, emotions, physical reactions and behaviours are closely interrelated because of the way the brain works.
- There are three different states of mind: reasonable (logical), emotional (instinctive) and wise (intuitive), depending on how different areas of the brain work together.
- The ability to think can be disrupted by stress. Stress can activate dormant core beliefs, trigger cognitive distortions and lead to a switch to the emotional mind. These processes apply both to individuals with intellectual disabilities and to the staff who support them.
- For individuals with intellectual disabilities, the development of thinking will be incomplete and these elements of their thinking will be 'hard wired' and not amenable to change. Some of their difficulties with thinking that arise from life experiences and stress may change in response to compassionate, containing support and appropriate interventions.
- Understanding an individual's typical thinking style and how this changes when they are stressed or distressed is helpful in making sense of their patterns of behaving and relating to others.
- When planning support, it is important to hold in mind that an individual's difficulties with thinking may be hard wired. Support should be designed to reflect their current functioning but with learning opportunities and supportive interventions designed to help their development progress.
- There are a range of practical strategies that can help to support individuals and compensate for intellectual deficits, thinking styles and cognitive distortions.
- For more able, motivated individuals who have reached the **R**eason stage, there are also options that may help them develop healthier patterns of thinking.

Intellectual Disabilities and 'Personality Disorder' © Pavilion Publishing and Media Ltd and its licensors 2023

Chapter 16: Building a positive and stable sense of self

This chapter explores what is meant by a positive and stable sense of self. It looks at how the development of self-image and self-esteem may be influenced by having intellectual disabilities and experiencing adversity, trauma and stigma. It explores the issues that can arise from having low self-esteem, high (unrealistic) self-esteem, or an unstable sense of self. It considers how these issues can be addressed within a compassionate and containing support style.

Key topics

- Sense of self
- Self-esteem
- Developing a sense of self
- Sense of self, self-esteem and intellectual disabilities
- Assessment and formulation
- The importance of everyday interactions
- Small steps build self-efficacy
- Interventions that promote a positive and stable sense of self

Sense of self

A sense of self is the mental picture an individual has of themselves. Other terms used for this picture include 'self-image', 'identity' and 'self-concept'. Sense of self is complex and encompasses a number of elements (see Box 16.1).

Box 16.1: How individual sees themselves. May be called self-image, identity, self-concept, sense of self	
Dimensions	Example characteristics
Physical	Height, weight, appearance, gender
Personality and temperament	Sociable, lively, quiet, grumpy, lovable, characteristic ways of behaving
Intellectual	Intelligence, common sense, memory, reasoning,

→

Skills	Social and technical skills, driver, dancer, cook, sewer, gardener, listener
Values and principles	Beliefs, attitudes, political and religious affiliations, opinions
Sexuality	
Roles	Worker, mother, son, friend
Affiliations, group membership	Working class, Welsh, Liverpool supporter
Core beliefs about self: These are the most central ideas about oneself. May not be consciously aware of them. Act like a lens through which every aspect of the self is viewed: *I am worthy of love, health and happiness. I am capable, determined and will win through.*	
Self-esteem: How individual evaluates themselves. ■ Across the dimensions of self e.g. too short, good listener, bad driver, too impatient. ■ Overall sense of worth (self-respect, self-esteem). ■ Belief in own abilities (self-confidence). ■ Belief about ability to succeed in different situations (self-efficacy). ■ Belief about responsibility for and ability to control own behaviour (agency).	
Self-compassion: being kind and understanding toward oneself. It comprises: ■ Recognising one's own hurts and difficulties. ■ Treating one's self with kindness, love, and compassion while going through challenging events. ■ Being less self-critical when life events do not go as planned. ■ To forgive one's self for not being perfect despite others' expectations.	

A sense of self is a broad picture of how someone sees themselves generally. For example, being in a bad mood would be a passing state but thinking of oneself as grumpy would be part of self-image. Self-image is never totally fixed; it is flexible and aspects are always adapting and developing in response to life events and the changes brought about by time. However, most people have a stable sense of self: they see themselves as the same person in the past, present, and future, despite the fact that sometimes they may behave in contradictory ways. A stable, flexible and coherent sense of self constitutes an important inner resource that facilitates self-regulation and mentalising, and helps navigate a complex social world (Jorgensen, 2020).

Intellectual Disabilities and 'Personality Disorder' © Pavilion Publishing and Media Ltd and its licensors 2023

An individual's self-image may or may not correspond to how other people see them. For example, someone most people consider short might consider themselves to be tall because they are the tallest member of their family. People may also value the same characteristic very differently. One individual may be happy being overweight, thinking 'big girls have more fun', while another may think 'I'll never be invited to a party, I'm too big'. This evaluation of personal qualities forms part of 'self-esteem' and is explored more fully below.

While some aspects of self-image are conscious, others have been absorbed over time and an individual may not be fully aware of them. These will form part of their core belief system. Core beliefs are important in shaping how people react emotionally and behaviourally and are explored in greater depth in Chapter 15.

Self-esteem

Self-esteem is the evaluative part of self-image and includes self-respect, self-confidence and self-efficacy (see Box 16.1). Self-esteem underlies an individual's beliefs about their right to be content, to be treated well by others and to respond to others as equals. It also underpins their belief in their abilities to cope with challenges and solve problems (self-efficacy). People with positive self-esteem are more resilient to setbacks and better able to face challenges. Positive self-esteem is linked with success in life and with mental well-being.

Both self-respect and self-confidence can fluctuate. For example, anyone's self-confidence can take a knock if they lose their job and are having difficulty finding another. However, having a wide range of roles and characteristics from which to derive a sense of worth helps protect self-esteem; strong areas can compensate for perceived weaknesses. Achievements, social standing, attractiveness and belonging to groups can all protect self-esteem.

Social comparison

One of the ways people form judgments about themselves is by comparing themselves to others (Festinger, 1954). If an individual sees themselves as lower than others on any attribute this can lower self-esteem. This is particularly likely to happen if the aspect found wanting is something that is important to the individual. For example, the widespread use of social media and exposure to photoshopped idealised images can result in negative self-appraisal of appearance (Tiggemann and Anderberg, 2019).

A 'downward comparison' is when an individual looks to another person or group that they consider to be worse off than themselves in order to feel better about themselves or their personal situation. Downward comparisons may also include denigrating others who are similar to themselves or denying their membership of a group that is seen as not socially valued. For example, someone with a mild physical disability may compare themselves to wheelchair users saying, *'I'm not a useless …'*, and refuse to engage with activities or services for people with physical disabilities. While this may boost their self-esteem, it comes at a cost; it isolates them from people who might otherwise be able to support them and undermines the development of a positive attitude towards their own disabilities.

Self-compassion

Self-compassion is the act of being kind and understanding toward oneself rather than judgmental. It is seen as a complex process with a number of elements (see Box 16.1). Self-compassion allows for positive self-worth in the face of adversity and is a significant predictor of happiness and optimism (Neff, 2021). Self-compassion is related to empathy and self-regulation and can also act to reduce negative thoughts and difficult emotions.

Developing a sense of self

Developing a sense of self is an interpersonal process embedded within and shaped by a cultural setting (Jorgensen, 2020). It begins within the emotional bond or attachment that develops between a baby and their parents (see Box 2.6). Babies have no sense of self or identity. Their self-image develops through interactions with other people and experience of the world. As they develop, they become aware of themselves as a separate being, differentiating themselves from others. They become aware of how others react to them and absorb or 'internalise' these reactions. Interactions between a parent and their baby have been described as 'mirroring'. Mirroring comprises a set of behaviours that accurately reflect what the child is thinking and feeling, for example by reflecting facial expressions, smiling and laughing together (Beacon House, 2022b). This conveys to the child that they are heard and that the parent understands their emotional state. When these responses are consistently validating (see Chapter 11), accepting, and show love, the child absorbs a positive sense of themselves.

Self-image and self-esteem continue to develop throughout life, with experiences and relationships outside the family becoming increasingly influential. Teenagers

Intellectual Disabilities and 'Personality Disorder' © Pavilion Publishing and Media Ltd and its licensors 2023

may experiment with different personas, making frequent changes to their style of dress, hairstyle, the groups they socialise with, the activities they take part in and their ambitions for the future. However, by early adulthood, most people develop a consistent sense of self – a stable sense of personal and sexual identity and consistent values, goals and ambitions.

Delays and disruptions

The development of self-image and self-esteem can be delayed or disrupted by many different factors (see Chapter 2). Some parents are not able to build a realistic, balanced sense of self in their children. This may be due to the parent's own experiences as children, to illness, problems with addiction or to circumstances surrounding birth and early childhood. Anything that disrupts or damages the bond between a child and parent will impact on the child's sense of self.

Childhood adversity disrupts normal identity development (Vartanian *et al*, 2018). Experiencing adversity may result in cognitive and emotional reactions that are difficult to integrate into a coherent self-narrative (Hayward *et al*, 2020). Experiencing abuse has a particularly disruptive effect on the development of a sense of self. Individuals who have experienced abuse in childhood have lower self-esteem than those experiencing other forms of adversity (Kim *et al*, 2022). In such situations, the parents' mirroring may be inaccurate, invalidating and inconsistent (Jorgensen, 2020) and the child is deprived of the positive interactions that provide the foundation of a positive view of the self (Haywards *et al*, 2020).

Abuse can lead to an image of the self as being flawed, damaged, dirty or bad. A child may feel they are unlovable and do not deserve to be treated well. This can make them vulnerable to further abuse as they grow up and lead to them accepting as 'normal' situations that most people would find intolerable (see also reciprocal roles, Chapter 7). Where parental responses are very inconsistent, it can lead to a fractured or unstable sense of self:

> *'If you determine who you are based on others' reactions to you, and those reactions have been unpredictable and / or scary, you have no framework for developing a strong sense of identity.'* (Ackerman, 2018)

Experiences outside the home, such as being bullied, can also undermine a child's sense of self, leading to low self-esteem and feelings of being unlovable and helpless (Choi and Park, 2021). These responses can create a negative cycle, making the child more vulnerable to future abuse.

Some individuals have characteristics that are not valued by society and that lead to them experiencing discrimination (see Box 1.5). The experience of stigma impacts on an individual's life experiences directly through the actions of others. If the distorted perception is internalised and believed to be a true reflection of the self, stigma can also shape an individual's sense of self and lower their self-esteem.

The cumulative effects of developmental and social experiences may result in individuals having low or unrealistically high self-esteem or an unstable sense of self and associated difficulties (see Box 16.2).

Box 16.2: Issues with self-concept/self esteem	
Unstable sense of self	■ Sense of identity may vary suddenly and dramatically. Shown outwardly in change to dress, hair, choice of activities and friendship groups. May be uncertain about or suddenly switch aims and personal preferences. May have no idea who they are or what they believe in. May feel like a 'chameleon', changing who they are depending on their circumstances and what they think others want from them: changes in image and self-esteem are often related to interpersonal triggers. May be unable to see their past self, present self, and future self as the same person. May feel they do not exist away from others. To those around them it can sometimes feel like an individual is not one but several different people. ■ May seek repeated reassurance, but not be comforted. May panic when alone. May self-harm in effort to reconnect with self/world. May lack hope for the future and struggle to learn from experiences.
Low self-esteem	■ Lack of confidence – exaggerating weaknesses and underestimating strengths. ■ Reduced ability to cope with everyday challenges. ■ External locus of control, feel helpless/powerless to achieve change, over-dependence on others. ■ Highly self-critical, negative self-talk, dissatisfied with many aspects of self. ■ Selective attention to feedback – focusing on negative comments, don't hear compliments but hyper-sensitive to criticism. ■ Low expectations – lack of belief that they can achieve a good outcome. ■ Indecision for fear of making the wrong choice. →

 Intellectual Disabilities and 'Personality Disorder' © Pavilion Publishing and Media Ltd and its licensors 2023

Low self-esteem	■ Fear of failure, may not start things or may give up easily. ■ May not enforce own boundaries. ■ Being a people-pleaser – going along with things they don't want do, being unable to say no. ■ Low mood or irritability, increased risk of anxiety, depression and suicidal thoughts. ■ May be insecure, constantly seeking reassurance but unable to accept and hold on to that reassurance.
Feelings of worthlessness	Can lead the individual to self-neglect. This may take the form of poor personal care and untidy appearance. Neglecting physical health can result in serious tooth decay, infected wounds, extreme weight loss or gain and non-adherence with treatment for illnesses such as diabetes or colitis. (See Chapter 17.)
High (unrealistic) self-esteem	■ Overconfident and overestimate abilities, attributes, and skills. Can put self at risk. ■ Disproportionate sense of personal rights/entitlement, thinks only of self. ■ Views self as special, may see self as above rules, contributing to offending behaviour. ■ An inability to accept criticism, being more prone to anger or aggression, or to dismissing negative feedback and externalising responsibility (blaming others). ■ Hinders ability to acknowledge difficulties or recognise the need for change.
References: Cherry (2022b; 2023), Jorgensen (2020)	

An unstable sense of self makes it difficult for individuals to integrate their past and present selves. They live in the present and struggle to learn from past experiences or avoid repeating past mistakes. They find it difficult to anticipate, plan for and invest in their own futures. An unstable sense of self is also associated with difficulties with mentalising and interpersonal difficulties (De Meulemeester *et al*, 2017). Low self-esteem is both a vulnerability factor for depression and anxiety and also a consequence of experiencing them (Fennell, 2016). Low self-esteem makes individuals underestimate their capabilities and to be overly critical of themselves while high (unrealistic) self-esteem leads to overconfidence.

Enduring problems in the functioning of aspects of the self, such as identity, is one of the criteria for being given a diagnosis of 'personality disorder' (see Box 1.9). It is likely that this reflects the high rates of trauma experienced by those given this diagnosis.

Sense of self, self-esteem and intellectual disabilities

Studies report mixed evidence regarding levels of self-esteem for individuals with intellectual disabilities compared with the general population (Lee *et al*, 2023). Some studies have found no difference, while others have found unrealistically higher (Davies *et al*, 2021) or lower self-esteem, depending on the characteristics of the study and the comparison group.

Individuals with intellectual disabilities will face many challenges to their sense of self and self-esteem as a result of their disabilities and experience of living with those disabilities. Chapter 2 explored how the bonding between parent and child with intellectual disabilities may be disrupted, leading to insecure attachments. It also explored the higher rate of trauma experienced by individuals with intellectual disabilities. These will impact on the development of a sense of self and self-esteem. It is likely that individuals with intellectual disabilities will experience frequent failure and they may not move through valued life stages at the same rate as their peers and siblings, for example finding a job, finding a partner, leaving home and having a family. These experiences shape their personality (see Chapter 1) and are likely to impact on their sense of self.

In addition to the direct consequences of living with intellectual disabilities, individuals are exposed to how others view those disabilities. Having a disability is not valued by Western society. This is reflected in how individuals with intellectual disabilities are treated. They are vulnerable to bullying at school, may be picked on in their local community and experience hate crime. Individuals with intellectual disabilities may take on society's view of them and develop a sense of being different and inadequate (Paterson *et al*, 2012) and express feelings of shame, anger and powerlessness about their disabilities (Logeswaran et al, 2019).

Sometimes, having intellectual disabilities may lead to an individual having a sense of being special and that society's rules do not apply to them. This can occur when individuals are not held accountable for their actions and are protected from the consequences that would usually be associated with inappropriate behaviour.

 Intellectual Disabilities and 'Personality Disorder' © Pavilion Publishing and Media Ltd and its licensors 2023

As issues with sense of self is one of the diagnostic criteria for 'personality disorder', individuals with intellectual disabilities given this diagnosis are likely to have difficulties with both their sense of self and self-esteem. They may have a strong sense of being flawed, dirty or bad (see Box 16.3).

Box 16.3: Unhelpful, unhealthy core beliefs about self	
Different/ defective	I am stupid, inferior, not good enough, defective. I am not like other people, not like my brothers and sisters.
Helpless/ dependent	I am ineffective, incompetent, unable to cope, powerless, out of control, trapped, vulnerable, needy, weak, a failure, useless, not good at anything, I don't measure up, I fail no matter how hard I try.
Unlovable	I am unlovable, unlikeable, unwanted, undesirable, unattractive, not good enough to be loved by others, ugly, boring, I will be rejected, abandoned, always alone, I have nothing to offer.
Worthless	I am bad, irresponsible, worthless, dangerous, toxic, evil, inhuman.
Undeserving	I can't have what I want, I don't deserve happiness, love, pleasure, to be healthy.
Entitled/ special	I should get what I want, restrictions/rules don't apply to me, I can't tolerate restrictions, my needs are more important than other people's, they are supposed to take care of me.

Feelings of being unlovable and undeserving of good treatment will shape their responses to others. They may have absorbed rigid negative reciprocal roles such as *'Abuser / Bully – Abused / Victim'* – *'Rejecting / Rejected'* (see Chapter 7). This makes them vulnerable to further abuse or neglect, which further reinforces their negative self-image. They may struggle to make sense of who they are, and this may be compounded by frequent moves with associated loss of a coherent narrative of their life story. These issues can undermine their abilities to form and maintain relationships, to recognise the need for and to seek help, and to engage with services.

Assessment and formulation

Within the multitude of issues experienced by individuals with intellectual disabilities who might be given a diagnosis of 'personality disorder', issues with self-concept and self-esteem may not seem of high priority and 'self-esteem' will rarely be the main focus of an assessment, intervention and formulation. However, issues with sense of self are pervasive and will impact on all aspects of an individual's functioning.

If a formal assessment is thought necessary, rating scales for assessing self-esteem have been successfully adapted for use with individuals with intellectual disabilities (Parks and Parks, 2019; Syropoulou *et al*, 2021). However, the most valuable insights are often gained from comments that individuals make, their responses to feedback and the consistency of their responses when talking about their past, present and future. Active listening may help individuals express some of the ways they feel about themselves. These insights can be fed into the formulation process to help understand an individual's thoughts, emotions and behaviour (see Chapter 4).

Taking time to reflect (see Chapter 7) on how an individual might see and judge themselves can give valuable insights into their patterns of relating and behaving. For example, 'disproportionate' anger to apparently neutral comments might reflect low self-esteem. Unconscious core beliefs about self-worth, might explain a need for constant reassurance or self-neglect.

Box 16.4 gives part of the outcome of a staff reflection for 'David'. Having made an initial formulation of the behaviours that lead to David experiencing a crisis in the pub (Box 9.14), his staff team met to reflect on other behaviours of concern, including his verbal aggression and unkind remarks to staff and other residents. This identified several issues related to core beliefs and self-esteem, which helped develop their initial formulation and were helpful in developing a strategy for building trust and engagement.

Box 16.4: Team reflective case discussion for 'David'*

The crisis relapse and contingency plan created for David following the incident at the pub highlighted the need for staff to gain his trust and help him engage more actively with them. It was agreed that a team reflective case discussion would be the first step in this process. As part of their reflection the team explored what it must have been like for David growing up and how this might have shaped his view of himself and other people. It seemed David's insecure attachment was acting to make him reject others before they rejected him. His verbal abuse might be acting to keep staff and other individuals at a safe distance. This suggested he might hold core beliefs about being different and unlovable and have low self-esteem. Staff also wondered if David's negative comments to others acted to help him feel he was better than them – boosting his self-esteem at the expense of forming relationships. They wondered if it was frightening for David to accept help as this undermined his sense of self-efficacy, confirmed he could not do everything alone and reminded him of how vulnerable he sometimes was.

They wondered if it was safer for David to express his fear as anger to cover his vulnerabilities. Understanding what might be behind David's comments helped to take the sting out of them.

 Intellectual Disabilities and 'Personality Disorder' © Pavilion Publishing and Media Ltd and its licensors 2023

It was decided to create a small team within a team to support David to help build his trust. David was enjoying woodwork and the team saw building things together as an opportunity to have fun, offer a non-threatening situation and provide opportunities to feedback positive comments to David.

*'David' is a composite example created from clinical experience and the literature. He is not based on a specific individual.

The importance of everyday interactions

It is important to be aware that an individual's difficulties with self-image and self-esteem have evolved over their whole life span, are embedded in both their thinking and emotional responding, and, sadly, *often continue to be reinforced by their encounters with others in their everyday lives.* Even if an individual has reached the **Reason** stage (Box 3.1), and is able to engage, it is unlikely that a few sessions of individual therapy (however good the therapist) will change an individual's long-term view of themselves, if all the other contacts in their life fail to challenge (or even actively reinforce) their negative view of themselves. The importance of addressing the 'how' as well as the 'what' of intervention (see Chapter 3) is particularly important when thinking about sense of self. *Patterns of everyday interaction both lead to and play a central role in addressing these issues.*

Every interaction with an individual, from their first to their last contact with a service (whatever the primary task), represents an opportunity to show them that they are valued and have many positive qualities. To facilitate this, it is important that staff have time to reflect on whether they have unconsciously absorbed negative stereotypes of individuals with intellectual disabilities and to ensure they are working in a genuinely person-centred way, tailored to individual need (see Chapter 7). Only when staff are seeing and responding positively to the individual as a unique human being will their interactions be genuine, validating and accepting, and hence help build a positive self-image. Given that individuals who might be given a diagnosis of 'personality disorder' can be highly sensitive to other people's non-verbal cues and general mood, offering *genuine* compassion is vital when building a reparative relationship.

Many of the measures taken to engage individuals and make them feel safe (Chapter 5) will also make them feel valued and cared for. The non-specific factors in interventions (Box 3.5) all work towards showing an individual that they are valued, cared for and have a positive future to look forward to. Techniques for *active listening* (Box 10.13) and *validating emotions* (Box 11.14) will help individuals feel heard and understood. These are reflected in positive attitudes and respectful behaviour (see Box 16.5). The PACE approach (Hughes, 2017, Box 5.10) and proactive compassionate containment (see Box 9.5) will also promote a positive sense of self. These approaches need to be embedded in the individual's PBS plan (see Chapter 8) so that positive experiences are repeated multiple times each day.

Box 16.5: Support style that can promote a positive self-image and self-esteem	
Positive attitude:	
Non-judgmental, curious, active interest Hopeful, long-term view Persistent – not giving up Genuine warmth Finding ways to have fun together	Respectful Realistic expectations Consistent and predictable Finding common ground – shared interests
Respectful behaviours:	
Polite Using someone's preferred name Answering questions honestly Believing that what they say is true to them Apologising for mistakes Using 'friendly' body language e.g. eye contact, smiling.	Punctual Listening to what they have to say Giving someone time Doing what has been agreed Using a warm, friendly tone of voice

Whatever intervention stage an individual has reached, even the simplest of actions can be done in ways that convey powerful messages about how the individual is viewed. For example, helping an individual clean their room can send the message that the member of staff cares about the individual, understands that they feel too low to do this alone, and that this does not make them bad or lazy. Alternatively, the staff member can convey that this is a waste of their precious time, that the individual is lazy and inconsiderate, and that the individual's feelings are exaggerated or silly. The first approach will help build self-esteem and self-compassion, the second will confirm the individual's view that they are not worthy of help because they are a bad person. Having fun, laughing, joking, playing games or dancing all create a positive atmosphere and give the message that the individual is someone worth spending time with.

Barriers to positive interactions

This may look like stating the obvious. However, in busy, high-pressured services, it is often very difficult to maintain respectful behaviour towards individuals and find

 Intellectual Disabilities and 'Personality Disorder' © Pavilion Publishing and Media Ltd and its licensors 2023

time just to be with them. For example, a conversation may be interrupted by an important phone call and then not resumed due to an unexpected visitor (message: '*other people are more important than you*'). A casual reference to a cup of tea 'later' can be forgotten amid a host of other tasks (message: '*you don't matter as much as my paperwork*'). Being person-centred needs to be built into the service (see Chapter 6) so that staff have the confidence to let the phone go to voicemail, say they will call back, keep the important visitor waiting and take other actions that show individuals they really do matter.

Being respectful can be particularly difficult when individuals behave towards staff in ways that can be experienced as disrespectful. Such behaviours might include: being verbally abusive, interrupting conversations with other individuals, repeatedly asking the same question or arriving late or not at all (see Chapter 13). Anyone can respond to politeness with respect, but it takes insight, self-regulation and a good support system (see Chapter 7), to continue to respond respectfully in the face of repeated inconsiderate behaviour. It is important to keep considering the individual's perspective; often they are so overwhelmed by their own needs that they do not consider the impact of their behaviour on others. Also, their ability to mentalise may be impaired, meaning they have little awareness of the impact of their behaviour on the other person. If there is evidence that the individual is aware of and takes some satisfaction in the impact of their behaviour on staff, it may be helpful to reflect on the traumatic things that might have happened to them to create this self-defeating need to put others down and treat them poorly. Maintaining respect in the face of all challenges (see Chapters 8, 9 and 10) sends a strong message that staff think that the individual matters. (Being respectful does not mean accepting verbal or physical aggression to others. Maintaining boundaries and compassionately containing unacceptable behaviour convey important messages that staff and other individuals are also people and deserve to be treated with respect.)

Small steps build self-efficacy

A big barrier to individuals making any changes can be the inability to translate heartfelt wishes into an achievable action plan. They aim high, for example, '*I will never self-harm again*' but underestimate the time and effort involved in achieving this when they have been self-harming frequently for many years. They may hold ambitions for a full-time, high-status job while getting up at mid-day and not engaging in any work-related activities. When they meet a setback, as they must if the goal is very ambitious, it confirms their sense of being 'useless' and they are likely to abandon their efforts to achieve the goal. Every time this happens, it is a setback for their self-efficacy, making it harder for them to try again in the future.

It is easy to fall in with such goals as they often reflect things that staff hope the individual will achieve. This adds to the individual's sense of letting others down when things go wrong. Rather than get caught up in the enthusiasm of a great goal, it is helpful to be quietly optimistic. Low-key responses might be: '*It's great you want to do that but it will be hard work*'. The aim is not to pour cold water on the idea but to set the scene for realistic goal-setting. This is easy to do first time round but needs to be maintained even if it is the fifth time someone has tried to change something and they have abandoned it every previous time. Some actions that can promote self-efficacy are given in Box 16.6.

Box 16.6: Actions that can promote self-efficacy:	
Encouragement and support	Gentle encouragement and support make a huge difference to how someone sees themselves. Remind someone of how far they have come, how good it will feel if they do have a go and listening when it feels too difficult will all make a difference. Let them know you believe in them even when they don't believe in themselves.
Praise and compliments	Let individuals know they have things to feel good about. Look for opportunities to give genuine positive feedback. Individuals may struggle to accept and remember positive comments, but it is still important that they hear them. Praising effort helps individuals learn to persist with tasks they find difficult and builds self-efficacy: '*Well tried, you keep working like that and you'll soon get the hang of it.*'
Constructive criticism	A way of helping individuals hear the difficult things they need to hear in order to make progress. Embed 'negative' comments within positive comments: Rule of thumb 5-6 positives for each 'negative'. Precede a negative with a positive: '*You've done a really good job of vacuuming the carpet but there are still some dirty socks under the bed.*' Be specific and say what needs to be done differently. Compare: '*Your bedroom is filthy*' with '*Your room will look great if you put those dirty clothes in the laundry basket and vacuum the carpet*'.
Achievable goals	Helping an individual identify a path towards idealistic goals creates the opportunity to succeed. Achieving small successes makes the foundations for improving self-efficacy, building skills and resilience. Words such as '*never*' and '*always*' give clues that a goal may need some un-packaging if it is not setting the individual up to fail.

 Intellectual Disabilities and 'Personality Disorder' © Pavilion Publishing and Media Ltd and its licensors 2023

Goal setting	A way of agreeing realistic targets and breaking them into achievable small steps (see box 16.7). Draw a ladder with a lot of rungs, putting where someone wants to be at the top and where they are now at the bottom. Working together, identify a number of small steps that make progress towards the goal. Each step can then be developed into a more detailed action plan. Once one step is achieved, a detailed action plan can be made for the next step. The ladder with rungs achieved provides a visual reminder of successes and progress.
Reactions to setbacks	Setbacks are a painful but inevitable part of trying to change – validate their emotional reaction but help individuals see setbacks as part of life and nothing to feel bad about. Calmly explore: Just how bad is this setback? Imagine a ladder: *Are they back at the beginning or have they just slipped a few rungs?* *Are the steps still too big – should the ladder have more rungs?* *Does the action plan need changing?*

If the individual enjoys board games, playing snakes (chutes) and ladders can be a good introduction to the concept of long-term goals and setbacks (or a favourite computer game that has multiple stages). This gives a concrete example of how a goal can be achieved despite multiple setbacks. Playing the game can make a safe space in which to talk about the individual's efforts to achieve seemingly impossible goals and move towards realistic goal-setting.

Goal-setting is a useful technique for turning dreams or distant goals into achievable short-term steps. Turning something 'impossible' or very long-term into lots of small tasks creates many opportunities to succeed and consequently to build self-efficacy. It also makes it easier to evaluate the seriousness of any setbacks; are they back one rung or two, or are they right back to the beginning? It is also a way of encouraging an individual to try things that they might reject if they were presented as an endpoint. Having tried them, they may then discover that they enjoy them and are content not to achieve the original goal. Example ladders are given in Box 16.7, but each individual's ladder will be unique to them and their goal.

Intellectual Disabilities and 'Personality Disorder' © Pavilion Publishing and Media Ltd and its licensors 2023

Box 16.7: Example of goal setting

Goal: Regulate emotions without the use of self-harm

Mostly able to self-regulate without use of self-harm.

Sometimes able to use other ways of regulating emotions – self-harm less frequent and/or less severe.

Learn and practice other ways of regulating emotions.

Identify other ways of addressing underlying needs.

Identify common triggers for self-harm and problem solving – can we make life less stressful and more fun?

Explore the pros and cons of self-harm. What purpose does it serve?

Co-write a safety plan to keep individual as safe as possible while working on this goal.

Starting point: severe and frequent self-harm

Goal: Having a full-time job

Build work seeking skills e.g. attending job interviews.

Work related experience e.g. voluntary work.

Build work skills e.g. attend college.

Take part in a range of daytime activities.

Build a daily routine that fits with going to work (may be a number of steps).

Identify job options; job centre interview.

Exploring the pros and cons of working – What does a full-time job mean?

Starting point: no daytime activities, getting up at mid-day.

Interventions that promote a positive and stable sense of self

For individuals who have reached the **R**eason stage and have a respectful and positive PBS plan in place, it may be helpful to explore specific interventions. There are a range of options, including individual and group work.

Intellectual Disabilities and 'Personality Disorder' © Pavilion Publishing and Media Ltd and its licensors 2023

It has long been established that it is possible to develop confidence and help individuals with intellectual disabilities feel more positive about themselves using general group approaches and CBT (Lindsay and Kasprowicz, 1987; Szivos and Griffiths, 1992; Whelan *et al*, 2007). DBT, a wide-ranging approach developed specifically for individuals with 'borderline personality disorder' involving both individual and group work, has been shown to help build a more coherent sense of self and improve self-esteem (Roepke, 2011) and has been adapted for use with individuals with intellectual disabilities (McNair *et al*, 2017). Compassion focused therapy (CFT) has been found to help individuals with intellectual disabilities view themselves more favourably (Goad, 2020), increase overall self-compassion, and reduce self-criticism and unfavourable social comparison (Clapton, 2016). All of these approaches require group leaders to be trained in the specific therapy approach.

Participation in self-advocacy groups (whose members speak up for themselves and work to improve the lives of their members) has also been found to improve self-esteem and increase confidence (Tilley *et al*, 2020). The skills and knowledge acquired in these groups may develop capacities to focus upon and celebrate strengths and may result in a more positive relationship with the label and experience of intellectual disabilities.

Whatever form it takes, group work offers individuals the chance to work together to help each other. There are opportunities to give and receive feedback, to give emotional support, and to share practical solutions. A well-run group creates the opportunity for individuals to realise that they are not alone and that other people have had similar experiences. It gives the opportunity to learn with and from other people in a safe setting. A group may also give individuals the opportunity to explore and challenge the views that society holds of them.

Where an individual does not have access to specialist groups, creating a 'tree of life' (see Box 4.7, Ncube, 2006), a life storybook (Ledger *et al*, 2022), a memory book or a survival story (see Box 16.8) can all help individuals build a more positive and coherent sense of self. These approaches have the advantage of creating a physical resource and hence can be accessed at any time of the day or night when an individual needs reassurance of their existence or to reconnect with positive past experiences. Self-compassion can be developed using exercises such as 'start being kind to yourself' and 'hand on heart' (Williams and Jones, 2022, pp45-50).

Box 16.8: Activities that can help build a positive stable sense of self

Tree of life: See Box 4.7

Life story:

An individual shares important episodes in their life with another person and they find ways of recording this that are meaningful for the individual e.g. objects, photos, video, drawing, writing. May involve co-detective work – finding things out, visiting places. May choose to share it with others.

Memory book:

- My achievements.
- My favourite things, activities, places, pets, people.
- My good qualities.
- Looking my best.
- Great days out.
- Holidays.
- People who care about me.
- Nice things people have said to me.

As the individual finds pleasant thoughts or memories, help them find ways to record them e.g. words (an account or poem), personal photographs, images from the internet, drawings or souvenirs such as ticket stubs. Take time creating the pages and make it fun. This way, the process of making the book will also be associated with positive memories.

Backup: there is a risk the book will be torn up if the individual becomes upset. This risk should be discussed openly and ways of reducing the impact of this should be identified e.g. take a photo of a treasured ticket stub for the book while keeping the original in a box where it is difficult to access. Artwork can be photocopied or scanned into the computer for safekeeping. This way the book can be recreated after a setback. It may also be helpful to have multiple copies of the book, each in different settings that the individual uses. In this way there will still be a copy available elsewhere. The setback will also not seem so bad as it had been anticipated and planned for and special keepsakes have not been destroyed.

Survival story: a way of recognising bad things that have happened in the past in a constructive way.

On (date) this (event) happened to me. The memory makes me feel (list feelings).
I will never forget what happened to me but **I have survived**.
These are things I have achieved:...
I am getting on with my life.
These are my plans...
My life may never be the same but I can have a good life and there is much to look forward to.

 Intellectual Disabilities and 'Personality Disorder' © Pavilion Publishing and Media Ltd and its licensors 2023

Where an individual struggles with a sense of being different, it may be helpful to use an exercise that explores their sense of difference and helps them see their good qualities. For example, 'feeling different from other people' (Williams and Jones, 2022, pp101-102). Social Stories™ can also be created to help individuals build a more positive understanding of their personal characteristics (see Box 12.13).

However, it is important to ensure that both individual and group work take place within a context that builds and reinforces a positive sense of self or the gains will be very limited.

Key learning points

- Sense of self or self-image is the mental picture a person has of themselves, including their evaluation of themselves.
- Positive self-image and self-esteem promote well-being and give people inner resources to help them face life's challenges.
- Low self-esteem can lead to a range of problems including hyper-sensitivity to criticism, reluctance to try anything new, self-neglect and depression.
- Individuals who have experienced adversity and trauma may have an unstable sense of self and difficulties with self-esteem. They may have a sense of being flawed, damaged, dirty or bad. Feelings of being unlovable and undeserving of good treatment may shape how they look after themselves and their responses to others.
- Individuals with intellectual disabilities face a number of barriers to building a stable and positive sense of self, including disruption to bonding with parents, experience of trauma, repeated failure and the experience of stigma.
- Reflecting on an individual's sense of self and self-esteem can give helpful insights that can enrich formulation and intervention plans for a wide range of difficulties.
- Building a positive and stable sense of self is a long-term project that requires staff to think as much about *how* they do things as about *what* they do.
- By adopting positive attitudes (non-judgmental, respectful and hopeful) and positive actions (such as having fun, goal-setting, giving praise, compliments and feedback), staff can create an environment that fosters a positive sense of self.
- For individuals who have reached the **R**eason stage, there are a range of individual and group interventions that can help to build a positive and stable sense of self, self-compassion, self-esteem and self-efficacy.

Chapter 17: Promoting health and well-being

This chapter looks at physical and emotional well-being and explores how these are interrelated in the experience of pain, chronic pain, the adoption of health-promoting behaviours and secondary gains of illness. It looks at health inequalities and the impact these have on individuals given a diagnosis of 'personality disorder' and individuals with intellectual disabilities. It explores the impact of childhood adversity on well-being. It highlights the importance of considering psychological factors when seeking to understand and address patterns of behaviour that are detrimental to well-being. It shows how positive health behaviours may be supported within a Positive Behavioural Support framework together with a Health Action Plan and Hospital or Care Passport.

Key topics

- Well-being
- Interrelationship between physical and psychological well-being
- Health inequalities
- Adversity, trauma and well-being
- Assessment and formulation
- Capacity, choice and human rights
- Promoting well-being and positive health behaviours
- Health Action Plans
- Hospital/care passports

Well-being

Well-being is often divided into physical and psychological or emotional well-being. Physical well-being includes the ability to get the most out of daily activities without undue fatigue, physical stress or pain. It includes taking care of one's body and adopting daily habits and behaviours that have a positive impact on overall health, well-being and quality of life. Psychological well-being is a combination of feeling good and functioning well; the experience of positive emotions such as happiness and contentment as well as the development of one's potential, having some control over one's life, having a sense of purpose, and experiencing positive relationships (Huppert, 2009).

The World Health Organization describes 'health' as being 'a state of complete physical, mental and social well-being' (WHO, 1946). Well-being is seen as arising, through complex and interrelated mechanisms, from the cumulative effect of factors within the individual's biology, external factors such as the environment, and health behaviours (see Box 17.1). *This definition recognises that the physical, psychological and social aspects of an individual are interwoven and cannot be addressed in isolation*. Many harmful factors affect both physical and mental health. Many actions intended to improve physical well-being also benefit psychological well-being and vice versa.

Box 17.1: Factors that influence well-being

External:

- Culture
- Education and literacy
- Social policy/discrimination
- Social class and status
- Social support networks
- Income/poverty
- Childhood adversity
- Health care services
- Housing
- Pollution (air, water, soil)
- Road safety
- Employment
- Work conditions
- Sanitation
- Immunisation

Biomedical:

- Gender
- Genetics
- Prenatal factors e.g. maternal nutrition

Health promoting behaviours:

- Eating a healthy diet
- Maintaining a healthy body weight (not over or underweight)
- Drinking plenty of fluids (water, squash etc)
- Drinking caffeinated drinks in moderation (tea, coffee, cola, 'power drinks')
- Drinking alcohol in moderation
- Taking regular exercise (e.g. 30 minutes a day)
- Sleeping well; the right amount (about 7 hours per night) and self-waking (rather than an alarm clock)
- Having a healthy life/work balance
- Managing stress positively e.g. practicing yoga
- Making positive social contact e.g. voluntary work
- Mental stimulation e.g. crossword puzzles, quiz games
- Not smoking
- Not misusing drugs
- Self-care e.g. attending check-ups/screening, cleaning teeth
- Adherence to medical advice e.g. following gluten free diet for Coeliac disease

 Intellectual Disabilities and 'Personality Disorder' © Pavilion Publishing and Media Ltd and its licensors 2023

Interrelationship between physical and psychological well-being

The interrelationship between physical and psychological well-being is complex and not yet fully understood. However, it is helpful to think about some of the ways this interaction shapes the experience of pain and health and illness-related behaviours. The experience of pain (see Box 17.2) is a complex neurological process which usually *but not always* has its origins in harmful stimuli.

Box 17.2: Pain

An unpleasant sensation caused by the brain's interpretation of signals from 'nociceptors', part of a system for detecting, responding to, repairing and preventing harm.

Pain covers a number of different unpleasant sensations that are the result of different tissues being damaged (e.g. nerves, joints, muscles, internal organs), different types of damage (e.g. burns, cuts) and the involvement of different types of nerves that convey pain messages.

Pain process:

- 'Nociceptors' work like smoke alarms, detecting signs of a problem and alerting the brain to the problem. (The signals themselves are not pain.)
- The brain receives these signals and automatically translates them into the feeling of pain.

Perceived intensity, unpleasantness and duration of pain is influenced by biological, social and psychological factors:

- Excitement and distraction reduce the perception of pain.
- Low mood/depression/anxiety make pain feel worse.
- Mindfulness/meditation reduces the extent to which pain is experienced as unpleasant.
- Social support reduces the impact of pain, social isolation increases it.

Pain does not always resolve when noxious stimulation stops and/or the damage has healed. It can also occur in the absence of noxious stimulation.

Mis-responding of the brain or receptors can cause 'real' pain (i.e. the pain experienced is indistinguishable from that arising from a physical injury):

- Nociceptors may continue to fire after the cause of harm is resolved.
- Nociceptors can become hyper-sensitive making pain more frequent and intense.
- Nociceptors sometimes activate on their own, when there's no actual harm. →

■ The brain can unconsciously create pain without nociceptor signals. (May be described as 'persistent somatoform pain', 'functional pain' or a 'functional somatic disorder'* or functional neurological disorder.)
The concept of pain thresholds can be unhelpful and can contribute to poor care: '*high pain threshold*' leads to pain control techniques being neglected as '*not needed*'; '*low pain threshold*' leads to dismissing genuine pain as an '*over reaction*'.
Individuals who self-harm experience physical pain of such an intensity that it can blot out unbearable emotional pain.
Chronic pain = long-term conditions e.g. arthritis, or when pain persists after damage has mended.
* Burton *et al* (2020); Covington (2000)

Social and psychological factors have an influence (usually unconscious) on how pain is experienced. Consequently, the experience of pain both influences and is influenced by emotional reactions and mental health. For example, there is a high co-occurrence of PTSD and chronic pain (Kind and Otis, 2019). Every individual's path to chronic pain will be different. Box 17.3 gives one example of how physical and psychological responses to a painful experience can interact to intensify and prolong pain, contributing to the experience of chronic pain.

An individual's pattern of health-related behaviours and whether they adhere to medical advice can have a significant impact on their well-being. Emotional and intellectual functioning and social factors have a significant impact on an individual's ability to engage in positive health behaviours with associated impact on health and well-being (see Box 17.4). It is thought that between a third and a half of all medicines prescribed for long-term conditions are not taken as recommended (NICE, 2009; 2019), either because of barriers to understanding what to do or a misfit between the prescribed actions and the individual's beliefs and preferences. The concept of 'concordance' (an agreement reached after negotiation between an individual and a healthcare professional that respects the beliefs and wishes of the individual in determining whether, when, and how medicines or other actions are taken) reflects the increasing recognition of the importance of collaboration to overcome psychological barriers to engaging in health-promoting actions.

 Intellectual Disabilities and 'Personality Disorder' © Pavilion Publishing and Media Ltd and its licensors 2023

Box 17.3: Chronic pain

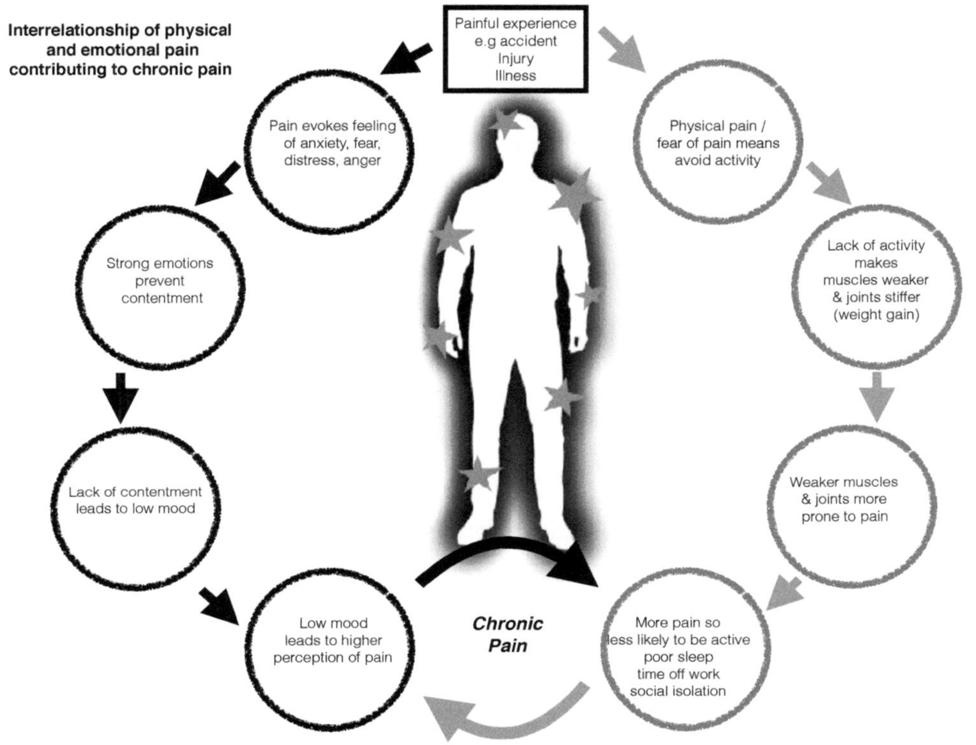

Adapted from Caver College of Medicine (2023). Image credit: Neus Brutal

Box 17.4: Factors influencing the adoption of health promoting behaviours

Early learning and establishment of routines and preferences.
Exposure to advertising, social media.
Social pressure e.g. peer group.
Belief systems.

Access to evidence-based health and well-being information i.e. knowing what to do:

- Access to health care.
- Access to other good quality sources of information e.g. NHS website.
- Ability to read, understand and retain that information.

Resources to enable action e.g.:

- Financial.

→

- Time.
- Skills.
- Intellectual – being able to understand, remember and implement recommendations.
- Regulation – being able to control emotions and impulses.

Developing positive health behaviours:

- Trusting the advice given/trusting the people giving the advice.
- Understanding the short and long-term consequences of choices.
- Acting on the basis of logical thinking rather than meeting emotional needs/ satisfying physical cravings.
- Sense of agency and locus of control – belief that one can influence their own behaviour and health.
- Self-esteem and belief that one deserves to be healthy and content.
- Putting long-term results ahead of immediate pleasurable consequences (delaying gratification).
- Being willing to undergo immediate minor discomfort to avoid possible greater discomfort in the future.
- Having the resources to put in the extra mental and physical effort needed to carry out the healthy option and create new daily routines.

This can be difficult enough when life is going well. It can seem almost impossible when faced with challenges such as negative life events.

Unmet psychological needs can also impact health-related behaviour through a process described as secondary gains (see Box 17.5). This process is particularly powerful in situations where psychological or mental-health needs are considered less 'real' or deserving of care than physical health needs, and where expressing emotional needs can lead to being stigmatised or blamed. Secondary gains do nothing to address underlying needs and, hence, an escalating cycle of physical-health-related issues can develop to maintain access to health interventions.

Box 17.5: Primary and secondary gains of health care and health behaviours

Primary gain: health care interaction addresses need that is conscious and arises directly from health problem e.g. getting an explanation for worrying stomach pains as 'acid reflux' and a treatment plan that resolves the issues.

Secondary gain*: when illness-related behaviours lead to unconscious needs being met e.g. seeing the GP about worrying stomach pains results in a caring interaction that makes the individual feel less lonely. So, unconsciously, they take no action but return two weeks later with the same concerns.

 Intellectual Disabilities and 'Personality Disorder' © Pavilion Publishing and Media Ltd and its licensors 2023

Examples of secondary gains from being ill:

- Increased social interaction: may see more people, be visited more often, escape loneliness.
- Increased positive interaction: people more likely to be interested/concerned about individual (physical pain is met with more sympathy than emotional pain, particularly if it is long lasting).
- Increased occupation: attending appointments fills empty time.
- Feeling special/interesting: If symptoms are difficult to 'diagnose'.
- Feeling cared about: others offer sympathy, ask about illness, may get visits, cards, flowers.
- Being cared for: others look after day to day issues like cooking, cleaning, doing the laundry.
- Escaping boring or stressful job: able to stay home and engage in preferred activities.
- Avoiding boring or stressful activities: being unwell is more acceptable than saying no.

As secondary gains do not resolve the underlying need, an individual may become trapped by their illness behaviour. There is a risk of a negative spiral developing which can intensify psychological needs and result in poorer health care.

Longer term consequences if underlying need is not identified and met in a more constructive way:

- Reduced motivation to engage in health promoting behaviours.
- Failure to adhere to interventions.
- Reduced opportunities to learn and engage in life enhancing activities.
- Risk of adopting a 'sick role' that prevents achieving potential and developing healthy inter-dependence.
- Risk of unconscious 'exaggeration' of symptoms.
- Risk of being unreliable informant of own symptoms and advice given in consultations.
- Risk of being given negative labels such as 'time waster', 'malingerer'.
- Risk of concerns being dismissed and health problems going undetected.
- Risk of continued or worsening health despite multiple interventions.
- Partial information may lead to misdiagnosis and inappropriate interventions.
- Over-medication (higher doses, multiple medications) with risk of side-effects.
- Sub-optimum control of chronic illness with increased risk of complications.
- Over-investigation with associated trauma increasing emotional distress.

→

- Receiving 'uncaring care' as a result of frustration in care providers.
- Misunderstandings, and possibly conflict, between different teams leading to uncoordinated care.

Factitious illness**: (or 'Munchausen's syndrome') This is where the need to be in the 'sick role' and to access sympathy and special attention is so overwhelmingly powerful that it drives an individual to fake symptoms and illnesses in order to be receive medical treatments including invasive and painful investigations and surgery.

Reference: *Fishbain (1994); **Carnahan and Jha (2023)

Health inequalities

The conditions in which people are born, grow, live, work and age, influence their physical and psychological well-being. Social determinants of health, such as education, housing and employment may not be equally distributed. When this occurs, 'health inequalities' may arise. Health inequalities are:

> '*... avoidable and unfair differences in health status and determinants between groups of people due to demographic, socioeconomic, geographical and other factors.*' (Public Health England 2018)

Individuals given a diagnosis of 'personality disorder' and individuals with intellectual disabilities are both disproportionately likely to experience issues with physical and mental well-being. Both experience reduced life expectancy compared to the general public (18-24 years less), with individuals given a diagnosis of 'personality disorder' also being at greater risk of death by suicide, homicide and accidents than the general population. Compared with the general population, people with intellectual disabilities are three to four times as likely to die from an avoidable medical cause of death (NICE 2021). Deaths are considered avoidable if they could have been prevented or treated given timely and effective healthcare or public health interventions (UK GOV 2023).

Individuals given a diagnosis of 'personality disorder' are more likely to report having poor health and have multiple illnesses (Dixon-Gordon *et al*, 2017). They have higher rates of asthma, migraines, musculoskeletal issues, dermatological issues (Reynolds *et al*, 2023), are more likely to be overweight (with associated risks for diabetes and arthritis) and experience chronic pain (Sansone and Sansone, 2012; Ghoshal, 2020). Individuals given a diagnosis of 'personality disorder' are also more at risk of experiencing factitious illness (Gordon and Sansone, 2013). They may

 Intellectual Disabilities and 'Personality Disorder' © Pavilion Publishing and Media Ltd and its licensors 2023

struggle to access preventative health care as the service model does not actively seek to engage or build trust. This means opportunities to detect problems early are missed. When individuals do access services, they may experience 'non-caring care', discrimination and diagnostic stigma (Warrender *et al*, 2021). Individuals given a diagnosis of 'personality disorder' are more likely to live in less safe neighbourhoods, have less access to healthy foods and fewer opportunities to be involved in healthy activities. They have difficulty gaining and maintaining employment and are over-represented in low-paid and temporary work. Difficult and fragile living arrangements and financial situations may result in chronically high levels of stress.

Individuals with intellectual disabilities also experience multiple health problems and face barriers to accessing good health care, including difficulties accessing services, failure of services to make reasonable adjustments, failure to recognise deteriorations in health, incorrect diagnoses, lack of co-ordination between care providers and inadequate follow up (Heslop *et al*, 2021; Mencap, 2023). When in a general hospital, individuals with intellectual disabilities may not receive the extra support they need with basic self-care such as washing and eating. During the COVID-19 pandemic, individuals with intellectual disabilities were disproportionately affected by the virus, lockdowns and the rapid shift to digital health care (Courtenay and Perera, 2020; Chadwick *et al*, 2022). They are more likely to be inappropriately or over medicated. Some medications prescribed for mental health problems increase the risk of physical illnesses, particularly diabetes and heart disease. They may also have an indirect effect on health by increasing appetite and therefore the risk of obesity. Individuals with intellectual disabilities are less likely to have access to factors known to have a positive impact on well-being such as work (paid or unpaid).

Service initiatives

NICE (2021) summarises initiatives aiming to reduce health inequalities for individuals with intellectual disabilities including annual health checks and co-produced Health Action Plans (HAP). Initiatives aimed at ensuring individuals get the help and support they need include the use of health liaison nurses (Brown, 2020) working with GPs, within acute hospitals and ambulance services (NHS England, 2019a), and 'reasonable adjustment flags' which alert staff to key information (NHS digital, 2023). Public Health England guidance on intellectual disabilities (2023) aims to provide accessible information to help frontline workers use their relationships with clients, families and communities to provide the best possible support for people with intellectual disabilities and their families, across an age continuum. However, there is much still to be done, for example only 50% of individuals access annual health checks (Perera *et al*, 2019). Other initiatives aim to access health-promoting activities such as work and address loneliness.

These initiatives are taking place within the context of a wider system that increasingly recognises the inter-relatedness of physical and mental health needs. The Community Mental Health Framework for Adults and Older Adults (NHS England, 2019a) recognises the need to break down the current barriers between mental health, physical health and social care services in order to improve well-being. Within primary health care, 'social prescribing' initiatives (NHS England, 2022) seek to connect people to activities, groups and services in their community to meet the practical, social and emotional needs affecting their physical health and well-being.

Adversity, trauma and well-being

Chapter 2 explored the high rates of childhood adversity and trauma experienced by individuals who might be given a diagnosis of 'personality disorder' and those with intellectual disabilities. Trauma in childhood can have a significant long-term impact on well-being, both by its direct impact on physical health and through disruption to the development of neurological and physiological systems that regulate arousal, emotions and behaviour (see Box 2.5). These changes in turn can lead to health-risk behaviours with associated illness, disability and social problems (NHS Education for Scotland, 2021). For example, individuals may attempt to cope with intense overwhelming emotions through responses such as over-eating, smoking or using drugs and alcohol. These may bring temporary relief but have a long-term negative impact on well-being. The combination of developmental issues and social disadvantage means that individuals struggle to engage in and sustain positive health behaviours within the context of overwhelming, unconscious psychological needs and social disadvantage.

Depression

Individuals who have experienced childhood adversity, particularly those who have experienced abuse, may have low self-esteem and are vulnerable to experiencing depression (Kim *et al*, 2022).

Individuals with intellectual disabilities may also be more likely to experience depression than the general population (Bakken, 2021). Depression impacts directly on mental well-being, for example through feelings of sadness, helplessness and hopelessness, preoccupation with negative thoughts and loss of enjoyment. It also affects physical well-being, changing appetite and sleep patterns. Experiencing

 Intellectual Disabilities and 'Personality Disorder' © Pavilion Publishing and Media Ltd and its licensors 2023

depression may make it more difficult for an individual to cope with pain and may also make it more difficult for them to take actions that might reduce the pain, such as engaging in mentally absorbing activities to provide distraction and taking gentle exercise. They may not have the motivation to carry out self-care activities. Strong negative feelings about themselves mean that they may feel that they do not deserve to be well, or that they deserve to be in pain (see Chapter 16). Consequently, they lack the motivation to manage chronic illnesses, take medication as directed or attend appointments consistently. This can lead to crises where an individual shuts down completely, with serious risks to their health.

Individuals with intellectual disabilities who might be given a diagnosis of 'personality disorder' are likely to have their physical well-being undermined by the interaction of all the factors described above and will experience many barriers to adopting positive health behaviours. From a baseline of poor physical health and intense psychological needs, they are vulnerable to experiencing negative spirals which can lead to chronic pain or the development of further illnesses such as diabetes. Some may develop factitious or somatic disorders. They are unlikely to be able to escape these negative spirals without the compassionate help of others. If the factors behind these patterns of behaviour are not understood, they are at risk of being blamed and held responsible for their health problems with further discrimination and exacerbation of health inequalities.

Assessment and formulation

There are two strands to assessment of these difficulties. First, gaining a clear understanding of the individual's physical and mental health needs by liaising with health professionals. This is particularly important for individuals with health issues that are supported by a number of different teams and services. Box 17.6 gives points at which support staff can promote the accuracy and effectiveness of assessing health needs.

Box 17.6: Promoting the accuracy and effectiveness of assessment of health needs

Accurate information of the full picture	Collaborating with an individual to compile an accurate summary of relevant information, rather than acting on what an individual may recall or is focusing on at the time of assessment. Details of all current medications: number, dose (side-effects and interactions – is this causing the health problem?)

→

Promoting adherence to preparation for tests	Collaborating with and supporting the individual to ensure instructions are understood and followed e.g. not eating before a fasting blood sugar test.
Adherence to medication	Collaboration and support to identify what medication is actually being taken and whether this adheres to the prescription.
Adherence to other medical advice	Collaboration and support to identify actions are actually being taken and whether this adheres to the prescription e.g. sugar intake and diabetes.
Identify barriers preventing services from meeting individuals needs*	These might include: knowledge and awareness, communication, fear and embarrassment, involvement in healthcare decision-making and time. Is support from health liaison nurse available?
Co-operation and co-ordination between different teams	Where individuals have complex and multiple needs, promoting well-being often involves a number of different teams and services, for example GPs, hospital consultants, nurse practitioners, community nurses and care staff. Is the individual being given different/conflicting advice by different teams? (If tensions arise, ideas for addressing them are explored in Chapter 7).
Reference *Doherty *et al* (2020)	

Second, it is important to assess and formulate the psychological and social factors that are shaping their health behaviours, following the same approach used for behaviours described as 'challenging'. This includes exploring psychological needs arising from childhood experiences, their patterns of thinking, feeling and relating, and how they are supported and responded to by health professionals (see Chapters 4 and 8). It is also important to consider the impact of service characteristics. The barriers to engagement explored in Boxes 5.5 and 5.6 apply equally to mental and physical health services. Box 17.7 gives some frequently encountered issues with health-related behaviours and some possible factors that might lead to these issues occurring (also see Box 8.2).

Box 17.7: Making sense of health risk behaviours: mechanisms that may be driving unhelpful behaviour

Issues	Possible underlying factors/emotional needs
Missing appointments.	Distrust, fear, denial, avoidance. Service model does not facilitate engagement for individuals with intellectual deficits, insecure attachments or distrust of others. Failure to make 'reasonable adjustments'.

 Intellectual Disabilities and 'Personality Disorder' © Pavilion Publishing and Media Ltd and its licensors 2023

Continually changing, vague health problems, go to GP appointment for one issue but discuss another.	Memory, communication skills, multiple sources of low level of discomfort, agreeing with GP rather than expressing real need, need to feel special, cared for and to be pampered, seeking compassion.
Poorly controlled/managed chronic health problems such as diabetes, epilepsy, skin problems.	Not understanding regimens, poor impulse control, cravings for processed foods*, difficulty delaying gratification, disorganised/lack of routine, low mood, low self-esteem.
Secondary issues arising as result of neglected personal care e.g. skin infections, tooth abscess.	Low self-esteem, denial/avoidance of issues, guilt, embarrassment – may believe they do not deserve to be healthy and be unable to cherish self.
Not following medical advice – may seem to do the opposite of positive health behaviours.	Need to feel in control, not believing advice, lack of trust, denial, high levels of stress – depleted resources. Intrinsic difficulty of giving up some unhealthy behaviours (e.g. hyper-palatable processed foods stimulate reward systems creating 'cravings' but have long-term negative effect on mood* creating a negative cycle), entrenched patterns, avoiding discomfort of tests e.g. finger pricks.
Misreporting of advice given, so that it appears to support continuing unhealthy behaviours.	To avoid pressure to make changes they feel unable to make, to avoid conflict, to continue to meet cravings/ addiction.
Repeatedly seeking advice but not acting upon recommendations.	Memory, not understanding advice, need for social contact, have fallen into 'sick role'.
Unreliable source of information on symptoms e.g. 'exaggerating' 'withholding' information, under-reporting.	Over-whelming feelings, need to get a reaction, forgetting, embarrassment, shame, fear.
Chronic pain.	Negative spiral of reduced activity, increased sensitivity, low mood and increased pain, hyper-sensitivity.
Over reliance on pain killers.	Lack of knowledge, skills, energy to use pain management, external locus of control.
Dramatic reaction to examination	Fear, pain, need to feel special, need to interact with special staff e.g. having paramedics called.
*References Firth *et al* (2020); Alonso-Alonso *et al* (2015)	

Collaboratively exploring the psychological and service-related factors behind a behaviour helps identify constructive approaches to changing it, or ways of supporting the individual that help achieve the desired outcome. Box 17.8 gives a formulation for Susan, exploring how her emotional well-being and history of trauma impacted on support for her diabetes.

Box 17.8: Formulation of 'Susan's'* diabetes

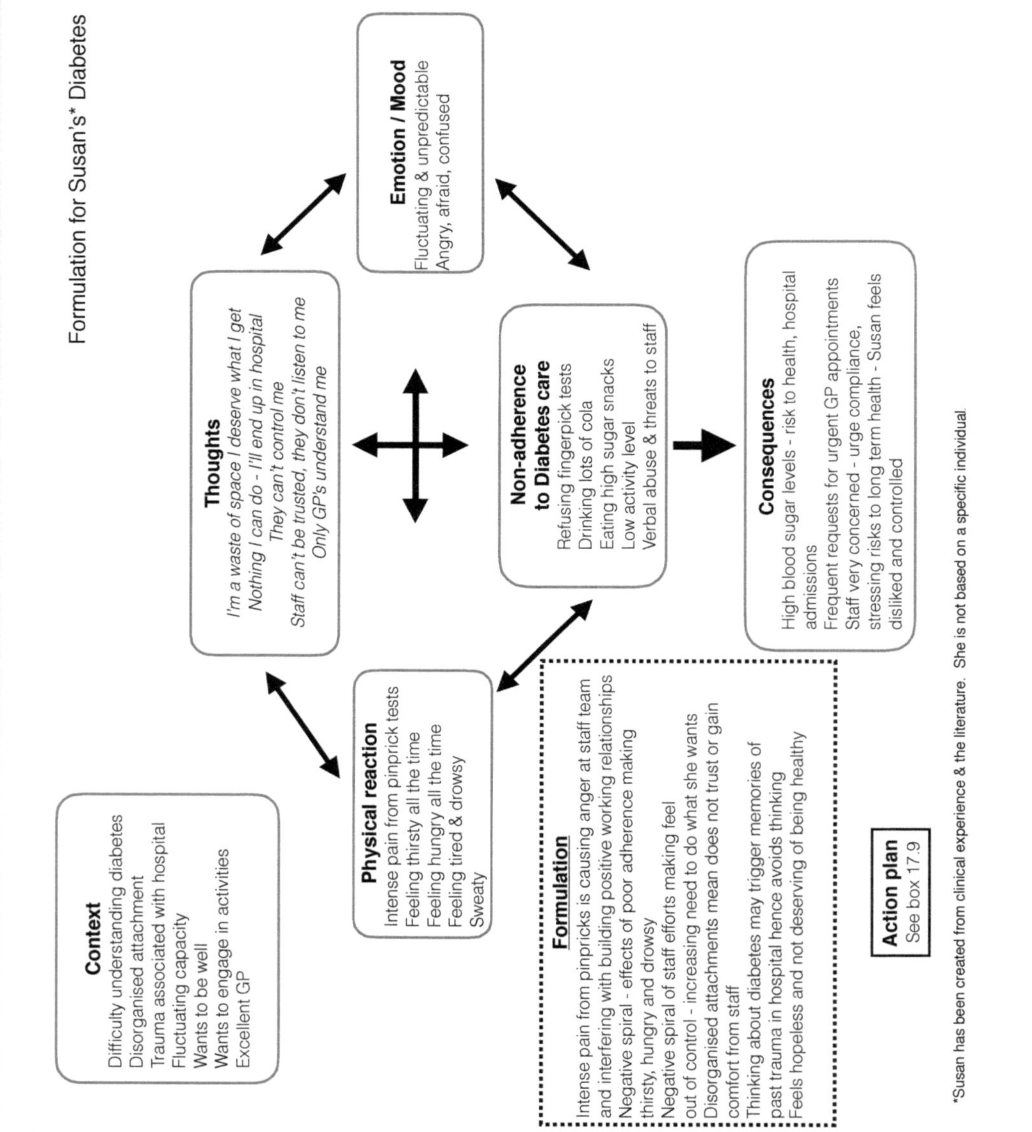

Intellectual Disabilities and 'Personality Disorder' © Pavilion Publishing and Media Ltd and its licensors 2023

Capacity, choice and human rights

One of the biggest barriers to promoting well-being is concerns about freedom of choice and human rights. Teams may be paralysed by indecision about whether they can or cannot intervene; there are many different perspectives on what constitutes a harmless indulgence compared to a health risk. Many members of the general public make unhealthy choices several times every day. There is no reason why anyone should not have the occasional cream cake or sometimes take the lift rather than walking up stairs. However, when behaviour has potentially very serious, life-changing or threatening consequences, it is important to be sure the individual has the capacity to make that 'choice' (see Box 14.5).

Within the framework of the Mental Capacity Act (2005), capacity must be assessed sensitively and in a non-judgmental way to encourage the individual to be open and honest about their behaviour. It is also important to be mindful of fluctuations in capacity, for example at times of intense distress or shutting down, an individual may lack the capacity to make decisions that they are capable of when functioning at their best. At times of crisis or where issues are complex, teams will need access to legal advice and ethical opinions.

If an individual does not understand their health problems and is unaware of the consequences of their behaviour, it does not necessarily mean that they lack capacity. Attempts can be made to help them understand. If, despite all efforts to inform them, they do not understand, this may be an indication that they lack capacity and that decisions must be made for them following the principles of best interest.

Individuals who are aware of the consequences of their behaviour may still not be making an active choice to behave in a harmful way, they may want to follow advice but find it difficult in some way. Only where the individual understands the consequences of their behaviour and would be able to behave appropriately if they wished, but actively chooses to behave in ways that are harmful to their health, can staff consider this to be an informed choice. Even in this situation, staff have a duty of care towards the individual. This would allow staff, for example, to say '*It is true that we cannot tell you what to drink when you are out alone. However, we can only offer you sugar-free drinks here, because of your diabetes.*' It is still essential to explore the factors driving the unwise choices, particularly unmet psychological needs, and continue to work to find healthier ways to meet these needs.

Where an individual is making unwise choices, staff teams should reflect on the approach they are taking and whether this is inadvertently reinforcing the individual's unhealthy behaviours. If this is found to be the case, then staff need to identify ways in which they can switch the balance so that reinforcement is given for healthier choices. Reflective case discussion (see Chapter 7) will be helpful in such situations.

Promoting well-being and positive health behaviours

It can be helpful to think about support for well-being using the same approach as the traffic light PBS plan (see Chapter 8). Actions, tailored to the appropriate intervention stage (see Box 3.1), include: health promotion (primary prevention), identifying and responding promptly to early signs of illness or deterioration (secondary prevention), and how to address a health crisis such as going into hospital (tertiary prevention). Many actions to meet underlying psychological needs can be integrated with the PBS plan. Box 17.9 gives an example of a way forward identified by formulating health-risk behaviours associated with Susan's diabetes.

Box 17.9: 'Susan'* – the way towards more positive health behaviours based on the formulation in Box 17.8

An alternative to pinprick tests would make everyone happier and more relaxed.	Liaising with GP led to Susan being given a Flash glucose monitor**. This eliminated the need for most finger-prick tests. Easy monitoring meant staff could take extra readings at times they hoped would show a 'good' reading giving praise and encouragement to Susan and proof there was something she could do to avoid going to hospital.
Capacity assessment showed Susan did not currently have capacity to make unwise decisions about diabetes.	Home decided to implement a service-wide 'healthy living' program so that everyone would benefit and Susan would not feel picked on. Team followed Diabetes UK advice on how to include treats in a healthy eating plan. With the aim of improving Susan's understanding of her health issues, a plan of fun activities to learn about healthy living was set up.
Sugar-free drinks and low GI snacks made readily available to break negative physical spiral.	Removal of temptation of high-sugar drinks and snacks meant staff did not need to try to control intake. Susan's mood improved with better control of sugar levels.

 Intellectual Disabilities and 'Personality Disorder' © Pavilion Publishing and Media Ltd and its licensors 2023

Staff agreed a different way of responding to health-risk behaviours to break the negative spiral around 'control'.	Responses to health-risk behaviours were low key. Positive health behaviours received praise, encouragement and 'high 5s'. GP also adopted an approach of focusing on positives.
Susan's low self-esteem and feeling she deserved to be unwell also needed to be addressed.	Staff aimed to do at least one fun activity a day with Susan, when they could laugh and feel good and actively looked for things to praise. A referral was made to psychology to address underlying issues.

*Susan has been created from clinical experience and the literature. She is not based on a specific individual.
**NHS England (2019)

Primary prevention includes creating an environment that promotes and supports positive health behaviours, seeks to meet underlying emotional needs and facilitates adherence to medical recommendations (see Box 17.10).

Box 17.10: Promoting positive health behaviours	
Address underlying need	View unhealthy behaviours as a warning light that psychological needs are not being met. Choose interventions to address underlying needs in parallel with health promotion actions. For example, pampering and cosseting. Everyone needs to feel special and cherished. Look at ways of meeting these needs through healthy rather than unhealthy behaviours and build them into the individual's PBS plan. This might include 'spa at home' sessions or cosying up to watch a film.
Knowledge	A good knowledge of heath promoting actions, e.g. diet and exercise, means staff can answer questions and suggest a wide range of healthy alternatives. A good knowledge of pain-management techniques can complement and reduce the need for pain-controlling medication. These can include looking at seating and positions, use of hot or cold compresses, creams and rubs, and gentle exercise. Distraction techniques, relaxation and self-soothing (see Boxes 15.15,11.16 and 11.17) may also be helpful. Shared knowledge of the individual's specific health problems and the recommended treatments will promote consistency and reduce the risk of conflicting messages. This in turn makes it more likely that the individual will adhere to advice.

→

Modelling	Social learning is a powerful influence: seeing those supporting them choosing healthy options creates an environment that promotes change.
Attitudes	Healthy choices can be seen as 'rabbit food', hard work and boring or as tasty, fun and life affirming. It helps if those supporting the individual hold positive attitudes.
Accessibility	Health information and teaching materials need to be accessible (see Box 5.6) and also fun to complete. Healthy options and health-promoting activities need to be easily available and built into the structure of the day.
Collaboration	Move from adherence to 'concordance'. Explore options rather than pressing one option e.g.: *'OK, you don't want to do X, how else can we work together to beat your (condition)?'*
Reduce temptation/ need	Think about situations where unhealthy behaviours occur and look to see if they can be changed to reduce temptations or need e.g. shop from a list, have healthy snacks at home (see Box 14.8), join a support group.
Reinforce healthy behaviour	Aim to notice and praise healthy behaviours and to be very low key in responding to unhealthy behaviours (never 'ignore' as this is disrespectful and leads to escalation). Where unhealthy behaviour appears to be 'seeking a reaction', look to see if the need can be met in other ways e.g. scheduling more regular 1:1 time, do something fun.
Intervention stage	Tailor interventions to the stage the individual is at: ■ **R**egulate – sensitively address health needs within compassionate containment. ■ **R**elate – prioritise building collaborative relationships and engaging individual. ■ **R**eason – collaboratively explore healthier options with the individual; where are they in the change cycle*? **Contemplation:** Thinking of making changes? Explore possible changes and 'road blocks' look at pros and cons (see Box 14.10). **Preparation:** Mind made up? Choose a goal and identify small steps (see Box 16.7). **Action:** Making changes? Getting going on agreed changes and overcoming blocks, healthy rewards for progress. **Maintenance:** Keeping it going? Build healthy routines, overcoming setbacks, problem solving.

 Intellectual Disabilities and 'Personality Disorder' © Pavilion Publishing and Media Ltd and its licensors 2023

Peer support	Health promotion groups can be great fun, provide peer support and reduce risk of an individual feeling controlled or punished by efforts to promote healthy behaviours.
*Prochaska *et al* (1994) Transtheoretical Model of change	

Support and monitoring

Many health problems can be resolved by encouraging individuals to accept greater support. For example, jointly preparing for a visit to the GP or specialist, writing down the current problem, symptoms and worries, can help ensure that important issues are not overlooked at the appointment. Individuals should be encouraged to let a trusted member of staff accompany them to appointments so that they are able to hear the advice given. If there are concerns that medication or other treatments are not being accurately followed, individuals should be encouraged to accept closer support for at least a few weeks to see if they are accurately taking medication. Staff may be able to help individuals keep a log of symptoms and responses to medication to provide the doctor with more accurate information. Techniques for helping individuals engage with and form positive relationships with staff and services are explored more fully in Chapter 5.

Support needs to be given within the caring and compassionate containment style described in Chapter 9. Particularly where health-risk behaviours have serious consequences, there is a risk of adopting restrictive practices. Where behaviours are driven by the need to be in control, this can cause a negative spiral and will always damage the trust that is essential for successful interventions. Losing sight of the individual's psychological needs risks leaving them feeling uncared for, vulnerable and alone.

Health Action Plans

An important part of promoting well-being is creating and implementing a Health Action Plan (HAP). As a result of the concerns about the poor health of individuals with intellectual disabilities, the Department of Health (2002; 2009a; 2009b) recommends that every individual has a HAP. This is a document that includes the actions needed to maintain and improve the individual's health, and any help they need to accomplish these actions. It should include ensuring that the individual has an annual health check from someone with expertise in intellectual disabilities (NICE, 2021). The HAP is intended to provide a link between the individual and the range of services they need for their physical and mental well-being.

The HAP is primarily for the individual with intellectual disabilities and is collaboratively created by health professionals and the individual in a format that the individual is able to understand and use.

The process of collaborating to develop the HAP can be productive, as it can help explore how an individual's psychological needs and cognitive profile are impacting on their physical health. The HAP can become a resource for the individual to use and also a means of promoting consistency within and between staff teams. In developing the plan, it is important that staff draw on accurate information about any health conditions. However well drawn up a HAP is, most individuals are unlikely to follow it without support from staff, and it is therefore important that staff provide active support. It is also important that actions in an individual's HAP and PBS plan are complimentary and consistent to avoid creating conflicts or confusion.

Hospital/Care passports

Physical healthcare professionals are increasingly recognising the importance of addressing psychological and social factors that influence an individual's ability to adhere to recommendations and the need for reasonable adjustments to the care offered (Ghosha, 2020; Reynolds *et al*, 2023). However, interventions are more likely to be effective if staff supporting the individual are able to liaise closely with healthcare staff.

It is also helpful to ensure that the individual has a Hospital or Care Passport (East Sussex Health Care trust, 2017; Mencap, undated). Hospital passports were developed in the 1990s due to concerns about staff in hospitals not knowing how to communicate with or support individuals with intellectual disabilities. They have evolved to be used to support individuals going into any setting where staff are unfamiliar with the individual and are also therefore called Care or Health Passports.

A passport aims to bring together key information about the individual, how to communicate with them and support them, in a form that is well organised and easy to read. They aim to include essential health information about current medication, allergies, dietary and religious requirements and important contact numbers. There are many different formats for passports with considerable variations, which can lead to key information being omitted or being difficult to locate (Northway *et al*, 2017). Hence, they are most effective when there is a service-wide initiative to agree a standard format. The use of hospital passports has been shown to have a positive

 Intellectual Disabilities and 'Personality Disorder' © Pavilion Publishing and Media Ltd and its licensors 2023

impact on care (Heifetz and Lunsky, 2018; McCormick *et al*, 2021; 2022), resulting in enhanced communication and more person-centred care experiences in a range of healthcare settings. However, hospital passports can only be effective if they are used. Issues that can arise include passports being lost as a person moves to a different ward, passports being filed without being read, passports not being easily accessed (ideally, they should be placed at the end of an individual's bed), and staff not having the time (or inclination) to read them (Unitt, 2018). It is also important that they are regularly updated.

Collaborative work with the individual to ensure that key information needed by general hospital staff is included in the hospital passport can also offer a less threatening and more empowering way to think about what might happen if an individual continues with health-risk behaviours. This may provide an opening to begin to address such behaviours.

Overall, a positive, proactive and compassionate approach that recognises the interrelationship between physical and psychological well-being can provide insights into health-risk behaviours and lead to interventions that address underlying psychological issues as well as overt physical health issues.

Key learning points

- Health is more than not being ill. It is a state of physical, mental and social well-being.
- Physical and mental well-being are determined by the complex interaction of multiple factors. These include biomedical (factors within the body), environmental/social (external factors that the individual has little or no control over) and health behaviours (factors over which the individual may have control).
- The interaction of psychological, social and physical factors can be seen in how pain is experienced, the development of chronic pain, whether individuals adopt health-risk or health-promotion behaviours, and in the secondary gains of ill health.
- Health inequalities are avoidable and there are unfair differences in health and access to determinants of health. Individuals given a diagnosis of 'personality disorder' and individuals with intellectual disabilities experience significant health inequalities including shorter life expectancy and poorer physical and mental health than the general population. They also receive poorer health care.

- Exposure to adversity and trauma in childhood can have a significant long-term impact on well-being through their direct impact on physical health, by increasing the risk of depression, and by disrupting the development of neurological and physiological systems that can lead to enduring distress and health-risk behaviours.
- Health-risk behaviours, self-neglect and difficulties adhering to medical advice have their origins in unmet psychological needs and difficulties with regulating emotions and behaviours. It is therefore essential to take a holistic approach to assessment and formulation of well-being needs. Physical health will often improve if emotional needs are met and vice versa.
- Clarity about mental capacity and close teamwork can help resolve the confusion and disagreements that may arise in teams about how problems relating to physical health and health-risk behaviours should be addressed. When addressing complex, life-threatening issues, swift access to legal and ethical advice is essential.
- It can be helpful to think about support for well-being using the same approach as the traffic light PBS plan: looking at health promotion (primary prevention), responding promptly to early signs (secondary prevention) and how to address a health crisis such as going into hospital (tertiary prevention).
- Health action plans and Hospital or Care Passports are helpful in promoting well-being and ensuring the individual's needs are met. It is important that these are regularly updated and readily accessible to ensure they are used.

 Intellectual Disabilities and 'Personality Disorder' © Pavilion Publishing and Media Ltd and its licensors 2023

References

Ackerman C E (2018) *What is Self-Image in Psychology? How Do We Improve it?* https://positivepsychology.com/self-image/

Agrawal H, Gunderson, J, Holmes, B and Lyons-Ruth K (2004) Attachment studies with borderline patients: a review. *Harvard Review of Psychiatry.* 12, 2, 94-104.

Akinola P and Rayner G (2022) Staff attitudes, beliefs and responses towards self-harm: a systematised literature review. *British Journal of Mental Health Nursing* 11, 1

Alexander RT, Green FN, O'Mahony B, Gunaratna IJ, Gangadharan SK, Hoare S (2010) Personality disorders in offenders with intellectual disability: a comparison of clinical, forensic and outcome variables and implications for service provision. *Journal of Intellectual Disabilities Research.* 54, 7, 650-658.

Alford M, O'Rourke S, Doyle P and Todd L (2020) Examining the factors associated with impulsivity in forensic populations: A systematic review. *Aggression and Violent Behavior*, 54, 101409

Alonso-Alonso M, Woods S, Pelchat M, Grigson P, Stice E, Farooqi S, San Khoo C, Mattes R and Beauchamp G (2015) Food reward system: current perspectives and future research needs, *Nutrition Reviews*, 73, 5, 296–307.

American Psychiatric Association (2022) *Diagnostic and Statistical Manual of Mental Disorders, Fifth Edition, Text Revision* American Psychiatric Publishing Inc

American Psychological Association (2023a) Social skills. *Dictionary of psychology*. https://dictionary.apa.org/social-skills

American Psychological Association (2023b) Impulse. *Dictionary of psychology*. https://dictionary.apa.org/impulse

American Psychological Association (2023c) Metacognition. *Dictionary of psychology*. https://dictionary.apa.org/metacognition

Andersen, H K (2015), Personality disorder and intellectual disability – concept and prevalence. *Advances in Mental Health and Intellectual Disabilities*, 9, 4, 63-173.

Anderson J, Pickard M and Rye E (2020) *The CaPDID training manual.* Shoreham by Sea: Pavilion Publishing and Media Ltd.

Aruma (2022) *Disability stereotypes in the media* https://www.aruma.com.au/about-us/blog/run-forest-run-disability-stereotypes-in-the-media/

Bach, B, First MB (2018) Application of the ICD-11 classification of personality disorders. *BMC Psychiatry 18, 351.* https://doi.org/10.1186/s12888-018-1908-3

Badcock P (2019) *Explaining how the mind works A new theory* https://researchoutreach.org/articles/explaining-how-the-mind-works-a-new-theory

Baird J, Hyslop A, Macfie M, Stocks R, and Van der Kleij T (2017) Clinical formulation: Where it came from, what it is and why it matters. *British Journal Psychiatry Advances*, 23, 2, 95-103.

Bakken T L (2021) Psychosocial treatment of major depression in people with intellectual disabilities. Improvements within the last four decades: points of view. *International Journal of Developmental Disabilities*, 67, 5, 366-370.

BakkenT L, Kildahl AN, Gjersoe V, Bakken T L, Kildahl AN, Gjersøe V, Matre E, Kristiansen T, Ro A, Tveter AL and Høidal S H (2014) Identification of PTSD in adults with intellectual disabilities in five patients in a specialised psychiatric inpatient unit. *Advances in Mental Health and Intellect Disabilities,* 8, 2, 91–102.

Ball M A (2020) Service user involvement and co-production in personality disorder services: an invitation to transcend re-traumatising power politics In Ramsden J, Prince S and Blazdell J (Eds) *Working Effectively with "Personality Disorder" contemporary and Critical Approaches to Clinical and Organizational Practice* Shoreham by Sea: Pavilion Publishing and Media Ltd.

Bandura A (1977) *Social learning theory.* Englewood Cliffs, NJ: Prentice Hall.

Barnhill J, Cooper S, and Fletcher RJ (Eds) (2017) *Diagnostic Manual--Intellectual Disability 2 (DM-Id): A Textbook of Diagnosis of Mental Disorders in Persons with Intellectual Disability*. NADD

Bateman, Fonagy and Campbell (2020) Mentalization-Based Treatment. In Livesley W J and Larstone R (Eds) *Handbook of Personality Disorders: theory, research and treatment.* Guildford Press New York pp 541-554.

Bates C, McCarthy M, Skillman KM, Elson N, Forrester-Jones R and Hunt S (2020) "Always trying to walk a bit of a tightrope": The role of social care staff in supporting adults with intellectual and developmental disabilities to develop and maintain loving relationships. *British Journal of Learning Disabilities* 48:4, 261-268.

Baumer N and Frueh J (2021) *What is neurodiversity?* Mind and Mood, 23 https://www.health.harvard.edu/blog/what-is-neurodiversity-202111232645 (accessed 20/10/22)

BBC *Panorama* https://www.bbc.co.uk/news/uk-england-manchester-63261476

Beacon House (2020a) *The Space In Between: How Is The Support You Offer Influenced By Your Attachment Strategies*. https://beaconhouse.org.uk/wp-content/uploads/2020/12/The-Space-In-Between-1.pdf

Beacon House (2022b) *Mirroring* https://beaconhouse.org.uk/wp-content/uploads/2022/12/Mirroring-1.pdf

Beahm L A, Ingvarsson E T, Funk N, Haskins L and Frazier J (2023) Using an App-Based Token Economy to Increase Engagement in Daily Living and Vocational Tasks with Adults with Developmental Disabilities. *Behaviour Analysis Practice,* 25, 1–14.

Beail N, Frankish P and Allen Skelly (Eds) (2021) *Trauma and Intellectual Disability.* Shoreham by Sea: Pavilion Publishing and Media Ltd.

Beail N (2021) Introduction to Trauma and Intellectual Disability: why this book is needed. In

Beail N, Frankish P and Allen Skelly (Eds) *Trauma and Intellectual Disability*. Shoreham by Sea: Pavilion Publishing and Media Ltd.

Beck, A T (1979) *Cognitive therapy and the emotional disorders*. Meridian.

Bell L (2005) Managing Intense Emotions and Overcoming Self-destructive Habits: A self-help manual. Hove: Routledge.

Benefield N and Haigh R (2020) Personality Disorder: Breakdown in the Relational Field. In Ramsden J,Prince S and Blazdell J (Eds) Working Effectively with "Personality Disorder" contemporary and Critical Approaches to Clinical and Organizational Practice Shoreham by Sea: Pavilion Publishing and Media Ltd. pp 35-52

Bijkerk L E, Oenema A, Geschwind N and Spigt M (2022) Measuring Engagement with Mental Health and Behavior Change Interventions: an Integrative Review of Methods and Instruments. *International Journal of Behavioural Medicine,* 30,155–166.

Bild (2023) *What is active support?* https://www.bild.org.uk/wp-content/uploads/2020/06/What-is-Active-Support.pdf

Bigby C and Beadle-Brown, J (2018) Improving Quality of Life Outcomes in Supported Accommodation for People with Intellectual Disability: What Makes a Difference? Journal of Applied Research in Intellectual Disabilities, 31, 2, e182-e200.

Biswas A, Gumber R and Furniss F (2022) Management of self-injurious behaviour, reducing restrictive interventions and predictors of positive outcome in intellectual disability and/or autism. *British Journal of Psychiatric Advances*, 1-5. doi:10.1192/bja.2022.49.

Blades C A, Stritzke W G K, Page A C and Brown J D (2018) The benefits and risks of asking research participants about suicide: A meta-analysis of the impact of exposure to suicide-related content. *Clinical Psychology Review*, 64,1-12.

Block L (2022) *Stereotypes About People With Disabilities*. Disability History Museum https://www.disabilitymuseum.org/dhm/edu/essay.html?id=24

Block V J, Haller E, Villanueva J, Meyer A, Benoy C, Walter M, Lang U E, Gloster A T (2022) Meaningful Relationships in Community and Clinical Samples: Their Importance for Mental Health. *Frontiers in Psychology,*12;13:832520. doi: 10.3389/fpsyg.2022.832520.

Bolton W, Lovell K, Morgan L and Wood H (2011) *Meeting the Challenge, Making a Difference. Publisher?* https://www.newhamscp.org.uk/wp-content/uploads/2016/11/Meeting-the-Challenge-Making-a-Difference.pdf

Booth T and Booth W (1992) Practice in Sexuality Mental Handicap. *Journal of the British Institute of Mental Handicap (APEX)* 20, 2 64 - 69.

Bountress K, Adams ZW, Gilmore AK, Amstadter AB, Thomas S, Danielson CK (2017) Associations among impulsivity, trauma history, and alcohol misuse within a young adult sample. *Addictive Behaviour* 64, 179-184. doi: 10.1016/j.addbeh.2016.08.031.

Bramston P and Fogarty G (2000) The assessment of emotional distress experienced by people with an intellectual disability: A study of different methodologies. *Research in Developmental Disabilities*, 21, 6, 487-500.

Brette R (2022) Brains as Computers: Metaphor, Analogy, Theory or Fact? *Frontiers in Ecology and Evolution* 29, 10 - https://doi.org/10.3389/fevo.2022.878729

British institute of Learning Disabilities (2022) *About PBS* https://www.bild.org.uk/about-pbs/

British Psychological Society (2017) *Incorporating Attachment Theory into Practice: Clinical Practice Guideline for Clinical Psychologists working with People who have Intellectual Disabilities*

BPS Leicester. *Towards the identification of patterns in emotional distress, unusual experiences and troubled or troubling behaviour, as an alternative to functional psychiatric diagnosis.* BPS, Leicester.

British Psychological Society (2018) *The Power Threat Meaning Framework*

Brown D, Shawe-Taylor M. and Swan S. (2017) Positive behaviour support for people with a diagnosis of personality disorder. *Clinical Psychology Forum* 290, February 25-39.

Brown H (1994) 'An Ordinary Sexual Life?': A Review of the Normalisation Principle as It Applies to the Sexual Options of People with Learning Disabilities. *Disability and Society*, 9, 2,123-144.

Brown M and McCann E (2018) Sexuality issues and the voices of adults with intellectual disabilities: A systematic review of the literature. *Research in Developmental Disabilities,* 74,124-138.

Brown M (2020) Learning disability liaison nurses: the provision of compassionate, person-centred care for people with learning disabilities accessing acute hospital care. *Nursing Standard,* 35, 10, 90-94. doi: 10.7748/ns.35.10.90.s41

Burton C, Fink P, Henningsen P, Löwe B and Rief W (2020) Functional somatic disorders: discussion paper for a new common classification for research and clinical use. *BMC Medicine* 3,18, 1, 34.

Bush A and Griffith G (2017) 'Sometimes they listen to me about what works best for me, but they don't always do it' – Challenging behaviour: What does the evidence base tell us about service users' perspectives of support they receive? *Clinical Psychology Forum* 290, 42-47

Byrne G (2022) A Systematic Review of Treatment Interventions for Individuals With Intellectual Disability and Trauma Symptoms: A Review of the Recent Literature. *Trauma, Violence, and Abuse*, 23, 2, 541–554.

Byrne G and O'Mahony T (2020) Acceptance and commitment therapy (ACT) for adults with intellectual disabilities and/or autism spectrum conditions (ASC): A systematic review. *Journal of Contextual Behavioral Science* 18, 247-255

Cameron L (2015) The thing is, we all have stories don't we? *Tizard Learning Disability Review* 20, 1, 37-40.

Callus A (2017) 'Being friends means helping each other, making coffee for each other': reciprocity in the friendships of people with intellectual disability. *Disability and Society,* 32:1, 1-16.

Cameron R and Maginn C (2009) *Achieving Positive Outcomes for Children in Care.* London: Sage.

Cannon J and Gould I (2022a) Debate: "the Diagnosis-that-must-not-be-named" - Professionals' fear of BPD is failing their patients. *Child and Adolescent Mental Health,* 27, 2, 201-202.

Cannon J and Gould I (2022b) Response: Sometimes we wish Chris and Sam had died of cancer - a response to Commentaries on the May 2022 debate. *Child and Adolescent Mental Health,* 27, 3, 256-258.

Care Act 2014. https://www.legislation.gov.uk/ukpga/2014/23/contents/enacted

Carnahan K T and Jha A (2023) *Factitious Disorder* https://www.ncbi.nlm.nih.gov/books/NBK557547/

Caver College of Medicine (2023) Making it easier for chronic pain patients to get help https://medicine.uiowa.edu/anesthesia/content/making-it-easier-chronic-pain-patients-get-help

 Intellectual Disabilities and 'Personality Disorder' © Pavilion Publishing and Media Ltd and its licensors 2023

Cassidy S, Au-Yeung S, Robertson A, Cogger-Ward H, Richards G, Allison, C and Baron-Cohen S (2022) Autism and autistic traits in those who died by suicide in England. *The British Journal of Psychiatry,* 221, 5, 683-691.

Ceschi G, Billieux J, Hearn M, Fürst G, Van der Linden M (2014) Trauma exposure interacts with impulsivity in predicting emotion regulation and depressive mood. *European Journal of Psychotraumatololgy*, 29, 5. doi: 10.3402/ejpt.v5.24104.

Chadwick D, Alfredsson Ågren K, Caton S, Chiner E, Danker, ,Gómez-Puerta M, Heitplatz V, Johansson S, Normand C (2022) Digital inclusion and participation of people with intellectual disabilities during COVID-19: A rapid review and international bricolage. *Journal of Policy and Practice in Intellectual Disabilities*, 9, 3, 242-256.

Challenging Behaviour Foundation (2020) *'Broken'* https://www.challengingbehaviour.org.uk/wp-content/uploads/2021/03/brokencbffinalreportstrand1jan21.pdf

Challenging Behaviour Foundation (2022) *INFORMATION SHEET Positive Behaviour Support Planning: Part 3* https://www.challengingbehaviour.org.uk/wp-content/uploads/2021/02/003-Positive-Behaviour-Support-Planning-Part-3.pdf

Challenging Behaviour Foundation (2023) *Reducing the use of restraint, seclusion and other restrictive practices*. https://www.challengingbehaviour.org.uk/wp-content/uploads/2021/03/010-Reducing-the-use-of-restraint-seclusion-and-other-restrictive-practices.pdf

Chanen A M (2022) Debate: It is time to stop turning a blind eye to personality disorder in young people. *Child and Adolescent Mental Health*, 27, 2, 194-195.

Cherry K (2022a) *Kohlberg's Theory of Moral Development.* https://www.verywellmind.com/kohlbergs-theory-of-moral-development-2795071

Cherry K (2022) *What Is Self-Esteem? Your Sense of Your Personal Worth or Value* https://www.verywellmind.com/what-is-self-esteem-2795868

Cherry K (2023) *Self Efficacy and Why Believing in Yourself Matters* https://www.verywellmind.com/what-is-self-efficacy-2795954

Christensen I E, Risør, M B, Grøn L (2022) Senses of Touch: The Absence and Presence of Touch in Health Care Encounters of Patients with Mental Illness. *Culture, Medicine, Psychiatry,* 47, 402–421.

Choi B and Park S (2021) Bullying Perpetration, Victimization, and Low Self-esteem: Examining Their Relationship Over Time. *Journal of Youth and Adolescence*, 50, 739–752.

Churchill R, Moore T H M, Furukawa T A, Caldwell D M, Davies P, Jones H, Shinohara K, Imai H, Lewis G and Hunot V (2013) 'Third wave' cognitive and behavioural therapies versus other psychological therapies for depression. *Cochrane Database Systemic Review*, 18;(10)

Clapton N (2016) *Growing Kind Minds: Adapted group Compassion Focused Therapy for Adults with Intellectual Disabilities* (CFT-ID) https://research.bangor.ac.uk/portal/en/theses/growing-kind-minds-adapted-group-compassion-focused-therapy-for-adults-with-intellectual-disabilities-cftid(ac32443c-d51b-482d-ab6e-b3d92eb5a2fb).html

Clarkson P (2003) *The Therapeutic Relationship*. 2nd edition Whurr London and Philadelphia

Chowdhury M R (2019) *What is Client Engagement in Therapy and How to Apply It?* https://positivepsychology.com/client-engagement/

Coleman S E and Sharrock E (2022) An exploration of the Personal Relationship Advisory Group in a community learning disability service: A service development project. *British Journal of Learning Disabilities*, 50, 3, 402-411.

Cocker F and Joss N (2016) Compassion Fatigue among Healthcare, Emergency and Community Service Workers: A Systematic Review. *International Journal of Environmental Research and Public Health*, 3, 6 :618.

Courtenay K, and Perera B (2020) COVID-19 and people with intellectual disability: Impacts of a pandemic. *Irish Journal of Psychological Medicine,* 37, 3, 231-236.

Cowan A (2018a) Borderline Personality Disorder in Individuals with Intellectual Disability. *Journal of Childhood and Developmental Disorders,* 4, 2:6, 1-5

Cowan A (2018b) Too Many Feelings: A Case Series of Individuals with Borderline Personality and Intellectual Disability. *Journal of Childhood and Developmental Disorders*, 4, 3:9

Cowen A S and Keltner D (2017) Self-report captures 27 distinct categories of emotion bridged by continuous gradients. *Proceedings of National Academy of Science USA,* 114, 38.

Coventry P A, Meader, N, Melton, H, Temple, M, Dale H, Wright, K and Brown J V (2020) Psychological and pharmacological interventions for post-traumatic stress disorder and co-morbid mental health problems following complex traumatic events: Systematic review and component network meta-analysis. *PLoS Medicine*, 17, 8, e1003262.

Covington E C (2000) Psychogenic Pain—What It Means, Why It Does Not Exist, and How to Diagnose It. *Pain Medicine*, 1, 4, 287–294.

CQC (2019) *KEMPLE VIEW Quality Report* 12/09/2019 https://api.cqc.org.uk/public/v1/reports/2836c4dd-9068-4bc9-8fc6-d557f287d2cd?20210115213608

Currie TL, McKenzie K and Noone S (2019) The Experiences of People with an Intellectual Disability of a Mindfulness-Based Program. *Mindfulness* 10, 1304–1314.

Dagnan D, Jackson I and Eastlake L (2018) A systematic review of cognitive behavioural therapy for anxiety in adults with intellectual disabilities *Journal of Intellectual Disability Research*, 62, 11, 974-991

Dallimore S, Christie, K and Loades M (2016) Improving multidisciplinary clinical discussion on an inpatient mental health ward. *Mental Health Review Journal*, 1, 2, 107-118.

Dall'Ora, C., Ball, J., Reinius, M. *et al*. (2020) Burnout in nursing: a theoretical review. *Human Resources Health* 18, 41

Davies L, Randle-Phillips C, Russell A, Delaney C (2021) The relationship between adverse interpersonal experiences and self-esteem in people with intellectual disabilities: The role of shame, self-compassion and social support *Journal of Applied Research in Intellectual Disabilities*, 34, 4,1037-1047.

Day N J, Hunt A, Cortis-Jones L and Grenyer B F (2018) Clinician attitudes towards borderline personality disorder: A 15-year comparison. *Personality and Mental Health*, 12, 4, 309-320

Deba S, Pererab B Krystac K, Ozerd M, Bertellie M, Novellf R, Wielandg J and Sappokh T (2021) The European guideline on the assessment and diagnosis of psychiatric disorders in adults with intellectual disabilities. *The European Journal of Psychiatry*, 36, 1, 11-25.

de Bruijn J, Vonk J, van den Broke A and Twint B (2021) Emotional Development and Intellectual Disability: introduction to a dynamic concept. In de Bruijn J, Vonk J, van den

Broke A and Twint B (Eds) *Emotional Development and Intellectual Disability*. Shoreham by Sea: Pavilion Publishing and Media Ltd. 27-42.

de Klerk A, Keulen-de Vos M and Lobbestael J (2022) The effectiveness of schema therapy in offenders with intellectual disabilities: a case series design. *Journal of Intellectual and Developmental Disability,* 47:3, 218-226.

De Meulemeester C, Lowyck B, Vermote R, Verhaest Y and Luyten P. (2017) Mentalizing and interpersonal problems in borderline personality disorder: The mediating role of identity diffusion. *Psychiatry Research*, 258,141-144.

DesNoyers-Hurley A (2002) Potentially lethal suicide attempts in persons with developmental disabilities: review and three new case studies. *Mental Health Aspects of Developmental Disabilities,* 5, 3, 90–95.

Department of Health (2002) *Action for Health. Health Action Plans and Health Facilitation* http://www.nwtdt.com/Archive/health/hap/hapsbook.pdf

Department of Health (2009a) *Valuing People Now: A three-year strategy for people with learning disabilities.* London: Department of Health (Chapter 3 having a life).

Department of Health (2009b) *Health Action Planning and Health Facilitation for People with Learning Disabilities: Good practice guidance*.http://webarchive.nationalarchives.gov.uk/20130107105354/http://www.dh.gov.uk/en/Publicationsandstatistics/Publications/PublicationsPolicyAndGuidance/DH_096505

Department of Health (2012) *Transforming care: A National response to Winterbourne View Hospital*. Department of Health, London: UK

Department of Health and Social Care (2021) *Guidance Information sharing and suicide prevention: consensus statemen*t https://www.gov.uk/government/publications/consensus-statement-for-information-sharing-and-suicide-prevention/information-sharing-and-suicide-prevention-consensus-statement

Desrosiers L, Saint-Jean M, Laporte L and Lord MM (2020) Engagement complications of adolescents with borderline personality disorder: navigating through a zone of turbulence. *Borderline Personality Disorder and Emotional Dysregulation*, 7,18.

Dibdin E (2022) *What Are Core Beliefs and How Do They Affect Your Health?* https://psychcentral.com/health/core-beliefs-examples

Dinsdale N and Crespi B J (2013) The Borderline Empathy Paradox: Evidence and Conceptual Models for Empathic Enhancements in Borderline Personality Disorder. *Journal of Personality Disorders,* 27, 2, 172-195.

Dion J, Geneviève Paquette G,Tremblay KN; Collin-Vézina D and Chabot M (2018) Child Maltreatment Among Children With Intellectual Disability in the Canadian Incidence Study. *American Journal of Intellectual Developmental Disability*, 123, 2, 176–188.

Division of Clinical Psychology (2011) *Good Practice Guidelines on the use of psychological formulation*. BPS Leicester.

Dixon-Gordon K L, Conkey L C, Whalen D J (2017) Recent advances in understanding physical health problems in personality disorders. *Current Opinion in Psychology*, 21, 1-5.

Dixon LB, Holoshitz Y and Nossel I (2016) Treatment engagement of individuals experiencing mental illness: review and update. *World Psychiatry*, 15,1,13-20.

Dodd K, Laute V and Daniel S (2021) The development and evaluation of an integrated intensive support service. *Advances in Mental Health and Intellectual Disabilities,* 16,1, 1-17.

Dodd K, Marlow L, Jones K and Livesey A (2010) Social-Moral Awareness Test (S M A T) Surrey and Borders Partnership N H S Trust.

Doherty A J, Atherton H, Boland P, Hastings R, Hives L, Hood K, James-Jenkinson L, Leavey R, Randell E, Reed J, Taggart L, Wilson N and Chauhan U (2020) Barriers and facilitators to primary health care for people with intellectual disabilities and/or autism: an integrative review *BJGP Open,* 4, 3: bjgpopen20X101030.

Dunn B and Bolton W (2004) The impact of borderline personality traits on challenging behaviour: implications for learning disabilities services. *The British Journal of Forensic Practice* https://www.emerald.com/insight/content/doi/10.1108/14636646200400021/full/html

East Sussex health care trust (2017) *My Care passport* https://www.esht.nhs.uk/wp-content/uploads/2017/10/This-is-me-My-Care-Passport.pdf

Ebrahim S and Sams P (Eds) (2022) *Team Formulation Key Considerations in Mental Health Services* https://acpuk.org.uk/wp-content/uploads/2022/07/ACP-UK-Team-Formulation-Guidance-v1.pdf

Ehsan A, Klaas H S, Bastianen A and Spini D (2019) Social capital and health: A systematic review of systematic reviews. SSM Population Health,7, 8:100425. doi: 10.1016/j.ssmph.2019.100425.

Ekman (1999) Basic Emotions. in Dalgleish T and Power M (Eds) *Handbook of cognition and Emotion*. John Wiley and sons pp 45-60

Elliott C and Smith L (2009) *Borderline Personality Disorder for Dummies*. Indianapolis, Indiana: Wiley.

ecl (2023) *Ways to manage anxiety for adults with intellectual disabilities*. https://www.ecl.org/about/latest-news/blog/ways-to-manage-anxiety-for-adults-with-learning-disabilities

Emerson E (1995) *Challenging behaviour: Analysis and intervention in people with severe intellectual disabilities*. First edition Cambridge Press.

Emerson E and Hatton C (2008) *Estimating Future Need for Adult Social Care Services for People with Learning Disabilities in England*. CeDR Report 2008:6. Centre for Disability Research Lancaster University. Available at: eprints.lancs.ac.uk/21049/1/CeDR_2008-6_Future_needs)for_People_with_Learning_Disabilities_in England.pdf (accessed January 2014)

Equality and Human Rights Commission (2018) *The Human Rights Act* https://www.equalityhumanrights.com/en/human-rights/human-rights-act

Evans O G (2023) *Primary And Secondary Emotions* https://www.simplypsychology.org/primary-and-secondary-emotions.html

Evmenova A S, Graff H J, Motti V G, Giwa-Lawal K and Zheng H (2018) Designing a Wearable Technology Intervention to Support Young Adults With Intellectual and Developmental Disabilities in Inclusive Postsecondary Academic Environments. *Journal of Special Education Technology,* 34, 2.

Faculty of Psychiatry of Intellectual Disability (2016) *Psychotropic drug prescribing for people with intellectual disability, mental health problems and/or behaviours that challenge: practice guidelines.* Royal College of Psychiatry.

Families and Menacap (2021) *Tea, smiles and empty promises: Winterbourne View, and a decade of failures - a collection of family stories.* https://www.mencap.org.uk/sites/default/files/2021-05/Tea%2C%20smiles%20and%20empty%20promises%20-%20family%20stories.pdf

Farmer T (2016) *Defining an unwise decision* https://todayswillsandprobate.co.uk/defining-unwise-decision/

Farrokhian S, Alamdarloo G H and Asadmanesh E (2020) The effectiveness of functional training on impulsiveness of females with intellectual disability. *Health Psychology Research,* 30, 8, 3, 9116.

Fennell M (2016) *Overcoming Low Self-Esteem, 2nd Edition: A self-help guide using cognitive behavioural techniques*. Overcoming Books.

Festinger L (1954) A theory of social comparison processes. *Human Relations,* 7, 117–140.

Fishbain DA (1994) The Secondary Gain Concept: Definition Problems and Its Abuse in Medical Practice. *American Pain Society Journal* 3, 264–273

Firth J, Gangwisch J, Borsini A, Wootton R, Emeran A and Mayer E (2020) Food and mood: how do diet and nutrition affect mental wellbeing? *British Medical Journal*, 369 doi: https://doi.org/10.1136/bmj.m2382

Fletcher RJ, Barnhill J, Cooper SA (2016) *Diagnostic manual- intellectual disability (DM-ID-2): a textbook of diagnosis of mental disorders in persons with intellectual disability.* National Association on for the Dually Diagnosed Press.

Folmo E J, Stänicke E, Johansen M S, Pedersen G and Kvarstein E H (2021) Development of therapeutic alliance in mentalization-based treatment—Goals, Bonds, and Tasks in a specialized treatment for borderline personality disorder. *Psychotherapy Research*, 31, 5, 604-618.

Fonagy P and Luyten P (2020) Attachment, mentalizing, and the self. In Livesley W J and Larstone R (Eds) *Handbook of Personality Disorders: theory, research and treatment.* Guildford Press New York. pp123 - 140

Frankish P (2019) *Frankish Assessment of the Impact of Trauma in Intellectual Disability.* Shoreham by Sea: Pavilion Publishing and Media Ltd.

Frankish P (2021) Early development affected by trauma. In Beail N, Frankish P and Allen Skelly (Eds) *Trauma and Intellectual Disability.* Shoreham by Sea: Pavilion Publishing and Media Ltd. 55-64

Freeman N C, Gray K M, Taffe J R, and Cornish K M (2016) A cross-syndrome evaluation of a new attention rating scale: The Scale of Attention in Intellectual Disability. *Research in Developmental Disabilities,* 57,18-28.

Freud S and Breuer J (1895) *Studies in hysteria.* Penguin Books.

Freudenberger H J (1974) Staff burn-out. *Journal of Social Issues*, 30, 1, 159–65.

Frick C, Lang S, Kotchoubey B, Sieswerda S, Dinu-Biringer R, Berger M, Veser S, Essig M, and Barnow S (2012) Hypersensitivity in borderline personality disorder during mindreading. *PloS one*, 7, 8, e41650. https://doi.org/10.1371/journal.pone.0041650

Fritscher L (2021) *What Is Counter-Transference?* https://www.verywellmind.com/counter-transference-2671577

Frothingham M B (2023) *Emotional Intelligence (EQ): Definition, Components and Examples.* https://www.simplypsychology.org/emotional-intelligence.html

Gallichan D J and George C (2014), Assessing attachment status in adults with intellectual disabilities: the potential of the Adult Attachment Projective Picture System. *Advances in Mental Health and Intellectual Disabilities,* 8, 2, 103-119.

Gelso CJ, Palma B and Bhatia A (2013) Attachment theory as a guide to understanding and working with transference and the real relationship in psychotherapy. *Journal Clinical Psychology.* 69, 11, 1160-71.

Ghoshal M (2020) The Connection Between Borderline Personality Disorder and Chronic Pain: Implications of Stress and COVID-19. *Practical Pain Management*, Aug 7.https://www.practicalpainmanagement.com/chronic-pain-borderline-personality-disorder-links

Giambarberi L, Munger Clary H M (2022) Suicide and Epilepsy. *Current Neurolology and Neuroscience Reports*, 22, 441–450.

Giesbers S, Hendriks L, Jahoda A, Hastings R, Embregts P (2019) Living with support: Experiences of people with mild intellectual disability. *Journal of Applied Research into Intellectual Disabilities*, 32, I2, 446-456.

Gill (2019) *The Importance Of Trauma-Informed Design.* https://www.forbes.com/sites/forbesnonprofitcouncil/2019/12/09/the-importance-of-trauma-informed-design/?sh=2fdf91836785

Goad E J (2020) Compassion-focused therapy groups for people with intellectual disabilities: An extended pilot study. *Journal of Intellectual Disabilities,* 25, 4 https://doi.org/10.1177/1744629520925953

Goad E (2021) Trauma-informed care in a service related context. In Beail N, Frankish P and Allen Skelly (Eds) *Trauma and Intellectual Disability.* Shoreham by Sea: Pavilion Publishing and Media Ltd.

Golding, K S and Hughes D A (2012) *Creating Loving Attachments. Parenting with PACE to nurture confidence and security in the troubled child.* London: Jessica Kingsley Publishers

GoodTherapy *Countertransference* https://www.goodtherapy.org/blog/psychpedia/countertransference

Gordon D K and Sansone R A (2013) A relationship between factitious disorder and borderline personality disorder. *Innovations in Clinical Neuroscience*,10,11-12,11-3.

Gray C (2014) *Social Stories* 10.2 https://carolgraysocialstories.com/social-stories/what-is-it/

Gray, C. (2015) *The New Social Story Book™: Over 150 Social Stories That Teach Everyday Social Skills to Children and Adults with Autism and Their Peers.* Future Horizons.

Greentree E and Beth Kruger B (2019) *Functional Analysis and Formulation.* PBS Network BiLD. https://www.bild.org.uk/wp-content/uploads/2020/07/Functional-Analysis-and-Formulation.pdf

Gregson N and Delaney C (2021) Drawing in not encouraging away: systemic team formulation to support the trauma-informed care of a lady with intellectual disabilities, in the context of COVID-19

Advances in Mental Health and Intellectual Disabilities. https://www.emerald.com/insight/content/doi/10.1108/AMHID-12-2020-0032/full/html

Griffith G and Hastings R (undated) *Good Practice Guidelines: Mindfulness-based programmes for people with Learning Disabilities* https://www.bangor.ac.uk/mindfulness/

documents/Good%20Practice%20Guidelines%20Mindfulness%20and%20Learning%20Disabilities%20V5.pdf

Gupta S (2023) *How to Develop a Strong Moral Compass* https://www.verywellmind.com/how-to-develop-a-strong-moral-compass-7482422

Hamadi L and Fletcher HK (2019) Are people with an intellectual disability at increased risk of attachment difficulties? A critical review. *Journal of Intellectual Disabilities*, 25,1. https://journals.sagepub.com/doi/full/10.1177/1744629519864772

Hang K L and Vernon P A (2020) Genetics. In Livesley W J and Larstone R (Eds) *Handbook of Personality Disorders: theory, research and treatment.* Guildford Press New York. pp 235-250

Hansen A, Hazelton M, Rosina R and Inder K (2020) Factors Associated with Seclusion Use in Forensic Mental Health Settings: An Integrative Review. *International Journal of Forensic Mental Health,* 19, 2,198-213.

Harding (2021) Providing emotionally aware care in the positive behavioural support framework. Beail N, Frankish P and Skelly A (Eds) *Trauma and Intellectual Disability.* Shoreham by Sea: Pavilion Publishing and Media Ltd.

Harflett N, Jennings Y and Linsky K (2017) *Introduction to the research on the impact and effectiveness of meaningful activity for people with mental health problems*. National Development Team for Inclusion.

Hartley S, Baker C, Birtwistle, Burgess J L, Chatburn E, Cobbaert L, Howley M, Huggett C, MacKenzie-Nash C, Newton A, Parry S, Smith J, Taylor C D J, Taylor P J and Timoclea R (2022) Commentary: Bringing together lived experience, clinical and research expertise - a commentary on the May 2022 debate should CAMH professionals be diagnosing personality disorder in adolescence? *Child and Adolescent Mental Health,* 27, 3, 246-249.

Hartney E (2023) *Understanding Motivational Interviewing* https://www.verywellmind.com/what-is-motivational-interviewing-22378

Hastings R P (2002) Do challenging behaviors affect staff psychological well-being? Issues of causality and mechanism. *American Journal on Mental Retardation*, 107, 455–467.

Hayes S C and Hofmann S G (2021) "Third-wave" cognitive and behavioral therapies and the emergence of a process-based approach to intervention in psychiatry. *World psychiatry,* 20,3, 363-375.

Hayward L E, Vartanian L R, Kwok C and Newby J M (2020) How might childhood adversity predict adult psychological distress? Applying the Identity Disruption Model to understanding depression and anxiety disorders. *Journal of Affective Disorders,* 265, 112-119.

HCPC *reflective practice template* https://www.hcpc-uk.org/globalassets/standards/meeting-our-standards/reflective-practice/templates/reflective-practice-template.pdf

Heifetz M and Lunsky Y (2018) Implementation and evaluation of health passport communication tools in emergency departments. *Research in Developmental Disabilities,* 72, 23-32.

Henderson P, Fisher N R, Ball J and Sellwood W (2020) Mental health practitioner experiences of engaging with service users in community mental health settings: A systematic review and thematic synthesis of qualitative evidence. *Journal of Psychiatric and Mental Health Nursing,* 27, 6, 807-820.

Herman J (1992) *Trauma and recovery: the aftermath of violence - from domestic abuse to political terror.* New York: Basic Books

Heshmat S (2022) Acting on Impulse Why do we continue doing things that we don't intend to do? *Psychology Today* https://www.psychologytoday.com/gb/blog/science-choice/202203/acting-impulse

Heslop P, Byrne V, Calkin R, Huxor A, Sadoo A and Sullivan B (2021) Deaths of people with intellectual disabilities: Analysis of deaths in England from COVID-19 and other causes. *Journal of Applied Research in Intellectual Disabilities* 34, 61630-1640.

Heslop P and Macaulay F. (2009) *Hidden pain? Self-injury and people with learning disabilities. Bristol Crisis Service for Women*. https://www.selfinjurysupport.org.uk/hidden-pain-resources-for-people-with-learning-disabilities.

Hibbins J (2017) *Please Don't Call Us 'Difficult to Engage'* https://www.huffingtonpost.co.uk/joy-hibbins/please-dont-call-us-diffi_b_10988746.html

HM Government (2021) *Preventing suicide in England: Fifth progress report of the cross- government outcomes strategy to save lives*. https://assets.publishing.service.gov.uk/government/uploads/system/uploads/attachment_data/file/973935/fifth-suicide-prevention-strategy-progress-report.pdf

Hoffman J J, Hoelscher M L and Sherif K (2005) Social capital, knowledge management, and sustained superior performance. *Journal of Knowledge Management,* 9, 3, 93-100.

Horsham S and Grantham H (undated) *Mentalising-based therapy with learning disabilities.* https://www.plymouthonlinedirectory.com/media/1807/Mentalising-Based-Therapy-for-people-with-Learning-Disabilities/pdf/10.07.19_Mentalizing_Based_Therapy_for_people_with_LD.pdf?m=637084753634470000 accessed November 2022

Hollingworth P and Johnstone L (2014) Team formulation: what are the staff views? *Clinical Psychology Forum,* 257, 28-34.

Houston E (2019) *What Are Attributional and Explanatory Styles in Psychology?* https://positivepsychology.com/explanatory-styles-optimism/

Howlin P, Baron-Cohen S and Hadwin J (1999) *Teaching Children with Autism to Mind-read.* Chichester: John Wiley.

Hukkelberg S, Keles S, Ogden T and Hammerstrøm K (2019) The relation between behavioral problems and social competence: A correlational Meta-analysis. *BMC Psychiatry,* 19, 354.

Hughes D A (2007) *Attachment-Focused Family Therapy.* New York: W.W. Norton.

Hughes D (2017) Dyadic Developmental Psychotherapy (DDP): An Attachment-focused Family Treatment for Developmental Trauma. *Australian and New Zealand Journal of Family Therapy*, 38, 4, 595-605.

Huppert F A (2009) Psychological well-being: evidence regarding its causes and consequences. *Applied Psychological Health and Well Being,* 1,2,137–64.

Hymers G, Dagnan D and Ingham B (2021) Change processes within team formulations in intellectual disabilities services: what do multi-disciplinary staff find helpful? *Advances in Mental Health and Intellectual Disabilities,* 15, 6, 241-252.

icommunicate therapy www.icommunicatetherapy.com/adult-communication-difficulties-2/adult-learning-difficulties-intellectual-disability/key-guidelines-creating-total-communication-environment/

Iversen T E, Horndalsveen K, Matre E, Henriksen T F, Fusche S, Kildahl A N and Bakken T L (2019) Inpatient treatment of borderline personality disorder in adults with intellectual disability: reflections on practice. *Advances in Mental Health and Intellectual Disabilities*, 13, 2, 67-75.

Jacob, G A and Arntz A (2013) Schema therapy for personality disorders—A review. *International Journal of Cognitive Therapy*, 6, 2, 171–185.

James M and Warner S (2005) Coping with their lives- women, learning disabilities, self-harm and the secure unit: a Q-methodological study. *British Journal of Learning Disabilities*, 33 120–127.

Jenaway A (2019) *Relationship Roles for ACAT* https://www.engage.acat.org.uk/relationship-roles/

Joint statement of support from Chief Executives of statutory regulators of health and care professionals(2019) *Benefits of becoming a reflective practitioner* https://www.hcpc-uk.org/globalassets/news-and-events/benefits-of-becoming-a-reflective-practitioner----joint-statement-2019.pdf

Johnson J A (2019) *Are All Personality Descriptions Social Constructions? Yes, personality is socially constructed—but that doesn't mean it isn't real.* Psychology Today Posted September 28, 2019 Accessed August 2022. https://www.psychologytoday.com/gb/blog/cui-bono/201909/are-all-personality-descriptions-social-constructions

Jones D E, Park J S, Gamby K, Bigelow T M, Mersha T B, Alonzo T, Folger A T (2021) *Mental Health Epigenetics: A Primer With Implications for Counsellors* Feb 26, 11 1. https://tpcjournal.nbcc.org/mental-health-epigenetics-a-primer-with-implications-for-counselors/

Jones N (2021) Adapting dyadic developmental psychotherapy (DDP) to support adults with an intellectual disability who experience complex developmental trauma. In Beail N, Frankish P and Allen Skelly (Eds) *Trauma and Intellectual Disability.* Shoreham by Sea: Pavilion Publishing and Media Ltd.

Jones V and Haydon-Laurelut M (Eds) (2019) *Working with People with Learning Disabilities: Systemic Approaches*. Red Globe Press

Jorgensen C R (2020) Identity. In Livesley W J and Larstone R (Eds) *Handbook of Personality Disorders: theory, research and treatment.* Guildford Press New York. 107-122

Kalb LG, Beasley JB, Caoili A, McLaren JLand Barnhill J (2021) Predictors of Mental Health Crises Among Individuals With Intellectual and Developmental Disabilities Enrolled in the START Program. *Psychiatric Services,*1, 72, 3,273-280.

Kaplan S G and Wheeler E G (1983) Survival Skills for working with potentially violent clients. *Social Casework,* 64, 339-374.

Kasmani H (2021) Tree of Life: A Tool for Therapeutic Growth? *Educational Psychology Research and Practice,* 7,1.

Khan A, Cowan C and Roy A (1997) Personality disorder in people with learning disabilities: a community survey. *Journal of Intellectual Disability Research,* 41, 4, 324–330.

Kim J H and Choi J Y (2020) Influence of childhood trauma and post-traumatic stress symptoms on impulsivity: focusing on differences according to the dimensions of impulsivity. *European Journal of Psychotraumatology*, 11,1.

Kim Y, Lee H and Park A (2022) Patterns of adverse childhood experiences and depressive symptoms: self-esteem as a mediating mechanism. *Social Psychiatry Psychiatry and Epidemiology,* 57, 2, 331-341.

Kind S and Otis J D (2019) The Interaction Between Chronic Pain and PTSD. *Current Pain Headache Reports*, 23, 91.

Klaver M, van den Hoofdakker BJ, Wouters H, de Kuijper G, Hoekstra PJ and de Bildt A (2020) Exposure to challenging behaviours and burnout symptoms among care staff: the role of psychological resources. *Journal of Intellectual Disabilities Research,* 65, 2,173-185.

Kreisman J and Straus H (1991) *I Hate You, Don't Leave Me: Understanding the borderline personality.* New York: Avon books.

Kreisman J and Straus H (2004) *Sometimes I Act crazy: Living with borderline personality disorder*. New Jersey: Wiley.

Kennedy E (2013) Orchids and dandelions: How some children are more susceptible to environmental influences for better or worse and the implications for child development. *Clinical Child Psychology and Psychiatry,* 18, 3, 319–321.

Kohlberg L (1984) *The Psychology of Moral Development: The Nature and Validity of Moral Stages (Essays on Moral Development, Volume 2)* Harper and Row.

Kolod S (2021) *How to Spot Projection: Are Those Their Feelings, or Yours?* https://www.psychologytoday.com/gb/blog/psychoanalysis-unplugged/202105/how-spot-projection-are-those-their-feelings-or-yours

Krohn A (1974) Borderline 'empathy' and differentiation of object representations: A contribution to the psychology of object relations. *International Journal of Psychoanalytic Psychotherapy,* 3, 2, 142–165.

Kushnick A (2018) *What is relational trauma, and can EMDR help?* https://andrewkushnick.com/blog/2018/12/9/what-is-relational-trauma-and-can-emdr-help

Ledger S, McCormack N, Walmsley J, Tilley E and Davies I (2022) "Everyone has a story to tell": A review of life stories in learning disability research and practice. *British Journal of Learning Disabilities*, 50, I4, 484-493.

Lee A, Kiemle G. (2015) 'It's one of the hardest jobs in the world': the experience and understanding of qualified nurses who work with individuals diagnosed with both learning disability and personality disorder. *Journal of Applied Research in Intellectual Disabilities,* 28, 3, 238-48.

Lee J Y , Patel M and Scior K (2023) Self-esteem and its relationship with depression and anxiety in adults with intellectual disabilities: a systematic literature review. *Journal of Intellectual Disability Research*, 67, 6, 499-518.

Leising D, Rogers K and Ostner J (2009) The undisordered personality: Normative assumptions underlying personality disorder diagnoses. *Review of General Psychology*, 13, 230–241. Cited in BPS (2018)

Leyin A (1992) Sexuality and Personal Relationships - Policies, Guidelines and Values. *Journal of the British Institute of Mental Handicap (APEX),* 20, 2 20 70-73.

Li P (2023) *How Co-regulation with Parents Develops into Self-Regulation in Children* https://www.parentingforbrain.com/co-regulation/

 Intellectual Disabilities and 'Personality Disorder' © Pavilion Publishing and Media Ltd and its licensors 2023

Lindsay W (2007) Personality disorder. In N Bouras and G Holt (Eds) *Psychiatric and Behavioural Disorders in Intellectual and Developmental Disabilities*, pp143–153. Cambridge: Cambridge University Press.

Lindsay W and Kasprowicz M (1987) Challenging Negative Cognitions: Developing Confidence in Adults by Means of Cognitive Behaviour Therapy. *Journal of the British Institute of Mental Handicap* 15 159–62.

Linehan M (1993) *Cognitive-Behavioral Treatment of Borderline Personality Disorder (Diagnosis and Treatment of Mental Disorders)* New York: Guildford Press.

Livesley W.J. (2005) Principles and Strategies for treating Personality Disorder. *Canadian Journal of Psychiatry,* 50, 442-450.

Livesley W J and Larstone R (2020a) Part IV Introduction - Etiology and development In Livesley W J and Larstone R (Eds) *Handbook of Personality Disorders: theory, research and treatment.* Guildford Press New York. pp 229-234

Livesley W J and Larstone R (2020b) Part VII Introduction - Empirically based treatment In Livesley W J and Larstone R (Eds) *Handbook of Personality Disorders: theory, research and treatment.* pp 481-487 Guildford Press New York.

Llewellyn G and Hindmarsh G (2015) Parents with Intellectual Disability in a Population Context. *Current Developmental Disorders Reports*, 2, 119–126.

Lloyd J and Clayton P (2013) *Cognitive Analytic Therapy for People with Intellectual Disabilities and their Carers.* Jessica Kingsley: London

Lock S (2016) The Tree of Life: A review of the collective narrative approach. *Educational Psychology Research And Practice,* 2, 1, 2–20.

Logeswaran S, Hollett M, Zala S, Richardson L and Scior K (2019) How do people with intellectual disabilities construct their social identity? A review. *Journal of Applied Research in Intellectual Disabilities*, 32, 3, 533-542.

Lundahl A, Torenfält M, Helgesson G and Juth N (2023) Patients with borderline personality disorder and the effects of compulsory admissions on self-harm behaviour: a questionnaire study, *Nordic Journal of Psychiatry,* 16, 1-8.

Lunsky Y (2004) Suicidality in a clinical and community sample of adults with mental retardation. *Research in Developmental Disabilities*, 25, 3, 231–244.

Lunsky Y, Raina P and Burge P (2012) Suicidality among adults with intellectual disability. *Journal of Affective Disorders* 40, 3, 292-295.

Lye C and Stedmon S (2020) *Is reflective practice a good use of time in a medically-minded CMHT?* https://www.bps.org.uk/psychologist/reflective-practice-good-use-time-medically-minded-cmht

Made by dyslexia https://www.madebydyslexia.org

Madeson M (2021) *Transference vs Countertransference in Therapy: 6 Examples* https://positivepsychology.com/countertransference-and-transference/

Mahler M, Pine F and Bergman A (1976, reprinted 2000) *The Psychological Birth of the Hunan Infant.* New York: Basic Books.

Markham D and Trower P (2010) The effects of the psychiatric label 'borderline personality disorder' on nursing staff's perceptions and causal attributions for challenging behaviours *British Journal of Clinical Psychology*, First published: 24 December 2010 https://bpspsychub.onlinelibrary.wiley.com/doi/abs/10.1348/014466503607033 66

Marshall D F, Passarotti A M, Ryan K A, Kamali M,SaundersE F H, Pester B, McInnis M G and Langenecker S A (2016) Deficient inhibitory control as an outcome of childhood trauma. *Psychiatry Research,* 235, 7 DOI: 10.1016/j.psychres.2015.12.013

Maslach C. (1999) A Multidimensional theory of burnout. In: Cooper CL, (Ed.) *Theories of Organizational Stress.* Oxford University Press Inc.

Maslow A (1943) A Theory of Human Motivation. *Psychological Review*, 50, 4, 370-396.

McCarthy J, Blanco RA, Gaus VL, Razza NJ and Tomasulo DJ (2016) Trauma and stress related disorders In Fletcher R, Barnhill J and Cooper SA (Eds) *Diagnostic Manual - Intellectual Disability* 2nd Edition New York: NADD press.

Matthies, SD and Philipsen, A (2014) Common ground in Attention Deficit Hyperactivity Disorder (ADHD) and borderline personality disorder (BPD)–review of recent findings. *Borderline Personality Disorder and Emotion Dysregulation,* 1, 1, 3.

Maybo. https://www.maybo.com

McCarthy, M., Milne Skillman, K., Elson, N. Bates C, Forrester-Jones R and Hunt S (2020) Making Connections and Building Confidence: A Study of Specialist Dating Agencies for People with Intellectual Disabilities. *Sexuality and Disability,* 38, 3–18.

McCarthy M, Bates C, Elson N, Hunt S, Milne-Skillman K and Forrester–Jones R (2021) 'Love makes me feel good inside and my heart is fixed': What adults with intellectual disabilities have to say about love and relationships. *Journal of Applied Research in Intellectual Disabilities,* 1-11

McCausland D, McCallion P, Carroll R, McCarron M (2021) The nature and quality of friendship for older adults with an intellectual disability in Ireland. *Journal of Applied Research in Intellectual Disabilities,* 34, 3, 763-776.

McHugh C and Balaratnasingam (2018) Impulsivity in personality disorders: current views and future directions. *Current Opinion in Psychiatry,* 31, 1,63-68

Mcleod S A (2015) *Stereotypes*. www.simplypsychology.org/katz-braly.html

Mcleod S (2023a) *Context And State-Dependent Memory.* https://www.simplypsychology.org/context-and-state-dependent-memory.html

Mcleod S (2023b) *Kohlberg's Stages Of Moral Development.* https://www.simplypsychology.org/kohlberg.html

Mcleod S (2023c) *Albert Bandura's Social Learning Theory* https://www.simplypsychology.org/bandura.htm

Mcleod S (2023d) *Brain Reward System* https://www.simplypsychology.org/brain-reward-system.html

McCormick F, Marsh L, Taggart L and Brown M (2021) Experiences of adults with intellectual disabilities accessing acute hospital services: A systematic review of the international evidence includes passports. *Health and Social Care in the Community,* 29, 51222-1232.

 © Pavilion Publishing and Media Ltd and its licensors 2023

McCormick F, Marsh L and Brown M (2022) Using a hospital passport from the perspective of adults with intellectual disabilities, family carers and health professionals: A qualitative study. *Journal of Intellectual Disabilities* https://doi.org/10.1177/17446295221145996

McDonnell C G, Boan A D, Bradley C C, Seay K D, Charles J M and Carpenter L A (2019) Child maltreatment in autism spectrum disorder and intellectual disability: results from a population-based sample. *Journal of Child Psychology and Psychiatry,* 60, 5, 576-584.

McFetridge M, Hauenstein A, Heke S, Karatzias T, Greenberg N, Kitchiner N and Morley R (2017) *Guideline for the treatment and planning of services for complex post-traumatic stress disorder in adults.* UK Psychological Trauma Society.

McNair L , Woodrow C and Hare D (2017) Dialectical Behaviour Therapy with People with Intellectual Disabilities: A Systematic Review and Narrative Analysis. *Journal of Applied Research in Intellectual Disabilities*, 30,5, 87-804.

McNally P, Taggart L, and Shevlin M (2021) Trauma experiences of people with an intellectual disability and their implications: A scoping review. Journal of Applied Research in Intellectual Disabilities. 34, 4, 927-949 https://doi.org/10.1111/jar.12872

McNichols N K (2021) *The Vital Importance of Human Touch* https://www.psychologytoday.com/gb/blog/everyone-top/202108/the-vital-importance-human-touch

Mehrabian, A. (1972) *Nonverbal Communication*. New Brunswick: Aldine Transaction.

Mencap undated *My hospital passport* https://www.mencap.org.uk/advice-and-support/health-coronavirus/health-guides

Mental Health Foundation (2022) *Relationships in the 21st Century* https://www.mentalhealth.org.uk/sites/default/files/2022-06/MHF-Relationships-21st-Century-Summary-Report.pdf

Merrick J, Merrick E, Lunsky Y and Kandel I (2006) A review of suicidality in persons with intellectual disability. *Israeli Journal of Psychiatry and Related Sciences*, 43, 4, 158–264.

Mesibov G B, Shea V and Schopler E (2004) *The TEACCH Approach to Autism Spectrum Disorders*. Springer: New York

Miller W R (1983) Motivational interviewing with problem drinkers. *Behavioural Psychotherapy,* 11, 2, 147–172.

Miller J, Flory K, Lynam D and Leukefeld C (2003) A test of the four-factor model of impulsivity-related traits. *Personality and Individual Differences*, 34, 8,1403-1418.

Miller WR and Rose GS (2009) Toward a theory of motivational interviewing. *American Psychologist*, 64, 6, 527-37.

MIND (2023a) *Dissociation and dissociative disorders*. https://www.mind.org.uk/information-support/types-of-mental-health-problems/dissociation-and-dissociative-disorders/about-dissociation/

MIND (2023b) *What are flashbacks?* https://www.mind.org.uk/information-support/types-of-mental-health-problems/post-traumatic-stress-disorder-ptsd-and-complex-ptsd/symptoms/#WhatAreFlashbacks

Mirabella G (2021) Inhibitory control and impulsive responses in neurodevelopmental disorders. *Developmental Medicine and Child Neurology,* 63, 5, 520-526.

Mithen J, Aitken Z, Ziersch A, Kavanagh AM (2015) Inequalities in social capital and health between people with and without disabilities. *Social Science and Medicine*, 126, Feb, 26-35.

Mollison E, Chaplin E, Underwood L and McCarthy J (2014) A review of risk factors associated with suicide in adults with intellectual disability. *Advances in Mental Health and Intellectual Disabilities*, , 8, 5, 302-308.

Momene R (2015) *Negative Stereotypes and Attitudes Linked to Disability.* https://atlascorps.org/negative-stereotypes-and-attitudes-linked-to-disability/

Moran H (2010) Clinical observations of the differences between children on the autism spectrum and those with attachment problems: the Coventry Grid. *Good Autism Practice*, 11,2 44 -57

Morgan J K, Santosa H, Conner K K, Fridley R M, Forbes E E, Iyengar S, Joseph H M and Huppert T J (2023) Mother-child neural synchronization is time linked to mother-child positive affective state matching. *Social Cognitive and Affective Neuroscience*, 28,18,1:nsad001.

Morgan T A and Zimmerman M (2020) Epidemiology of personality disorders. In Livesley W J and Larstone R (Eds.) *Handbook of Personality Disorders: theory, research and treatment*. Guildford Press New York.

Morris D J, Webb E L, Parmar E, Trundle G and McLean A (2020), Troubled beginnings: the adverse childhood experiences and placement histories of a detained adolescent population with developmental disorders. *Advances in Mental Health and Intellectual Disabilities*, 4 6, 81-197.

Morsella E (2012) *What Is a Thought?* https://www.psychologytoday.com/gb/blog/consciousness-and-the-brain/201202/what-is-thought

Mulder (2020) Cultural aspects of personality disorder. In Livesley W J and Larstone R (Eds) *Handbook of Personality Disorders: theory, research and treatment*. Guildford Press New York.

Mulligan K and Scherer K R (2012) Toward a Working Definition of Emotion. *Emotion Review*, 4, 4, 345-357.

Murphy J (1998) Talking Mats: Speech and language research in practice. *Speech and Language Therapy in Practice*, Autumn, 11-14.

Nahapiet J and Ghoshal S (1998) "Social Capital, Intellectual Capital, and the Organizational Advantage." *Academy of Management Review*, 23, 2, 242-266.

Nankervis K, Ashman A, Weekes A and Carroll M (2020) Interactions of Residents Who Have Intellectual Disability and Challenging Behaviours, International Journal of Disability, Development and Education, 67, 1, 58-72.

Ncube N (2006) The Tree of Life Project. Using narrative ideas in work with vulnerable children in Southern Africa *The International Journal of Narrative Therapy and Community Work,* 1, 3-16.

Neff KD (2021) Self-Compassion, Self-Esteem, and Well-Being. *Social and Personality Psychology Compass*, 5,1, 1-12.

Ng F Y Y, Townsend ML, Miller C E, Jewell M and Grenyer B (2019) The lived experience of recovery in borderline personality disorder: a qualitative study. *Borderline Personality Disorder and Emotion Dysregulation*, 6, Article 10 .

 Intellectual Disabilities and 'Personality Disorder' © Pavilion Publishing and Media Ltd and its licensors 2023

NHS England (2016) *Stopping overmedication of people with a intellectual disability (STOMP)* https://www.england. nhs.uk/learning-disabilities/improving-health/stomp/

NHS England (2018) *Guide to making information accessible for people with a learning disability.* https://www.england.nhs.uk/wp-content/uploads/2018/06/LearningDisability AccessCommsGuidance.pdf

NHS England and NHS Improvement and the National Collaborating Central for Mental Health (2019) *The Community Mental Health Framework for Adults and Older Adults.* https://www.england.nhs.uk/wp-content/uploads/2019/09/community-mental-health-framework-for-adults-and-older-adults.pdf

NHS Education for Scotland (2021) *Trauma-Informed Practice: A Toolkit for Scotland*

NHS Education for Scotland (undated) *Nurture, adverse childhood experiences and trauma informed practice: Making the links between these approaches.* https://education.gov.scot/improvement/Documents/inc83-making-the-links-nurture-ACES-and-trauma.pdf accessed 29/10/22

NHS England (2019b) *Bradley's life-changing Flash Glucose Monitor* https://www.england.nhs.uk/diabetes/case-studies/bradleys-life-changing-flash-glucose-monitor/

NHS England (2022) *Social prescribing* https://www.england.nhs.uk/personalisedcare/social-prescribing/

NICE (2009 CG76) *Medicines adherence: involving patients in decisions about prescribed medicines and supporting adherence* www.nice.org.uk/guidance/cg76

NICE (2009) *Antisocial personality disorder: prevention and management* CG77 https://www.nice.org.uk/guidance/cg77/chapter/Introduction (under review - may be withdrawn because of changes to the diagnosis of 'personality disorder')

NICE (2009) *Borderline personality disorder: recognition and management* CG78. https://www.nice.org.uk/guidance/cg78/chapter/Introduction (under review - may be withdrawn because of changes to the diagnosis of 'personality disorder')

NICE (2015a) *Challenging behaviour and learning disabilities: prevention and interventions for people with learning disabilities whose behaviour challenges* NG11 https://www.nice.org.uk/guidance/ng11

NICE (2015b) *Violence and aggression: short-term management in mental health, health and community settings* NG10 https://www.nice.org.uk/guidance/ng10

NICE (2016) *Mental health problems in people with learning disabilities: prevention, assessment and managemen*t NG54 https://www.nice.org.uk/guidance/ng54

NICE (2018) *Decision-making and mental capacity* NG108 https://www.nice.org.uk/guidance/ng108

NICE (2020) *Self-harm: What are the risk factors?* https://cks.nice.org.uk/topics/self-harm/background-information/risk-factors/

NICE (2021) *NICE impact people with a learning disability* https://www.nice.org.uk/about/what-we-do/into-practice/measuring-the-use-of-nice-guidance/impact-of-our-guidance/nice-impact-people-with-a-learning-disability

NICE (2022) *Self-harm: assessment, management and preventing recurrence* NG225 https://www.nice.org.uk/guidance/ng225/resources/selfharm-assessment-management-and-preventing-recurrence-pdf-66143837346757

Nicoll M, Beail N and Saxon D (2013) Cognitive Behavioural Treatment for Anger in Adults with Intellectual Disabilities: A Systematic Review and Meta-analysis. *Journal of Applied Research in Intellectual Disabilities,* 26, 1, 47-62.

Northway R, Rees S, Davies M and Williams S (2017) Hospital passports, patient safety and person-centred care: A review of documents currently used for people with intellectual disabilities in the UK. *Journal of Clinical Nursing*, 26,(23-24), 5160-5168.

Nortje A (2021) *Piaget's Stages: 4 Stages of Cognitive Development and Theory*. https://positivepsychology.com/piaget-stages-theory/.

Nowicki S, Gregory S, Iles-Caven Y, Ellis G and Golding J (2018) Early Home-Life Antecedents of Children's Locus of Control. *Frontiers in Psychology Section: Developmental Psychology*, 9 https://doi.org/10.3389/fpsyg.2018.02032.

Ockenden J, Ashman B and Beadle-Brown J (2014) Active Support – Fundamental to Positive Behaviour Support. *Research and Practice in Intellectual and Developmental Disabilities* ,1, 2, 98-107.

Ofrat A, Krueger R F and Clark L A (2020) Dimensional Approach to Personality Disorder Classification. In Livesley W J and Larstone R (Eds) *Handbook of Personality Disorders: theory, research and treatment.* Guildford Press New York. pp 72-87.

OHID Office for Health Improvement and Disparities (2022) *Working definition of trauma-informed practice* https://www.gov.uk/government/publications/working-definition-of-trauma-informed-practice/working-definition-of-trauma-informed-practice

Oostermeijer S, Brasier C, Harvey C, *et al* (2019) Design features that reduce the use of seclusion and restraint in mental health facilities: a rapid systematic review BMJ Open 2021;11:e046647. doi: 10.1136/bmjopen-2020-046647

Ordetx K (2018) *Teaching Theory of Mind A Curriculum for Children With High Functioning Autism, Asperger's Syndrome, and Related Social Challenges*. Jessica Kingsley.

Oumaya M, Friedman S, Pham A, Abou Abdallah T, Guelfi JD, Rouillon F. (2008) Borderline personality disorder, self-mutilation and suicide: literature review. *Encephale,* 34,5, 452-8.

Padesky C (1986) In Beck A, Greenberger D and Padesky C (1995) *Mind Over Mood: Change how you feel by changing the way you think.* New York: The Guildford Press.

Page H (undated) *Total communication resource pack.* https://www.sussexpartnership.nhs.uk/sites/default/files/documents/total_communication_resource_pack.pdf

Paley B and Hajal NJ (2022) Conceptualizing Emotion Regulation and Coregulation as Family-Level Phenomena. *Clinical Child Family Psychology Review,* 25, 1, 19-43.

Park J and Park E (2019) The Rasch Analysis of Rosenberg Self-Esteem Scale in Individuals With Intellectual Disabilities. *Frontiers in Psychology*, 10 https://doi.org/10.3389/fpsyg.2019.01992

Paris J (2019) Suicidality in Borderline Personality Disorder. *Medicina (Kaunas)* 28, 55, 6:223.

Paris J (2020) Childhood adversities and personality disorder. In Livesley W J and Larstone R(Eds) *Handbook of Personality Disorders: theory, research and treatment.* Guildford Press New York, pp 301-308.

Paterson B, Young J and Bradley P (2017) Recognising and responding to trauma in the implementation of PBS? *International Journal of Positive Behavioural Support*, 7,1, 4-14

Paterson L, McKenzie K and Lindsay B (2012) Stigma, Social Comparison and Self-Esteem in Adults with an Intellectual Disability. *Journal of Applied Research in Intellectual Disabilities,* 25, 2, 166-176.

Patterson C W, Golightly M (2023) Adults with intellectual disabilities and third-wave therapies: A systematic review and meta-ethnography. *Journal of Applied Research in Intellectual Disabilities*, 36,1, 13-27.

Patterson C W, Williams J and Jones R (2019) Third-wave therapies and adults with intellectual disabilities: A systematic review. *Journal of Applied Research in Intellectual Disabilities*, 32, 6, 1295-1309.

PELICAN (undated) *Promoting Emotional Literacy in Children with Additional Needs* https://www.learningdisabilities.org.uk/learning-disabilities/our-work/employment-education/pelican

Pelleboer-Gunnink H A, van Weeghel J and Embregts P J (2021) Public stigmatisation of people with intellectual disabilities: a mixed-method population survey into stereotypes and their relationship with familiarity and discrimination. *Disability and Rehabilitation*, 43, 4, 489-497.

Penketh V, Hare D J, Flood A and Walker S (2013) Attachment in Adults with Intellectual Disabilities: Preliminary Investigation of the Psychometric Properties of the Manchester Attachment Scale–Third Party Observational Measure. *Journal of Applied Research in Intellectual Disabilities*, 1-13.

Perera B, Audi S, Solomou S, Courtenay K and Ramsay H (2020) Mental and physical health conditions in people with intellectual disabilities: Comparing local and national data. *British Journal of Learning Disabilities*, 48, 1, 19-27

Perry B D (2020) *4. Regulate, Relate, Reason (Sequence of Engagement): Neurosequential Network Stress and Trauma Series*. https://www.youtube.com/watch?v=LNuxy7FxEVk

Perry E and Flood A (2016) Autism Spectrum Disorder and attachment: A clinician's perspective. In H Fletcher, A Flood and D Hare. (Eds) *Attachment in intellectual and developmental disability: A clinician's guide to practice and research.* New York: Wiley.

Personality Disorder Commission (2018) *'Shining lights in dark corners of people`s lives' : the consensus statement for people with complex mental health difficulties who are diagnosed with a Personality Disorder.* https://www.mind.org.uk/media-a/4408/consensus-statement-final.pdf

Piaget J (1971) The theory of stages in cognitive development. In D R Green, M P Ford and G B Flamer. *Measurement and Piaget*. McGraw-Hill.

Pisani A R, Murrie D C and Silverman M M (2016) Reformulating Suicide Risk Formulation: From Prediction to Prevention. *Academy of Psychiatry*, 40, 623–629.

Pitonyak D (2008) *Jumping Into the Chaos of Things. Version 28*. www.dimagine.com/Jumping.pdf.

Pitonyak D (2009) *Upside Down and Inside Out: Supporting a person in crisis / supporting the people who care*. www.dimagine.com/Upside.pdf

Point of care foundation (2016) *About Schwarts Rounds* https://www.pointofcarefoundation.org.uk/our-programmes/staff-experience/about-schwartz-rounds/

Porcelan J A, Caujolle-Alls K E and Gentile J P (2019) Dismantling Fears Associated with Intellectual Disability Psychotherapy: An Evidence-based Practice. *Innovations in Clinical Neuroscience*,1,16, 14-18.

Porter C, Palmier-Claus J, Branitsky A, Mansell W, Warwick H and Varese F (2020) Childhood adversity and borderline personality disorder: a meta-analysis. *Acta Psychiatrica Scandinavica*, 141, 1, 6-20.

Prochaska J, and DiClemente C (1983) Stages and processes of self-change of smoking: toward an integrative model of change. *Journal of Consulting and Clinical Psychology*, 51,3, 390–395.

Prochaska J O, Norcross J C and DiClemente, C C (1994) *Changing for Good*. New York: Avon Books.

Psaila C and Crowley V (2005) Cognitive Analytic Therapy in People with Learning Disability: An investigation into the common reciprocal roles found within this client group. *Mental Health and Learning Disabilities Research and Practice,* 2, 2. doi: https://doi.org/10.5920/mhldrp.2005.2296

Public Health England (2018) *Health matters: reducing health inequalities in mental illness.* https://www.gov.uk/government/publications/health-matters-reducing-health-inequalities-in-mental-illness/health-matters-reducing-health-inequalities-in-mental-illness

Public Health England (2023) *Guidance Learning Disability - Applying All Our Health* https://www.gov.uk/government/publications/learning-disability-applying-all-our-health

Ramsden J (2020) Access to services: Moving beyond specialist provision while applying the learning. In Ramsden J,Prince S and Blazdell J (Eds) *Working Effectively with 'Personality Disorder' Contemporary and Critical Approaches to Clinical and Organizational Practice*. Shoreham by Sea: Pavilion Publishing and Media Ltd. pp137-146

Randle-Phillips C, Farquhar S and Thomas S (2016) Adapting and evaluating a tree of life group for women with learning disabilities. *British Journal of Learning Disabilities*, 44, 4, 301-308.

Raypole C (2022) *30 Grounding Techniques to Quiet Distressing Thoughts*. https://www.healthline.com/health/grounding-techniques#soothing-techniques

RDasH Rotherham, Doncaster and South Humber NHS trust (2014) *The 17 Step Plan* https://www.rdash.nhs.uk/wp-content/uploads/2014/04/17-Step-Behaviour-Risk-Management-Plan.pdf

Reasonable Adjustment Flag. https://digital.nhs.uk/services/reasonable-adjustment-flag

ReGain Editorial Team (2022) What Is Projection? Psychology, Example, And Application For Your Relationships Updated October 9 https://www.regain.us/advice/psychology/what-is-projection-psychology-example-and-application-for-your-relationships/

Reidbord S (2010) *Counter-transference, an overview: What is counter-transference*. http://www.psychologytoday.com/blog/sacramento-street-psychiatry/201003/countertransference-overview

Reynolds K, Rew J, and Nakamura M (2023) Personality Disorders in Dermatology: a Review of Patient Characteristics, Associated Dermatologic Conditions, and Pearls for Management. *Clinics in Dermatology,* March 4:S0738-081X(23)00036-6.

Rinaldi R, Batselé E and Haelewyck M (2022) Attachment and Challenging Behaviors in Adults with Intellectual Disability: A Scoping Review. *Journal of Mental Health Research in Intellectual Disabilities*, 15:3, 197-216.

Rishede M Z, Juul S, Bo S, Gondan M, Møeller S B and Simonsen S (2021) Personality Functioning and Mentalizing in Patients With Sub-threshold or Diagnosed Borderline Personality Disorder: Implications for ICD-11. *Frontiers of Psychiatry*, 12, https://doi.org/10.3389/fpsyt.2021.634332

Roepke S, Schröder-Abé M, Schütz A, Jacob G, Dams A, Vater A, Rüter A, Merkl A, Heuser I and Lammers C (2011) Dialectic behavioural therapy has an impact on self-concept clarity and facets of self-esteem in women with borderline personality disorder. *Clinical Psychology and Psychotherapy,* 18, 2, 148-158.

Rogers C. (1957) The Necessary and Sufficient Conditions of Therapeutic Personality Change *Journal of Consulting Psychology*, 21, 95–103.

Rogers C (2012) *On Becoming a Person: A Therapist's View of Psychotherapy*. Houghton Mifflin Harcourt.

Rose A and Webb Z (2012) Birthday cake mindfulness exercise. Unpublished.

Rossiter R and Arena R (2021) What's in a name? Findings, issues and refections on diagnosis – an update from a Faculty Survey . *Clinical psychology Forum*, 339, 56-66.

Roy M, Retzer A and Sikabofori T (2015) Personality development and intellectual disability. *Current Opinion in Psychiatry*, 28,1, 35-39.

Royal College of Nursing (2023) *Duty of care*. https://www.rcn.org.uk/Get-Help/RCN-advice/duty-of-care

Royal College of Psychiatrists (2001) *LD DC-LD: Diagnostic criteria for psychiatric disorders for use with adults with learning disabilities / mental retardation (occasional paper)* London RCP.

Royal College of Psychiatrists (2006) *Challenging Behaviour: A unified approach*. http://www.rcpsych.ac.uk/files/pdfversion/cr144.pdf (accessed January 2014).

Royal College of Psychiatry (2020) *Self-harm and Suicide in adults*. https://www.rcpsych.ac.uk/docs/default-source/improving-care/better-mh-policy/college-reports/college-report-cr229-self-harm-and-suicide.pdf?sfvrsn=b6fdf395_10

Royal College of Psychiatrists (2021) *Mental health services for adults with mild intellectual disability*. College Report

Royal College of Psychiatry (2021) *Attention deficit hyperactivity disorder (ADHD) in adults with intellectual disability.* https://www.rcpsych.ac.uk/docs/default-source/improving-care/better-mh-policy/college-reports/college-report-cr230---attention-deficit-hyperactivity-disorder-(adhd)-in-adults-with-intellectual-disability.pdf

Ruiz-Aranda D, Cardoso-Álvarez S and Fenollar-Cortés J (2021) Therapist Attachment and the Working Alliance: The Moderating Effect of Emotional Regulation. *Frontiers in Psychology*, 12 https://doi.org/10.3389/fpsyg.2021.784010

Salgado RM, Pedrosa R, Bastos-Leite AJ. (2020) Dysfunction of Empathy and Related Processes in Borderline Personality Disorder: A Systematic Review. *Harvard Review of Psychiatry*, 28, 4, 238-254.

Salovey P, and Mayer J D (1990) Emotional intelligence . *Imagination, Cognition and Personality*, 9, 3,185-211.

Salters-Pedneault K, (2023) *What Is Impulsivity?* https://www.verywellmind.com/impulsive-behavior-and-bpd-425483

Samaritans (2020) *Depiction of suicide and self-harm in literature*. https://media.samaritans.org/documents/Suicide_and_self_harm_Literature_FINAL.pdf

Samaritans (2023) *If you are worried about someone else.* https://www.samaritans.org/how-we-can-help/if-youre-worried-about-someone-else/how-support-someone-youre-worried-about/

Samaritans *Safety plan* https://www.getselfhelp.co.uk/docs/SafetyPlan.pdf

Samways B (2022) Professionals' attitudes towards people with intellectual disabilities who self-harm: A literature review. *Journal of Intellectual Disabilities*, 26, 4, 954–971.

Sansone R A, Sansone L A (2012) Chronic pain syndromes and borderline personality. *Innovations in Clinical Neuroscience*, 9, 1,10-14.

Sappok T and Conty M (2021) The Scale of Emotional Development - Short In de Bruijn J, Vonk J, van den Broke A and Twint B (Eds) *Emotional Development and Intellectual Disability*. Shoreham by Sea: Pavilion Publishing and Media Ltd. 207-218.

Sappok T, Barrett BF, Vandevelde S *et al* (2016) Scale of Emotional Development - Short. *Research in Developmental Disorders,* 7,166-175.

Schmeck K (2022) Debate: Should CAMHs professionals be diagnosing personality disorder in adolescents - 'no rationale to deprive adolescents of effective treatment'. *Child and Adolescent Mental Health*, 27, 2, 192-193.

Schenk N, Fürer L, Zimmermann R, Steppan M and Schmeck K . Alliance Ruptures and Resolutions in Personality Disorders. *Current Psychiatry Reports* 23. https://doi.org/10.1007/s11920-020-01212-w

Sellars C (2011) *Risk Assessment in People with Intellectual Disabilities* (2nd edition) Chichester: BPS Blackwell.

Sheehan L, Gaurean B and Corrigan P W (2022) Debate: Stigma implications for diagnosing personality disorder in adolescents. *Child and Adolescent Mental Health*, 27, 2, 203-305.

Shiner RL and Allen TA (2020) Developmental Psychopathology. In Livesley W J and Larstone R (Eds) *Handbook of Personality Disorders: theory, research and treatment.* Guildford Press New York. pp 309-323

Sibbald S (2020) Life and Labels: Some Personal Thoughts about Personality Disorder. In Ramsden J,Prince S and Blazdell J (Eds) *Working Effectively with "Personality Disorder" contemporary and Critical Approaches to Clinical and Organizational Practice*. Shoreham by Sea: Pavilion Publishing and Media Ltd.

Siegel D (1999) *The Developing Mind: How Relationships and the Brain Interact to Shape Who We Are*. The Guildford Press.

Sineson V (2021) The history of trauma. In Beail N, Frankish P and Allen Skelly (Eds) *Trauma and Intellectual Disability*. Shoreham by Sea: Pavilion Publishing and Media Ltd.

Singh N N and Hwang Y S (2020) Mindfulness-based programs and practices for people with intellectual and developmental disability. *Current Opinion in Psychiatry*, 33, 2, 86-91.

Skelly A (2017) Maintaining bonds: Positive behaviour support and attachment theory. *Clinical Psychology Forum,* 290, 36-41

Skilling G D, Sclare P D, Watt S J, Fielding S (2008) The effect of catalytic converter legislation on suicide rates in Grampian and Scotland 1980-2003. *Scottish Medical Journal*, 53, 4, 3-6.

Skills for Care and Skills for Health (2013a) *National Minimum Training Standards for Healthcare Support Workers and Adult Social Care Workers in England*. NHS England: Leeds.

 Intellectual Disabilities and 'Personality Disorder' © Pavilion Publishing and Media Ltd and its licensors 2023

Skills for Care and Skills for Health (2013b) *Code of Conduct for Healthcare Support Workers and Adult Social Care Workers in England* https://www.skillsforhealth.org.uk/wp-content/uploads/2020/11/Code-of-Conduct-Healthcare-Support.pdf

Smith K E and Pollak S D (2020) Early life stress and development: potential mechanisms for adverse outcomes. *Journal of Neurodevelopmental Disorders*, 12:34 https://doi.org/10.1186/s11689-020-09337-y

Solace (2022) *Domestic Abuse experienced by Adults with a Learning Disability and Autistic Adults* https://respond.org.uk/wp-content/uploads/2022/04/Solace-Guideline-on-Domestic-Abuse.pdf

Stannis R L, Crosland K A, Miltenberger R and Valbuena D (2019) Response to bullying (RTB): Behavioral skills and in situ training for individuals diagnosed with intellectual disabilities. *Journal of Applied Behaviour Analysis*, 52, 1, 73-83.

Stubbe D E (2018) The Therapeutic Alliance: The Fundamental Element of Psychotherapy *Focus The Journal of Lifelong Learning in Psychiatry,* Fall, 402-403.

Substance Abuse and Mental Health Administration (SAMSHA) (2014) *Concept of trauma and guidance for a trauma informed approach SAMSHA trauma and justice strategic initiative.* U.S. Department of Health and Human Services, Office of Policy, Planning and Innovation. SAMHSA's Concept of Trauma and Guidance for a Trauma-Informed Approach (nasmhpd.org)

Syropoulou A, Vernadakis N, Papastergiou M and Kourtessis T (2021) Psychometric evaluation of the Rosenberg Self-Esteem Scale in primary school students with mild intellectual disability: First evidence. *Research in Developmental Disabilities*, Jul;114:103964. doi: 10.1016/j.ridd.

Szivos S and Griffiths E (1992) Coming to terms with learning difficulties: the effects of group work and group processes on stigmatised identity. In A Waitman and S Conboy-Hill (Eds) *Psychotherapy and Mental Handicap*. London: Sage.

Talking Mats www.talkingmats.com/about/our-story; www.talkingmats.com/research/free-resources

Tanaka G, Tang H, Haque, OS and Bursztajn HJ (2019) How Catastrophe Can Change Personality. *Psychiatric Times*, 36, 9, https://www.psychiatrictimes.com/view/how-catastrophe-can-change-personality

Taylor J (2022) *What Are Your Emotional Hot Buttons?* https://www.psychologytoday.com/gb/blog/the-power-prime/202211/what-are-your-emotional-hot-buttons

Thompson D (2018) *Sex, Personal Relationships and the Law for Adults with Learning Disabilities*. Shoreham by Sea: Pavilion Publishing and Media Ltd.

Thompson D and McCarthy M (2016) *Sex and the 3 Rs: Rights, Risks and Responsibilities* (4th edition) Shoreham by Sea: Pavilion Publishing and Media Ltd.

Thompson J (2011) *Is Nonverbal Communication a Numbers Game?* https://www.psychologytoday.com/gb/blog/beyond-words/201109/is-nonverbal-communication-numbers-game

Thompson R A (2019) Emotion dysregulation: A theme in search of definition. *Developmental Psychopathology*, 31,3, 805-815.

Tiggemann M and Anderberg I (2019) Social media is not real: The effect of 'Instagram vs reality' images on women's social comparison and body image. *New Media and Society*, 22,12.

Tilley E, Strnadová I, Danker J, Walmsley J, and Loblinzk J (2020) The impact of self-advocacy organizations on the subjective well-being of people with intellectual disabilities: A systematic review of the literature. *Journal of Applied Research in Intellectual Disabilities*, 33, 6, 1151-1165.

Timmins S (2018) *Successful Social Articles into Adulthood: Growing Up with Social Stories™* Jessica Kingsley.

Toogood S (2017) Positive behavioural support and borderline personality disorder. *International Journal of Positive Behavioural Support,* 7, 1, 24-30.

Turnbull O H and Salas C E (2021) The Neuropsychology of Emotion and Emotion Regulation: The Role of Laterality and Hierarchy. *Brain Science,*17,11, 8,1075.

Tyrer P (2022) Debate: Young people with personality disorder should be recognised and appropriately managed. *Child and Adolescent Mental Health*, 27,2, 199-200.

UK GOV (2020) *National statistics. Avoidable mortality in the UK*: 2020https://www.gov.uk/government/statistics/avoidable-mortality-in-the-uk-2020

UK Pods (2022) https://ukpodsltd.co.uk/case-study/100-reduction-in-ground-restraint-copy-3-copy-3/

United Response (2015) *Active Support. An Essential Component of the Way We Work* https://s33156.pcdn.co/wp-content/uploads/2015_UR_Active_Support_final_low.pdf

Unitt I (2018) The time has not yet come to stop talking about hospital passports. *Nursing times* blog 24 December.

Unwina G, Tsimopouloua A Biza, Kroesea S and Azmib S (2016) Effectiveness of cognitive behavioural therapy (CBT) programmes for anxiety or depression in adults with intellectual disabilities: A review of the literature. *Research in Developmental Disabilities*, 51–52, 60-75.

van den Bogaard K, Nijman H, Palmstierna T and Embregts P (2018) Self-Injurious Behavior in People with Intellectual Disabilities and Co-Occurring Psychopathology using the Self-Harm Scale: A Pilot Study. *Journal of Developmental and Physical Disabilities,* 30, 5, 707–722.

Vanwalleghem S, Miljkovitch R and Vinter A (2021) Attachment representations among school-age children with intellectual disability. *Research in Developmental Disabilities*,118,104064

Villines Z (2022) *Core beliefs: What they are and how to identify them*. https://www.medicalnewstoday.com/articles/core-beliefs

Vonk J (2021) Seven stages of emotional development from birth to adulthood. In de Bruijn J, Vonk J, van den Broke A and Twint B (Eds) *Emotional Development and Intellectual Disability*. Shoreham by Sea: Pavilion Publishing and Media Ltd. 57-82.

Wang Z, Xu X, Han Q, Chen Y, Jiang J and Ni G (2021) Factors associated with public attitudes towards persons with disabilities: a systematic review. *BMC Public Health,* 21, 1058.

Wareham K and Alex Kelly A (2020) *Talkabout Theory of Mind: Teaching Theory of Mind to Improve Social Skills and Relationships*. Routledge

 Intellectual Disabilities and 'Personality Disorder' © Pavilion Publishing and Media Ltd and its licensors 2023

Warrender D, Bain H, Murray I and Kennedy C (2021) Perspectives of crisis intervention for people diagnosed with "borderline personality disorder": An integrative review. *Journal of Psychiatric and Mental Health Nursing,* 28, 2, 208-236.

Weerasekera P (1993) Formulation: a multiperspective model. *Canadian Journal of Psychiatry*, 38, 5, 351-8.

Wegner, D M, Schneider, D J, Carter, S R and White T L (1987) Paradoxical effects of thought suppression. *Journal of Personality and Social Psychology,* 53, 1, 5–13.

Weight E J and Kendal S (2013) Staff attitudes towards inpatients with borderline personality disorder. *Mental Health Practice*, 17, 3, 34-38.

Whalley M (2019) *Cognitive distortions: an introduction to how CBT describes unhelpful ways of thinking*. https://www.psychologytools.com/articles/unhelpful-thinking-styles-cognitive-distortions-in-cbt/

Whelan A, Haywood P and Galloway S (2007) Low self-esteem: group cognitive behaviour therapy. *British Journal of Learning Disabilities*, 35 125–130.

While A (2021) Touch: knowledge and considerations for nursing practice. *British Journal of Community Nursing,* 26, 4, 190-194.

Wigham S, Emerson E (2015) Trauma and Life Events in Adults with Intellectual Disability. *Current Developmental Disorders Report*, 2, 93–99.

Wiginton K (2021) *What Is Neurodiversity?* https://www.webmd.com/add-adhd/features/what-is-neurodiversity.

Wijnroks L (2021) The relationship between cognition and emotion in people with an intellectual disability: a neurological approach. In de Bruijn J, Vonk J, van den Broke A and Twint B (Eds) *Emotional Development and Intellectual Disability*. Shoreham by Sea: Pavilion Publishing and Media Ltd. 97-114.

Wilcox E (2013), "Biscuits and perseverance: reflections on supporting a community intellectual disability team to reflect", *Advances in Mental Health and Intellectual Disabilities*, 7, 4, 211-219.

Williams J and Jones R (2022) *Living Your Best Life*. Shoreham by Sea: Pavilion Publishing and Media Ltd.

Wink L, Erikson C, Chamers J and McDougle C (2010) Co-morbid intellectual disability and borderline personality disorder: a case series. *Psychiatry*, 73, 3, 277–287.

World Health Organisation (1946) *Preamble to the Constitution of the World Health Organisation as adopted by the International Health Conference, New York.* www.who.int/about/definition/en/print.html

World Health Organization (2022) ICD-11: International Classification of Diseases (11th revision) https://icd.who.int/

Wong S PC (2020) A Treatment Framework of Violent Offenders with Psychopathic Traits. In Livesley W J and Larstone R (eds) *Handbook of Personality Disorders: theory, research and treatment*. Guildford Press New York. pp 629-644.

Vartanian L, Hayward L, Smyth J, Paxton S and Touyz S (2018) Risk and resiliency factors related to body dissatisfaction and disordered eating: The identity disruption model. *International Journal of Eating Disorders*, 51, I4, 322-330.

Intellectual Disabilities and 'Personality Disorder' © Pavilion Publishing and Media Ltd and its licensors 2023

Yashinsky D (2022) *15 Psychological Projection Examples*. https://helpfulprofessor.com/psychological-projection-examples/

Yeandle J, Fawkes L, Beeby R, Gordon C, and Challis E (2015) A collaborative formulation framework for service users with personality disorders. *Mental Health Practice*, 18, 5, 25-28.

Zero Suicide Alliance (undated) *SHARE: consent, confidentiality and information sharing in mental healthcare and suicide prevention*. https://assets.publishing.service.gov.uk/government/uploads/system/uploads/attachment_data/file/1013010/zero-suicide-alliance-share.pdf

Zigler E, Bennett-Gates D, Hodapp R and Henrich (2002) Assessing personality traits of individuals with mental retardation. *American Journal on Mental Retardation,* 107, 3, 181–193.

Zilcha-Mano S, Roose SP, Brown PJ and Rutherford BR (2019) Not Just Nonspecific Factors: The Roles of Alliance and Expectancy in Treatment, and Their Neurobiological Underpinnings. *Frontiers in Behavioural Neuroscience*, 12.

 Intellectual Disabilities and 'Personality Disorder' © Pavilion Publishing and Media Ltd and its licensors 2023